BUSHMAN LETTERS

Interpreting |Xam Narrative

MICHAEL WESSELS

Much of the material in this book has appeared in a different form and in various journals as listed below:

Antjie Krog, Stephen Watson and the Metaphysics of Presence, *Current Writing*, 118 (3), 2007: 24-48 (www.ukzn.ac.za/currentwriting);

The Discursive Character of the lXam Texts: A Consideration of the lXam 'Story of the Girl of the Early Race Who Made Stars', *Folklore*, 119 (1), 2007: 307-324 (www.tandf.co.uk/journals/titles/0015587X.asp);

Myth of Origin or Play of Difference: A Discussion of Two Versions of the lXam Story of the Moon and the Hare, *Current Writing*, 20 (1), 2008: 54-68 (www.ukzn.ac.za/currentwriting);

New Directions in lXam Studies: Some of the Implications of Andrew Bank's *Bushmen in a Victorian World: the Remarkable Story of the Bleek-Lloyd Collection of Bushman Folklore*, *Critical Arts: A Journal of North-South Cultural Studies*, 22 (1), 2008: 69-82 (www.tandf.co.uk/journals/rcrc);

The Story in which the Children are Sent to Throw the Sleeping Sun into the Sky: An Exploration of Power, Identity and Difference in a lXam Narrative, *Journal of Southern African Studies*. 34 (3), 2008: 479-494 (www.tandf.co.uk/journals/carfax/03057070.html);

Text or Presence: On Rereading the lXam and the Interpretation of their Narratives, *Journal of Literary Studies*, 24 (3), 2008: 20-39 (www.tandf.co.uk/journals/RJLS);

The lXam Narratives: Whose Myth of Origin? *African Studies*, 67 (3), 2008: 339-364 (www.tandf.co.uk/journals/titles/00020184.asp);

Religion and the Interpretation of the lXam Narratives. *Current Writing*, 20 (2), 2008: 44-66 (www.ukzn.ac.za/currentwriting);

The Universal and the Local: the Trickster and the lXam Narratives, *English in Africa*, 35 (2), 2008: 7-33 (www.journals.co.za/ej/ejour_iseaeng.html);

Foraging, Talking and Tricksters: a Critical Appraisal of Mathias Guenther's Contribution to Reading the lXam Narratives, *Journal of Folklore Research*, 45 (3), 2008: 299-328 (www.indiana.edu/~jofr);

Reading the Hartebeest: a Critical Appraisal of Roger Hewitt's Interpretation of the lXam Narratives, *Research in African Literatures*, 40 (2), 2009: 82-108 (http://inscribe.iupress.org/loi/ral).

BUSHMAN LETTERS

Interpreting |Xam Narrative

MICHAEL WESSELS

WITS UNIVERSITY PRESS

Published in South Africa by

Wits University Press
1 Jan Smuts Avenue
Johannesburg
2001
http://witspress.wits.ac.za

Copyright© Michael Wessels 2010

First published 2010

ISBN 978-1-86814-506-5

The original cover images are **San** (the 'dancing' Kudu) and **Khoekhoen** (the abstract figures) art at Twyfelfontein, Namibia accessed on http://commons.wikimedia.org/wiki/File:San_-_Khoekhoen_rock_art_-_Namibia.jpg#file. The cover art for *Bushman Letters* has been reworked by Arlene Mahler-Raviv.

Edited by Alex Potter
Indexed by Elaine Williams
Cover design and layout by Hothouse South Africa
Printed and bound by Ultra Litho (Pty) Ltd.

The Bushmen's letters are in their bodies. They (the letters) speak, they move, they make their (the Bushmen's) bodies move. They (the Bushmen) order the others to be silent .... A dream speaks falsely, it is (a thing) which deceives.

||Kabbo (Bleek & Lloyd, *Specimens of Bushman Folklore*, 1911)

CONTENTS

FOREWORD

It is difficult to compose a preface for a brilliant book. In one sense, there is nothing more to say, as what the book contains reflects its own perfection. Yet the very essence of Michael Wessels' extraordinary and rich study of |Xam narrative is that nothing is ever closed and final. The interpretive act is never complete; indeed, the book is about multiplicities. |Xam narrative exists, Wessels tells us, as something in process, something unfinished, never to be cast in stone. His chapters in the section, 'Reading the Narrative' constantly force us away from a single and singular reading. Instead, he emphasises the rich and intricate texture of the narratives and shows us the ways in which they invite multiple interpretation and elicit multiple meanings. He invites us to concede difference and to understand that there is no easily marked out common Khoisan tradition. His approach thus takes us away from what he rightly sees as the 'generalising tendency in the field that holds that all Bushmen (or even all Khoisan) belong to a single culture'. Instead, the book focuses our minds on particularities – the specificities of the |Xam language, out of which his study comes, within the wider sweep of Khoisan languages. He reminds us too of the particular delineations of the individual speakers who passed on their often rich and detailed knowledge and creativities to their interlocutors, Wilhelm Bleek and Lucy Lloyd, at their home in Mowbray in Cape Town. Through his meticulous research in the Bleek and Lloyd archives and his use of Andrew Bank's work on the Bleek and Lloyd families and the |Xam informants themselves, Wessels presents for us the quite substantial differences between Bleek and Lloyd in their working habits and views of their informants' culture. Lucy Lloyd emerges as a woman increasingly interested in the specificity of local cultures and the particularities of |Xam culture, thus moving away from her brother-in-law Wilhelm Bleek's belief in the dominant theories of social evolution and racial differentiation of his era.

Alongside the close gaze that Wessels asks us to engage in, we are taken into a new critical world. *Bushman Letters* sweeps away the stockades of an old critical habitus that has largely fenced off the study of what was/is often regarded as 'traditional' literature from texts seen as 'modern'. This approach has also assumed that 'oral literature' should be regarded as being linked to the past and not fully part of contemporary literary discourse. Wessels, however, wants an understanding of 'the signifying practices of the |Xam discursive tradition itself'. He argues most convincingly that earlier hermeneutic practices have been most interested in overarching patterns and structures, and not in the essence of 'the thing itself'. He brings to bear on the productive world of the |Xam narratives and their mediators the work of key contemporary thinkers such as Spivak, Foucault and Bourdieu. He sees the texts themselves as sites of creativity and contestation, which critics and readers have to keep in mind as they engage with the narratives – and, indeed, with similar cultural forms and traditions across the region.

Like all fine scholars, Wessels does not see his own work in isolation, but situates it in a wider critical tradition, in his case one that has grown up around the |Xam archive and the hermeneutic principles that inform that tradition. He draws illuminatingly on the classic seminal work of scholars such as Hewitt and Guenther, and interrogates their positions. Finely, carefully and generously, he critiques these interpretations through offering alternative modes of reading, thus providing a kind of metacriticism of what has gone before. He asks us to assume that there may perhaps not have been a social function to the narratives. Neither, he argues, can we assume that the narratives fit into patterns of universal storytelling – this particularly for the stories around the 'trickster' figure, |Kaggen, and his family. And neither, he assures us, can we assume that the narratives mesh in some way with the archives of rock painting or sit comfortably with the narratives of other San people. Examine their textuality, he tells us, and do not always see them as the representation of something else – particularly as a representation of lost origins. In connection with the idea of the myth of origins, he engages in particular with the deconstructionist ideas of Derrida, who is one of the main influences on his work. Observe also the narratives' intertextuality within the broader context of |Xam discourse, he urges.

Startlingly, Wessels argues that the stories on which he focuses from the huge Bleek and Lloyd corpus, now digitised, belong not to the past, but to the present. There is the tendency of certain forms of scholarship – in spite of the work of historians of the nineteenth century such as Penn and Bank – to position the |Xam and their culture in a timeless past. In this reading, therefore, they do not impinge on the present and on the construction of the South African 'Now'. Yet we understand from Wessels' book that this narrative world and its dense context are still with us. The |Xam language itself has not survived and its last speakers died at the beginning of the twentieth century, yet the wider world of the Khoisan is very much present. How is this? Many of the contemporary inhabitants of the Cape can claim some Khoisan ancestry. The book, therefore, in its wider vision is a call for both inclusivity and hybridity within the paradigm of the modern South African nation. Most of the groups that make up South Africa: Xhosa, Zulu, Afrikaner, Tswana, Cape Coloured and so on possess in genetic, linguistic and cultural terms a strong Khoisan inheritance. In this sense of a hybrid identity within and part of an African society, therefore, the Khoisan past is part of the living present of South Africa. Moreover, the Khoisan inheritance deserves far greater centrality in discussions of what it is to be African.

I want to thank Michael Wessels for the graceful complexity of his path-breaking work. I predict that the book will become a classic text and will shape future research in the field of 'Bushman letters' and more widely in the field of contemporary literary criticism and critical discourse. It may also shape public knowledge, which, after all, is the site where history and culture are continually interpreted and reinterpreted.

Liz Gunner
WISER,
University of the Witwatersrand, Johannesburg.
February 2010

ACKNOWLEDGEMENTS

Generous funding from the National Research Foundation (South Africa) and the American Council of Learned Societies has made it possible to write this book.

I should like to single out Liz Gunner, Duncan Brown, Cheryl Stobie, Mbulelo Mzamane and Barbara Barkhuizen from among the many scholars whose support and encouragement have been invaluable to me.

Anne Solomon's incisive comments and intellectual friendship have been a major contribution to the development of this book.

All writers probably owe a special debt to librarians. I am grateful to the skilful and friendly assistance given me by the librarians of the Cecil Renaud Library, University of KwaZulu-Natal, Pietermaritzburg; and the librarians of the Manuscripts and Archives Department and the African Studies Library at the University of Cape Town.

Much of the material in this book has appeared in different forms over the years in various journals as listed on page ii of *Bushman Letters*. I thank the editors and publishers of these journals for granting me permission to use material from the articles. The editorial staff of these journals and the reviewers who read my work have all contributed to the process that culminated in this book, as have the reviewers who reviewed the manuscript of this book and suggested revisions that have greatly improved it.

I am especially grateful to Veronica Klipp, Julie Miller, Melanie Pequeux and the staff of Wits University Press, and to Alex Potter for his editing.

I could never adequately acknowledge the places of sea, mountain and forest in which this book has been written.

And finally, my heartfelt thanks to Linzi, Akira, Tao and Cynthia — for the days, the days.

NOTE ON TERMINOLOGY

The term 'Khoisan' refers to the pre-colonial inhabitants of southern Africa whose languages formed part of the same wide linguistic family and who can be distinguished linguistically from speakers of the Bantu family of African languages. A distinction is frequently made between Khoi pastoralists and San hunter-gatherers, but this division is not clear cut. Solomon (n.d.) notes that the term 'San' more usefully 'describes language, not phenotype or economic identity'. The Nharo of the central and western Kalahari region, for example, were mostly hunter-gatherers, but spoke a Khoi or Khoe language. The hunter-gatherers of the region are commonly referred to as San or Bushmen. Both these terms have denigratory histories, and neither was invented by the people denominated by it. 'San' is a Khoi-derived term that refers in an insulting fashion to people without cattle (Bennun 2005: 30), while 'Bushman' (or its Afrikaans equivalent, 'Boesman') is a term that was introduced by the settlers to the Cape to refer dismissively to the hunter-gatherers of the region. Lucy Lloyd was told by her informant |Han#kass'o that the |Xam and the Korana referred to each other as 'Saa', a term that Bank (2006: 289) notes 'was a derivation of "San", meaning "thief" in the language of the Korana'.

This book follows, where possible, the practice of writers who use the names that particular groups of 'Bushman' or 'San' people give themselves, names such as Jul'hoan or |Xam. This signals an attempt to distance the study from the generalising tendency in the field that holds that all Bushmen (or even all Khoisan) belong to a single culture, with only minor variations. It also represents an attempt to avoid choosing between the terms 'Bushman' and 'San'. It is impossible to avoid this choice altogether, however. Any discussion of the wider field in which a study of the |Xam narratives has to be conducted by reason of inescapable intertextual histories requires the use of one or other of the words. The terms 'Bushman' and 'San' are used interchangeably in the recent literature. Both have enjoyed at different times and for different reasons the status of politically correct signifiers. At present, the use of one or other of them seems a matter of the writer's preference.

My decision to use the term 'Bushman' has been influenced by the fact that it is the term used in my primary source, the archive known as the Bleek and Lloyd Collection. In addition, this book explores the ideological component of the category of person to which the words 'Bushman' and 'San' refer. Both terms have the ability to carry the idealised version of the figure of the southern African hunter-gatherer that is examined in the book, but the term 'Bushman', in my view, is more appropriate a term to employ in the discussion, also conducted in the book, of earlier views of the 'Bushman' — views that were either explicitly racist or were coloured by Darwinian evolutionary ideas

NOTE ON REFERENCES TO THE BLEEK AND LLOYD NOTEBOOKS

I have followed generally accepted practice when quoting from the unpublished notebooks of the Bleek and Lloyd Collection, my primary source. The letter B or L, respectively, is used to indicate whether the notebook was compiled by Wilhelm Bleek or Lucy Lloyd. The Roman numeral, in the case of Lloyd's notebooks, refers to the informants: |A!kungta (I), ||Kabbo (II), #Kasin (IV), Dia!kwain (V), !Kweiten-ta-||ken (VI) and |Han#kass'o (VIII). The Arabic number following the Roman numeral indicates the number of the notebook collected by Lloyd from a single informant. The final number(s) after the colon refers to the page(s) of all the materials collected in a set of notebooks from a particular informant. An apostrophe following this number indicates that reference is being made to the reverse pages that Bleek and Lloyd used to record information or make observations that illuminated the main text. Thus, a reference to the Lloyd notebooks might read: L.II.32:5506–13'.

The Roman numerals that accompany references to Bleek's notebooks refer to the number of the notebook rather than to an informant.

INTRODUCTION

THE BLEEK AND LLOYD COLLECTION

For a very considerable period of time, probably, the |Xam language, in many forms and variations, was spoken across a broad region of present-day South Africa, west of Port Elizabeth and south of the Orange River. In the semi-arid area of the present-day Northern Cape province, home to the |Xam adults whose narratives form the subject of this book, |Xam speakers lived in small bands of between ten and thirty people near waterholes, ownership of which was passed down from generation to generation. Their economy was largely based on hunter-gathering, although they also traded and, increasingly, by choice or coercion, were drawn one way or another into the colonial economy.

|Xam was just one of many Khoisan languages that existed in pre-colonial southern Africa.[1] It was, however, the San or Bushman language that possessed the largest number of speakers, a position that is currently held by the Ju|'hoan (or !Kung) language of Angola, Namibia and Botswana. By the beginning of the twentieth century,[2] almost all the speakers of |Xam had been either killed by settler commandos or incorporated into the Afrikaans-speaking population of the Cape Colony, a process that frequently involved the separation of children from their parents. The language's demise was swift.[3] Only a few decades earlier, in the 1870s, German linguist Wilhelm Bleek and his sister-in-law, Lucy Lloyd, who grew up in the new British colony of Natal, had quite easily been able to find |Xam speakers from whom

1

to learn the language and obtain a large and varied body of material. The fact that Bleek and Lloyd drew their informants from prisoners in Cape Town's notorious Breakwater Prison, however, was in itself symptomatic of the forces that would rapidly lead to the destruction of the |Xam language as a spoken medium. From the second half of the nineteenth century, |Xam-speaking people had found themselves alienated from their land as farmers claimed the area as their own, and the former had, as a consequence, become subject to constant harassment and arrest as poachers or stock thieves.

It is somewhat ironic that |Xam survives only in written form, since the Bleek and Lloyd Collection is generally celebrated as the literature of an oral culture. In fact, the disappearance of the language and its transcription were linked. Part of Bleek's motivation, as we shall see, in preserving the language and its mythology was what he saw as the inevitable extinction of Bushman languages and their speakers, a view that was an integral part of his theory of development. In this respect, the Bleek and Lloyd project can be understood as an example of 'ethnography's tendency to become an imperial culture's rite of mourning of what it destroys' (Moran 2009: 127). It should also be noted that it has not been the |Xam language texts themselves that have been subjected to scholarly scrutiny, for the most part, but English translations of them. This is indicative of the fact that the |Xam materials are a highly mediated phenomenon. They exist by virtue of a complex series of interactions over centuries between European colonial-ism and |Xam-speaking hunter-gatherers in the Cape. These interactions culminated, albeit indirectly, in the establishment of the ethnographic relationship between several |Xam adults and Bleek and Lloyd and the compilation of the |Xam notebooks in Cape Town in the 1870s and 1880s. The broader context of this history has been charted by Nigel Penn (1996; 2005), while Andrew Bank (2006) has meticulously investigated the histories of the |Xam informants themselves, as well as those of the Bleek and Lloyd families. The intellectual climate in which Bleek and Lloyd pursued their project has also been explored in some depth, again by Bank (1999), while Shane Moran (2009) has meticulously dissected Bleek's theory of language and its place in colonial ideology.

The process of the collection of the |Xam materials, Bank's and Moran's work makes clear, entailed more than the recording of extant traditions; it involved their invention and construction, whether as mythology, folklore or literature. Theoretical expectations and scholarly and aesthetic practices preceded and determined the course of the collection of the |Xam materials. They accompanied, in turn, their translation and form, as well as the history of their subsequent consumption, interpretation and classification. Bleek himself claimed that he and Lloyd transcribed directly 'from the lips of the Bushmen', and accompanied the |Xam texts by 'as literal an English translation as could yet be achieved' (Bleek & Lloyd 1911: 444). Nevertheless, the Bleek and Lloyd translations clearly reflect nineteenth-century European ideas about the content and rendition of folklore. Bleek elicited particular kinds of materials from the informants that supported his views about the importance of mythology in general, and of stories about the sun, moon and stars in particular (Guenther 1996: 89; Bank 2006: 155, 158; Moran 2009: 114–27). While the peculiar word order of the translations might be attributable to an attempt to faithfully reproduce |Xam syntax; or even, as some have claimed (Krog 2004: 10), to the influence of Cape Dutch (Afrikaans) on the texts; the use of Elizabethan archaisms, for example, must be seen as a rhetorical device for situating traditional lore in antiquity. Bleek and Lloyd not only recorded the |Xam narratives; in a sense, they created them.

The materials in the Bleek and Lloyd Collection archive, our chief source of |Xam oral literature, are commonly referred to as narratives. They consist, however, of a range of biographical and historical material and information about |Xam life and culture in addition to actual narratives. The materials that can be considered as chiefly narrative can be separated into stories that have been directly experienced by the narrators themselves or by someone they know, and traditional narratives that feature talking animals and fantastical events. The |Xam themselves, it should be noted, do not make such a distinction, referring to all their 'stories, news, talk, information, history and what English-speakers call myths and folklore' as *kukummi* (Lewis-Williams 2000: 9). The traditional stories are set in a mythical or formative time that preceded the present order of existence. This period is usually referred to as the First Times or the First Order, and its inhabitants as the people of the Early Race. These people display characteristics of people and animals; the separation of species had not yet

3

occurred; and the story of this separation itself forms the subject of many of the narratives. About half the stories are animal tales that often include information about how particular animals acquired certain characteristics — the baboon its bare buttocks or the hyena its stooped shoulders, for example. A great many stories concern the antics and escapades of the character |Kaggen (the Mantis), who lives with his family, the dassie, the porcupine, the ichneumon (a species of mongoose), the blue crane and Kwammang-a (|Kaggen's son-in-law, who is associated with the rainbow).[4]

The Bleek and Lloyd Collection could be said to have its beginnings in Bleek's interest in the origin of languages and in the evolutionary racial theory that preoccupied the period. The immediate impetus for the project, however, was Governor Henry Barkly's decision to agree to Bleek's request for a few carefully selected |Xam prisoners to be released into his custody at his home in Mowbray, Cape Town, so that he might conduct his research into the |Xam language and its mythology (Bank 2006: 69–73). Bleek himself died in 1875, but the work was continued by Lucy Lloyd until her death in 1913, although the last of the |Xam informants had left by the end of 1879. Lloyd also worked with !Kung informants from what is now Namibia in the early 1880s.

THE |XAM INFORMANTS

Bleek and Lloyd's main informants were five men who had been convicted of various offences and under different pretexts. At this time, the diminishing pool of |Xam speakers was being rapidly incorporated into the farm labourer population, and those who led an independent existence were frequently criminalised as stock thieves and poachers. In addition to the five men, a woman, !Kweiten-ta-||ken, the sister of one of the informants and wife of another, also provided materials. The first informant, a man of about 18 years of age named |A!kungta, was released into Bleek's custody from the Breakwater Prison, where he had been imprisoned for receiving stolen goods (he had been apprehended participating in the eating of a stolen ox) at the end of August 1870 (Bank 2006: 73). Much of the foundation of Bleek's knowledge of the |Xam language was laid in his early sessions with |A!kungta.

|A!kungta was joined in February 1871 by ‖Kabbo, another 'Flat Bushman' from the same area of |Xam-ka !au (Bank 2006: 153) who had been imprisoned for cattle theft.[5] A man of about 55, ‖Kabbo was the first informant with an extensive knowledge of what we might call |Xam literature. In a chapter entitled 'Science and sentiment', Bank (2006: 179–203) notes the difference in the way that Bleek and Lloyd approached their work with ‖Kabbo. Bleek was especially interested in eliciting fables and myths from him, since he believed that these sorts of materials would provide a direct insight into the Bushman mentality — information he required as evidence for his theories of social evolution and racial differentiation (Moran 2009: 124–25). Lloyd, by contrast, was as interested in learning about everyday |Xam life in her interactions with ‖Kabbo as she was in |Xam literature and beliefs. ‖Kabbo's sessions with Lloyd were also less formal than his sessions with Bleek (Bank 2006: 161). ‖Kabbo himself frequently decided what he would talk to Lloyd about. He also collaborated more with Lloyd on translating the materials into English than he did with Bleek.

‖Kabbo's narratives are notable for their hunting references and metaphors, a reminder that ‖Kabbo, the oldest of the informants, had spent more time living a hunting-gathering life than the other informants had. Suitably, for someone whose name translates as 'Dream', his stories and information were sometimes prompted by dreams. Hewitt (1986: 240) remarks that ‖Kabbo uses a lot of reported speech in his narratives, a feature that contributes both to characterisation in them and to the presentation of multiple perspectives on the same events. He also 'rarely gave a narrative from beginning to end', departing from a story to tell another related one or to give information about |Xam life, before returning to the main narrative:

> He talked about anything that interested him and wandered from natural history into narrative and out again in a kind of 'stream of consciousness' where a word or allusion could spark off a narrative, or a narrative with a certain theme could lead him into a description of some practical activity such as hunting, for which he had a great relish (Hewitt 1986: 239).

‖Kabbo's narratives are also notable for their length and complex plot development. One story, notes Bank (2006: 171), about Jupiter and his child, 'runs over five notebooks, 300 pages and five months'. Lloyd herself observed of ‖Kabbo that he was 'an excellent narrator, and patiently watched until a sentence had been written down, before proceeding with what he was telling. He much enjoyed the thought that the Bushman narratives would become known by way of books' (Bleek & Lloyd 1911: x).

‖Kabbo and |A!kungta left the Bleek household in October 1873 to return to the northern Cape Colony. The next major informant, Dia!kwain, arrived a few weeks after his brother-in-law, #Kasin, in November 1873 (Bank 2006: 224). The two men had been imprisoned for murdering a farmer who had threatened to kill them. They had already lost several family members to settler violence at the time of the incident (222).[6] Even the colonial magistrate recognised that they had acted in self-defence, and found them guilty of culpable homicide rather than murder. Dia!kwain stayed until March 1876, about six months after Bleek's death (273), and, like ‖Kabbo, proved to be an accomplished storyteller.

Dia!kwain's childhood seems to have been quite traditional in terms of culture and economic practice. He was able to supply a great deal of information to Bleek and Lloyd about the |Xam way of life, including rock art, music and dance. His knowledge of the observances surrounding hunting, for example, was very detailed. Often these involved certain people avoiding eating specific body parts of particular animals. Dia!kwain also possessed an intimate knowledge of |Xam narrative. His early narratives concentrate on explaining 'how things appear in nature' (Bank 2006: 240). These include a number of animal fables that describe how the different animals attained their distinctive characteristics.

Many of Dia!kwain's narratives are based on real-life events. He tells a number of stories that involve a relative's encounter with lions, for example, although these accounts also display some elements of legend (Bank 2006: 244–51). He concentrates on recounting events from his childhood and reiterating the 'parental advice' he received (Bank 2006: 251). He might have avoided talking much about his adult years, since these were characterised by traumatic conflict with settlers and experiences of dislocation and displacement. He focuses quite often on the figure of the *!gi:xa*, translated as 'sorcerer' or 'sorceress' in the materials, and as 'people' or 'spirits' in some interpretations (Solomon 2007: 157), who specialised in skills such as healing, rainmaking and controlling the movement of game.

Dia!kwain lived in the Bleek household during the period of Bleek's final illness and death, which came in August 1875. Not surprisingly, much of the material that Lloyd collected from Dia!kwain at this time is centred around the theme of death (Bank 2006: 255–75). Dia!kwain stayed on another six months after Bleek's death, leaving in March 1876. He travelled extensively after leaving Cape Town, working as he went and probably visiting his sister, !Kweiten-ta-llken, before becoming a shepherd on a farm. In all likelihood, he was reunited with his wife, Johanna. He was probably murdered by friends of the farmer that he and #Kasin had killed in 1869 on his return to the Kenhardt district from a trip to the Free State with another farmer (275).

Although Dia!kwain was too young at the time of his arrest to have practised much as a storyteller himself, his memory of the stories he had heard as a child was extremely extensive. He was able to relate these narratives in a way that often showed more concern with narrative struc-ture, according to Hewitt (1986: 244), than that displayed by the other two major informants, llKabbo and lHan#kass'o, although his general storytelling skills do not seem as developed as theirs. They also showed more innovation and creativity. Dia!kwain was primarily interested in conveying cultural information and often used narratives to illustrate this information. Lucy Lloyd encouraged this aspect of his testimony as she herself became as interested in lXam culture in general as in their mythology or folklore (Bank 2006: 158). Hewitt (1986: 244-245) remarks that Dia!kwain's lKaggen stories 'have great energy and, like, llKabbo's versions, quarry a lot of interest out of lKaggen's bantering dialogue with members of his family'. He also observes that Dia!kwain had a 'special capacity for the serious rather than the humorous' (Hewitt 1986: 246). Dia!kwain's sister, !Kweiten-ta-llken, joined her brother for a few months at the end of 1874 and provided the only testimony that Bleek and Lloyd were able to obtain from a woman (Bank 2006: 225).

A few months after Dia!kwain's departure, llKabbo's son-in-law, lHan#kass'o, who had been arrested and released with llKabbo, arrived back in Mowbray from the northern Cape Colony. He had left the Bleek household after a short stay in 1871 to go and fetch his and llKabbo's wives. Bleek and Lloyd were keen to interview women, and the isolated informants were eager to have some of their family members with them. This journey itself was symptomatic of the conditions faced by the subjugated peoples of the colonial Cape. |Han#kass'o set out on the journey back to Cape Town with ||Kabbo's wife, !Kwabba-an; his own wife; ||Kabbo's daughter, Suobba-||kein; and a baby. Only |Han#kass'o survived the trip. !Kwabba-an fell ill and perished on the way; then the baby died; while Suobba-||kein was beaten to death by a policeman in Beaufort West (Bank 2006: 301).

Hewitt (1986: 242–44) ranks |Han#kass'o as the best of the narrators along with ||Kabbo. |Han#kass'o's narratives, however, were much more tightly structured than ||Kabbo's and he seldom interrupted his stories with digressions. Hewitt (242) notes that he 'had a fondness for using the same number of repetitions in different narratives'. He made frequent 'use of chanted phrases and song', always timing them carefully so as to enhance the story that he was telling (243–44). In Guenther's opinion, |Han#kass'o was a 'masterful' storyteller, the best of the |Xam storytellers, despite the fact that ||Kabbo is more widely celebrated:

> |Han#kass'o's narratives … are well composed and the plot is free of the deviations so frequent in |Xam story telling. It unfolds fluently and gathers momentum and suspense. Dialogue is used skillfully and repetition appears regularly to underscore the drama of the story (Guenther 1989: 28–29).

|Han#kass'o's storytelling, even in the ethnographic context of Lloyd's interviews in Cape Town, were lively affairs. Bleek's daughters, Edith and Dorothea, remembered that he '"was great in storytelling" allowing them to "feel more than know what was happening." They remembered his "eloquent gestures" and dramatic re-enactments' (Bank 2006: 364). |Han#kass'o made good use of hand gestures, and he used 'exclamations for dramatic effect' (Bank 2006: 365). He altered his tone frequently, sometimes whispering, sometimes crying and so on. He used particular click sounds for specific animals, and these were often related to the shape of the animal's mouth.

|Han#kass'o assumed the role of an informant very soon after arriving in Mowbray at the beginning of 1878. One of his first tasks was to comment on a series of rock paintings that Lloyd showed him (Bank 2006: 304, 322–39). When the governor, Bartle Frere, asked Lloyd in February

1878 if her informants could shed any light on the relations on the frontier between the settlers and the indigenous population, she reported that, according to |Han#kass'o, conditions were very bad. There were only two farmers who treated the Bushman well in the region. She also mentioned to Frere that ||Kabbo had earlier expressed the wish that the governor at the time, Barkly, would authorise the expulsion of the settlers from his ancestral homeland (341–42). |Han#kass'o cuts an isolated figure in the Bleek household, but he does, at least, seem to have enjoyed a relatively relaxed and informal relationship with Lucy Lloyd, as well as the children in the household, for whom he sometimes made presents (343).

Bank (2006: 351–53) argues that Lucy Lloyd increasingly became interested in the specificity of local cultures, instead of seeing the study of culture as consisting of 'mapping the local onto a global chart', the common ethnographic approach of the time, and also the comparative approach to both linguistics and culture of Wilhelm Bleek, the 'universal philologist' (Moran 2009: 24–27). Lloyd's work with |Han#kass'o in the late 1870s reflects her growing fascination with the particular character of |Xam culture itself. While |Han#kass'o still recounted traditional stories, he accompanied these with a great wealth of general cultural information. |Han#kass'o left Cape Town in December 1879, when he returned to his home district to search for his son (Bank 2006: 373). No-one knows what happened to him after that. Bank guesses that he found his surviving son and worked on a farm.

Just before his departure, |Han#kass'o was joined in the Bleek household by several !Xun children. Lucy Lloyd studied their language, discovering that it was very different from |Xam, although she also detected points of convergence. She recorded a number of !Xun narratives featuring the shape-shifting character |Xué. The children also drew detailed pictures of animals and an astonishing variety of plants from memory.

PUBLISHED SELECTIONS FROM THE BLEEK AND LLOYD COLLECTION

The year 1911 saw the publication of Bleek and Lloyd's *Specimens of Bushman Folklore*, a selection of extracts from the notebooks. The 76-year-old

Lucy Lloyd had spent decades preparing the manuscript and trying to persuade the intellectual community of the importance of the materials it contained. *Specimens of Bushman Folklore* reproduces the format of the notebooks with the |Xam and English translation side by side, a feature consistent with the importance Bleek and Lloyd attached to language. The emphasis is on stories, especially those of a 'mythological' character. The book also contains sections on legends, personal history, and customs and superstitions.

In 1923 Bleek's daughter, Dorothea, published another, more heavily edited, selection from the notebooks. *The Mantis and His Friends* concentrates on the |Kaggen narratives and leaves out the |Xam language text. Dorothea Bleek's editorial interventions frequently extend to constructing a single narrative from several different texts. In the process, events are made to occur in the same story that do not coexist in any single account in the notebooks (Hewitt 1986: 213–14). Dorothea published further extracts from the materials in the anthropological journal *Bantu Studies* between 1931 and 1936 (Hollmann 2004: 2–3). These extracts concern beliefs and customs rather than stories.

A few more selections of Bushman stories appeared in the decades that followed. These drew on the materials published by Lucy Lloyd and Dorothea Bleek, as well as on other sources such as Joseph Orpen (1874), Gideon von Wielligh (1919–21) and materials from the Kalahari.[7] Arthur Markowitz (1956) recounts 35 narratives, drawn chiefly from the |Xam sidereal materials that were published in *Specimens of Bushman Folklore*. He rewrites the stories in order to give them literary appeal, but eschews the use of modern language in favour of preserving their 'primitive' character. The notebooks themselves disappeared until the British researcher Roger Hewitt managed to have them located in the University of Cape Town Library by some library assistants in the early 1970s. Today the handwritten notebooks form the core of the Bleek and Lloyd Collection housed in the Manuscripts and Archives Department of the University of Cape Town. The materials are very much part of the public domain. In 1997 the collection 'was entered into UNESCO's Memory of the World Register' (Bank 2006: 389). Thanks to the indefatigable efforts of Pippa Skotnes and her team, the entire Bleek and Lloyd Collection is now available online and on a DVD that accompanies Skotnes's book, *Claim to the Country* (2007).

In 1989 anthropologist Mathias Guenther published 16 |Xam stories from the Bleek and Lloyd Collection in *Bushman Folktales: Oral Traditions of the Nharo of Botswana and the /Xam of the Cape*. By publishing stories from two Bushman traditions together, he 'sought to illustrate the extent to which they were part of a single Khoisan mythological tradition' (Bank 2006: 391). Most of the |Xam stories had not been published before. Guenther noted that half the hundred or so narratives that can be assembled from the collection remained unpublished. Further selections and extracts from the notebooks followed, notably David Lewis-Williams's *Stories that Float from Afar* (2000) and a collection of the materials published in the 1930s by Dorothea Bleek in *Bantu Studies*, edited by Jeremy Hollmann (2004) and entitled *Customs and Beliefs of the /Xam Bushmen*. Hollmann's book presents both the |Xam texts and the English translations as they appeared in *Bantu Studies* in the 1930s, and also supplies notes to the text and introductions to each section.

In addition, several volumes of poetry have appeared in the last 15 years that are based on extracts from the notebooks. They were preceded in 1969 by a number of versions in poetry of |Xam materials by Jack Cope, included in *The Penguin Book of South African Verse* (Cope & Krige 1968). Stephen Watson's volume, *Return of the Moon: Versions from the /Xam*, appeared in 1991. This was followed in 2001 by James's *The First Bushman's Path: Stories, Songs and Testimonies of the /Xam of the Northern Cape* and in 2004 by Antjie Krog's *The Stars Say 'Tsau': /Xam Poetry of Dia!kwain, Kweiten-Ta-//Ken, /A!kunta, Han#kass'o, and //Kabbo*.

All the published selections and versions have reordered the original materials of the notebooks considerably. Narrative, information and autobiography run into each other in the notebooks. Stories often 'lack' clear beginnings and ends. The |Xam used the term *kukummi* (plural of *kumm*) to signify things that were told (see above) and did not maintain 'rigid generic distinctions between verse forms and narrative, or between sacred and profane genres' (Brown 1998: 26). Narrative and history were 'regarded as equally true or untrue' (Hewitt 1986: 56). The selections, on the other hand, order the materials thematically and generically, and the stories are supplied with names. This process already involves a degree of interpretation and predisposes, in turn, particular readings, a phenomenon I explore at some length in later chapters. Solomon (n.d.: 14) notes that '[t]he ways we imagine and understand San arts are echoed in the ways they are presented and reproduced in the present'. Presenting the materials in the form of poetic extracts, especially, both aestheticises them and results in their removal 'from the larger body of narratives of which they are part ... many are stories within a bigger story' (Solomon n.d.: 14). Elana Bregin (1998: 87) has described the difference between reading the notebooks and the edited collections:

> Encoded in their convoluted, repetitive and aesthetically untidy structure
> is a far better sense of the cultural 'strangeness' and perceptual and expres-
> sive 'difference' of the Bushman worldview than is offered by the more
> lyrically flowing versions of the later collections.

THE WRITING ON THE BLEEK AND LLOYD COLLECTION

The |Xam texts, both as they appear in the notebooks and in the published selections or reworkings, provide the chief focus of this book. I consider, in particular, the question of their interpretation and accompany this discussion with a detailed analysis of several of the texts. At the same time, a careful examination of the work that has provided interpretation of the texts is also undertaken. In this section I provide an overview of the body of writing that subsequent chapters will scrutinise more closely.

Most of the writing that has been produced in relation to the Bleek and Lloyd archive describes the origins, development and history of the project. A smaller body of writing seeks, in some way, to explicate the narratives. Much of this work is pioneering and insightful. It is a comparatively small body of work, however, if one considers both the range of the materials in the notebooks and the quantity of other sorts of writing about the collection. In this regard, Solomon (n.d.: 12) maintains that the stories 'remain rather under-researched'. She notes, too, that scholarship concentrates on 'issues of authenticity and presentation [of the materials] at the expense of further understanding of the narratives themselves'

(Solomon n.d.: 244). Of the analysis that does exist, relatively little has attempted a close reading of the texts (Brown 1998: 36–37). Lewis-Williams (1998a: 195) observed ten years ago in an article in *African Studies* that 'given the rich heritage of indigenous southern African folklore, it is surprising that so few scholars have attempted detailed exegesis of specific myths'. His statement is still largely applicable to the study of the ǀXam narratives today.[8] It is partly to address this gap that I attempt a close and theoretically self-conscious reading of selected texts, mostly in the second half of this book, readings that aim not only to discuss the materials, but to engage in a metacriticism that is inspired by them and that attempts to discern an indigenous exegesis in the materials and to build on it.

As I pointed out at the beginning of this chapter, the limited body of work that has interpreted the ǀXam narratives has not been subjected to the sustained, close and critical scrutiny that, to my mind, is of particular significance in cross-cultural studies. Solomon (n.d.: 254) writes: 'Neglected in all recent literary studies is an appreciation of the interpretation that has already gone into them. The criticism that does exist consists of comments rather than sustained analysis. It is rather amazing …' In the course of the book, I attempt, therefore, to initiate an extensive critique of the ways in which the ǀXam texts have been analysed. Too often, broad statements and assumptions about the stories have been unquestioningly reproduced in works by later authors, attaining in the process the status of reified truths.

Bleek and Lloyd themselves might be seen as the first interpreters of the materials that they assembled (Bank 2006: 184). The translation of the texts into ǀXam entailed hermeneutics, while the reports they presented to parliament, the articles that Bleek wrote, the particular kinds of narrative that they tried to elicit and the categorisation of the materials they collected all involved acts of interpretation.

In 1929 Dorothea Bleek published an article about the ǀXam narratives called 'Bushman folklore' in which she sets out to give some idea of the scope and nature of the materials. She notes that 'very few ǀKham stories concern human beings alone, the greater part centre in animals, by which I mean members of the animal kingdom, some in heavenly bodies or forces of nature often in connexion with animals' (Bleek 1929: 302). In the course of the article, she manages not only to provide summaries of a considerable number of tales, but also to discuss the place of |Kaggen and !Khwa in |Xam narrative and belief and the role of storytelling in |Xam social life.

Roger Hewitt's 1986 book *Structure, Meaning and Ritual in the Narratives of the Southern San* was the first book-length study of the materials to be published and remains to date the only book that is devoted chiefly to interpretation of the narratives. A reading of this work forms the subject matter of chapter 5 of this book. Hewitt's work both brought the materials back into the public domain and formed the foundation of much of the work that has followed. Twenty years after his book was published, it still represents 'perhaps the most detailed and insightful study' of the narratives (Solomon n.d.: 245). His study is taxonomic, structuralist and functionalist. A feature of Hewitt's work is his investigation of the 'way in which a relatively restricted set of motifs and themes are configured into an abundance of individual stories' (56). He also provides extensive ethnographic background to the narratives. In his own words, Hewitt (1986: 20) sets out to situate 'individual narratives within their narrative tradition and that tradition, within a cultural context extending from the material world to the conceptual frameworks evinced in custom and belief'. Although he discusses a number of stories in considerable detail, he concentrates on classifying narratives according to type rather than attempting close analysis of individual stories. Hewitt's work, observes Brown (1995: 79), 'tends to emphasise the creation of structural typologies over the analysis of texts in terms of their symbolic resonance within their society and beyond'.

As the title of Guenther's *Bushman Folktales: Oral Traditions of the Nharo of Botswana and the /Xam of the Cape* (1989) suggests, he adopts a comparative approach to interpretation in this book. Although Guenther provides commentaries that contain hermeneutic statements, his main project in the book is to present selections of texts from the two Bushman traditions. His subsequent study of the |Xam narratives in *Tricksters and Trancers: Bushman Religion and Society* (1999), however, contains an extended discussion of the interpretation of Bushman narrative. His argument in the book rests chiefly on a reading of the |Kaggen narratives as trickster tales. Guenther, as I will show in chapter 6, contends that these stories reinforce a foraging ideology that encourages individualism and flexibility. His book also brings together the |Xam trickster and Kalahari trance practitioner, whom he regards as different manifestations of a single Bushman complex. Guenther's treatment of individual texts in this book is generally quite brief, although he does examine the story of 'The Origin of Death' in some detail.

David Lewis-Williams (1996a; 1998a) has provided two of the most detailed readings of |Xam narratives. He extends Hewitt's structuralist dissection of the narratives by including a vertical level of meaning that he identifies especially with shamanistic experience. Chapters 3 and 11 of this book include a closer look at Lewis-Williams's analysis of |Xam stories.

Andrew Bank (2006) offers not only a history of the Bleek and Lloyd Collection, but readings of particular texts as well. The particular importance of these readings, I will argue in chapter 7, is the way that they draw attention to the social and historical contexts of the production of specific texts, as well as to the presence of performative aspects in the process of the collection of the |Xam materials in Cape Town.

Besides the work of these writers, which I will examine especially closely in the course of this book, many other writers also comment on the narratives and their interpretation in various ways. This book takes this writing into account as well. The introduction and notes to the major collections, such as Bleek and Lloyd's *Specimens of Bushman Folklore* (1911), Dorothea Bleek's *The Mantis and His Friends* (1923), Lewis-Williams's *Stories that Float from Afar* (2000) and Jeremy Hollmann's *Customs and Beliefs of the /Xam Bushmen* (2004), all contain observations of an interpretive nature, even though interpretation is not their main business.

Alan James's versions in poetry of extracts from the Bleek and Lloyd Collection, *The First Bushman's Path: Stories, Songs and Testimonies of the |Xam of the Northern Cape* (2001), are accompanied by detailed commentaries on each poem. Although James provides many useful insights into individual texts, his approach does not consist of close textual reading, as his commentaries are intended to enhance appreciation of the poetry.[9] He does, however, provide a detailed intertextual map by cross-referencing the materials he has chosen with others in the collection. This method enables the materials, to some degree, to begin to interpret themselves. With regard to James's (2001: 24) stated intention to 'highlight an aspect of that text, such as a structure or imagery, that might be passed over by the reader if it were not emphasized', Solomon (n.d.: 251) notes that 'the poetic form in this scenario may function as an "analysis" in itself'. In a similar way, the manner in which a photograph of a rock painting is framed entails an interpretation of the painting (Solomon n.d.: 119).

Literary critic Duncan Brown has written in some detail on the narratives and their interpretation. The |Xam texts, he emphasises, challenge our ability to listen across 'social and historical distances' (1995: 79) to the perspectives of the |Xam themselves. Brown (1995: 80) also argues for a reading that situates the texts 'within the signifying practices of their society'. In *Voicing the Text: South African Oral Poetry and Performance*, Brown (1998: 71) contends that the '|Xam texts represent not the primordial child-man, nor an idyllic African past but a complex imaginative response to pressing social and economic needs'. He advocates a dialectical strategy to reading the texts that attempts to both recover their past meanings and situate them in the context of South Africa's 'human, social and political reconstruction' (Brown 1998: 2).[10] 'Present needs and ideologies' impel the retrieval of history that the reading and interpretation of the narratives implies. The past can become a radical agent that questions and judges the present (Brown 1998: 24–25). This, for Brown, provides a 'moral purpose' for studying the |Xam texts. The narratives, asserts Brown (1998: 54), following Biesele (1976: 303), allow for the processing in discourse of social and political problems. Brown's work has influenced my own approach to reading the narratives in ways that I describe most fully in chapter 3.

The central concern of Anne Solomon's work (1997; 1999; 2007; 2008; 2009; n.d.) is the rock art of the Drakensberg. She shows that the evidence that has been extracted from the |Xam narratives in order to support the dominant trance theory of rock art interpretation has to be questioned on several grounds. In order to do this, she undertakes a careful examination of the |Xam texts. Her readings produce important new insights into the place of the spirits of the dead in the materials, for example, and emphasise the value of paying close attention to the texts themselves.

The title of Elana Bregin's 1998 MA dissertation, 'The identity of difference: A critical study of representations of the Bushmen', is deliberately ambiguous, for she examines in her study not only the process of 'othering' involved in the representation of the Bushmen by others, but the processes by which the Bushmen themselves represented the world. She considers the lXam narratives and the rock art of the Drakensberg from the perspective of representation *by* the Bushmen rather than *of* the Bushmen. This project involves the retrieval of 'a more authentic and "human" Bushmen identity from the welter of myths — both derogatory and idealised — which have contributed to their long history of "othering"' (Bregin 1998: 29). This necessitates an acknowledgement by the critic that alterity is a function of the critic's project of the self rather than a characteristic of the people being 'othered' (28). It also requires a recognition of the complexity of the 'mythological systems and psychic spaces' being considered (26).[11] The project of trying to understand the tales entails the critic's undergoing a considerable 'paradigm shift' (25).

Bregin's reading of the stories is mostly wide and general. She follows Hewitt (1986) in asserting that the chief theme of the tales is the main- tenance of 'a stable social order' (Bregin 1998: 91), and Brown (1998), Guenther (1996) and Biesele (1993) in emphasising the role of narrative in the mediation of the recurrent concerns of a foraging way of life. These include 'food-sharing, uncontrollable weather, interpersonal relationships and social protocol' (Bregin 1998: 91). Stories, she believes, serve a didactic function that goes far beyond their entertainment value. Bregin considers the stories of the sun, moon and stars, for instance, as hunter-gatherer attempts to account philosophically for 'the great imponderables of their existence', such as mortality and 'the origin of the heavenly bodies' (Bregin 1998: 102).

Belinda Jeursen's MA dissertation (1994), 'Gender in lXam narratives: Towards an unidealised reading of the community', focuses on the stories that concern !Khwa and menstruating girls. Her article in the journal *Alternation* (Jeursen 1995) covers some of the same ground. Jeursen pays special attention to the texts gleaned from !Kweiten-ta-llken, the only lXam woman who contributed substantially to the Bleek and Lloyd Collection. Her study is unusual in that it discovers asymmetrical relations of power in a culture usually presented as egalitarian. She reads the stories that are related to female initiation rites, in particular, as a conflict between individual freedom and 'gender-based' traditions (Jeursen 1995: 40). She

17

notes that, in the context of ritual, conflict occurs between individuals and power structures rather than between two individuals. She maintains that punishment in the narratives for the breaking of taboos is reserved for women (41), and she emphasises the masculinity of both !Khwa and |Kaggen (42). Jeursen provides a fairly detailed analysis of 'The Girl of the Early Race who Made Stars', reading the story in terms of power and sexuality rather than as a story of the origin of the stars, as most other interpreters have done. A feature of Jeursen's work is the strong emphasis she places on the didactic and ideological function of stories. 'All the |Xam stories', she asserts, 'share the function of education in belief and survival' (40). In relation to 'The Girl of the Early Race who Made Stars', for example, she contends, that the 'narrative is an account aimed at instructing people, especially young girls, about puberty rites and the corresponding observances' (52).

Harold Scheub's *Story* (1998) brings together three South African storytellers from different written and oral traditions. ||Kabbo is included, along with Nongenile Masithathu Zenani, a Xhosa storyteller, and the novelist Pauline Smith. Scheub provides details of the |Xam informant's biography and examines his storytelling techniques. Scheub relates and discusses several of ||Kabbo's stories. His commentaries on the stories of 'The All-devourer' and 'The Mantis and the Ticks' are particularly detailed (213–17). Stories function, in Scheub's view, as mechanisms for the production of emotions. This is their meaning and the 'essence of story-telling' (8). Misinterpretation often results from critics placing too much attention on the ethical or formal aspects of a story and ignoring the fact that stories are always emotionally interpreted by their auditors. The emotional life of the teller is layered in the story. Each telling is resonant with the affective life of the narrator and the audience, as well as the echoes of all its previous tellings. Although 'story is a major means of communication' in which 'a message is conveyed from one generation to another' and 'is the vehicle whereby essential historical and social values … are retained', it accomplishes this task 'not in didactic ways, not on the literal level of the sequence of events, but in the form of emotion' (22). The very 'building blocks of storytelling', images, are 'felt actions or sets of actions' (23).

STORIES OF IKAGGEN AND STORIES OF THE SUN, MOON AND STARS

I concentrate in this book on the IXam narratives that feature IKaggen, the Mantis, and those that concern the sun, the moon and the stars, both when I discuss the work of other writers and when I analyse the IXam materials myself. The IKaggen and sidereal materials lend themselves to the purposes of this study for several reasons.[12] They are particularly suitable for investigating the concepts of the trickster and the myth of origin, two recurring ideas that frame the reading of the stories that I seek to question in this book. They form a substantial corpus of materials that have invited the attention of those critics who have attempted to interpret the IXam stories. Since previous critics have written about them, my own interpretation of these kinds of narrative can either build on or question the work of these predecessors. Most of these stories also appear in the early selections from the collection (Bleek & Lloyd 1911; D. Bleek 1923) and can, thus, easily be read as discrete texts and located as particular kinds of story, even as the editorial interventions that resulted in these textual arrangements are questioned. These materials are also more readily available to readers than are the unpublished materials from the notebooks. I make extensive use of these unpublished sources, too, however, in order to support my contention that the narratives should be read in the context of an intertextual IXam discursive field rather than as myths.

I am aware that by focusing on the sidereal and IKaggen ('trickster') materials at the expense of others in the collection I might be reinforcing a bias that is grounded in the ideological and theoretical preoccupations of collectors and interpreters, even as I seek to critique them. Moran (2009: 97) argues in his examination of Bleek's theory of language that the latter's preoccupation with sidereal materials was integral to his hierarchical theory of race and culture. Sidereal worship, in Bleek's view, represented an advance on ancestral worship as practised by the African people further north in southern Africa and was the precursor of more advanced forms of religion. Guenther (1996: 89) observes that, under the influence of Max Müller, Bleek was predisposed to consider sidereal materials of particular importance and to elicit them from his informants as much as he could. Hewitt (1986: 91) notes, too, that despite the best efforts of the collectors, the sidereal materials only comprise a relatively small part of the narratives.

Although the same could not be said of the |Kaggen materials, I will argue in later chapters that the centrality of |Kaggen has been inflated through a process whereby several features that recur in the |Kaggen narratives tend to be ascribed to a |Kaggen complex, when they actually form part of a |Xam broader discursive field that includes |Kaggen himself.

Although I cross-reference them quite extensively, I have somewhat neglected the many stories of the First Times that feature animal characters, but which do not feature |Kaggen and his family. This omission does not imply that I consider these narratives of less interest or consequence than the cosmological materials or the 'trickster' tales that I have chosen to focus on for the reasons outlined in the previous paragraph. The Bleek and Lloyd corpus is so wide that I necessarily have to be selective, especially since I advocate detailed readings rather than broad comparative treatment. I have also not provided close readings of the biographical, historical and cultural material in the notebook for the same reason. Once again, however, I do refer to these materials extensively when discussing the narratives that I have chosen to examine closely. This accords with my argument that one of the first steps in beginning to understand particular |Xam texts is to situate them within the broader field of |Xam discourse.

THE PROJECT OF THIS BOOK

The Bleek and Lloyd Collection, it will have become evident, has attracted a considerable amount of attention, particularly in the last 40 years. Several selections from the archive have been published with varying degrees of editorial intervention. Some of the materials have been reworked into poetry. The history of the production of the collection has been written and the biographies of the major |Xam and European protagonists recreated. Scholars have analysed the colonial context in which the |Xam project proceeded, both in terms of the frontier history of the Cape at the time and in terms of Bleek's ideological and theoretical concerns. Attempts have been made to link the |Xam notebooks with rock art from other parts of the region and with the practice of shamanism. Several studies also exist in which the materials themselves are classified and interpreted. It is with this last aspect of |Xam studies, in particular, that this book concerns itself, and it seeks to inaugurate a critique of the way in which the |Xam texts have been read. Only comments have so far been offered about the relatively small but influential body of work that has attempted to understand the materials and it has not yet been subjected to sustained critical analysis. This book also attempts to offer a fresh approach to reading the |Xam texts, one that engages with their textuality and takes cognisance of more recent developments in literary, cultural and post-colonial theory.

The book consists of four sections and 12 chapters. In section 1, comprising chapters 1, 2, 3 and 4, some of the theoretical and methodo- logical questions that attend the analysis of the |Xam narratives are discussed. Chapter 1 consists of an overview of the work of the theorists whose work has most influenced the reading of the |Xam materials: Claude Lévi-Strauss, Bronislaw Malinowski and Vladimir Propp in particular. It also includes a discussion of some of the ideas of Michel Foucault, Pierre Bourdieu and Gayatri Spivak that have informed the enquiry that I conduct in the book. Chapter 2 contains an argument for the application of particular aspects of contemporary theory to the interpretation of both the |Xam texts themselves and to the writing that has been produced in relation to them. The chapter focuses on aspects of the work of Jacques Derrida. Chapter 3 investigates the idea of the myth of origin in the field of comparative mythology as this idea appears in the reading of the |Xam narratives. This is followed in chapter 4 by a critique of the notion of the trickster. Some of the theories regarding the trickster are set out, before the way in which the term has been applied to the |Xam figure |Kaggen is explored.

Section 2 examines some of the most influential writing about the |Xam narratives. I describe and examine Roger Hewitt's pioneering work on the |Xam narratives in chapter 5, concentrating specifically on his reading of the |Kaggen stories. Chapter 6 discusses Mathias Guenther's reading of the |Kaggen materials and compares it to Hewitt's. Guenther's notion of a foraging ideology that underlies Bushman narratives is critiqued at some length. This is followed in chapter 7 by a consideration of the implications for interpreting the narratives of Andrew Bank's historical research on the Bleek and Lloyd Collection.

Section 3 primarily investigates the materials that concern the sun, moon and stars and explores different ways of reading these texts. Chapter 8 provides a reading of different versions of a story that features the moon, as well as the different versions of a narrative that features |Kaggen. I discuss the way in which discursive objects are ordered in these narratives, as well as the narratives' relation to power and their ability to elicit multiple interpretations. Chapter 9 analyses 'The Children are Sent to Throw the Sleeping Sun into the Sky', with particular attention to the story's aetiological status, its chain of speaking and its presentation of identity. Chapter 10 investigates 'The Girl of the Early Race who Made Stars', according special attention to the intertextual field in which the narrative participates.

Section 4 consists of a discussion of two of the many controversies that have attended Bushman studies over the years. Chapter 11 critiques David Lewis-Williams's shamanistic interpretation of a |Xam narrative, while chapter 12 investigates the furore that attended Stephen Watson's accusation that Antjie Krog's *The Stars Say 'Tsau'* constituted plagiarism.

1 For a discussion of the various terms that have been used to designate the people whose narratives form the subject of this study, see the 'Note on terminology' at the start of the book.
2 The last known trace of |Xam was spoken by the elderly Hendrik Goud in the mid-1980s (Deacon 1996: 113).
3 See Anthony Traill's (1996) analysis of the rapid destruction of the |Xam language.
4 Dorothea Bleek (1929: 305) says of Kwammang-a that he is 'a being seen in the rainbow' and 'a quiet, brave man, whose behaviour forms a great contrast to that of the talkative, nervous Mantis'.
5 The |Xam were divided into Flat Bushmen, Grass Bushmen and Mountain Bushmen, depending on which region of the area in the northern Cape south of the Orange River and in the vicinity of present-day Kenhardt they came from.
6 When the same source is referred to throughout a paragraph, only the first reference gives full details, and the remainder of the references given only page numbers.
7 In 1873 Joseph Orpen, recently appointed as magistrate of a new district in the Drakensberg, recorded a number of narratives involving Cagn (Orpen's spelling) that were told to him by his interpreter, Qing (Bank 2006: 305). These materials were published in the *Cape Monthly Magazine* (Orpen 1874) with a commentary by Wilhelm Bleek. After the Bleek and Lloyd Collection, the largest corpus of Bushman narratives from the area falling within the boundaries of present-day South Africa was collected by Gideon von Wielligh. His informants included some |Xam speakers near Calvinia. Von Wielligh published his narratives in Afrikaans between 1919 and 1921. Hewitt (1986: 18) remarks of this body of materials that they represent 'an often illuminating supplement to the Bleek and Lloyd Collection. However, Von Wielligh was a popular writer who sought to encourage poor Afrikaners to read. His simplified stories, pub-

lished in Afrikaans, were re-modelled by him to these didactic ends and, unfortunately, cannot be taken as reliable versions of |Xam narratives'. Van Vuuren (1995) notes that Hewitt relies quite heavily at times on Von Wielligh's materials, despite his qualified dismissal of them. The fact that Von Wielligh's narratives are in Afrikaans accounts, in Van Vuuren's opinion, for the relative lack of recognition they have been accorded.

8   There are notable exceptions, however. Hewitt (1986: 91–104) provided a detailed analysis of 'The Story of the Dawn's Heart and His Wife the Lynx' more than ten years before Lewis-Williams's observation. Lewis-Williams himself (1996a; 1998a) analyses two stories in considerable detail. Guenther (1999) analyses 'The Moon and the Hare' in some depth in a book that is otherwise general and comparative in its approach to the materials, as was his earlier work (1989). Belinda Jeursen (1995) interprets the story of 'The Girl of the Early Race who Made Stars' in terms of gender and power. Duncan Brown (2006) provides an innovative reading of ||Kabbo's discourse on returning home, treating it textually. Andrew Bank (2006) examines several of the narratives in a way that establishes a much more concrete historical context for them than was previously attempted. Anne Solomon (2009) provides a fine revisionist reading of Dia!kwain's 'The Broken String'.

9   Solomon (n.d.: 14) argues that presenting the narratives as extracts, as James does, necessitates the use of extensive introductory and explanatory materials, whereas 'the stories are intelligible when seen within the larger body of narratives of which they are a part'.

10 Solomon (n.d.: 217) notes that the question of establishing a relationship between the past of the stories and the present of interpretation is complicated by the fact the |Xam past is not monolithic: '|Xam narratives ... belong not only to the nineteenth century past of the narrators and recorders, but also to a tradition that may be of great antiquity — perhaps even millennia old — as well as to the present in which we read them'. With regard to rock paintings, she cautions that scenes of conflict between Bushmen and colonists do 'not provide us with any new historical information', nor do they 'give the other side of the story told in official colonial papers and other historical literature' (225).

11 Bregin emphasises the challenge of interpreting complex Bushman representational arts. Solomon (n.d.: 215), too, notes that Bushman art and stories must be understood on their own terms: 'San arts are imaginings of past, present and future worlds, not documentary records left behind.' She insists on the point that '[s]tories and images were made *as* stories and images, not as information repositories, and their status as artworks inevitably shapes the kind of "data" they may comprise or evoke' (Solomon n.d.: 216, original emphasis).

12 The stories of the sun, moon and stars are commonly referred to as the sidereal materials in the literature.

SECTION 1

Text, Myth and Narrative

CHAPTER 1

READING NARRATIVE:
Some Theoretical Considerations

THEORIES OF MYTH AND FOLKLORE

As is only to be expected, the writers who have provided interpretation of the
|Xam materials draw on theories of interpretation. This theory is generally
implicit in their work and has to be extracted from it. |Xam studies have, for
the most part, been characterised by an absence of direct theoretical debate,
and categories such as the trickster, myth, literature and folklore are generally
deployed without discussion or qualification, as though they were natural
and uncontroversial. This is true despite the fact that the categories of
literature and mythology served as potent ideological markers in Bleek's
theory of language and race, as Moran's (2009: 119–27) analysis of this aspect
of Bleek's writing has shown. Interpreters of the |Xam narratives tend to draw
liberally, eclectically and uncritically from different theories of mythology, a
practice that frequently leads to inconsistencies in their contentions about
the |Xam materials. This is not surprising when, as Strenski (1987: 3)
observes, the different theorists propose 'theories and concepts of myth
[that] are so different that little can usefully be argued among them'.

Although there is little discussion of theory in the writing on the |Xam
materials, certain writers and their theories recur quite often in this
literature. In the first part of this chapter I will briefly introduce the
theories of these writers as a prelude to the critique of these theories that is
offered in the rest of the book. Hewitt and Guenther make use of both
functionalist and structuralist analysis in their discussion of the |Xam

materials. Hewitt draws explicitly on the work of Claude Lévi-Strauss and Vladimir Propp, while Guenther follows trends in Lévi-Strauss's writing, as well as that of Bronislaw Malinowski, but is also critical of them. Lewis-Williams's analysis of |Xam stories refers to Mircea Eliade and Lévi-Strauss. The writing of Paul Radin, Carl Jung and others on the trickster has also influenced the interpretation of the narratives and will be explored in some detail in chapter 4.

Malinowski based most of his conclusions about myth on the evidence of the Trobriand society in which he lived during the First World War and the distinctions that people there made between different genres of oral literature. The pragmatic functionalist position for which he is most well known, however, emerged more strongly later in his career, when he tried to convince colonial administrations about the importance of employing the findings of scientific anthropology in order to better understand their subjects. His motives seem to have aimed not so much at increasing the efficacy of colonial control as at enhancing sympathy for cultural diversity and the protection of indigenous institutions.

Malinowski (1926: 11) approaches myth chiefly in terms of the practical role it plays in a particular society: 'an intimate connection exists between the word, the mythos, the sacred tales of a tribe, on the one hand, and their ritual acts, their moral deeds, their social organization, and even their practical activities, on the other.' This means that he is not primarily concerned with what one might describe as the intrinsic meaning that a myth might contain outside its social context or with its relationship with mythology from different regions of the world — the focus of an earlier generation of anthropologists who were chiefly interested in comparison and synthesis. Malinowski takes some trouble to define the characteristics of myth, arguing that not all the oral literature of a society fulfils the same sort of function. Myths are of a serious and sacred character and contain a truth value for all the members of the society in which they occur (35–36). Myth is not simply a type of fiction: 'Myth as it exists in a savage community, that is, in its living primitive form, is not merely a story told but a reality lived' (21).

Malinowski argues that the different elements of a culture constitute an interpenetrating whole, and interference with one aspect undermines the others. Myth is a vital ingredient of a cultural system and is essential to the preservation of its institutions and the fulfilment of the needs of human individuals that have a biological basis. He accords myths of origin or charter myths a critical role in sanctioning the social order. A myth 'comes into play when rite, ceremony, or a social or moral rule demands justification, warrant of antiquity, reality and sanctity' (Malinowski 1926: 36). A myth provides more than an aetiological explanation; it is 'a warrant, a charter, and often even a practical guide to the activities with which it is connected' (38). Malinowski (2001: 326) imputes to myth a conservative function that is connected with his conception of the conservative nature of traditional societies: 'The main social force governing all tribal life could be described as the inertia of custom, the love of uniformity of behaviour.' Malinowski's ideas about myth appear in different forms in the writing of the chief interpreters of the |Xam narratives, where they are generally reproduced without comment. Guenther, however, as I will show in chapter 6, is critical of aspects of Malinowski's functionalism.

The other theorist of myth who appears frequently in the writing on the |Xam narratives is, of course, Claude Lévi-Strauss. Although his ideas about mythology are entirely different from Malinowski's, his conception of the conservative and unchanging nature of traditional societies is quite close to Malinowski's. Nor does Lévi-Strauss altogether abjure functionalist explanation, despite his insistence that a myth is not a reflection of the social order, but gains its meaning from its relation to other myths. His remarks about the role of myth relate to intellectual and symbolic orders rather than to practical and social life, Malinowski's focus. Myths function, in Lévi-Strauss's view (1955: 443), to 'provide a logical model capable of overcoming a contradiction'.

Lévi-Strauss sought to challenge many of the ideas about 'primitive' cultures that served to position them at the bottom of the cultural evolutionary ladder by arguing that such cultures were different, not inferior. Indeed, in many respects, he implies, they are to be preferred to modern societies, since they are egalitarian and value social balance and harmony more than competition. Humans have always thought equally well, argues Lévi-Strauss, even though the content of thought might vary considerably, at least as far as external appearances are concerned.

People in pre-modern, small-scale societies are bricoleurs, using the sensory data that is at hand in their environment in order to elaborate signifying systems that enable them to think about the world in a fashion that might be described as concrete, as opposed to the abstract reflection that characterises scientific and philosophical thought (Lévi-Strauss 1966: 16–22). This 'savage' mentality does not seek to change the world or to interpret it in radically new ways so much as to reaffirm it through a process of transformation that re-orders an established and finite symbolic system. Myths, for example, display this process of transformation as they are told and reworked within the framework of a structure of finite possibilities.

Derrida (1976), as I describe in the next chapter, argues that Lévi-Strauss perpetuates a form of ethnocentrism, even as he challenges it, by positing a radical opposition between pre-colonial and modern societies and positioning the former as closer to pure presence. What Lévi-Strauss (1966) terms 'cold societies' are characterised not only by the sort of mythological and artistic bricolage to which I have referred, but by their resistance to history. Such societies, according to Lévi-Strauss, seek to maintain their character rather than develop in time. They are more orientated to an inaugural event that separates humans from animals than to history itself. One of the most striking characteristics of cold societies is the absence of writing. In Lévi-Strauss's view, writing is a necessary condition of social stratification and the asymmetrical distribution of power. This contention famously provoked the criticism of Derrida, who argued that in effect no society exists without writing, even if it does not have a formal writing system. Both speech and writing display a tension and instability between signifier and signified that can be called textual and that characterises all human signifying systems. Foucault (1980) has argued that power is always present in human relations in myriad forms. It does not require the formal political structures whose absence from certain societies is invoked by Lévi-Strauss and linked to freedom from writing.

Much of the writing on the |Xam narratives, I will argue, reproduces Lévi-Strauss's views about small-scale societies, power and writing. The reading of the narratives themselves also exhibits his influence, especially in relation to his contention that human thought is built on a system of binary oppositions: 'all mythemes of whatever kind, must, generally speaking, lend themselves to binary operations, since such operations are an inherent feature of the means invented by nature to make possible the functioning of language and thought' (Lévi-Strauss 1981: 559). Myth explores the contradictions that result from binary thinking through a process of analogical reproduction and dialectical synthesis.

Lévi-Strauss is more concerned with the synchronic aspects of myth than their location in history. In accordance with this bias, he focuses on the connections that link myths together at the deep structural level of mythemes, the basic units of myth that are combined or separated in various ways in order to make life's contradictions intelligible. He is not as interested in the sequence of events of individual narratives as in the paradigmatic links among narratives that often occur in geographically different places. A narrative, he maintains, that does not make much sense on the syntagmatic level might be illuminated by a paradigmatic comparison with another myth form far afield.[1] Lévi-Strauss's methodology is clear and his aims universal:

> By dividing the myth into sequences not always clearly indicated by the plot, and by relating each sequence to paradigmatic sets capable of giving them a meaning, we eventually found ourselves in a position to define the fundamental characteristics of a myth (Lévi-Strauss 1979: 199).

The perspective that is gained from following this procedure is not available to the purveyors of myths themselves. Lévi-Strauss (1969: 12) claims to be able to show 'how myths operate in men's minds without their being aware of the fact'. The structuralist critic explicitly adopts a privileged position in relation to knowledge, enjoying an objective, external perspective — a stance that has been contested by post-structural and post-colonial critics.

Lévi-Strauss is a ubiquitous presence, not only in relation to the study of myth, but in his influence on a generation of thinkers in a variety of fields. What might broadly be called post-structuralist thought is critical of Lévi-Strauss's structuralism, while also relying on many of his insights. My own study of |Xam narratives similarly owes much to aspects of Lévi-Strauss's structuralism, but also engages in a critique of it, something that could be said, too, of Michel Foucault's early work, an important source of the approach I adopt to reading the |Xam texts.

Roger Hewitt's analysis of the |Xam materials relies quite heavily on Lévi-Strauss's work, especially for his reading of the |Kaggen stories in terms of the nature–culture binary and also for his reading of |Kaggen as a mediator. His structural breakdown of these same stories, however, is based on Vladimir Propp's *Morphology of the Folktale*. Lévi-Strauss suggested that Propp's method would have worked better with myths than with the Russian folktales that he actually used because of their stronger oppositions (Dundes 1997: 42). Hewitt might be seen to be adopting Lévi-Strauss's advice by concentrating on |Xam myths — materials in which he finds the strong oppositions to which Lévi-Strauss refers. As I will argue in chapter 3, however, the |Xam narratives do not altogether conform to the traditional definitions of myth. Alan Dundes (1997: 42) has pointed out that Lévi-Strauss himself deals as often as not with what folklorists would describe as folklore rather than myth in the four volumes of *Introduction to a Science of Mythology*. Be this as it may, Hewitt reads the narratives in terms of a nature–culture opposition that is inspired by Lévi-Strauss, but adopts as his primary method of approach to the |Kaggen narratives a Proppian-style syntagmatic breakdown of their recurring functions. A function, in this context, 'is understood as an act of a character, defined from the point of view of its significance for the course of the action' (Propp 1968: 21). One of the defining characteristics of functions is that their 'sequence' is 'always identical'. I shall deliver a critique of this method in relation to Hewitt's work in chapter 5, arguing against its relegation of the textual detail of a narrative to mere 'verbal surface'. It could be noted here, however, that one of the salutary effects of the adoption of this method in Hewitt's work is the focus he maintains on the |Xam corpus itself, resisting the comparitist and universalising tendencies that are evident in some of the other writing on the narratives. This is consistent with Propp's empiricist approach to the study of Russian folktales, which might be contrasted with Lévi-Strauss's deductive approach. Lévi-Strauss's method tends to ignore the sequence of events in individual narratives and to concentrate instead on discovering the underlying paradigmatic oppositions that characterise human thought. Propp (1984:

76) himself said of this difference: 'My model corresponds to what was modeled and is based on a study of data, whereas the model Lévi-Strauss proposes does not correspond to reality and is based on logical operations not imposed by the data.' My own approach to analysis, as will become evident in the course of the book, is to forego both Lévi-Strauss's universalism and Propp's focus on the plot elements that are common to all the narratives of a local genre and to concentrate instead on the discursive detail of the texts.

GENERAL THEORY

In this book, I deliver a critique of the existing body of writing that concerns itself with reading the |Xam texts, and also read some of these texts myself. Both of these tasks rely on the work of a number of theorists. The overarching framework for my study has been inspired by the work of Derrida, particularly his reading of the writings of Rousseau and Lévi-Strauss in *Of Grammatology* (1976). The conception of a pre-lapsarian world of pure presence, Derrida argues, has determined, to a considerable degree, the European view of its own history and its construction of the pre-modern. An obsession with a primordial state of unity, proclaimed or repressed, has provided the principal impetus for the study of 'aboriginals', as well as a perennial source of images for successive installations of the 'primitive' in the modern and postmodern imaginative galleries. A myth of a lost origin underlies Western thought and invests it with unacknowledged metaphysical premises. Derrida contends that the evidence incriminates the materialist and empiricist discourses and practices that claim to exclude a metaphysical dimension as much as it does those systems of thought that base themselves within one.

I will discuss in this book the influence that this 'metaphysics of presence' has exerted on the way the figure of the 'Bushman' has been constructed and viewed. In particular, I examine the impact of this ideological complex on the collection and interpretation of the |Xam narratives. I also attempt to indicate the complexity — the impossibility, perhaps — of discovering a hermeneutics that eludes the 'metaphysics of presence'. In the next chapter I discuss the implications of my reading of

Derrida on the analysis I undertake in much greater detail. In the remainder of this chapter I should like to discuss the work of three other theorists who have particularly influenced the writing of this book: Michel Foucault, Pierre Bourdieu and Gayatri Spivak.

FOUCAULT

My approach to the analysis of the lXam texts has been especially informed by Foucault's relatively early work on discourse, particularly in *The Order of Things: An Archaeology of the Human Sciences* (1970) and *The Archaeology of Knowledge* (1972). Even though these works do not mention oral narrative as such, they have provided much of the technical inspiration for the manner in which I have attempted to read the lXam narratives, i.e. as discourse with their own modes of intertextuality. My investigation of the links between knowledge and power, in relation to both the lXam texts and to the texts in which they have been interpreted, also owes much to Foucault's writing on power.

Power, for Foucault, is enmeshed with knowledge, which always appears within the context of socially legitimated systems of thought. Foucault argues in the context of Europe that systems of thought or epistemes consist of the possible discourses that dominate an era. They are demarcated by the exclusion of certain categories such as insanity, sickness and criminality (Foucault 1973; 1975; 1977). Edward Said (1991; 1993), Gayatri Spivak (1988; 1999) and others have argued that the enterprise of imperialism relies on a similar mechanism of exclusion of the 'other'.[2] The notion of the primitive has been central to the delineation of reason (as was a particular formulation of madness) and to the ideas of civilisation and modernity. Wilhelm Bleek, the 'colonial intellectual', as Moran describes him, contributed to the framing of modernity with his studies of Bushman literature and language. 'The very idea of modernity ... is inseparable from the construction of the Bushmen,' writes Moran (2009: 127). Bleek's work encompassed not only the establishment of a hierarchically ordered scheme of language and literature, but also of physical type. He was directly involved in the anthropometric project in which photography was used in order to classify races in terms of physical type (Godby 1996; Webster 2000). The anthropometric method was used also, as Foucault describes, in studies of the criminal and the insane, for similar reasons.

Foucault investigates how specific individuals gain the authority to produce particular kinds of discourse. This would include the processes of academic legitimation, whereby individuals become the source of truths and authoritative statements about the |Xam and their narratives, beginning with Bleek and Loyd themselves. Who is qualified to make such pronouncements? '[F]rom whom ... does he receive ... the presumption that what he says is true? What is the status of the individuals who ... have the right, sanctioned by law or tradition, juridically defined or spontaneously accepted, to proffer such a discourse?' (Foucault 1972: 50). Beside the institutional factors, which I will discuss in a consideration of Bourdieu's work in the next section of this chapter, part of the answer lies within the field of discourse itself. Statements organised in particular ways gain their legitimation from their location within the discursive formation and from their adherence to particular relations. They belong always to a series and play a role among other statements. There are established '*procedures of intervention* that may be legitimately applied to statements' (58; original emphasis). These 'rules of formation operate ... on all individuals who undertake to speak in this discursive field' (63). This does not mean that a discourse is a static and rigid system. Although it possesses 'its own rules of appearance', it has 'also its own conditions of appropriation and operation' and these are 'the object of a struggle, a political struggle' (120), a phenomenon that is evident, as we shall see, in Bushman studies with its many controversies.

The limits that apply to the enunciating subject in all discourses apply also to the Bushman storyteller who

> brings into existence outside himself an object that belongs to a previously
> defined domain, whose laws of possibility have already been articulated,
> and whose characteristics precede the enunciation that posits it. ... the
> subject of the statement ... is not in fact the cause, origin, or starting-point
> of the written or spoken articulation of a sentence (Foucault 1972: 95).

||Kabbo himself could be said to be articulating something similar when he talks about 'stories that float from afar' (L.II.32:2875–77).[3] However, the

existence of this domain, I argue, not only sets limits to what a storyteller can say, but also constitutes a signifying field that enables multiple meanings to be generated. These meanings are not necessarily consistent. Contradiction is not an anomaly in discourse, but its necessary condition since, in Foucault's words (1972: 151), it is in order 'to overcome it that discourse begins to speak'. A discursive formation is 'a space of multiple dissensions' (155) whose 'purpose is to maintain discourse in all its many irregularities' (156). The IXam narratives are not, I would argue, timeless, archetypal artefacts, as their designation as folklore or myth suggests, but discourse, and thus sites of ideological production and contestation.[4]

Foucault claims that conventional histories of ideas ignore the properties of discourse and follow a linear narrative in which periods follow each other in necessary succession. Temporal dislocation and discontinuity disappear when such histories of ideas are viewed against a vast, unified backdrop, as each generation of ideas gives birth inevitably to its successor. He maintains, however, that abrupt interruptions of, and peremptory ruptures with, what has gone before are the characteristic properties of epistemes (8). The sort of history of ideas, he charges, that charts a gradual, seemingly inevitable progression of thought through the ages is an example of the proclivity to distinguish the unifying categories of a field of study as the prelude to their apparent discovery in the analysis that follows (25). The grand narrative of the history of ideas, Foucault asserts, fabricates unities and relationships through time, whereas the sort of archaeological excavation he offers exposes ruptures within seemingly homogeneous fields of study at the same time as it reveals synchronic relationships between apparently quite different contemporaneous discourses. Seemingly similar epistemological complexes from different periods belong to very different structures of meaning, depending on the epistemic context. Only a retrospective assembly of dispersed elements unites these diverse phenomena into a history.

Both the IXam narratives and the analytical approaches that seek to apprehend them occur within particular epistemes, creating a state of affairs in which different modalities and bodies of knowledge are juxtaposed through the practice of the researcher's hermeneutics, a situation that demands, I would contend, as much conceptual self-reflexivity on the part of the researcher as is possible. The epistemic contexts in which the interpretations have occurred determine, or strongly influence, what appears within the field and which claims can be made, validated and invalidated in relation to it. This book does not, therefore, attempt to replace the interpretations that have emerged in the course of the history of engagement with the Bleek and Lloyd Collection with other, 'truer' ones so much as to explore how different regimes of truth have produced particular kinds of knowledge about the |Xam narratives and to describe the contours of that knowledge. It also seeks to explore the types of knowledge about the |Xam narratives that beckon the contemporary researcher. While I argue for a particular approach to the |Xam texts and illustrate it in my own interpretive practice, I attempt always to foreground the limitations of the tools at my disposal (the result of their cultural, linguistic and historical specificity) and the temporary status of the statements I can make about the narratives. An episteme functions, maintains Foucault, not to distinguish the true from the false so much as to demarcate what can or cannot be authorised as knowledge. Inevitably, in the era of the globalisation of capital, and postmodern and post-colonial thought, present-day scholars view the narratives from a different vantage point from the one offered by the Victorian milieu in which they were collected or the modernist one in which much of their interpretation has been framed. Foucault's work suggests that 'knowledge' concerning the |Xam should be seen not as having resulted from an ever closer and more accurate understanding of the field so much as from the different discourses that have produced intellectual knowledge over the course of the last 125 years. It becomes important to locate ideas, interpretations and theories within these broader regimes of truth and relations of power rather than simply within the history of the ideas and theories that constitute Bushman studies.

Foucault's writing on epistemes has consequences, too, for the way in which the narratives themselves are considered. It cannot be presumed that the materials in the Bleek and Lloyd Collection all belong to a single |Xam episteme. Even if it could be shown that the narratives had remained the same over long periods of time, it would not mean that they produced the same kinds of meaning at different times in |Xam history. It is probable that the narratives would already have contained different discursive possibilities for the recently released prisoners who narrated the stories in the alien setting of Mowbray — with the dispossession of the |Xam already far advanced — than those they would have borne for members of an intact |Xam band (if such a thing ever existed) following a way of life close to that described in the stories. It is difficult to discern epistemic ruptures in a corpus of narratives like those collected by Bleek and Lloyd. A comprehensive knowledge of |Xam history and culture over a significant length of time would be necessary in order to detect breaks of the kind Foucault discovers between the Renaissance concern with taxonomy and the birth of humanism, for example. Such an exercise might be conducted with materials from a linguistic group with an extant oral literary tradition such as the Jul'hoansi for which written and historical records also exist. It is difficult to see how Foucault's method could work without them. Nevertheless, to suggest that the |Xam are exempt from the operation of epistemes would, in my view, be to locate their systems of thought outside history and power.

Most commentators have argued for the |Xam narratives' educative or explanatory utility in one way or another. Jeursen (1995: 40), for example, emphasises the didactic function of stories, asserting that 'all the |Xam stories … share the function of education in belief and survival'. Hewitt highlights the role of the stories in reinforcing social values. 'Educational narratives', he maintains, often work through the reflection and learning that follows on disaster (Hewitt 1986: 49). Guenther has argued, correctly in my view, that it is a mistake to discover ethical concerns, covert didacticism, organic philosophical treatises and social commentary in the stories. He maintains that one should not overemphasise 'the normative influence of folklore on the behavior of people' or underestimate 'the ludic, recreational' aspects of myth (Guenther 1999: 161). The terms of this debate largely fall away when knowledge is understood in the broader sense in which Foucault considers it. It does not matter whether or not the narratives are directly didactic. They form part of the |Xam archive of possible statements that together constitute a discursive formation, the precondition for the production and authorisation of knowledge. It is not the narrative discourse's capacity to hold knowledge and information that needs to be considered in this regard so much as the ways in which its statements make meaning possible and produce and legitimate truth.

According to Foucault (1972: 49), the rules of discursive practice 'define not the dumb existence of a reality ... but the ordering of objects'. I attempt to show in the following chapters how the practice of hermeneutics itself brings together objects in accordance with the rules of particular analytical discourses rather than discovers meanings inherent in the interpreted materials. The narratives, too, arrange and bring together a great many dispersed objects. Women and meat, for instance, are often juxtaposed in the |Xam narratives, as they are in the Ju|'hoan stories in which Biesele (1993) tracks this congruence. A correspondence between certain stars and animals provides another example, as does the sympathetic complex surrounding the relationship between a hunter and a large game animal he has shot. Accordingly, I attempt to pursue a line of enquiry in relation to the |Xam narratives that considers the ways in which the narratives form and order objects. Instead of trying to decode the narratives in order to discover traces of deeper meanings they carry from a world beyond themselves, I attempt to keep their surfaces in view and describe the field of their statements. Discourse, asserts Foucault (1972: 120), appears not as 'a providence which has always spoken in advance' but as 'an asset — finite, limited, desirable, useful — that has its own rules of appearance'.

It is also a productive exercise, I will attempt to show in later chapters, to approach the |Xam materials in terms of Foucault's analysis of power. If, as Foucault suggests, 'each society has its régime of truth' (Foucault, 1980: 131) and, moreover, 'specific effects of power are attached to the true', then an enquiry into the narratives could begin to reveal the effects of truth through which |Xam society distributed power and employed power's creative potential. This is an important line of enquiry in the context of a society[5] that, in its usual form, contained no formal social stratification and was predicated on the absence of asymmetrical relations of power.[6] '[P]ower', writes Foucault (1980: 142), 'is co-extensive with the social body; there are no spaces of primal liberty'. Power is ubiquitous; it pervades all social relations and is interiorised by individuals. 'Between every point of a social body, between a man and a woman, between the members of a family ... there exist relations of power' (187). The normative regulatory mechanisms that give Bushman bands and their relations with other bands the loose cohesion they possess could be understood in terms of power in this sense. Foucault, as is well known, relates modern modalities of power to methods of surveillance, most famously figured in Bentham's panopticon, a structure that enables a 'mode of operation through which power will be exercised by virtue of the mere fact of things being known and people seen in a sort of immediate, collective … gaze' (154). In Bushman bands, everyone sees everyone. A certain kind of power is manifested by means of this constant scrutiny, which the individual interiorises 'to the point that he is his own overseer' (155) and superintends his own behaviour. Guenther (1999: 42) points out, in relation to the !Kung and other Bushman groups, that a mechanism of deflation is consistently mobilised whereby any individual who becomes too self-assertive is subjected to group ridicule. Foucault maintains, moreover, that power is always present in the medium of discourse itself and within the processes of subjectivisation and objectivisation.

BOURDIEU

The writing of the French sociologist Pierre Bourdieu also offers, in my opinion, several invaluable concepts and strategies with which to contextualise a contemporary intellectual engagement with the world of the |Xam texts. Of particular importance to this study has been his notion of fields. Bourdieu's work has especially helped me to analyse the questions that pertain to the location of this book within the field of Bushman studies and within the wider academic field that enfolds Bushman studies, a necessary consideration in a study that aims to be self-reflexive.

A singular theoretical and ethical unease attends the project of this book. Interpretation of the narratives unavoidably re-represents both them and their narrators. A particular |Xam 'other' has to be constructed — a move that has a fraught history. The work of Thornton (1983b), Bank (1999; 2006) and Moran (2009) has shown that Bleek and his generation of scholars were often motivated to study materials like the |Xam narratives by their fascination with human evolution, an interest that fed an ideology of scientific racism that helped legitimate imperialism. However, while the ongoing interest in the 'primitive other' can be linked with a nostalgia for the lost origin and with the desire to recover some part of the earlier history of humankind — and still, therefore, constitutes a form of ethnocentrism

— the sort of motivation that impelled Bleek and his contemporaries could no longer be ascribed in any direct way to present-day scholars, none of whom would argue for the innate superiority of Western culture. In *Orientalism*, Edward Said (1991) links the systematic study of 'others', which assumed a new level of sophistication during Napoleon's invasion of Egypt, with imperial hegemony. Knowledge of the people one wishes to dominate is an essential component of power,[7] and the anthropological and colonial enterprises were inextricably interwoven. It would be an oversimplification, however, to situate the contemporary study of |Xam texts in this way. For a start, even if the living descendants of the |Xam were identified, they would now form part of a wider post-colonial population whose life practices bore little resemblance to those described in the nineteenth-century |Xam narratives. Detailed anthropological information of the sort required by the earlier phase of colonialism with its direct deployment of power is, in any case, not relevant to the project of contemporary capital. It could be argued, however, as De Certeau (1986) has done, that any assertion of Western rationality's hegemonic sway over the 'other' is relevant to the unequal relations of power that characterise the phase of global capitalism. Moran (2009: 117) has identified another sort of motivation behind the popularity of Bushman studies, one that also modifies the conventional view of the role of ethnographic knowledge. He links continued interest in the Bleek and Lloyd archive, for example, by white South African academics to a desire for 'access to a restitutive and collective history', an identification with a marginalised people that corresponds to their own sense of 'marginalization'.

Bourdieu's work offers another angle of approach to the question of the relation between power and knowledge in a study such as the one undertaken in this book. It is necessary, maintains Bourdieu, to analyse societies and the way power is distributed in them in terms not only of class, but also of fields, i.e. the social spaces in which agents manoeuvre for position and compete for resources. A cultural field is a 'series of institutions, rules, rituals, conventions, categories, designations, appointments and titles which constitute an objective hierarchy' (Webb, Schirato & Danaher 2002: 21) and which produces and authorises 'certain discourses and activities' (44). A field, such as academia, possesses a certain autonomy and its own ways of accumulating and legitimating power. Within this field, individuals accrue the prestige that comprises symbolic capital; enjoy access to the forms of social capital that come from membership of the networks that characterise the field; and accumulate the cultural capital and forms of knowledge, taste and sensibility that give agents in the field access to particular forms of power and prestige in the wider society. Although the agents within these fields usually understand themselves to be engaged in a quest for objective and disinterested truth, they are in fact, maintains Bourdieu, primarily engaged in competing for intellectual capital, resources, contacts, publications and so on that constitute the currency of the field. Bourdieu's analysis revolves, for the most part, around the national academy, but it could, in the present context, be extended to describe a global academic network. Just as capital in the form of wealth has been globalised, so has intellectual capital. The power to 'know' the world, to make authoritative statements about it and accrue capital from this power occurs on the supra-national level of international journals, research institutes and conferences to a much greater degree than ever before, a process greatly facilitated by electronic communication and air travel, and linked in intricate ways with the field of development and its experts. Despite the globalisation of this sort of capital, however, the centres of its authority are still the traditional metropolitan institutions.

Bourdieu's writing situates anthropology — and the other disciplines of the humanities relevant to the concerns of this book — within the context of the academic field, and explores the ways in which this field competes for space in the wider power structures of contemporary society. The field of education 'is overdetermined by the political field' (Webb, Schirato & Danaher 2002: 132). Disciplines such as law and medicine are 'centrally located in terms of this relationship'. The humanities or the 'pure' sciences, on the other hand, serve the essential role of masking the political nature of the universities and their role in the reproduction of social stratification and the authorisation of knowledge. This dynamic is clearly evident in Bushman studies. The 'recuperation' of the Bushman by scholars and the elevation of their narratives to the status of South African literature masks the continued subjugation of real people in South Africa, the descendants of the |Xam included (Voss 1987; 1995). Despite 'the vicissitudes of historical encounter, the belief is that a common set of values can be gleaned from the aesthetic legacy' (Moran 2009: 118).

Bourdieu also describes another, more hopeful, aspect of intellectual practice, one that is particularly apposite to a contemporary study of the products of 'other' cultures such as the |Xam narratives. Generally, in the era of globalisation, people encounter experiences and images that clash with the received ideas of their habitus.[8] This invites a degree of reflexivity that is especially reinforced in fields that allow for or dispose 'its agents towards, "the systematic exploration of the unthought categories of thought which delimit the thinkable and predetermine the thought"' (Bourdieu & Wacquant 1992: 40). A notion of 'radical doubt', the existence of 'an ethical imperative' and the ability to historically contextualise 'social issues and objects of knowledge' within a field all contribute towards a high degree of reflexivity (Webb, Schirato & Danaher 2002: 52). The fields of cultural studies and Bushman studies (the fields most relevant to this book) both display high levels of reflexivity, a phenomenon that is heightened in a study conducted in the period of globalisation. One of the first consequences of the sort of reflexive approach that characterises these fields in this period is the realisation that the field itself creates research problems. They are not waiting to be discovered in the world, but are produced by agents deploying historically situated forms of rationality.

Bourdieu maintains that it is especially through the acquaintance with other societies that intellectual reflexivity is stimulated with regard to such matters as the sexual division of society. A 'detour through an exotic tradition is indispensable in order to break the relationship of deceptive familiarity that binds us to our own tradition' (Bourdieu 2001: 3) and to the perspectives on the world it produces.[9] This provides one rationale for the project with which I am engaged in this book. Its aim is as much to allow the |Xam materials to interrogate the truth claims and authority of the tradition that seeks to comprehend them as it is to elucidate the materials themselves. Accordingly, I devote much time to the critique of the body of interpretation that has grown up around the Bleek and Lloyd Collection. More unusually, perhaps, I subject my own interpretation of |Xam texts to a critique. In some sense — often quixotic, perhaps — this methodology attempts to question the authority of the tradition of Western rationalism to construct and offer knowledge about the 'other'.

SPIVAK

The writing of Gayatri Spivak has shaped the analysis in this book in a variety of ways. The questions that Spivak asks about who speaks for whom in regard to the voices of the marginal and dispossessed are critical to the investigation that is conducted in this book, an investigation that spans the colonial and post-colonial eras, from the period in which the materials were transcribed, through their history of various sorts of interpretation and appropriation, to their privileged place in contemporary scholarship and South African national culture. Spivak's discussion of the native informant (1999), especially, has implications for the consideration of the web of relationships among the |Xam texts, their narrators, their collectors, and their readers and interpreters.

Spivak (1999: 6) traces the genesis of the figure of the native informant from the earlier ethnographic native informant who was a 'blank, though generative of a text of cultural identity that only the West (or a Western-model discipline) could inscribe' to 'the self-marginalizing or self-consolidating migrant or postcolonial masquerading as "native informant"'. The prime example of the latter is the migrant Third World intellectual who delivers inside 'knowledge' about his own people. The position of native informant is not always sought after by the migrant intellectual him-/herself, and is often conferred by the academic establishment on a person without his/her complicity by virtue of his/her national origin. It thus forms part of the wider mechanism by which the 'centre' masks the exclusion of the margin by admitting selected representatives of it. The |Xam informants and the way they have been positioned display characteristics of the two types of native informant that Spivak describes. Although the pieces in *Specimens of Bushman Folklore* (Bleek & Lloyd 1911) are attributed to individual narrators and some biographical information about them appears along with their photographs, the |Xam narrators very much fit the type of the ethnographic informant, the representative of a traditional culture and society. They delivered their information outside their native realm for the benefit of a Western intellectual audience on terms over which they had, at best, only partial control. With time, however, a scholarship of reclamation has repositioned them as the other sort of informant — agents who deliver inside and expert information from a world that is distant in time and space.

Spivak asserts that two untenable assumptions underlie the expectation that the migrant intellectual can deliver inside knowledge about the nation in which he/she originates, i.e. the assumption that the heterogeneous mass of people who exist in the section of the Third World under consideration can be spoken of by a single voice and the assumption that individuals are qualified to represent this voice because they belong to the same national group. These assumptions about essentialised subaltern collectivities on whose behalf Third World intellectuals can speak parallel, I believe, the assumption that an essentialised Bushman identity and culture can be repre-sented by five or six informants and the texts that emerged from their forced collaboration with Bleek and Lloyd. An individual is set up as 'an authentic ethnic fully representative of his or her tradition' (Spivak 1999: 60). The move whereby individuals become the voice or face of whole cultural traditions ignores the fact that 'an ethnicity untroubled by the vicissitudes of history and neatly accessible as an object of investigation is a confection' (60).

Spivak (1999: 114) has cautioned that a view of the 'Third World as distant cultures, exploited but with rich intact literary heritages waiting to be recovered, interpreted and curricularized in English/French/German/ Dutch translation; delivering the emergence of a "South" that provides proof of transnational exchange' fosters the emergence of 'the Third World' as a signifier that encourages the forgetting of the formative processes of 'worlding'[10] even as it expands the hegemonic reach of the literary discipline. A process such as the canonical incorporation of the |Xam texts is a way in which the epistemic violence of Western dominance becomes naturalised and hidden. It enables the misrecognition of the fact that 'liberal multiculturalism is determined by the demands of contemporary transnational capitalisms' (397). In addition, the 'worlding' process of imperialism is obscured by terms such as 'the Third World' and 'native', since these terms become categories that can be spoken of apart from the history of imperialism. I will argue, in a similar way, that terms like 'myth', 'trickster' and others that recur in relation to the |Xam materials serve the same function. They imply a universal order of cultural reality that exists apart from the colonial and neocolonial structures of economic and epistemic domination.

Spivak demonstrates at length how the categories of enlightenment thought and its notions of pure, disinterested reason were conditional upon the relationships of imperialism. Thinkers were involved in 'the "scientific" fabrication of new representations of self and world that would provide alibis for the domination, exploitation and epistemic violation entailed by the establishment of colony and empire' (Spivak 1999: 7). I have already mentioned Bleek's part in this project. Spivak examines the cases of Kant, Hegel and Karl Marx, among others. The figure of the native 'other' and his/her radical difference from modern humans are central, for example, to Kant's delineation of reason and morality. At the same time, his discourse, which promotes itself as humanism, relies on a universal concept of humankind in order to construct a teleology in which the '(auto)biography of the West ... masquerades as disinterested history' (208). This requires that the 'other' be given partial access to the 'being-human'. 'This limited access' of the non-European to culture and, consequently, to 'being-human', becomes 'the itinerary of the native informant into the post-colonial' (30) — and, I would argue, of the |Xam narrators and their legacy into the mainstream of the South African national imaginary.

I shall conclude this chapter by briefly mentioning some of the other implications for this study of aspects of Spivak's work. As indicated by her use of the subtitle, *Toward a History of the Vanishing Present*, Spivak (1999) is interested in the vantage point from which the past is surveyed in the context of post-colonialism. This makes, as I have indicated, many of her insights and concepts especially valuable in relation to a contemporary consideration of the |Xam texts. She offers, in addition, a hermeneutic strategy that is political. Every reading, she suggests, could become 'an upheaval parasitical to the text' (153). Instead of merely celebrating 'global hybridity', it is possible, she maintains, 'to anthropologize the heritage of the Euro-United States' (157). Finally, she suggests 'that a different standard of literary evaluation, necessarily provisional, can emerge if we work at the (im)possible perspective of the native informant as a reminder of alter-ity' (351–52). The mobilisation of this perspective necessarily offers a critique of imperialism in its past and present forms. In the context of this study, this entails the deployment of a strategy of reading that attempts to allow the |Xam texts to interrogate and judge the forms of rationality that have been used to interpret them.

Spivak, as is well known, first came to prominence with her translation of Derrida's *Of Grammatology* and the lengthy preface that she attached to it. The next chapter considers the ways in which *Of Grammatology* and some of Derrida's other writing have informed the project of this book.

NOTES

1 Guenther (1989: 49) perhaps exhibits the influence of this approach when he writes of Nharo and |Xam tales that possess similarities that 'some of the narratives can, with caution and within fairly confined limits, be treated as complementary and gaps in one tale can be filled in with the details from the corresponding other tale'.

2 Spivak (1999: 278) goes so far as to suggest that Foucault's 'clinic, the asylum, the prison, the university — all seem to be screen-allegories that foreclose a reading of the broader narratives of imperialism'.

3 For an explanation of how quotes from the notebooks are referenced, see the 'Note on references to the Bleek and Lloyd notebooks' on page x.

4 In this regard, Barber (1991: 3) observes that 'literary texts' are 'inherently discursive'. Oral texts are no exception, and she notes the presence of struggle in the *oriki* texts she studies (Barber 1991: 5).

5 Guenther (1999: 229) has gone so far as to question the description of |Xam social configurations as societies.

6 According to Guenther (1999: 19), the |Xam and other Bushmen became more hierarchically organised and centralised when they had to fight colonial forces. They returned to their usual egalitarian ways when the threat had passed.

7 It is important to bear in mind in this study of the texts translated by Bleek and Lloyd that translation was an essential part of the constitution of the knowledge to which Said refers (Bassnett & Trivedi 1999: 3).

8 Habitus refers to the set of dispositions of class-based agents that generate particular practices, attitudes and ideas. Habitus results from socialisation and education, but comes to be embodied in individuals and to be seen as natural.

9 The effectiveness of a study of the |Xam narratives in breaking the patterns of familiarity Bourdieu describes is, I believe, contingent upon the deployment of an interpretive strategy that is based on an awareness of its own ideological and historical foundations. While the encouragement to use such a strategy itself results partly, in

Bourdieu's view, from the study of other cultures, I would maintain that in the past the study of other cultures has served as often to reinforce the acceptance of Western forms of rationality. My reading of the literature related to the |Xam and related studies in later chapters leads me to conclude that the study of other cultures can stimulate or retard intellectual reflexivity. It is to be hoped that, in the context of globalisation, the other factor Bourdieu identifies as stimulating intellectual self-examination, i.e. the study of 'exotic' traditions, is more likely to have the consequences Bourdieu imputes to it.

10 A term Spivak uses to refer to the processes by which people are forcibly included in global networks of economic and political domination.

CHAPTER 2

TEXT OR PRESENCE?
On Re-reading the |Xam and the Interpretation
of their Narratives

THEORY AND ITS ABSENCE IN THE ANALYSIS
OF |XAM MATERIALS

The close interpretation of the |Xam texts remains, as I have noted, a task that
surprisingly few scholars have attempted. It is also true to say that, with some
exceptions, the interpretation that has been conducted does not employ or
engage with the theoretical insights that have resulted from the debates of the
last 40 years in the fields of cultural and literary studies. Nor, again with some
exceptions, has the interpretation that has been produced itself been
subjected to the type of critical scrutiny that takes these theoretical develop-
ments into account. A number of reasons might be advanced for why
Marxist, feminist, post-structuralist or post-colonial theory has had relatively
little impact on the interpretation of the |Xam narratives. The ground-
breaking analysis of the |Xam narratives by Roger Hewitt was produced in
the 1970s, although only published in the late 1980s. It preceded, therefore,
much of the theoretical activity to which I am referring. In addition, several
of the readers of the |Xam stories have been anthropologists, historians,
archaeologists and art historians rather than literary critics, and academics in
these disciplines have not always been preoccupied with theoretical
questions to the same degree as cultural and literary scholars. The general
field of folklore and mythology, moreover, within which much of the
interpretation of the |Xam texts could be located, remains largely rooted in
the comparative, functionalist and structuralist paradigms of an earlier era,

partly, perhaps, because the object of its study has often been positioned as traditional and timeless. Another possible factor is that contemporary theorists have rarely shown much interest in analysing 'traditional' oral texts themselves and have not, therefore, provided a lead as to how to apply their insights to texts of this sort (Csapo 2005: 290).

Despite the relative lack of impact of contemporary theory on the interpretation of the |Xam materials, the insights produced by this theory have potentially profound consequences for the ways in which the texts are read. Work such as that of Henry Gates (1988) or Karin Barber (1991; 1999) has demonstrated the effectiveness of employing some of the theoretical insights of the last 50 years when reading both traditional oral texts and the more contemporary texts that are directly related to older oral traditions. These insights involve, chiefly, the textual nature of language, the ideological character of cultural production and the importance of locating texts within an internal discursive economy rather than, for example, analysing them in terms of ahistorical, cross-cultural plot structures or situating them within a universal genre of archetypal myths.

Although most of the interpreters of the |Xam texts have not systematically concerned themselves with the theoretical aspects of interpretation, they have generally applied themselves to understanding the texts in such a tenacious and intelligent fashion that they have often, it seems to me, encountered the limitations of the interpretive schools or theoretical frameworks within which they were working. This can be seen in various ways in their work. While Hewitt, for instance, uses Radin's writing on the trickster in order to discuss the |Xam mantis figure, |Kaggen, and has also been influenced by Lévi-Strauss's idea that myths are structured in terms of a nature–culture binary, he qualifies his use of their concepts in very significant ways. He distances himself, for example, from Radin's Jungian universalism by insisting that |Kaggen's 'role *qua* trickster [be] elucidated within a very specific ethnographic context' (Hewitt 1986: 19–20). His detailed examination of a story concerning the Dawn's Heart Star and the Lynx leads him to conclude that the binaries in the narrative are mediated differently from the way Lévi-Strauss claims they are in myth (102).

Hewitt's struggle to fit his analytical tools to the materials is replicated in other work on the narratives. Andrew Bank (2006: 354) notes that Lucy

Lloyd herself moved away from a preoccupation with mythology to concentrate on |Xam culture in general. Her change in focus could be interpreted in terms of a progressive departure from Bleek's theories of cultural evolution, a move that was prompted by her increasingly close acquaintance with |Xam discourse itself. Mathias Guenther (1999) questions the ability of structuralist and functionalist approaches to adequately engage with Bushman narrative, at the same time as demonstrating how easily the materials can be accommodated within these explanatory frameworks. He argues that none of the theoretical paradigms that have been applied to the |Xam narratives is able to illuminate more than particular aspects of them (Guenther 1999: 232). Duncan Brown (1995; 1998), whose work is informed by recent literary theory and to which I will return in the next chapter, explicitly criticises the limitations of certain approaches to the narratives and suggests that the texts could be read as distinctive 'rhetorical acts' and not simply 'as evidence of social practices and belief systems' (Brown 1998: 36).

JACQUES DERRIDA AND THE |XAM NARRATIVES

The work of many theorists could be used to illustrate the relevance of aspects of contemporary theory to the interpretation of oral literature. I mentioned several of the implications of the ideas of Foucault, Bourdieu and Spivak for reading this sort of literature in the last chapter. In this chapter, I will focus chiefly on some of the writing of Jacques Derrida in *Of Grammatology* (1976). There are a number of reasons that could be given for this choice. I will argue in chapter 4, for example, that the term 'trickster' has been widely applied with little qualification to |Kaggen, the central protagonist in a great many |Xam stories of the First Times. Anne Doueihi (1984; 1993) draws on *Of Grammatology* in order to deliver an incisive critique of the identification of figures from diverse cultures as tricksters. Derrida's work was also a major influence on Henry Gates's (1988), *The Signifying Monkey: A Theory of Afro-American Literary Criticism*, a seminal text, as I argue in chapter 4, for the reading of oral literature and non-Western texts in general. Derrida's critique of Lévi-Strauss and the ethnological project in *Of Grammatology* is also closely connected to the concerns of this book, as I pointed out in the previous chapter.

49

The relative absence of recent theory from interpretation of the ǀXam texts has not been replicated in other writing about the collection, particularly that which concerns representation of the Bushmen and the ideological basis of Bleek's Bushman project. Here, Derrida's work sometimes features directly, as in the writing of Moran (1995; 2001; 2009). Even where it is not mentioned explicitly, the work of Wilmsen (1996), Bregin (1998; 2000), Brown (1995; 1998) and others on both the ǀXam narratives and the Bushmen more generally accords, in important respects, with Derrida's delineation in *Of Grammatology* of a complex in Western thought that is characterised by nostalgia for a lost origin. The examination in this chapter of some of the repercussions of his work for reading the ǀXam narratives does not occur in a vacuum, therefore.

One of the major themes *Of Grammatology* is the contention that a system of binaries recurs in European thought. One of the terms of the binary is privileged, and its ability to signify relies largely on its opposition to the suppressed or negative pole of the binary. The favoured pole is located close to an origin and invested with presence. The primary opposition in Western thought is the one between speech and writing. A written sign supposedly symbolises a spoken sign, which in turn symbolises a concept. Writing, therefore, is only the representation of a representation. While Western thought positions all signification as secondary, as only the outward sign of an inner signified, it tries to mask the derivative character of the sonic sign by erecting an opposition between speech and writing. Speech is then located, in terms of its opposition to writing, as proximate to the signified.

This phonocentric move — in which the voice is considered as contiguous with presence and being, while writing is positioned as supplementary — paves the way for the gap between the order of the signifier and the realm of the signified to be similarly narrowed in regard to the privileged pole of a number of other sets of binaries. Such binaries include an opposition between nature and culture in which nature is aligned with authentic life and placed against the artificial realm of culture. The wider complex in which signifiers and signifieds are considered as belonging to the orders of the sign and meaning respectively is called logocentrism, since it is based on the view that graphic or sonic signs are the outward representation of the logos, a realm of conceptualisation that precedes or is interior to all signification. Signification, in this structure, results from the relationship between a sign and the concept it signifies rather than from the relations among signs themselves.

Before going on to discuss the presence of an opposition between speech and writing in some of the literature that has interpreted the |Xam materials, I should like to make some observations about the implications that the system of antithetical binaries has had for the way that the Bushman in general has been represented in colonial and contemporary thought. The opposition between nature and culture has been central to this history. Broadly speaking, nature, like speech, is situated as close to an origin in which presence is directly accessible, while culture, like writing, is seen as a necessary, but unfortunate, product of the lack that distance from the origin has produced. The Bushman is frequently considered, in terms of this complex, to be closer to the origin and to nature than is modern humankind, both literally, in the sense that he|she is supposed to belong to an earlier phase in the development of humankind in which economic activity involved the natural activities of hunting and gathering, and figuratively, since he|she symbolises a more natural way of life, one that is closer to the one that prevailed before the fall from presence. Rousseau singles out the primitive people of the warm passionate South who still inhabit a time before time as living closest to nature and to the state of full presence (Derrida 1976: 251). Although they have been partially wrenched from nature, they are not yet in society (253).

The |Xam, 'illiterate' foragers and inhabitants, literally and metaphorically, of the South come as close at is possible to fulfilling the conditions for the 'natural man' that Derrida finds in Rousseau and in the literature he has inspired. Since, however, the view of the Bushman as emblematic of natural humankind is based on an untenable opposition between nature and culture, and is also the product of an ideological complex in which Bushmen exist chiefly as objects or symbols in a Western teleology, it comes as no surprise to find that interactions with historically situated Bushman contradict many of the expectations of the Western construct 'Bushman'. This dynamic, as Bank's (2006) work has shown, was already a feature of Wilhelm Bleek's interactions with the |Xam interlocutors.

51

Bleek's ideas about the |Xam, their language and their mythology changed once he got to actually know them. In a similar way, as I have already suggested, several scholars have discovered the limitations of their interpretive frameworks when applying them to specific |Xam texts. But since it is impossible for critics to think entirely outside the structures of thought that has generated these frameworks, and even more so if the critiques of them that have appeared in the theoretical debates of the last half century are ignored, this contradiction can never be properly resolved in their work.

Derrida observes that the nostalgia for an origin, and the association of the primitive with it, occurs within a wider European narrative:

> Non-European peoples were not only studied as the index to a hidden good Nature, as a native soil recovered, of a 'zero degree' with reference to which one could outline the structure, the growth and above all the degradation of our society and our culture. As always, this archaeology is also a teleology and an eschatology; the dream of a full and immediate present closing history ... (Derrida 1976: 114–15).

This complex produces its own paradoxes. The simple condition of natural humankind must be returned to in order to reunite with presence. On the other hand, nature has also to be left behind. The difference between nature and culture must be maintained in terms of the structure, and yet collapsed if presence is to be reclaimed. 'On several levels, nature is the ground, the inferior step: it must be crossed, exceeded, but also rejoined. We must return to it, but without annulling the difference' (Derrida 1976: 197). The difference must be maintained, for it is the alienation from nature represented by societies and language that 'permitted the actualisation of the potential faculties that slept inside man' (257).

This marks the limits of the sympathy with the 'non-European' that follows from the attraction his/her closeness to the origin exerts and the pathos-ridden knowledge that contact with civilisation must inevitably precipitate a fall away from presence. Modern humankind's interest in this primal human is its interest in a part of itself that is no longer present. The primitive human can never be allowed to exist as a reciprocating, self-representing, contemporary individual. The difference between the savage and the civilised must be maintained, for it is precisely the modern human's distance from the origin that has resulted in his/her development. Modern humankind might be further from presence than the primitive, but it is also closer to the endpoint of the teleological trajectory in which full presence will be reclaimed on the higher level that has been put in play through the fall from innocence. When the point of total alienation is approached, the 'total reappropriation of presence' becomes possible (Derrida 1976: 295).

This structure goes some way towards explaining the inconsistent ways in which people such as the |Xam have been regarded and treated. They have been both vilified and idealised at different points in history. Wilmsen (1996: 186) describes the conflicting but related impulses to preserve 'a mythic image of the childhood of mankind' and to expunge the 'sub(human) remainder' of 'the childhood of human nature'. The Bushmen are animal-like, since they are low on the ladder of ascent to contemporary humankind, but also godlike, in that they are closer to the origin and the age of innocent purity. In the first case, they clearly mark the divide between civilised and uncivilised humans in that, as hunter-gatherers, they are nearer to animals than to human cultivators and pastoralists. In the second case, they preserve and embody the attributes that modern humankind has lost: authenticity, simplicity, spiritual innocence and spontaneity.

This Janus-faced complex can justify persecution or inspire fascination, depending on the way in which the unstable opposition between nature and culture is construed. Both impulses were in evidence in the Cape Colony during the period in which the |Xam materials were assembled. The view that the Bushmen were virtually animals who should give way to more civilised people predominated, however, at a time when the struggle for land and resources was paramount and the Bushmen were still capable of offering stiff resistance to incursions into their areas. Nor, incidentally, was the genocidal impulse confined to colonial opinion in southern Africa. After Charles Dickens had seen an exhibition of Bushmen in London, he wrote: 'I have not the least belief in the Noble Savage ... I call a savage something highly desirable to be civilised off the face of the earth' (quoted by Maughan Brown 1983: 59). The lives of the |Xam informants, as the materials make clear, were played out in this murderous milieu in which persecution and dispossession were everyday experiences.

Bleek's theories of cultural, racial and linguistic evolution perfectly exemplify Derrida's contention that the Western intellectual tradition is positioned within a particular myth of origin, one that turns on a fall from presence and a teleology. These theories provided the intellectual context in which the Bleek and Lloyd Collection was assembled. Bleek's interest in the lXam and their mythology was closely linked to his interest in human origins and the history of the unequal rates of evolution of different peoples. Understanding this history required a comparative study to be made among different languages. He believed that language, culture and race could be correlated in an evolutionary scheme within which he positioned Bushman languages close to the way in which non-human primates communicated (Bank 1999: 9). The study of Bushman mythology, in Bleek's view, was an important source of evidence for his evolutionary theories, especially since he believed that mythology provided direct access to a people's mental structure.

Derrida's work indicates that the idealisation of the primitive is as much a form of ethnocentrism as is racial discrimination. The ethnocentric basis of racism is obvious, but the ethnocentric nature of the romanticised version of the Bushman is less apparent, since it constitutes itself as 'anti-ethnocentrism, an ethnocentrism in the consciousness of a liberating progressivism' (Derrida 1976: 120). The core of this attitude depends, however, on the ethnocentric 'desire for the Other to REMAIN "other," not to become too much like us' (Zizek 2001: 69; original emphasis). 'Bushman' is a term that must often be understood as referring to the 'other' of 'South African historiography' (Bregin 2000: 37) rather than to an actual category of historically situated people. For most of South Africa's colonial past, this 'other' was 'sub-human'. Much of the obsession with racial difference was driven, as we have seen, by Social Darwinism, which 'postulated a linear or teleological model of human development, from degenerate native child to adult white man' (Bregin 2000: 39). This scheme allowed for 'a slide backwards through "racial decline"', and the Bushman, it was commonly thought, represented the actualisation of this possibility. They were a 'degraded species', while the Zulu occupied the ideo-logical position of the noble savage.

The idealisation of the Bushman is more consistently a twentieth-century phenomenon than a nineteenth-century one. Tony Voss (1987) has traced the passage in South African literature of the depiction of the Bushman from vermin to original, quintessential human beings. In writing such as that of Laurens van der Post (1961), the Bushmen become not only part of common humanity, but quintessential human beings (Brown 1998: 63–64). They are closest to the origin — the pure embodiments of natural humankind. This phenomenon characterises not only literature, of course: Wilmsen (1989; 1995; 1996) emphasises its presence in anthropology and other forms of scholarship. Bank (2002) has shown how this stereotype of the Bushman has sometimes been inadvertently strengthened by scholarly writing on the Bleek and Lloyd Collection. The informants, for example, are commonly said to have lived in huts in Bleek's garden, whereas they actually lived in the house. In this way, 'the world of the house, site of the colonial culture of Bleek and Lloyd' is separated conceptually from 'the natural world, site of huts and traditional stories' (Bank 2002: 71), and 'addressor and addressee are overdetermined as civilized Western man and natural savage' (Moran 1995: 31).

Most contemporary academic writing on the |Xam archive is critical of the legacy I have been describing.[1] It attempts to find ways with which to engage the tangible realities of rock art and the verbal materials in the Bleek and Lloyd Collection that do not reproduce ethnocentric or romanticised ways of viewing the Bushmen. Nevertheless, this writing, as Bank's observation about the huts in the garden demonstrates, still sometimes unwittingly contains some of its patterns. Brown (1998: 27) maintains that the influence of both the idealised and the overtly racist way of thinking about the Bushmen can only be weakened if 'the songs and stories of the |Xam' are allowed to '"talk back" back to modern understanding'. In this way, Bushmen can begin to speak for themselves, to some extent, rather than exist as a product of the distorted representations of others. I would argue also that addressing the materials in the Bleek and Lloyd archive in a way that incorporates the insights of contemporary theory can contribute to this project in a variety of ways. I shall discuss some of them towards the end of this chapter. For now, I should like to return to Derrida's critique of the opposition between speech and writing.

SPEECH AND WRITING

In terms of the 'metaphysics of phonetic writing', as we saw, the voice is positioned as close to the pre-textual realm of being, while writing, the preserve of the signifier, merely represents speech. It is alienated from presence, to which its signs can only gesture. The way that language works, however, argues Derrida, renders the quest for absolute origin, or for fullness of being and presence within it, impossible. No sign, verbal or written, is pure; it always carries the traces of all the other signs. This entails not only a spatial relationship of difference and relationship, but also a temporal one of deferral. Meaning is never absolutely present, fixed or univocal, as it was understood to be in the theological 'age of the sign' (Derrida 1976: 14); it is always, to some degree, postponed. This is as true of the spoken word as it is of the written one. Speech and writing, thus, both rely on an interplay of presence and absence, the respective qualities attributed to speech and writing, rather than on their opposition. This contention has major implications, in my view, for the way in which 'traditional' oral narratives are read. They have generally been identified as folklore or myth and treated in very different ways from texts that have been produced in the written tradition. Derrida's work suggests, however, that the products of both voice and pen deal in signs and are equally susceptible, therefore, to being approached as texts.

The insight that oral literature exhibits both the characteristics that are usually separately associated with writing or speech is contained in the title of Duncan Brown's study of South African oral literature, *Voicing the Text* (1998). Brown (1998: 17–18) would like to see the development of interpretative

> models that acknowledge simultaneously the textuality and historicity of oral texts, of combining a sociology with a poetics of oral literature ... the crucial questions for criticism become: what does the text seek to accomplish in the spheres of social and political action, and how does it accomplish this (by what rhetorical features/formal strategies)?

He argues elsewhere that the stark separation of orality and writing obscures the fact that a form of signification such as rock art 'uses an "alphabet" of symbols, signs, colours, shapes and images in making its meaning, and which demands intelligent "reading"' (Brown 2006: 22). The activity of tracking 'requires decoding, involving the analysis of signs in context, the creation of hypotheses, and so on: the same cognitive processes as reading printed texts'.

Brown's position is unusual in the context of the analysis of the IXam materials. Much of the writing on the IXam narratives is implicitly predicated, in my view, on a radical distinction between orality/presence and writing/textuality. In the Western intellectual tradition, contends Derrida, the very notion of history is defined by the possibility of writing. Since the Bushmen have no history — the consequence of their having no writing — it follows that their oral narratives are timeless myths or folklore rather than historically and culturally situated texts that provide a dialogical discursive space in which meanings are generated and contested: 'a mythic time is reserved for them, while real time ticks on impartially for us all' (Wilmsen 1996: 187).

Much of the writing on the IXam and other Bushmen either directly separates speech from writing or has been influenced by intellectual traditions that do. Dorothea Bleek (Bleek & Stow 1930: 47), for example, writes that '[h]alf or more than half of each day was spent lounging about watching bird and beast, and talking — always talking'. Natural humans are largely free from the imperative to work:

> It is difficult for us to realize how large a part talking, and hence story-telling, makes in primitive man's life. Where a man's only labour is hunting, which occupies only a few hours of a day, and probably not of every day, there is an amount of leisure unparalleled among civilized people (D. Bleek 1929: 311).

Are Bleek's statements simply ethnographic observation or do they carry the ideological whiff of the metaphysics of presence? Why, one might ask, does she describe the Bushmen's use of their surplus time as 'lounging about'? What is the rhetorical effect of conflating speech, proximity to nature ('watching bird and beast') and idleness? Hewitt (1986: 47) explicitly separates speech from writing when he notes that narrative formed 'part of daily living to an extent unknown in literate societies where leisure time is limited'. Are people in literate societies always busier than those in speech-based ones? To which particular literate societies is Hewitt alluding? Is he suggesting that writing itself produces an alienation from direct experience or is he merely saying that people in more complex societies enjoy less leisure time?

Mathias Guenther unequivocally embraces a radical opposition between oral and written cultures, a position that determines, to a significant degree, in my opinion, his reading of the materials. In an article, Guenther (2006: 255) emphasises the centrality of speech to Bushman culture: 'In talking and telling stories, not only are the concerns and issues of the foraging lifeway and society dealt with, but also the ethos or ideology upon which they rest is reiterated and reconstituted.' Storytelling is only one aspect, albeit an important one, of a speech-based society: 'Talking is pervasive and is found in all of the San's institutional domains. ... All of this talk greases the wheels of society in what is an inherently loose and labile collectivity' (255). Once again, Guenther might simply be making the point that a great deal of the surplus time that attends a foraging economy is devoted to conversation, discussion and storytelling. He is, after all, like Dorothea Bleek, a field anthropologist who has closely observed the interactions that he describes. When, however, these statements about Bushman speech and orality are placed in the context of his writing generally, they can be seen, I would argue, to contain strong echoes of the logocentric complex that Derrida delineates in *Of Grammatology*.

Although it is not always directly stated in his work, the polar opposite of the oral, speech-based social and cultural practice that Guenther celebrates in much of his own work is writing. Every now and then, this opposition is brought into the open, as when he claims, in relation to religion, that orality invites more variety than does writing, whose style is fixed (Guenther 1999: 85). In Guenther's view, orality is so different from written literature that it eludes interpretation by literate Western critics. The difference between speech and writing is primary and ontological. Writing, for example, focuses attention on the meanings of actual words, while oral cultures concentrate on the 'message'.

In this framework, writing, Derrida's work indicates, is more than a technique of inscribing words: it describes the process of the production of meaning through artifice. It always occurs at a remove. Speech, on the other hand, is the direct manifestation of consciousness and truth. By bringing this opposition into play, Guenther signals his approach to reading the |Xam narratives, a strategy that relies heavily on oppositional binaries. These include speech and writing, orality and textuality, and simple foraging societies and complex contemporary societies, as well as egalitarianism and power. Bushman speech and orality are aligned with spontaneity, flexibility and an absence of power, while writing belongs to rigid, complex social formations that are characterised by structure and power.

Guenther (2002: 15) locates Bushman narrative and figures such as the |Xam character |Kaggen firmly in the world before the fall:

> This early pre-Genesis world of chaos and ambiguity, which God's divine creation has displaced from the Judeo-Christian cosmic purview, is the world of the trickster. He is its premier inhabitant, along with the early animals, humans, and animal-humans. It is also the world of Bushman mythology ….

Guenther's choice of words, in the context of Derrida's discussion of the Western complex of the lost origin, is revealing. This complex, as we have seen, is a way of thought that is predicated on a fall from presence. The narrative of Genesis is the prototypical narrative in the Western tradition of the fall into experience. Guenther explicitly inserts Bushman narratives into this wider, 'universal' narrative, positioning them at a point even before the creation. The contours of this pre-creation world, he suggests, have been suppressed in the dominant Judeo-Christian account. The |Xam tales, it is commonly asserted, chart a movement from the state of 'chaos and ambiguity' of the First Times to a present state that is, in most respects, an improvement on the First Times. If we follow Guenther's logic, as well as his assertions about the Bushman foraging way of life generally, we would have to conclude that the present order of the Bushman — the post-mythological world of the hunter-gatherer — corresponds to the pre-lapsarian phase of creation in the Genesis narrative.

I cannot in the space of this chapter provide an in-depth analysis of Guenther's statements concerning speech, orality and power. I will examine his work at greater length in chapter 6. What I would like to suggest here, however, is that a similarity exists between many of them and the writing of Jean-Jacques Rousseau and Claude Lévi-Strauss that Derrida investigates in *Of Grammatology*. In *Tristes Tropiques* (1961), Lévi-Strauss expresses the belief that his introduction of the idea of writing to the Nambikwara has corrupted the immediacy of their existence and the purity of their ways. Where before they knew only speech, that almost unmediated secretion of the soul, they have now been introduced to the artificial order of writing. Derrida (1976: 109) claims that Lévi-Strauss's support of Rousseau's attack on writing leads to his inability to see that there is no 'society without writing', whereas all 'societies capable of producing, that is to say obliterating, their proper names, and of bringing classificatory difference into play, practice writing in general'. Lévi-Strauss's failure to see this and his scorn of writing lead to an ethnocentrism in which the absence of writing is equated with innocence and non-violence, and the primitive 'other' is constituted as the 'model of original and natural goodness' (Derrida 1976: 114). Rousseau himself applies this model especially to foraging people, for he considers that writing 'is born with agriculture'. 'The furrow of agriculture', as Derrida (1976: 287) puts it, 'opens nature to culture (cultivation)'.

Rousseau and Lévi-Strauss both link orality to community and writing to a lack of authentic relationships. A particular view of hunter-gathering societies is presupposed, at once pure and peculiarly susceptible to outside corruption:

[O]nly a micro-society of non-violence and freedom, all the members of which can by rights remain within range of an immediate and transparent, a 'crystalline' address, fully self-present in its living speech, only such a community can suffer, as the surprise of an aggression coming *from without*, the insinuation of writing, the infiltration of its 'ruse' and of its 'perfidy'. Only such a community can import *from abroad* 'the exploitation of man by man' (Derrida 1976: 119, original emphasis).

Such a society is pre-political for politics presupposes that liberty has already been lost; politics is 'always the supplement of a natural order somewhere deficient' (Derrida 1976: 298). Writing and political enslavement, in this scheme, necessarily accompany each other. Writing is an instrument of power, commanding 'by written laws, decrees and literature' (302). Lévi-Strauss follows Rousseau, whom he hails as his antecedent and the founding father of anthropology (105), in claiming that exploitation of man by man is peculiar to literate societies.

Guenther's (1999) position comes close to the views that Derrida ascribes to Rousseau and Lévi-Strauss. He asserts that Bushman societies are 'free of hierarchy and power structures' (Guenther 1999: 5). He links this freedom to orality and the hunter-gathering way of life. His reading of Bushman narrative is tied to this phenomenon: Bushman myth 'is able to remain within its proper, mythic time, where order is inchoate and power absent, rather than be called upon to spin out charter myths that legitimate temporal order and power' (84). Speech in Guenther's work is consistently aligned with freedom, spontaneity and egalitarianism; writing belongs to structure, order and power.

DECONSTRUCTING THE |XAM TEXTS

So far in this chapter I have referred to Derrida's work in order to discuss some of the writing that has been produced in relation to the |Xam. His work has equally important implications, in my view, for the reading of the |Xam texts themselves. It is not a simple matter of deriving a methodology from his work, however, and transferring it to the interpretation of the |Xam texts. Derrida himself argues that his strategy — deconstruction — is not properly a method. It does not comprise a set of rules and practices that can be repeated and used in different contexts. Deconstruction 'does not settle for methodological procedures, it opens up a passageway, it marches ahead and marks a trail' (Derrida 1992: 337). It does not replace metaphysical philosophy with a new kind of philosophical framework in terms of which the unified themes in texts can be discovered and explicated. Whereas analysis traditionally seeks to attain a resolution, deconstruction continues to disassemble the elements it exposes. It must be stressed that this is not the same as attempting to reduce a narrative to its basic constituent elements, as Hewitt, for example, does when he breaks the narratives down into types and then the individual narratives down into functions. This sort of approach, in Derrida's view, is a regression 'toward an indissoluble origin'. The apparently basic elements that structuralism isolates are themselves subject to deconstruction (Derrida 1985: 2).

The type of reading a deconstructive approach generates is always provisional. Deconstruction, Derrida asserts, cannot operate outside the logocentric structure. It depends on the old structure's 'strategic and economic resources of subversion', with the result that 'the enterprise of deconstruction always in a certain way falls prey to its own work' (Derrida 1976: 24). Of necessity, a language is employed whose premises are not subscribed to. We are so tied to the categories of logocentrism that 'nothing is conceivable for us without them' (Derrida 1976: 13). The authority of a reading is, therefore, fleeting: 'we must learn to use and erase our language at the same time' (Spivak 1976: xviii).

Although Derrida's work does not embody replicable methodological procedures in the conventional sense, methodological consequences do arise from his work, however. I shall briefly discuss some of those that, in my view, are important for |Xam narrative studies. Deconstruction is a way of reading without recourse to a 'natural' hierarchy of signifiers (Derrida 1976: 44) and one that is not founded on an idea of language as guaranteed by a transcendental signified, a signified that transcends all signifiers such as God or some other first cause. It follows that all the signifiers in a narrative could be given detailed attention. They are not merely verbal decoration, and a reading should, moreover, investigate the way that signifiers work within the |Xam texts themselves. Where functionalist and structuralist readings of the |Xam narratives have suppressed the textual details in the interests of submitting the texts to overarching analytical paradigms and tended to discuss them in comparative and general terms, Derrida's work invites the sort of rigorous reading that investigates their singularity.

A reading produced in a deconstructive spirit does not claim to be able to represent the 'real' world of the texts. It disassociates itself from the essentialist notion that a 'true' meaning exists beneath the surfaces of the stories that can be deciphered. It does not suppress the elements in the stories that do not fit a particular interpretive scheme or dismiss them as marginal. A reading that takes into account Derrida's critique of the metaphysics of presence also foregrounds the fact that the reader is always implicated in a reading. Derrida draws attention to the highly mediated nature of texts. This is especially true of our reception of the |Xam texts, which is filtered by a complex series of events that includes transmission, translation, and a history of interpretation situated within particular traditions of reading and ethnology.

Derrida's contention (1976: 14) 'that there is no linguistic sign before writing' has important consequences, as I indicated earlier, for the way in which the oral aspect of the |Xam materials is considered. Even if we had access to the spoken performance of |Xam narrative rather than to the translated texts, we would still, according to Derrida's logic, have to read these performances as texts, in spite of the fact that the context of the performance would mobilise a range of meanings in the form of gestures and other non-verbal codes of performance that are excluded from written texts. In Rousseau's thinking, the gesture is closer to presence, more natural even than voice (Derrida 1976: 233). Derrida maintains, by contrast, that gestures, too, should be interpreted primarily as text — part of the interaction of speech and writing from which signification emerges.[2]

To summarise and conclude: Derrida's work suggests that the |Xam narratives can be read textually in terms of their situation within a discursive economy rather than as a body of oral literature that is purportedly closer to the origin of things than are written texts. Meaning is generated from the multiplicity of signs within the texts and their circulation within a discursive order rather than from the proximity of privileged signs to the origin of things. In the next chapter, I shall extend this discussion to a discussion of the concept of mythology in relation to both the |Xam materials and their interpretation.

NOTES

1 Popular culture still, of course, purveys an idealised image of the Bushman. This is largely true, too, of the better non-academic writing on the Bushmen and the |Xam such as Bennun (2005) and Martin (2008).

2 This is not to underestimate the importance of performance, of course. Karin Barber (1991; 1999) argues persuasively, I think, that a reading of oral texts is required that takes into account their textuality and also emphasises their performative and dialogical qualities. She asserts, for instance, that 'for an *oriki*-text to be apprehended as a

text, it must be heard and seen in action' (Barber 1991: 7). This is not possible when it comes to |Xam narrative. The performative components of the narratives have to be gleaned from the texts and guessed at on the basis of more contemporary story-telling practice. Neither of these strategies comes close to fulfilling Barber's require-ments for understanding a performance as text. These absent components of the story constitute for interpreters the 'real' of the stories, in the Lacanian sense — those aspects of them that necessarily evade re-representation and which, as a result, can-not be read. The 'real', in this case, is not pre-textual or extra-textual, but simply the irretrievable absence of an important component of the narratives — a consequence of the context in which they were recorded.

CHAPTER 3

WHOSE MYTHS ARE THE |XAM NARRATIVES?

INTRODUCTION

Controversy has attended rock art interpretation and the applicability of the category of hunter-gatherer to the Bushmen in the Kalahari and Namibia.[1] However, as I have noted before, controversy has been curiously absent from discussions about the reading of the |Xam narratives. In this chapter, I wish, at least, to stimulate some theoretical discussion in relation to these narratives by considering one of the recurring questions in the broader field of folklore and mythography, that of the distinction among genres of oral literature. I will focus, in particular, on the designation of the |Xam materials as mythology. My interest is not so much in mythology itself, however, as in the ideological and hermeneutic act of reading the narratives in terms of this category. I do not hope to discuss all the implications of describing the |Xam materials as myths, nor can I provide an exhaustive examination of the way in which different writers have used the term in relation to the |Xam texts. What I wish to do, rather, is point out some of the theoretical and ideological implications of the use of such a term and initiate a debate about its deployment in the study of the |Xam narratives. By doing so, I hope to provoke discussion rather than present a watertight case. The chapter also includes a consideration of fresh approaches to reading the narratives and a short examination of a narrative that has been identified as a myth.

'Mythology' was a potent ideological sign for Wilhelm Bleek. In his report to parliament in 1873, Bleek maintained that the importance of the |Xam materials 'lies in the mythological character of the stories', a characteristic that separates Bushman from Bantu literature since the latter have 'legends, but, strictly speaking, no mythologies' (Bleek & Lloyd 1911: 445). Bank (2006: 158) argues that Bleek was more interested in myths than in 'legends or information of an everyday kind', since he believed that the 'Bushman mind' was more closely related to the European mind of distant times and was of a far more poetic cast than '"the mind" of Bantu-speakers'. Their possession of mythology, and the imaginative faculty that myth requires, was proof to Bleek that Bushmen are closer to Europeans on the cultural evolutionary ladder than Africans are. Myth also, of course, marks a difference between Bushman and Europeans. Bushmen only have mythology; Europeans possess forms that are the products of the higher forms of reason.

Despite the importance of mythology in Bleek's thought, there has been little attempt by critics to critically discuss the consequences of describing the materials as myths. As Moran (2009: 126) notes:

> The moral-aesthetic anthropology of contemporary re-readings of the Bleek and Lloyd archive aiming to counter the racializing interpretations of the past are distinguished by a marked incuriosity about the nature and history of *mythos* or its place within Eurocentric modes of thought (original emphasis).

Most writers tend to use the terms 'myth', 'folklore' and 'narrative' interchangeably. Lucy Lloyd separates the narratives into mythology, fables and legends in *Specimens of Bushman Folklore* without defending the use of these categories. She uses the term 'folklore' in the title of this collection, but earlier referred to the narratives as mythology in her report of 1889 (Lloyd 1889: 4–5). Dorothea Bleek (1929) is more conscious of a distinction between folklore and mythology than most of the writers who have written about the materials. She describes the materials in the collection as a whole as folklore, but notes that 'some of the Lion stories bear more the character of myths' than do the other animal tales (Bleek 1929: 304). She argues that the ǀKaggen narratives, in contrast to many of the other stories in the collection, cannot be called 'fables; they form a cycle of myths' (Bleek 1929: 305). Mathias Guenther (1989) describes the materials as folktales in the title of his book about |Xam and Nharo narratives, but frequently characterises them as myths in the body of his text (49). He particularly links mythology with creation: fundamental to 'Bushman Mythology' is the 'idea of double creation'. He argues that there is a close correspondence between Nharo and |Xam mythology, since 'they derive from a common stock of mythological and mystical ideas and perceptions'. The idea of myth is also central to his investigation in *Tricksters and Trancers* of narrative as part of Bushman religion (Guenther 1999), as we shall see in chapter 6. David Lewis-Williams (2000) refers to the 'ancestral folklore of the San of southern Africa' in the subtitle of his selection from the Bleek and Lloyd Collection, but uses the term 'myth' to describe the stories he analyses in two of his essays (1996a; 1998a). We might assume that mythology is a more suitable vehicle for the shamanistic themes he discovers in the narratives than folklore would be.

The lack of debate about the distinctions between mythology and folklore in |Xam studies provides a contrast with the writing of the folklorists and mythographers in other parts of the world, who have devoted considerable attention to separating folklore from myth. We saw in chapter 1 that the distinction was important to Lévi-Strauss. He asserts that only myths adequately reveal the structures of human thought, since they mediate stronger oppositions than folktales do; i.e. they contain cosmological and natural oppositions, in contrast to the social and moral ones that characterise folktales. Myths, in consequence, exert an orthodox and conservative force, while folktales are often critical of the status quo. William Bascom (1984) discusses the differences among myth, legend and folklore at length. The three genres differ, for instance, 'in their settings in time and place, in their principal characters and, more importantly, in the beliefs and attitudes associated with them' (Bascom 1984: 12). Myths often have an aetiological function and are set in creation time, but folktales can occur at any time. The protagonists in folktales often rely on magic in order to escape from difficult situations, while the heroes of mythology have to rely much more on their own efforts and resources. Myths are accepted as true; folktales are considered to be fiction. Trickster tales are usually folklore, whereas creation tales can generally be classified as myths.

Even if writers in the field of |Xam studies were concerned with the precise classification of folklore and myth, the materials would still resist easy classification. The |Xam stories that feature |Kaggen, the Mantis, are commonly read as both trickster and creation tales. They do not neatly conform, therefore, to the characteristics of folklore or mythology as set out by Bascom. The chief classifier of Khoisan oral literature, Sigrid Schmidt (2001: 194), has noted in relation to Nama narrative — but she could just as easily be writing about |Xam narrative — that it is difficult to tell where 'myths end and other genres begin'. Many Bushman tales treat serious matters in a comical and entertaining way, and '[i]t is difficult to classify them either as fictitious or as true stories' (Schmidt 2001: 195). Isidore Okpewho (1983: 55–56) questions the validity of the distinction among myth, legend and folklore in relation to African oral literature in general.

While writers in the field of Bushman studies frequently refer to the |Xam materials as stories, narratives, folklore, folktales or the |Xam word *kukummi* rather than as myths, none of them rejects or questions the use of the term 'myth', and it appears frequently in their work.[2] The actual word that is used to describe the narratives is not, in any event, the critical question. Certain recurrent strains in the interpretation of the narratives, I would argue, originate in the field of mythology, as I described in chapter 1 when I dealt with Lévi-Strauss's and Malinowski's theories of myth. The dominant tendency in the reading of the |Xam narratives has been to regard them as myths rather than as discourse, a point on which I will elaborate later in this chapter.

Many of the narratives are described as aetiological, a feature that is commonly ascribed to myth. 'The narratives which deal with the sun, moon and stars are, with few exceptions, entirely aetiological constructions' (Hewitt 1986: 93). Alan James (2001: 148) describes stories such as the one that tells how the sun was thrown into the sky by a group of boys as 'creation myths'. Duncan Brown (1998: 64), too, refers to 'creation tales' that are 'concerned with mythological origins'. It is probably Guenther (1989), however, who most emphasises the status of a large set of narratives as creation myths. He matches |Xam creation stories with their Nharo equivalents, claiming that they 'derive from a common stock of mythological and mystical ideas and perceptions' (Guenther 1989: 49). Derrida's linking of the Western intellectual tradition with a myth of origin lends the description from within this tradition of materials such as the

|Xam narratives as aetiological, to my mind, a certain circularity. The question arises as to how thinking that has been shaped by a particular myth of origin, and which is predicated on nostalgia for a lost origin, can identify and interpret another myth of origin in terms that do not merely reflect its own longing to return to an origin. I noted in the last chapter that the association of Bushmen and their narratives with the origin of humankind is one that most contemporary scholars would reject. It is my view, nevertheless, that the power of the notion of origins encourages a characterisation of the |Xam narratives as primarily 'myths of creation'. At the same time, it needs to be recognised that it is the work of the writers who sometimes describe the |Xam materials as 'creation myths' that provides the resources for an understanding of them that complicates and undermines this categorisation.

MYTHS: What are they and what do they do?

Lévi-Strauss, as we have seen, maintains that there are no inherent meanings in individual myths; myth itself enables meaning. Karin Barber, by contrast, finds a meaning in narratives themselves. Importantly, this meaning is not dependent on structural elements that underlie all myth, but on the discursive conventions that allow texts to enunciate 'the *conventions* in accordance with which the text|utterance is generated ... it is by means of these conventions that any meaningful utterance is formed, recognised as such, and its meaning grasped' (Barber 1999: 28). These discursive conventions or genres are culturally and historically specific, unlike Lévi-Strauss's universal structures. Is myth a universal genre, as Lévi-Strauss's position implies, and the very condition of meaningfulness, or are there a multiplicity of local genres, as Barber suggests, a contention that robs so wide and universal a category as 'myth' of much of the meaning that has traditionally been accorded it?

The word 'myth' is, of course, used in many different ways nowadays. It has become necessary to specify the analytical context in which the term is being employed, for it can no longer be assumed that its meaning is universal and transparent. The way in which the sign is understood influences the choice of methodological approach and determines the object of study itself: 'Definition is never the innocent first step in a process of empirical discovery ... theories of myth themselves to a large degree constitute mythologies' (Csapo 2005: 1).

The study of myth accompanied the birth of the discipline of anthropology in the era of colonial expansion. Myth was interesting insofar as it provided a basis for comparison with contemporary European thought. The use of the term 'myth' in this context related more to the tale of 'European self-discovery' (Csapo 2005: 11) than to the intrinsic nature of particular indigenous discourses. Myths, in this view, not only described origins, but themselves belonged to the origins of humankind. Csapo (2005: 7) notes that 'Westerners invented the concepts of science, history, myth, and literature partly to distinguish our own cultural thought and expression from that of mythmaking societies'. He points out that the category of myth is not derived from the societies whose literature is described as myth. This creates a problem of 'equatability of concepts across cultures' (7), a problem that did not overly trouble nineteenth-century thinkers, who tended anyway to conflate the level of development of 'primitive' societies and their myths with the phase of childhood in the life of the individual. Cultures at a similarly low level of evolution would produce similar myths. It was assumed that a great many cultures were at a similar stage of development and thus produced a common sort of literature. The great diversity of these cultures was largely ignored.

The ethnocentrism that attended comparative mythology has mostly dissipated. In my view, however, some of its legacy persists in a diluted form. An example is the readiness of certain writers to downplay differences among societies, a phenomenon that exists in most schools of myth analysis. The comparatists' method relies on the correspondence between stories from a wide region or even from around the world. The different schools of structuralism also depend on the premise that the same stories reappear in different guises in different societies. The functionalists, by contrast, emphasise the need to locate narratives within specific societies. The function they so often impute to narratives, however, namely that of reinforcing the social order, is itself so general that it, too, tends to work as a universal. The differences among stories from different cultures become inconsequential, since almost all stories possess the same function.

What draws theories of myth together, according to Csapo (2005: 189), whether they are psychological, structuralist or assert the symbiosis of ritual and myth, is that they all assume that there is a latent or hidden meaning in myth that is mostly not consciously 'received by the societies in which the myths are actively transmitted'. The ethnocentric and hegemonic character of this assumption has, of course, been a preoccupation of post-colonial critics. Godzich (1986: xiii) provides a metaphorical description of it:

> Western thought has always thematized the other as a threat to be reduced, as a potential same-to-be, a yet-not-same. The paradigmatic conception here is that of the quest in romances of chivalry in which the adventurous knight leaves Arthur's court — the realm of the known — to encounter some form of otherness, a domain in which the courtly values of the Arthurian world do not prevail. The quest is brought to an end when this alien domain is brought within the hegemonic sway of the Arthurian world: the other has been reduced to (more of) the same. The quest has shown that the other is amenable to being reduced to the status of the same.

Until the 1970s the term 'myth' was generally used in the universal and comparative way that I have been describing and was reserved for certain types of traditional cultural expression of an imaginative, 'sacred' and narrative nature from all eras and all parts of the world. In more recent times, the term 'myth' has been employed by Marxists, poststructuralists and other constructivist critics in relation to certain products of modern mass culture. These writers seldom discuss 'traditional myth' itself. In the work of Barthes, for example, the term is given an application that includes the description of a kind of bourgeois thinking that sees itself as the only valid type of thinking (Coupe 1997: 157). My focus in this chapter, however, remains the more orthodox use of the word 'myth'.

As preparation for the arguments for a discursive approach to the narratives that I will introduce later in the chapter and pursue in the rest of the book, I will briefly examine more closely, in relation to both hermeneutic practice in general and to the |Xam narratives in particular, a definition of myth that would probably not invite a great deal of opposition from most of the schools of thought that have concerned themselves with myth: myth 'is typically a traditional sacred story of anonymous authorship and archetypal or universal significance' (Cupitt 1982: 29). I do not want to suggest that this definition should have priority over others. I simply wish to use it as an example in order to show that signifiers like 'myth', 'traditional', 'sacred' and 'story' whose meanings seem transparent are weighted by structures of thought, some of which bear the traces of the colonial era. I am not claiming that it is possible to avoid using these terms altogether. I am proposing, rather, that they be used with particular circumspection and certain qualifications in |Xam studies.

As we saw in chapter 1, Gayatri Spivak (1999: 114) has argued that the 'worlding' process of imperialism — the way in which people find themselves included in global networks of economic and political domination through processes over which they have no control — is obscured by the use of terms that become essentialised categories that can be spoken of apart from the history of imperialism. The definition of myth I am considering here (Cupitt 1982: 29) explicitly excludes the specific historical contexts in which the term was mobilised by scholars such as Bleek by appealing to 'the universal significance' of myth. The word 'typically' establishes the power of the analytic gaze and constitutes the term — 'myth' — as an object with finite parameters, even as it is invested with a timeless and boundless significance. The definition establishes the authority of an institutionally sanctioned tradition of reason to universalise, categorise and fix within a taxonomic order. It affirms the capacity of this tradition to reduce to type and to exert its hegemony over other discursive practices, such as 'myth', through its power to bring them within the domain of its own critical practice.

The term 'traditional' posits a relationship between things that can only be discerned by modernity's teleological gaze — that peculiar vantage point from which the past is surveyed from a point in the future. 'Tradition' here refers to a locality outside history that is beyond rearrangement. Lévi-Strauss's positing of societies 'without history' (Leach 1989: 9) — people who experience themselves as sealed off in time or as a succession of time presents — comes to mind. The term 'traditional' works in this context as a 'less offensive' substitute' for 'primitive' (Okpewho 1983: 225).

The correlative of this positing of the timeless narrative realm of myth is the delineation of a modern space characterised by notions of dynamic literature and culture. The |Xam narratives, it is commonly supposed, with the obvious exception of the historical and biographical materials, belong to a pre-modern cultural complex and have been repeated in recognisable form from time immemorial. Their traditional nature is authenticated by the almost complete absence of untraditional elements. Very little intrudes from the colonial or modern eras. None of this, however, is as obvious as it might seem. Guenther (1986) has shown how Nharo narrative has adapted to the changed economic and linguistic circumstances of life in the colonial and post-colonial eras. Can we assume that this was unprecedented and that prior to colonial penetration the traditional existed uncontaminated by history? There is also the question of the contexts of reception. Brown (1998: 62) suggests that some of the narratives could have been employing a technique of analogy with which to comment on contemporary events; i.e. a story with a traditional form might be a response to the present. The expectations of the interviewers may also have encouraged the narrators to relate more 'old' stories and fewer stories that related to their present circumstances, such as those dealing with boers, commandos and Koranas, than they might have told in the contemporary context of the farms of the colonial north-west Cape. Guenther (1996: 93) also considers the possibility that the 'alienation and oppressiveness of the narrators' lives in colonial Cape society evoked a sense of the integrity of their own culture' and inspired them to tell more traditional stories.[3]

Durkheim argued that all societies need to distinguish between the sacred and the profane (2001). The particular basis for this distinction in any single society might seem random and arbitrary, but it is rigidly enforced in all societies by interdictions. The realm of myth, which belongs to the sacred, is separated from the profane and everyday in a manner that is absolute. For Dundes (1984), as is indicated by the title of the book that he edits, it is primarily its sacred character that distinguishes myth from other forms of narrative. Once again, much of the interpretation of the |Xam materials that has been conducted suggests that |Xam narrative cannot be aligned with the sacred and separated from the profane in this way. Guenther (1999), in his study of Bushman religion and the figure of |Kaggen, the Mantis, insists that |Xam narrative and religion revel in ambiguity and contradiction, and that the sacred and profane coexist and interpenetrate in ways that are bewilderingly multiple and various.

The characterisation of myths as sacred also suggests that they are artefacts that are unchanging and impervious to history rather than the fluid products of discourse. If stories belong to the realm of the sacred, they might be expected to be performed or told in a ritualised space clearly separate from the everyday. If this is the case, then once again the ethnographic and historical evidence as assembled, for example, by Hewitt (1986: 47) suggests that the IXam narratives do not conform to the sacred character of the myth, for they were told in all sorts of contexts and were often an extension of everyday speech. Guenther (2006: 241) notes that '[s]tories are told not only to children, but also to adults as a cherished recreational pastime and an element of socializing and inter-camp visiting'.

The category of the sacred in the anthropological literature has also been identified with what a society believes to be true. A myth is a sacred tale because it is believed to be true by people living in the culture in which it occurs. Bascom (1965: 4) actually distinguishes myth from folktale chiefly on the grounds that myths are considered true, whereas folktales are not. However, a belief in the truth of a myth, it is implied, is objectively erroneous or, at the very least, unverifiable. It is no coincidence that the word 'myth' in everyday contemporary usage is used to refer to a falsehood that presents itself as the truth. Pre-scientific experiences of truth, the sacred and the mythical, it is imputed by mythologists, were based either on unfounded beliefs or on misinterpretation of empirical experience. One of the hidden implications, then, of describing certain IXam narratives as myths is that the IXam considered these stories to be literally true. A related assumption is that all the members of a society such as the IXam held the same beliefs, since a story would lose its status as a myth once its truth value began to be disputed.

The connotations that the word 'story' carries in the definition also need to be examined more closely. I shall assume that the term refers to a text that is presented in narrative form rather than to a distinction between fiction and non-fiction. Many of the IXam narratives, however, do not easily fit the usual description of a story, if form is the chief criterion. They are often embedded in much longer discourses that do not have a clear beginning or ending. It is frequently the editing process that precedes their inclusion in selections of IXam myths and folktales that gives them the

74

formal features of tales. Dorothea Bleek (1923), as we shall see in chapter 11, constructed stories from several pieces in the notebooks, none of which contains all the elements found in the stories as they appear in her published version of them.

The term 'anonymous authorship' distinguishes the performative storyteller from the individual author with a biography and a documented identity. It carries with it a great many other imputations as well, however. It creates a contrast between the enlightenment subject; i.e. a deliberate agent; a conscious, differentiated individual; and an author, on the one hand, and the anonymous, pre-modern purveyor of myths, on the other. In this context, the term performs several ideological tasks, I would argue, besides referring to the fact that in oral traditions the 'original' inventor of a story is usually not known. It obscures the fact that all writing, and not just myth or traditional narrative, participates in a discourse that precedes it. It separates myth from the realm of the privileged artist — the work of art as the manifestation of private genius. Myths emerge almost fully fledged from the primitive mind which experiences rather than creates them. Moran (2009: 126) notes in this regard 'that Lloyd entitled their book *Specimens of Bushman Folklore*, not literature, thus retaining the idea of the collective mind'.

This issue of authorship is one of no small consequence. Csapo, who subjects many views of myth to a wide-ranging critique, concludes at the end of his investigations that one of the chief defining features of myth is its social character. It belongs to and is produced by a society rather than an individual. If a story is told once, it is not a myth. It becomes a myth once a society decides to transmit it (Csapo 2005: 161). This question has certain twists in regard to the Bleek and Lloyd Collection. We know the names of the narrators and their sources, and they are historically located individuals. They have identifiable styles and participated in the translation of their work. They have been presented sometimes as authors or even as individual poets (Krog 2004). Were they authors or were they simply representatives of the collective who transmitted timeless myths, before fate in the form of their arrests and the presence in Cape Town of Wilhelm Bleek led them into history and authorship? Is it not likely that their status as performers and 'producers of texts' is more complex than either of these positions suggests?

While most of the writers who write about the |Xam narratives label them as myths of origin or creation tales, in one way or another, their own description of the narrative process, as I have pointed out, often belies the implications of this designation. Hewitt himself accords the |Xam narrators a role that is close to that of the writer, even though his structuralist breakdown of the stories underplays their influence. The narrators did not simply repeat timeless accounts. They created narratives by bringing together discursive elements and ordering them within the space of the performance. Hewitt (1986: 217) traces this process in regard to a number of versions of different stories, concluding that 'there is no one authentic version of this story, but rather a number of combinable elements'. The narrators apply not only humour (208) and stylistic devices to the materials, but organise them in uniquely individual ways (239). As a result, their narratives exhibit different interpretations of characters and events. |Han#kass'o, for example, organises the materials in such a way as to 'emphasise the creative and benevolent side of |Kaggen's character' (220), while ||Kabbo foregrounds |Kaggen's ambiguous nature (Hewitt 1986: 241). Hewitt (231–32) notes how ||Kabbo organises the elements in his version of the story of the all-devourer (L.II.33:2966–3149) in a manner that articulates: 'how far not to go in the direction of culture as represented by non-San groups'.

Guenther (1996: 77–99) provides an important insight into the performative aspects of oral narratives. Even if the content of a story remains the same, each telling is a unique event. Its meanings are produced in part by the performance context, and the style and content of a narrative are to a significant degree dependent on the physical and social setting in which it is performed. Also, the purpose of the storytelling session influences the rhetorical strategy and intent. All of this suggests that a story, while not a unique work, can be seen as a historically contingent event rather than as an unchanging sacred object of anonymous authorship.

Most writers have emphasised the conservative social role of myth, an emphasis that is consistent with the sort of definition of myth that I have been considering. Malinowski, as we saw in chapter 1, was of the view that myth 'justifies the social order, its institutions, practices, customs, and moral codes' (Csapo 2005: 142). The purpose of myth is to reinforce tradition. This is connected to the relationship between myth and an origin, since myths confer weight to traditions by linking them to inaugural events or a 'supernatural reality'. Lévi-Strauss, as I note in chapter 1, also endows myth with a conservative function, arguing that myths operate to resolve cultural contradictions (Csapo 2005: 224). Laurence Coupe (1997) describes how myth has frequently been seen to produce an affirmation of order and perfection through the deployment of a mechanism by means of which it contrasts the disorder of finite life as experienced from day to day with the order and plenitude of mythical time. If the |Xam stories are indeed stories of the affirmation of order — and Hewitt (1986) has read them in this way — then it must be conceded that they elicit this affirmation by following an inverse procedure to the one Coupe describes. They show the confusion of categories that occurs in mythical time and contrast this with the order of present time.

The dominant view is that myths reinforce social codes, and they carry the weight of age-old traditions. In order to qualify as myths, oral narratives should be considered as socially important (Csapo 2005: 9). Very often they lend institutions and practices particular authority by aligning them with an aetiological event. The idea that myth preserves the status quo in one way or another is also a feature of some of the more recent constructivist accounts of myth in which the term, identified with the products of contemporary commodified culture, is used to describe the ideological complexes that work to conceal the constructed nature of power. Myth belongs to the sphere of mystification and the naturalisation of bourgeois ideology (278). The constructivist reading of myth as ideology locates myth in history, however, while the older accounts of myth tend to consider myths as timeless artefacts. The constructivist position also suggests that myths are contested sites. They work to maintain ruling-class power, but also elicit counter-hegemonic responses.

However, it should be emphasised that not all writers regard myth as a conservative force. Ricoeur (1991: 490) contends that although mythical narratives may model a social and cosmic order, they are also 'a disclosure of unprecedented worlds, an opening to other *possible* worlds which transcend the established limits of our *actual* world'. Raymond Firth (1961: 175–79, cited by Okpewho 1983: 231) remarks that myths of origin can be 'divisive' or 'unitive'. They might 'be not so much a reflection of the social structure itself as of organization pressures within the social structure'. The view that the type of narratives that are described as myth can be a dynamic rather than a conservative social force is proposed chiefly in lXam studies by Guenther (1999), as we shall see in chapter 6. His reading of lKaggen is premised on the view that lXam myths are accounts of the permeability of order, crucial to the production of the type of flexible individuality required by an uncertain hunter-gathering economy. Lewis-Williams (1996a: 141), too, remarks that lXam myth may be 'one of the battlefields on which the struggle to reproduce or transform society ... was contested'.

INTERPRETING THE lXAM NARRATIVES

Common patterns can be found in the lXam narratives themselves and among them and other narratives from the southern African region and around the world (Guenther 1989; Schmidt 1989; 1996). These similarities, which include motifs, characters and plots, invite the application of a universal descriptive term such as myth to the narratives. The problem, I would argue, lies in separating the discovery of such patterns, surface or deep text from an expectation of finding them that precedes a reading of the narratives. An approach that seeks first and foremost to establish a framework in which particular patterns are made to surface from beneath the world of appearances could miss the fact that the stories themselves might be foregrounding the play of appearance, as Henry Gates (1988) maintains the African American materials he studies are doing, or offering a metadiscourse about other signifying practices in the culture, a property Barber (1991) attributes to the Yoruba *oriki* she analyses.[4] Brown (1998: 17–18) calls for an approach to the analysis of oral narrative that does justice to its textual, sociological and historical characteristics. A hermeneutic strategy that reads stories primarily as myths tends to overlook not only their discursive and metalinguistic properties, but their relationship with the specificities and contingencies of history and society.

Lévi-Strauss emphasises the central importance of the auditors in the storytelling context. Meaning only exists through listeners who, as in a musical performance, decide what the message is (Leach 1989: 130). The question then arises as to what extent it is possible to recover the ways in which historically and socially situated |Xam participants would have received the narratives that have been preserved in the Bleek and Lloyd Collection. Karin Barber (1999: 45) argues that it is feasible, even imperative, to grasp 'what a text is constituted for, and how people within its circuit of signification seize it'. The reward of doing so is that literary texts 'tell us things about society and culture that we could learn in no other way' (Barber 1991: 1). It is the recognition of the discursive nature of texts that makes them amenable to interpretation: 'literary texts are revealing because they are inherently discursive' (Barber 1991:3). Barber's chief method of gaining an insight into indigenous texts is to examine 'the prevailing and culturally established modes of interpretation'. 'Texts', she claims, 'are set up to be interpreted in particular ways; they engage the hearer in specific kinds of hermeneutic activity' (Barber 1999: 28). Brown (1998: 20) similarly stresses the importance of conducting 'research into the aesthetic strategies and critical practices of the specific societies in relation to their performance genres'.

This position contrasts starkly with Lévi-Strauss's distrust of 'native distinctions' (Okpewho 1983: 53) or of the common view that 'the analyst can afford to ignore the views of the informant since, being a primitive anyway, he has far less understanding of the import of the images of his tale than the scholar with his wider frame of reference' (Okpewho 1983: 29). While none of the scholars who analyse the |Xam narratives would consciously subscribe to such a position, it persists, I would argue, as a concealed premise in some of the interpretive approaches that they employ. Functional, structural and comparative treatments of the narratives all discover layers of meanings in the texts that are inaccessible to indigenous storytellers and their audiences. Hewitt's reading of the narratives, for instance, is based on Lévi-Strauss's view that myths exhibit 'a system of binary differentiation' and conceal a code that 'operates at a more or less *unconscious* level' (Okpewho 1983: 37; original emphasis); i.e. the deeper structure and import of the tales are available only to the interpreter. It would be impossible, of course, to divest an interpretation that occurs within the framework of the academic tradition altogether of this asymmetrical epistemological structure. Nevertheless, it is possible, I would argue, to incorporate indigenous exegesis to a more significant degree into an analysis while simultaneously exposing the inability of the analytical tools developed in the tradition of Western rationalism to provide a definitive understanding of lXam discourse.

Barber argues for the autonomy of a signifying practice: it has to be understood in terms of its own discursive codes if elementary interpretive errors are to be avoided. She observes that oral texts are 'accompanied by well-developed indigenous methods and techniques by which their interpretations are carried out' (Barber 1991: 4). The acknowledgement of indigenous systems of exegesis is a salutary antidote to academic claims to a hermeneutic monopoly. As Barber (1999: 27) asserts, knowledge of the way in which the praise poetry she discusses in her essay is received and interpreted is an essential preliminary step to an analysis of the materials. The lXam materials do, however, present particular difficulties in following Barber's method. In the absence of live performance, it is difficult to do more than acknowledge the importance of the non-verbal elements of the stories: the dramatisation, mime, character-specific locutions and vocabularies, and interactive techniques (Hewitt 1986: 51). The absence of contemporary lXam speakers, storytellers and listeners means that the meanings that the narratives evoked in their auditors have to be reconstructed on the basis of educated conjecture.[5] This not only involves reading the notebooks in new ways, but considering present-day Bushman storytelling practice and reception as models, a comparative procedure that has been criticised in relation to rock art interpretation in which contemporary Bushman cultural practice in the Kalahari has been used as evidence in support of particular readings of the paintings of the Drakensberg (Solomon 1997; 1999; 2008). The social context, whose presence, in Barber's view, is necessary for the emergence of the textuality of oral texts (Barber 1991: 8), has to be reconstructed in ways that the social contexts of the praise poetry (1999) and the *oriki* (1991) studied by Barber do not. Nor do the lXam appear to have possessed an exegetical tradition comparable to the one described by Barber (1999) in relation to Yoruba praise poetry. The meanings the stories might have produced were not socially sanctioned and monitored in the same semi-formalised manner. The stories appear to have been truly popular mediums, and there were no specialist storytellers (Hewitt 1986: 49). Although Hewitt (1986: 50) implies that certain stories were reserved for adult audiences, the listeners to stories were generally of all ages and both genders. There was no special time or place for storytelling, and narrative was 'part of sociability' (Hewitt 1986: 50). Nor do the |Xam appear to have formally recognised different genres with different conventions (Hewitt 1986: 56),[6] a contributing factor to the types of exegetical practices that Barber describes. Moreover, the |Xam texts do not appear to contain obscure historical references and allusions or in-house riddles whose meanings can only be unravelled by secret, specialist or initiate information and knowledge.

The Bleek and Lloyd notebooks do, however, contain an 'indigenous' metanarrative of the stories, since the narrators provide extensive background information to and explanations of the narratives, sometimes, no doubt, as a result of the knowledge the narrators gained of their new auditors' ignorance of many of the features of |Xam life and sometimes in answer to specific questions from the collectors (Bank 2006: 173). The explanatory information was frequently noted on the pages facing the main text. It also sometimes formed a new discourse in its own right. Dia!kwain, especially, often provided more information than story (Hewitt 1986: 244). Bank (2006: 167) notes that many of the explanations and notes were added after the actual process of dictation. They were 'part of the collaborative work of translation'. The employment of dialogue in the narratives, as Hewitt points out, also allows for the existence of multiple perspectives and exegetical commentary in the stories themselves: 'when the action is over, events may be endlessly discussed by the characters, argued about, seen from different points of view and told from the perspective of even quite peripheral characters' (Hewitt 1986: 55).

Along with this explicit exegesis, offered by the informants in notes to the materials or in explanatory digressions and by the perspectives allowed by the technique of dialogue in the stories, critics following Barber's approach can also exploit the fact that literary texts themselves frequently offer hermeneutic tools. It 'is often through literary texts that exegetical commentary is directed towards systems of signification' (Barber 1991: 2). This is a feature of their literariness: 'literary texts function like nodal points in the flow of speech. They are salient and enduring landmarks in the field of discourse, reference points to which speakers orient themselves or from which they take their departure' (2). An understanding of how the |Xam texts themselves interpret the broader discursive field in which they are situated can become a valuable tool in interpreting them. Fresh meanings become available from a reading of the texts if their exegetical qualities are mobilised. In addition, the limitations of many of the interpretive tools that have previously been applied to the texts begin to be exposed in new ways.

It could be argued that the |Xam texts contain the sorts of hermeneutic tools to which Barber refers in several forms. Hewitt (1986: 192) notes of the |Kaggen narratives that '|Kaggen's ambiguous nature must have often presented individual narrators with the task of interpretation ...'. |Kaggen's flouting of social convention creates critical perspective. In regard to |Kaggen's predictive dreaming, Hewitt (178) observes that '[b]y being an outsider who nevertheless has such an access to the real shapes behind appearances, he shares something of the position of the blind seer or the hermit magician in the fictions of other cultures'. |Kaggen thus operates as a sign that mobilises a metacommentary on |Xam signifying systems.

Hewitt (1986: 119) also describes the presence of mediating figures in the stories: 'the child-informant, featuring in many of the narratives, and mediating figures such as the Partridge and the Lynx ... are ciphers functioning as part of the mechanics of the plot.' I would argue that such figures do more than facilitate the unfolding of the plot, as Hewitt suggests. Nor are they chiefly concerned, in my opinion, with the negotiation of contradictions, as Lévi-Strauss, from whom Hewitt derives the notion of the mediator, contends. They foreground, rather, the discursive and textual nature of a narrative, either through providing different perspectives on the narrative events or by crossing the borders between realms, highlighting, in the process, the constructed nature of boundaries, and by, extension, the play of difference that produces signification. These figures thus contribute to the exegetical commentary to which Barber refers, a commentary that can be turned on other signifying systems beyond the narratives. Humour, a strong feature of the |Xam narratives, could be regarded as another distancing mechanism that encourages exegesis on the part of audience and narrator. The representation of |Kaggen and an array of other figures in the stories is often satirical; satire invites a critical perspective.

Barber (1991) argues that oral literature is ideological. One of its features is struggle (5). Recognising the ideological nature of |Xam texts allows them to signify in ways that have been closed to them in most of the commentary that regards them as myths. The influence of the metaphysics of presence predisposes critics to underestimate the role of conflict and power in the narratives, since, in terms of the intellectual structure it produces, people like the |Xam are located as ideal communities that exist outside history. When ideology and power are returned to the texts, they emerge as sites in which different versions of truth are tested and contested. Instead of discovering the single 'truth' behind an oral text, as functionalist or structuralist explanations often seek to do, an interpretive strategy can be pursued that encourages the enunciation of a multiplicity of |Xam voices.

Helize van Vuuren (1994: 63) reads one of ‖Kabbo's discourses as a piece of 'meta-discourse' that relates to |Xam cultural production, an example of 'indigenous literary theory'. In the text to which Van Vuuren refers, ‖Kabbo emphasises that stories require expansive social interaction: 'The Flat's people do visit their fellow's houses; that they might smoking sit at the door (of) them. Therefore, they hear stories, at them. For they feel that they are used to visit, for they feel that smoking's people [they] are' (L.II.32:2880–81). This suggests that for ‖Kabbo the discursive space is socially bounded; it is dialogical. He might agree with Bakhtin that language always 'manifests itself in discourse, the word oriented towards another' (Dentith 1995: 32). Stories require social equality and compatibility:

> I do feel, this time, it is here, I ought to sit together with my fellow men ...
> I must visit; I must talk with my fellow men; for, I do work here, with
> womenfolk; whom I do not talk with them; for they do verily send me to
> work (L.II.32:2882–84).

‖Kabbo situates the source of stories within a community of belonging and within discourse:

> I do not hear stories, while I feel that I do not visit, that I might hear stories
> which sail along, while I feel that another place's people are those which are

here, those do not hear my stories. They do not talk my language; for they
do visit their fellows (L.II.32:2876–79).

‖Kabbo's celebrated piece about storytelling is not the only place in the
materials in which visiting and stories are linked. In the narrative by
|Han#kass'o that Lloyd called 'The Mantis and Kwammang-a Visit the
Dassie's House', and which I discuss in chapter 8,[7] |Kaggen's wife describes
the different attitudes towards visiting strangers displayed by Kwammang-a
and her husband:

> For he felt that strangers' houses they were, those at which they were.
> Therefore, Kwammang-a was quiet, he only spoke to get stories. These
> stories were what he listened to, for the other people were those, from
> whom he had gone to talk, getting these stories were what he went to talk
> about, but this man was the one who played tricks (L.VIII.2:6190).

This extract indicates that ‖Kabbo's much-quoted thoughts about stories
are part of a wider |Xam discourse about storytelling and listening. Stories
bring strangers together, not just one's 'fellows'. Refusing to listen, as
|Kaggen does, drives people apart. One visits in order to obtain stories;
discourse creates a wider community. As we can see, however, if we
compare ‖Kabbo's piece with |Han#kass'o's story, the category of the
stranger in this context excludes those whose culture and language are
completely alien, as well as those who, like |Kaggen, are unable to listen.
Listening here is an indicator of the sort of discursive reciprocity that, for
‖Kabbo, is not possible in colonial Cape Town. More crucially, perhaps, the
people among whom ‖Kabbo finds himself stranded cannot give him
stories. Their discourse is closed to him. Without turning ‖Kabbo into a
spokesperson for the colonised, we could comment that the asymmetry of
the colonial encounter precluded the sort of exchange that occurs between
strangers when they meet on an equal footing and become fellows.

How can we 'listen' to the |Xam texts? Levinas, writes Godzich (1986:
xvi), identifies 'a form of truth that is totally alien' to the self and yet calls
out to the self. It requires the self 'to leave the realms of the known and of
the same'. The 'truths' the |Xam stories might offer summon from beyond

the confines of the intellectual tradition that seeks to apprehend them. These 'truths' must be allowed their inaccessibility and their difference, even as we seek to comprehend them. The awareness of how a historically situated method of interpretation projects its own concerns onto historically situated texts, allied to the realisation that these texts themselves offer hermeneutic tools, is the precondition, in my view, for the practice of the sort of dialectic that Brown (1998: 2) proposes in which text and interpretation, as well as past and present, question each other.

'THE MANTIS, THE ELAND AND THE MEERKATS':
Reading a narrative as myth or text

The question naturally arises as to how the remarks I have made so far in this chapter would translate into reading an actual piece of IXam text. Although I have been critical of the manner in which structuralist, functionalist and comparative analytical preconceptions have sometimes determined the way in which the materials have been viewed, I do not wish to propose that the insights these approaches have to offer should be rejected out of hand. I am suggesting, rather, that the statements produced by these analytical pro-cedures should be rigorously investigated, as should their relationship with the various schools of myth studies. As with all interpretive statements about the texts, they can, I would contend, only be accorded an insecure and relative authority. This is partly because of the fluid, elusive and multivocal nature of discourse itself, a property of the IXam narratives that is often suppressed when they are treated as myths. The distance between the discourse of hermeneutics and IXam discourse and practice only increases the speculative status of the statements an interpreter can make about the texts. I would argue that it is possible to put new statements about the narratives into play, but not to produce final truths about them, at least as far as their meaning is concerned. I do not wish to imply, however, that all statements about the narratives have an equal weight. As Hewitt's work exemplifies, interpretation of the texts should be based on close engagement with the materials and make carefully considered strategic claims about them.

As I have stated several times, the work of Hewitt, Guenther, Lewis-Williams, Brown and others contains elements of the sort of interpretive approach that I think could be pursued further. In the remainder of this chapter, I will offer some comments regarding Lewis-Williams's (1998a) analysis of 'The Mantis, the Eland and the Meerkats'. The approach to interpretation in this article is, in my opinion, salutary in certain respects. For the most part, though, it is highly problematic, for reasons that I will explore in the remainder of this chapter, the most serious of which is that Lewis-Williams's reading seems to impose a meaning on the text in order to illustrate a theory of shamanism rather than allow the narrative to signify on its own terms. Lewis-Williams (1998a: 194) begins his paper by lamenting the absence of a close reading of 'southern African folklore' and proceeds to offer just such a reading. He argues that the text 'communicates simultaneously on a number of different levels' (198) and provides at least two interpretations of the narrative. He gives all the elements in the piece that he analyses extended attention. Instead of dismissing many of the elements in the story as extraneous to the deep structure of the story, as some readers of 'myth' do, he shows how they all contribute to the overall meaning of the piece. A strong feature of the paper is the manner in which he investigates particular signs. These include 'shoe', 'gall', '|Kwammang-a' (|Kaggen's son-in-law) and 'waterhole.' He observes of the shoe, for example, that:

> The shoe itself has various significances. One is that the San are able to recognise people from their bare footprints in the sand. ... By wearing a shoe made of antelope hide, |Kwammang-a was able to alter his footprints, thus masking his identity as a pawed creature and concealing his anom-alous position in |Kaggen's family. When the Mantis stole his shoe, his true spoor (and thus identity) was revealed (Lewis-Williams 1998a: 203).

This investigation of the significations attached to shoes is one of the factors that leads him to conclude that the narrative concerns the mediation of an inherent tension in |Xam society, namely the relations between affines who are united by marriage, but belong to different groups. These groups had to 'share' or compete for scarce resources. He goes on to observe that the shoe in question — that of |Kaggen's son-in-law, Kwammang-a — was made from 'antelope hide', and suggests that this might have been an eland skin. |Kaggen steals the shoe and fashions an eland from it. He hides the baby eland in the reeds next to a waterhole and rears it on a diet of honey. The possibility that the shoe is made from eland skin, as well as the fact that |Kaggen produces an eland, which in a sense can be understood as his offspring, leads Lewis-Williams to reach his second major conclusion about the narrative, namely that it centrally concerns |Xam shamanic practice. He argues that the 'eland will become the shamans' power-animal *par excellence*' (Lewis-Williams 1998a: 204, referring to Lewis-Williams 1981: 75–102). The story, he asserts, is actually the myth of the origin of |Xam shamanism: 'in making this mediatory, potent animal, the Mantis created the basis for |Xam shamanism' (Lewis-Williams 1998a: 205). He reinforces this interpretation of the text by the examination of some of the symbolism that is connected to other signifiers in the story, such as honey and the waterhole.

I have already commented that the strength of this analysis is its method of investigating the different elements in the story. Its chief limitation, however, in my view, is that it does not proceed nearly far enough with this enterprise. Lewis-Williams only assembles the evidence that supports his overall reading of the story as a myth of the origin of |Xam shamanism. The more open-ended intertextual approach for which I am arguing would include even the significations of a word that might, at first sight, seem irrelevant to the text being considered. Often these other significations and the chains of associations they produce subvert the interpretation already arrived at or suggest others that might coexist with it. Lewis-Williams (1998a: 198), we might assume, would not be averse to such an outcome, for he notes that his analysis of the story is not 'the only possible' one.

The signifier 'shoe' occurs in several places in the notebooks, apart from the ones to which Lewis-Williams refers. Some of these references could be used to reinforce his reading, while others, I think, qualify or even contradict it. To illustrate this point properly is beyond the scope of this chapter. Here I can only describe some of the instances in which the sign 'shoe' occurs in the materials and offer a few remarks as to how these could be taken into account when analysing the narrative that Lewis-Williams discusses in his article.

The moon speaks like a shoe because it is created from |Kaggen's shoe:

Thus speaks the moon. He speaks because the Mantis made him speak. The Mantis spoke to the Moon because he was the Mantis' shoe. At that time the Mantis' shoe spoke. His shoe had always known how to speak, it had spoken whenever the Mantis shod himself. Both shoes spoke when the Mantis had shod himself. Therefore the Moon speaks feeling within him the speaking Mantis shoe (Guenther 1989: 73).

The moon's aptitude for speech is not the only attribute it possesses that is related to its origin as |Kaggen's shoe. It is red because |Kaggen's shoe was covered in red dust and cold because it is made from leather (L.II.4:484). |Kaggen also makes his favourite animal, the eland, from a shoe. He does not use his own shoe, though, but steals one of the shoes of his son-in-law, Kwammang-a.

The |Xam seem to have made shoes from a range of animal skins, including springbok, elephant and fox (B.I.198). But it is the gemsbok that is most celebrated for its leather. In a long discourse that the ichneumon delivers to the Mantis after one of his escapades, he relates how two men rejoice after they have killed a gemsbok. On coming across the poisoned antelope, the man asks, 'Is that a shoe lying there?' The other man says to him: 'A gemsbok lies there'. The other one rejoices to the first: 'Yes! My brother, do thus to us; that we are shod; for we have not been shod; for we have walked upon our (bare) feet; the sticks have been piercing them' (L.II.24:2171–72).

Other references to the sign 'shoe' in the materials include #Kasin's removing his shoes and turning up his trousers when looking into a hyena's hole (B.IV:3537). People also beat shoes together during a solar eclipse in order to bring the sun back so that they are not caught out in the veld in the dark (Hollmann 2004: 196).

Lewis-Williams (1998a: 203–4) maintains that Kwammang-a wears shoes in order to conceal his identity as a carnivore who has inappropriately married into a vegetarian family. Shoes signify the concealment of identity, since they cover up spoor. Although Lewis-Williams's statement is a little ambiguous, it could be read to suggest that the wearing of antelope hide shoes in particular is linked to the concealment of carnivore identity: 'By wearing a shoe made of antelope hide, |Kwammang-a was able to alter his footprints, thus masking his identity as a pawed creature and concealing his anomalous position in |Kaggen's family' (Lewis-Williams 1998a: 203). Why does #Kasin remove his shoes before looking into the hyena's hole? If shoes signify the cloaking of identity, does #Kasin, by removing his shoes, intend to reveal his true identity to the hyena rather than conceal it? Or is this context so different from that of the piece Lewis-Williams considers that these questions are inappropriate? Why does |Kaggen himself wear shoes? Is his wearing of shoes linked specifically to his shape-shifting prowess, the ability to mix identities, or is it simply that the animal|people of the First Times resembled humans and behaved to a large extent like them? People on the whole, the evidence of the materials suggests, wore shoes.

Why are both the eland and the moon made from shoes? Is this connected to concealment or to its opposite, revelation, in some way? Does dispelling the darkness and bringing back the sun by beating shoes have anything to so with the magic power that is derived from |Kaggen or antelope? Lewis-Williams (1998a: 204), as I have said, links the creation of the eland from a shoe to the power that was released from using an object belonging to an affine's shoe and to the shamanic qualities inherent in antelope hide and the relationship between |Kaggen and shamanism. The moon, derived as it is from a shoe, could also then be read as part of a shamanic complex. It is linked after all to |Kaggen, as it is said to be a |Kaggen thing that speaks (Hollmann 2004: 367), and is thus an archetypal symbol of transformation. In some versions of the moon and hare story, e.g. 'The Origin of Death' (see chapter 8), the moon has power over life and death itself. Trance is often described as a type of dying and resurrection (Biesele, Katz & St. Denis 1997). Although its potency cannot be said to derive from the illicit deployment of an affine's possession in the way that the eland's can, its potency could be attributed to its origin as an antelope hide, a trance animal, worn by the archetypal shaman, |Kaggen. Its redness could be linked to blood and thus to trance, which produces nose bleeding.

This is all possible and should not be discarded from a consideration of the text. The |Xam narrators themselves, however, never make these links explicit in the materials. Shoes are linked to protection from sharp sticks and they feature in the materials as everyday wear. They are not worn predominantly to conceal spoor. #Kasin removes his shoes when following the hyena, and it is their removal rather than their presence that is commented on. It is true that |Kaggen's shoes are capable of transformation and flight, but then so are all his things. It should be remembered, in this respect, that a |Xam hunter only wore or carried a few things. While it is probable that the shoes were made of antelope hide — most commonly, according to the materials, gemsbok or springbok, two of the big game animals associated closely with |Kaggen — they are also made from other animals' skins as well, including elephant and fox (although the notebooks are a bit ambiguous on this point).

It is certainly likely that these skins were used as much for their suitability and availability as for their symbolic purchase. This, of course, does not mean that they could not also serve as ritual or power objects, as when they are beaten together to prevent an eclipse. The cross web of signifiers allows multiple meanings to be carried simultaneously. I would argue, however, that their everyday signification and use should not necessarily be subordinated to esoteric and symbolic meanings. The surfaces of a text should be explored before underlying meanings are extracted from them. When I conjecture that the red shoes and moon might be connected to blood, this is at the expense of accepting the mundane |Xam explanation that their red colour is derived from the colour of the earth.

Lewis-Williams's essay displays, I would argue, several of the analytical tendencies that are associated with the reading of the materials as myths. He repeatedly refers to and consistently treats the piece as a myth. His approach, not surprisingly, therefore, reproduces some of the dominant strands in the study of mythology. He seeks to discover a latent meaning in the narrative, the quest that draws 'modern theories' of myth together (Csapo 2005: 189). His position that the text is a coded account of shamanic experience echoes the position towards myth of the ritualists who generally posit a significant correlation between myth and ritual, often giving the latter priority over the former. Lewis-Williams's reading of the story accords in this respect with his influential reading of rock art, which has been criticised by Anne Solomon (1997; 1999; 2008) precisely for its assertion that rock painting reflects ritual and the trance experiences that attend it rather than itself producing meaning. Lewis-Williams's essay also displays the influence of the structuralist approach to myth. He cites and echoes Lévi-Strauss when he argues that the story involves the resolution of conflict between affines and blood relatives. Lewis-Williams's method draws on the comparatist approach to the analysis of myth. Many of his statements are based not on the |Xam materials themselves, but on information about other southern African Bushmen. This is a feature

90

of his rock art analysis as well, in which he regularly transposes information from the |Xam materials or the Kalahari to the Natal Drakensberg. Sometimes this information is drawn from distant parts of the world, and the figure of the shaman itself is borrowed from Siberia.

I have argued, in the course of this chapter, that when the intertextuality of the materials is foregrounded by inserting each signifier in a narrative into the chain of signifiers with which it interacts in the rest of the materials, the discursive character of the texts begins to emerge and a rich and multivocal play of meanings is mobilised. When, on the other hand, the materials are treated as distinct genres, such as myth, legend, biography and history, the interpretive thrust is more towards containment and classification. The material's ability to generate multiple kinds of meaning is also limited, in my view, when a unified myth cycle is extracted from them. All the narratives of the First Times are then considered to form part of a consistent and coherent account of creation. I would contend instead that the |Xam stories are not primarily accounts of origin or creation, although they possess aetiological information. They are concerned more with the way things are or will be than with investigating how they originated. Nor are they articulated with a teleology. The stories mobilise overlapping possibilities, I believe, rather than chart a line of cause and effect or reveal a cosmic design unfolding in time from an origin. They can be read, instead, as heterotopian, sometimes dystopian, speculations in which the plastic shape of the present is projected into the parallel social imaginary of the First Order. Above all, they are discourse, constituting rather than reflecting experience and 'reality'.

This discussion is resumed in the next chapter. The focus shifts, however, from the category of mythology to the figure of the trickster, another of the universals that has, in my view, been uncritically transported into the interpretation of the |Xam studies.

NOTES

1 See, for example, Wilmsen (1989), Gordon (1992), Lee and Guenther (1993), Solomon (1997; 1999; 2008; n.d.), Lewis-Williams and Dowson (1994) and Lewis-Williams (1998b).

2   See, for example, D. Bleek (1929: 304, 305, 309), Hewitt (1986: 201), Watson (1991: 19),
    Brown (1998: 71), Guenther (1999: 4), Lewis-Williams (1996a; 1998a: vi; 2000: 9),
    Bank (2006: 146) and Solomon (1997; 1999).
3   Guenther (1986) maintains that modern Nharo deliberately and consciously employ
    the trance dance as a means of reinforcing a traditional identity. Bank (2006: 365)
    notes that both ‖Kabbo and |Han#kass’o told more traditional stories towards the
    end of their stay in Mowbray, and conjectures that this was partly attributable to
    cultural nostalgia and homesickness.
4   ‘Oriki are a genre of Yoruba oral poetry that could be described as attributions or
    appellations: collections of epithets, pithy or elaborated, which are addressed to a
    subject’ (Barber 1991: 1).
5   The work of Ansie Hoff (1998; 2007) suggests, however, that it is still possible to find
    descendants of the |Xam who can shed light on the Bleek and Lloyd materials. My
    statement thus might apply more strictly to desktop literary critics like myself than it
    does to anthropologists.
6   Brown (1998: 26) notes that ‘Bushman societies have generally not maintained rigid
    generic distinctions between verse forms and narrative, or between sacred and profane
    genres’. He links the absence of ‘institutionalized generic distinctions’ to the absence
    of social stratification (50).
7   Dorothea Bleek calls her composite story ‘The Dasse and the Crow’s Story’, part of
    which is taken from ‘The Mantis and Kwammang-a Visit the Dassie’s House’. The
    former will be discussed in chapter 8.

CHAPTER 4

THE QUESTION OF THE TRICKSTER:

Interpreting ǀKaggen

The study of the figure of ǀKaggen, the Mantis, has been central to the project of interpreting the ǀXam texts. Although critics differ about his role in ǀXam narratives and ǀXam culture, the characterisation of ǀKaggen as the ǀXam trickster is reproduced in nearly all the writing on him.[1] This chapter seeks to question this reading of ǀKaggen. I argue for an interpretive strategy that locates ǀKaggen within ǀXam discourse itself rather than one that identifies him as the local representative of a universal type. The arguments against the identification of ǀKaggen with a universal trickster draw on arguments that have been elaborated by other writers in order to question the attribution of the term 'trickster' to specific characters in local literatures from across the world. The first part of my discussion is, therefore, general in nature. I examine the broader trickster literature and its influence on ǀXam studies. This is followed by a consideration of some of the criticism that the trickster literature has elicited and the identification of this literature with a wider tendency towards universalising thought, a tendency that has elicited criticism from a range of contemporary thinkers. I conclude with an examination of the ǀXam hunting observances in which ǀKaggen appears in order to illustrate some of my earlier contentions about ǀKaggen's place in ǀXam discourse.

ǀKAGGEN, THE TRICKSTER

Stephen Watson (1991: 32) begins his poem 'The nature of ǀKaggen' with a line that reads: 'ǀKaggen, old trickster, magician, also called Mantis'. Most of the poems in Watson's collection can be linked directly to specific texts in the Bleek and Lloyd materials. This poem, however, employs a different strategy. It assembles common elements from many of the stories that feature |Kaggen in order to provide an overall picture of |Kaggen's 'nature.' But the actual designation of |Kaggen as a trickster is not derived from the source materials at all. It is fair to assume, I think, that Watson's character- isation of |Kaggen as a trickster exhibits the influence on him of the writing on the |Xam narratives by Roger Hewitt and Mathias Guenther. Both these writers, drawing directly on the broad trickster literature, describe |Kaggen as a trickster. Watson (1991: 4) acknowledges both of them: 'The books of Hewitt and Guenther were especially useful; in fact, they became my indispensable guides.'

The contribution of scholars such as Hewitt and Guenther to the study of the |Xam texts is, of course, indispensable to anyone who seeks to engage more closely with the texts. This does not mean, however, that this body of critical work is not open to contestation and reappraisal. There has been a tendency in the field to take Hewitt's statements, especially, as facts and to reproduce them uncritically. One of the chief manifestations of this ten- dency, in my opinion, is the acceptance that |Kaggen is a trickster. No-one, to my knowledge, has questioned the suitability of the term 'trickster' as a description of |Kaggen. Only Hewitt himself, as I observed in the previous chapter, displays a certain unease about the use of the term in relation to |Kaggen. Although Hewitt's reading of |Kaggen is strongly influenced by Paul Radin's (1956|1972) celebrated study of the Winnebago figure, Wakdjunkaga, he takes some trouble to distance his interpretation of |Kaggen from Radin's universal claims about the trickster. |Kaggen, insists Hewitt (1986: 210), should be located within a specifically |Xam cultural context.

Hewitt's reliance on Radin's view of the trickster and his close engagement with the |Xam materials are not comfortably reconciled in his writing. Radin presents the trickster as an archetype, the embodiment of a particular phase of consciousness, while Hewitt situates the trickster as a structural device within the materiality of language. |Kaggen, in Hewitt's view, is an enabling mechanism that allows core cultural themes to be translated into story. Hewitt's trickster is local; Radin's trickster is universal. Insofar as he is not a product of universal consciousness, but the product of the sphere of |Xam social relationships, Hewitt's trickster could even be described as materialist. Hewitt, nevertheless, links his reading of the trickster to Radin, whom he refers to or quotes extensively, and usually approvingly, establishing thereby an intertextual link with a particular tradition of writing on the trickster (Hewitt 1986: 131, 138, 145, 211n). Within the idealist context of the notion of a universal trickster, |Kaggen becomes the local manifestation of an ideal type. The trickster then becomes not only a device to articulate |Xam social messages — the role that Hewitt's functionalist reading usually ascribes to |Kaggen — but 'the Transformer, the establisher of the present order of things, utterly non-ethical, only incidentally and inconsistently beneficent; approachable and directly intervening in a very human way in the affairs of the world' (Hewitt 1986: 131, quoting Radin 1924: 22f).

A good example of the difficulty Hewitt finds in reconciling his acceptance of Radin's work on the trickster and his own location of |Kaggen within |Xam culture is to be found in his discussion of the dual nature of |Kaggen. Hewitt, as I shall describe in detail in the next chapter, distinguishes between two broad groups of |Kaggen narratives. One set of stories features a trickster sort of |Kaggen, while the other presents |Kaggen as a priestly saviour figure. Hewitt (1986: 138) poses the question as to how far the two aspects of |Kaggen's personality 'can be seen to be unified'. He claims that 'no absolute answer to this question can be given with regard to |Kaggen on the basis of the evidence available'. He notes that this problem presented itself also to Radin with respect to the Winnebago trickster. Radin (1956: 25, cited by Hewitt 1986: 138) wonders whether the Winne-bago figure represents a merging of two distinct figures, a deity and a trickster, or whether he was originally 'a deity with two sides to his nature, one constructive, one destructive, one spiritual, one material'. Hewitt decides that the existence of two deities in other Khoisan cultures suggests that Radin's first conjecture about the Winnebago trickster might be applicable to |Kaggen. He notes that Marshall (1962: 233) posits a syncretic origin in order to explain the dual nature of the Zu|wasi trickster deity, Gao!na (Hewitt 1986: 139).

Even though Hewitt finds an explanation of |Kaggen's dual nature impossible due to the lack of |Xam ethnographic evidence, he is tempted by

Radin's reading of the trickster into immediately offering one. It is, moreover, an explanation that runs counter to statements elsewhere in his book. Earlier he strongly — and correctly, in my view — rejects the common notion that |Kaggen is a deity (Hewitt 1986: 40). He also, as I have already mentioned, explicitly rejects Radin's universal view of the trickster and insists that |Kaggen was 'embedded in and integrated with the ideas and attitudes found in one San group, the |Xam' (210). Only a few pages after implying that Radin's statements apply to |Kaggen, he actually distances the |Kaggen narratives from the Winnebago ones precisely with regard to the hybridism of the central character. Radin, maintains Hewitt (145), argues that the Winnebago trickster cycles exhibit 'the intrusion of one distinct group of culture-hero narratives upon another purely trickster-centred cycle'. Hewitt (145) decides that 'there are more grounds for assuming that the |Xam narratives reveal genuine ambiguity concerning |Kaggen's character than that they represent a welding together of disparate groups' of stories.

Guenther displays none of the unease with the designation of |Kaggen as a trickster that can be detected in Hewitt's text. He is also more consistently drawn to the comparative perspective that much of the literature on the trickster invites than is Hewitt. His *Bushman Folktales: Oral Traditions of the Nharo of Botswana and the |Xam of the Cape* not only brings together materials from two different traditions in a common study, but also provides readings of individual narratives that find similarities between these narratives and others in the Khoisan cultural sphere. In one of his chapters, which he calls 'Trickster', Guenther (1989: 116–51) links |Kaggen with several Nharo figures such as 'Eyes-on-his-Feet' (116) and with a |Xam example of 'the Khoisan-wide Jackal Trickster' (147). According to Guenther (115), 'the trickster is the central figure in Bushman — as in Khoikhoi — mythology'. 'Ambiguity,' he continues, 'the quality at the core of this being universally, is the fundamental characteristic also of the Khoisan trickster'.

Guenther's later *Tricksters and Trancers: Bushman Religion and Society* (1999), which I discuss at some length in chapter 6, is chiefly a celebration of |Kaggen as a trickster. He states at the beginning of this book that he wishes to make a contribution to a project that brings together trickster figures from around the world (Guenther 1999: 6) At various points in his text he points out the ways in which |Kaggen exhibits general trickster attributes. He discerns similarities between him and the Winnebago figure, Wakdjunkaga, studied by Radin, for example (Guenther 1999: 103). In a chapter entitled 'The Bushman trickster', Guenther (1999: 95–125) conflates |Kaggen with a list of other Khoisan trickster figures.

By identifying |Kaggen as a trickster, writers enter, often inadvertently, the wider debates that revolve around the nature and role of the figure of the trickster. By not questioning the deployment of this universal category and its applicability to a specific cultural context, they place themselves, in my view, against those writers who maintain that the cross-cultural figure, the trickster, is little more than an idealist fabrication. In Guenther's case, it must be assumed that his position on the trickster is a considered one. He refers several times in *Tricksters and Trancers* to the essays in Hynes and Doty's (1993) book on the trickster. Revealingly, he hardly attempts to describe the positions of the writers in this book who argue against the use of the trickster 'term' and the universal approach this use invites, while adopting the position of those contributors to the book who champion the use of the term and the comparative approach to mythology.

The debate about the universality or cultural specificity of the trickster is, to my mind, a debate that is directly relevant to studies of the |Xam materials. In this chapter, I will critically review some of the anthropological and critical literature on the trickster whose influence can be found in the writing of those who, like Hewitt (1986), Guenther (1989; 1999) and Lewis-Williams (1996a; 1998a; 2000), have written about the |Xam narratives that feature |Kaggen. The general writing on the trickster is wide, and I will not attempt to provide a comprehensive survey of it. Instead I will concentrate on the trickster literature that is usually referred to in the body of work that comprises |Xam studies.

Implicit or explicit in all the discussions of the trickster are different positions regarding the figure's function and meaning, questions that also preoccupy both Hewitt and Guenther. Hewitt argues that the role of the |Kaggen narratives is the reaffirmation of the social order. This takes the form of an admonitory lecture by a family member after |Kaggen has violated the codes that regulate |Xam society. Guenther, on the other hand, maintains that |Kaggen's role is to provide a model of flexible individuality, a mode of selfhood that is required, in Guenther's view, by a foraging way of life. Both these positions, as I will show, echo influential strands in the general literature on the trickster.

Hynes and Doty (1993) characterise the history of trickster studies as dominated by the difficulty of comprehending the nature of the trickster. They quote Ricketts to the effect that understanding the trickster is 'one of [our] most perplexing problems', and Kroeber, who states that the trickster figure is 'perhaps the most bewildering to a modern reader' of all the aspects of Native American literature (Hynes & Doty 1993: 13). This difficulty has not, however, prevented the proliferation of writing about the trickster. 'More has probably been written about "tricksters" than about any other single category of character that appears in the myths and folktales of the world' (Carroll 1984: 105). In the eighteenth century, when it was first used, the signifier, 'trickster' designated 'one who deceives or cheats' (Hynes & Doty 1993: 14).[2] Today it more commonly refers to a wide variety of cultural and religious figures, and the term occurs in a range of literary, scholarly and popular contexts. It has been applied not only to characters from myth and folklore, but to a range of figures from sources as far apart as the gospels and contemporary film. Tricksters in Hynes and Doty's book include the Winnebago figure Wakdjunkaga, the Yoruba character Eshu, Hermes and Saint Peter. Guenther (2002) specifically endorses this all-encompassing, transcultural, ahistorical view of the trickster.

The writers who have written about the trickster display a variety of attitudes towards him. Some, following Carl Jung, regard the trickster as the manifestation of universal psychological material. Other commentators abjure the notion of a trickster with 'archetypal roots in a transcendental human psyche' (Hynes & Doty 1993: 2), but still consider the term a useful descriptive designation for a figure who, they maintain, displays enough common characteristics across cultures to justify its use. Another, smaller, group of writers argue against the 'generalizing, comparativist view' (Hynes & Doty 1993: 2) of culture that the deployment of the category 'trickster' presupposes. In this chapter, I will argue that the views of this last group of writers carry important interpretive implications for the study of oral literature in general and the |Xam narratives in particular.

JUNG AND RADIN: The trickster and his habitats in the primitive, the popular and the repressed

Paul Radin's *The Trickster: A Study in American Indian Mythology* (1956|1972) is a book that has been of seminal significance in the treatment of the 'trickster' figure ever since it appeared. Guenther (1999) extols Radin's book. Hewitt quotes from the book quite liberally in a work not characterised by extensive citation. Radin's work, maintain Hynes and Doty (1993: 2), offers the 'first comprehensive portrait of the trickster'. They contend that all the ensuing work on the trickster follows from Radin's book and locates itself within this tradition: 'In the editors' perspective as well as that of many of the contributors, we seek to build upon Radin in a critical manner' (Hynes & Doty 1993: 2). Carl Jung (1972) contributes an influential essay to Radin's volume, which Guenther (2002: 13) approvingly refers to in his essay, 'The Bushman trickster: Protagonist, divinity and agent of creativity'.

In Jungian psychological evolutionism, which is the framework for Jung's essay on the trickster in Radin's book, the trickster is an archetype that appears at certain stages of the development of the individual psyche and also inhabits the collective consciousness of a group at particular stages of social and cultural development. Jung conflates the period of childhood ego formation with a specific state of societal, pre-technological evolution (Pelton 1980: 233). The trickster, he maintains, forms part of the shadow of every individual and also has a social and cultural manifestation: 'all mythical figures correspond to inner psychic experiences and originally sprang from them' (Jung 1972: 195).[3] Mythical characters such as the trickster feature prominently in 'primitive', societies since their members still directly experience the sorts of psychic experiences that more 'advanced' societies repress.[4] Trickster tales are told by societies whose collective consciousness has evolved relatively recently from 'an absolutely undifferentiated human consciousness, corresponding to a psyche that has hardly left the animal level' (Jung 1972: 200).

The trickster, maintains Jung, appears in unalloyed form in the tales of cultures whose members possess a

> primitive or barbarous consciousness [that] forms a picture of itself on a
> much earlier level of development and continues to do so for hundreds or

even thousands of years, undeterred by the contamination of its archaic qualities with differentiated, highly developed mental products (Jung 1972: 200).

However, the trickster is not the sole preserve of the 'uncivilized'.[5] He might
be culturally suppressed in advanced societies, but the trickster survives in
the individual psyche of their members. Among those 'spoiled by
civilization' (201), the possessors, presumably, of 'differentiated, highly
developed mental products' (200), the trickster persists, albeit in a
modified, less enjoyable and more purely psychological form. Whenever

> the unsuspecting modern man ... feels himself at the mercy of annoying
> 'accidents' which thwart his will and his actions with apparently malicious
> intent, he speaks of 'hoodoos' and 'ginxes' ... Here the trickster is repre-
> sented by countertendencies in the unconscious, and in certain cases by a
> sort of second personality, of a puerile and inferior character ... the *shadow*
> (202; original emphasis).

The repressed shadow often expresses itself in pathological ways. This is the
price of civilisation and mental progress, the Jungian version of the myth
of the lost origin. As a collective figure, the trickster is shattered by the
'impact of civilization', although he is preserved, in vestigial and reduced
form, in popular culture. Jung mentions, in this regard, the circus clown,
the carnival figure of Pulcinella, the puppets, Punch and Judy, and jokes
that contain racial stereotyping.[6]

Jung identifies typical qualities of the universal trickster, an endeavour
that has been pursued in the trickster literature ever since. He notes the
trickster's 'fondness for sly jokes and malicious pranks, his powers as a
shape-shifter, his dual nature, half animal, half divine, his exposure to all
kinds of tortures' (Jung 1972: 195). He emphasises the trickster's blend of
the supernatural and the natural:

> The trickster is a primitive 'cosmic' being of *divine-animal* nature, on the one
> hand superior to man because of his superhuman qualities, and on the other
> hand inferior to him because of his unreason and unconsciousness. He is no
> match for the animals either, because of his extraordinary clumsiness and

lack of instinct. These defects are the marks of his *human* nature (Jung 1972: 203–4; original emphasis).

Jung's view of the properties of the trickster has been widely followed in the general trickster literature, as well as in some of the writing on the IXam narratives. Guenther (1999) and Lewis-Williams (2000), for example, both emphasise the blend of the divine and the human, animal or profane in the IXam trickster, IKaggen.[7]

Another influential result of Jung's thinking on the trickster is his identification of a range of figures from different cultures and 'levels' of culture as tricksters. In his essay, Jung (1972: 196) identifies Mercury, shamans and medicine men as tricksters. Even God displays trickster traits: 'If we consider, for example, the daemonic features exhibited by Yahweh in the Old Testament, we shall find in them not a few reminders of the unpredictable behaviour of the trickster' (196).[8]

Paul Radin, whose work, as I have observed, is cited in relation to IKaggen by both Hewitt and Guenther, shares Jung's view that the trickster is a universal archetype that can be found in the individual psyche and in the myths of all cultures, even as he applies these notions to the particular figure of Wakdjunkaga, the Native American Winnebago trickster at the centre of his study. Radin also locates the origins of the trickster in the early phases of human development. He is a sort of proto-human: 'an inchoate being of undetermined proportions, a figure foreshadowing the shape of man' (Radin 1972: xxiv). He belongs to a time in which consciousness is still a complicated unity, and good and evil have a single source. Dualism is an aspect of civilisation. Here again we have all the familiar elements of the metaphysics of presence and the lost origin that Derrida exposes in the works of Rousseau and Lévi-Strauss. Primitive cultures are closer to the origin, but are also underdeveloped. Although Radin (xxiii) maintains that the trickster is a universal figure, he contends that North American cultures possess the 'earliest and most archaic form' of the trickster. The archaic provenance of tricksters means that they might provide special insights into 'man's struggle with himself and with a world into which he had been thrust without his volition and consent' (xxiv).

Most of the writers who have written more recently about the trickster have distanced themselves from Radin's and Jung's scheme of cultural evolution and its implication that certain cultures are at a 'childhood' stage of development. Nor do they regard the trickster as a metaphysical or transcendental phenomenon. Nevertheless, they follow Radin and Jung in proclaiming the universality of the figure. These writers also share their predecessors' preoccupation with the nature and function of the trickster, often repeating Jung's and Radin's descriptions of his basic qualities. This is largely true, too, of the writing on the |Xam 'trickster', |Kaggen.

OTHER WRITING ON THE TRICKSTER

William Hynes and William Doty (1993: 2) argue for the kind of universalism that allows for comparative cultural and mythological studies. They maintain that a cross-cultural figure, the trickster, exists who exhibits similar characteristics. The object of working with an individual story, they maintain, is to explore its meaning, the product of two contexts: 'the specific, local, tribal, historically bounded context' and 'the wider phenomena of general human cultural expression' (3). In the process of arguing for this dual approach, they distance themselves from what they consider to be the extreme positions represented, on the one hand, by those who 'see the trickster as so universal a figure that all tricksters speak with essentially the same voice and those who counsel that the tricksters belonging to different societies are so culture-specific that no two of them articulate similar messages' (2). Hynes and Doty (5) attempt to bridge this divide, whose roots they trace to the old epistemological debate regarding 'universals and particulars'.[9]

Hynes and Doty follow Radin in attributing a conservative and educational function to trickster stories, a position also adopted by Hewitt in his reading of the |Kaggen materials. Although the trickster himself operates within the realm of contingency and potentiality, trickster stories 'provide a fertile source of cultural reflection and critical reflexivity that leaves one thoughtful yet laughing' (Hynes & Doty 1993: 4). They hold that this aspect of the stories is easily misunderstood, since Western thinking does not readily reconcile the comic with the serious. Although trickster stories are entertaining and elicit laughter, they are also 'instructive' (Hynes & Doty 1993: 7; original emphasis). They 'map' for members of the societies in which they occur how they 'ought' to behave (Hynes & Doty 1993: 7). In this context, Hynes and Doty refer to Brian Street's (1972) volume of essays dedicated to Edward Evans-Pritchard's study The Zande Trickster, in which Street maintains that in modern cultural contexts trickster-like characters are seen as individually motivated deviants, whereas in traditional contexts they are 'socially sanctioned' figures (Hynes & Doty 1993: 7). Even as the trickster violates social codes, he reaffirms them. The Zande tales of the trickster Ture 'serve as a model for these rules, demonstrating what happens if the prescriptions laid down by society are not observed' (Hynes & Doty 1993: 6–7, quoting Street 1972: 85). The way in which the trickster serves this function is complex, since the stories have to preserve a balance between 'creativity and destructiveness', between the chaos that ensues from questioning all the social codes and the stagnation that attends rigid adherence to them (Hynes & Doty 1993: 19). The trickster, accordingly, operates at the boundaries. He confirms the need for these boundaries by demonstrating the consequences of going beyond them: 'By acting at the boundaries of order the trickster gives definition to that order' (Hynes & Doty 1993: 19, quoting Street 1972: 101).

As suggested by its title: 'The exception who proves the rules: Ananse the Akan trickster', Christopher Vecsey's essay on the Akan trickster is close to Street's line of thinking about trickster tales. In violating codes, maintains Vecsey (1993), the trickster reaffirms them. The stories lead to an affirmation of the status quo through questioning it. Ananse is not a cultural hero who brings direct benefits to the Akan. Rather, the socially beneficial aspect of the tales lies in the process whereby the Akan draw 'ethical conclusions' from Ananse's failures and shortcomings (Vecsey 1993: 118). This is reminiscent of Hewitt's reading of |Kaggen: 'By violating social norms within the narratives,' maintains Hewitt (1986: 137), |Kaggen re-enforced 'the idea of society'. |Kaggen's 'response to the world ... makes it necessary for the family ideologues to articulate those norms' (Hewitt 1986: 149).

Robert Pelton, by contrast, accords a creative role to trickster tales rather than one that seeks to preserve social codes. He contends in his study of the West African tricksters Ananse, Legba, Eshu and Ogo-Yurugu that 'the trickster is a symbol of the liminal state itself and of its permanent accessibility as a source of recreative power' (Pelton 1980: 35). Pelton considers the trickster integral to the process whereby West African societies create a non-dualistic religious sensibility and culture, which includes all the contradictory aspects of life. The trickster demonstrates the sacredness of ordinary life. Pelton (1980: 266) also comments on the way in which the trickster delivers and invites 'metasocial commentary'. In many respects, Guenther's (1999) view of the trickster is close to Pelton's. They both locate the trickster in a religious context, and neither ascribes a conservative social function to the trickster. The figure of |Kaggen, in Guenther's view, is central to the formation of a flexible, creative and autonomous mode of individualism.

The trickster plays an important role, too, in Lévi-Strauss's analysis of mythology. He begins his consideration of the trickster by observing that 'the trickster of American mythology has remained so far a problematic figure' (Lévi-Strauss 1955: 440). For Lévi-Strauss (440), the puzzle is not the ambiguous nature of the figure so much as the fact that 'throughout North America his part is assigned practically everywhere to either coyote or raven'. In order to explain this phenomenon, Lévi-Strauss introduces the influential notion of the mediator. His theory of mythology, as we have seen, argues that myths provide the forum in which oppositions are explored in a manner that seeks their dialectical resolution. When this is not possible, the terms of the intractable binary will 'be replaced by two equivalent terms which allow a third one as a mediator' (440). The core opposition in trickster stories is that between life and death. Life is associated with agriculture and death with war, which in turn can be linked with vegetarian and hunting animals, respectively. Between these poles stand carrion eaters such as the coyote and the raven. It makes perfect symbolic sense, therefore, that the coyote and the raven should become mediating tricksters who span the opposition that the myths in which they appear attempt to resolve. Hewitt, as I mentioned in the previous chapter, identifies several mediating figures in the |Xam texts.

An ongoing project in trickster studies has been that of constructing typologies of the figure broad enough to encompass all his local manifestations. I have already alluded to the lists of trickster characteristics produced by Jung and Radin. Hynes presents such a typology in his and Doty's volume, advancing 'six characteristics common to many trickster myths' (Hynes 1993: 33). Laura Makarius (Hynes 1993: 34) suggests that such a scheme could help form 'a matrix by which to survey all known examples of tricksters and to judge their degree of "tricksterness"'. IKaggen has sometimes been ascribed characteristics that have been drawn from such typologies, I would contend, rather than from his place within IXam discourse itself. It becomes important to reconsider the applicability of these general characteristics to him and to investigate the degree to which trickster typologies have influenced the way in which he has been read.

WRITING AGAINST THE TRICKSTER

Several scholars criticise the general and comparative approach that characterises the writers whose notions of the trickster I have outlined so far in this chapter. They consider general typologies such as Hynes's reductive and unhelpful. In his study *The Zande Trickster*, Evans-Pritchard (1967) emphasises the need to locate trickster tales within specific cultural contexts. He argues also that in the Zande materials 'there is nothing buried. All is on the surface and there are no repressed symbols to interpret' (Beidelman 1993: 175, quoting Pritchard 1967: 29). This position undermines the generalised approach to interpretation, one of whose symptoms is the identification of the universal figure of the trickster in disparate tales, since this approach relies on going beneath the surface of the particular story in order to discover the universal pattern and motifs that underlie it.

Tom Beidelman (1993: 174) questions the use of 'the comparative method to understand the meaning of collective representations in other societies'. He briefly surveys some of the contributions to the discussion of the trickster figure and concludes that no fresh insights are to be gained from the 'general, global approach' (175). He proposes that instead of beginning with an analytical grouping into which disparate characters are fitted, it would be more helpful to study 'particular tricksters and their contexts well' (175). He mentions Geoffrey Kirk's (1974) criticism of the propensity to locate a disparate body of texts as myth and argues that the use of the global term 'trickster' is an equally reductive hermeneutic strategy. The category *'trickster'* itself 'may be merely the product of a series of false translations, much as terms such as *family* and *witchcraft* seem incomparable cross-culturally when taken out of context' (175; original emphasis). He proceeds to demonstrate his point by providing a local and particular reading of certain Kaguru figures, noting the paradox that in 'presenting material in order to criticize a global definition, one is drawn into using the very terms and references which one is subjecting to question' (176).

Anne Doueihi (1984; 1993) also delivers a critique of trickster analysis, one that draws, as I mentioned in chapter 2, on the work of Derrida. She argues that a confusion of categories, the result of a failure to distinguish between story and discourse, has led in the trickster literature to narratives being taken 'at their referential (face) value' (Doueihi 1993: 193). The assumption that the language of the stories is a 'transparent medium for the communication of some meaning or another, consequently leads to the search for some univocal meaning to which the trickster and his stories might be reduced' (Doueihi 1993: 194). This has resulted in trickster stories being seen as meaningful to the degree they 'figure in the great story of human civilization' (Doueihi 1993: 194). The trickster is located in a history that is either a fall away from presence or an 'increasing revelation' of it. In either case, the point of reference is 'a moment of presence that lies outside history, a moment that is conceived as the ultimate origin of the world' (Doueihi 1993: 194).

Doueihi maintains that most trickster analysis remains tied to this ideology of presence. Consequently, the trickster's meaning is sought in his origin (Doueihi 1993: 195), and this structure is imposed on the narratives. This results in a discourse of domination in which 'Western conceptions of the sacred and profane, of myth and literature, and of origin, evolution, and degeneration, are used to frame the trickster' (195). The 'terms set by the narratives themselves' (195) are ignored. The beginning is either privileged as proximate to the origin or is seen as 'a fall into history, and is represented as a primitive, chaotic, and underdeveloped period, which gradually leads to order and civilization' (196).

Doueihi (1993: 196) proposes that close attention be paid to individual narratives instead of turning the trickster into 'a hypothetical figure invented to fit a theory'. Such a strategy, she suggests, will show that stories undermine the single meaning commentators discover in the course of imposing their discourse of domination. Instead, it will be found that texts 'open into a plurality of meanings, none of which is exclusively "correct"' (199). Language generates multiple meanings through complex sets of relationships. It is not a transparent medium reflecting a single reality outside itself: 'It is in the reversals and discontinuities in language, in the narrative, that meaning is produced — not one meaning, but the possibility of meaningfulness' (199).

Henry Gates's *The Signifying Monkey: A Theory of Afro-American Literary Criticism* (1988) exemplifies, to my mind, the sort of critical approach that Doueihi (1993: 201) advocates when she suggests that a text be approached not as a story, but as 'a play of discourse with its own possibilities of being meaningful'. Gates (1988: 52) identifies the Afro-American figure, the signifying monkey, as a trickster, the 'functional equivalent' in Afro-American profane discourse of the divine Yoruba Esu figure of West Africa who assumes various, but linked figurations across the new world. Although he gives this figure a regional range, Gates refuses to position him within a universal narrative of the trickster that is susceptible to an analysis of the sort that assumes a privileged universal perspective. Gates argues instead that the Afro-American materials he deals with themselves embody a sophisticated hermeneutical system, one that revels in the materiality of language.

According to Gates, the difference between this tradition of interpretation and the Western critical one is illustrated in the meanings the term 'signify' mobilises in the two discourses. '"Signification" in standard English denotes the meaning that a term conveys, or is intended to convey' (Gates 1988: 46). This 'fundamental term in the English linguistic order' whose conventions have been established, 'at least officially, by middle-class white people' (46–47), is contrasted with the use of the term by blacks, who use it to refer to a range of rhetorical tactics. In using the term in this way, the black vernacular tradition marks its 'difference from the rest of the English community of speakers' (47). Gates refers to the white sign and simultaneously distances black usage from it by using the lower case for the white signs 'signification' and 'signify' and the upper case for the black signs. Black signification undermines white signification in a profound linguistic way, for it denotes 'the rhetorical structures of the black vernacular' and, therefore, replaces a semantic relationship with a rhetorical one (48). It belongs to a way of using language that calls attention to itself 'as an extended linguistic sign' (53), the antithesis of the conventional view in the West of the relationship between signifier and signified, which is predicated on a view of language as a transparent medium, a bridge between the world and the realm of signification.

The signifying Monkey, argues Gates (1988: 52), exists not as a character in stories, 'but rather as a vehicle for narration itself'. If misunderstood, this aspect of the signifying Monkey, contends Gates, can lead to serious hermeneutical errors when interpreting the poems and tales in which the figure appears. A reading that seeks to uncover their allegorical meaning misses their 'repeated stress on the sheer materiality, and the willful play, of the signified itself' (59). These materials have no underlying meaning to which they can be reduced, for they exist purely 'as a play of differences' (61). Gates also emphasises the intertextuality of the literature he discusses. Texts refer to others of the same genre. '[I]ntertextuality represents a process of repetition and revision' (60), a process that devalues meaning and valorises the signifier (61). Value resides in the foregrounding of the signifier 'rather than in the invention of a novel signified' (61).

Although Gates uses the trickster term and does not attempt to institute a discussion as to the legitimacy of the linking of the concept of the trickster with the figures he explores from the African and Afro-American traditions, the whole thrust of his work is away from the universalising Western mode of thought to which the idea of the trickster owes its existence. His labelling of the Western tradition as 'white' indicates the regional scope of this tradition, despite its pretensions to universality. His explication of the black tradition illustrates the existence of a realm of literature and interpretation that is not readily amenable to the traditional categories of Western criticism, since the two traditions are predicated on fundamental linguistic differences at the level of the sign itself. Afro-American literature operates happily within the play of difference of signifiers, whereas, as Derrida's work shows, the Western critical tradition depends on a metaphysics of presence in which the sign points to a truth beyond itself. The Jungian trickster illustrates this point clearly, since it is explicitly linked to a transcendental signified, the universal archetype 'trickster'. The more modest signification of the term in the work of writers such as Hynes and Doty still falls, I would argue, within this metaphysics of presence, since it is rooted in the idea of a general human culture in which the figure of the trickster makes repeated appearances, albeit in different guises and roles, as a signified.

Gates's work, in my view, has profound implications for the way in which the |Xam stories are read. If the critical tools developed in the West are inadequate to the task of interpreting Afro-American texts for the reasons so carefully explicated by Gates, is it not reasonable to question their applicability to the |Xam materials? Gates's work also reminds us of the importance of foregrounding the intertextuality of the |Xam narratives. |Kaggen, his work suggests, should be treated as a signifier that works in the material sphere of discourse rather than as a universal type.

|KAGGEN: Universal type or |Xam signifier?

As I have observed a number of times in this chapter, one of the effects of lumping disparate figures together as tricksters is to elide the differences among signifying systems. The ability of the |Xam stories to generate meaning does not reside, in my opinion, in the presence within them of a universal trickster, but in their intertextual relationships and their position within a |Xam discursive formation. The |Xam texts, I would argue also, signify directly from their surfaces, in accordance with an internal economy of difference, which is a difficulty for a critical interpretive tradition that instinctively delves beneath the surface, seeking universals and general patterns. I will examine this contention in relation to the appearance of |Kaggen in the |Xam hunting observances in the rest of this chapter.

Besides the |Kaggen who features in the narratives that are set in the world of the First Times when animals were still people, |Kaggen also appears in the contemporary world of the |Xam, the world that succeeded that of the First Times. |Kaggen, in this context, operates chiefly as the pro-tector of certain game animals. Hewitt identifies |Kaggen as a trickster in the First Order and as a supernatural being in the present order. The divide is not absolute, however. He argues that an understanding of the super-

109

natural being of the hunting observances is critical to an understanding of the |Kaggen of the narratives (Hewitt 1986: 40). Other commentators locate |Kaggen as a trickster in both types of discourse, even though they often note that the |Kaggen of the hunting beliefs and the |Kaggen of the tales display very different characteristics (see, for example, Schmidt 1996: 102–3). For Guenther, it is precisely the contradictory characteristics that |Kaggen displays in all the discourses in which he appears that marks him as a trickster. However, his more serious supernatural side, which he shares with several other Khoisan figures, makes him a 'trickster-god' rather than a simple trickster (Guenther 1999: 111). Lewis-Williams (2000: 8), too, as mentioned earlier, characterises |Kaggen as a 'trickster-deity'.

I will examine the place of both |Kaggen and the hunting observances in the broader |Xam discursive field before arguing that |Kaggen should be considered primarily in the context of the other signifying elements in |Xam discourse. Whether or not |Kaggen is seen as a supernatural being, a trickster or a trickster-deity in relation to hunting practices is not central to this discussion. My enquiry here investigates whether the discourse is dependent on |Kaggen as the representative of a universal figure or archetype, or whether the figure of |Kaggen is itself rather a product of |Xam discourse.

Although the |Kaggen of the hunting observances is a shape shifter and deceiver, a trait often identified with the trickster, he does not, in contrast with the |Kaggen of the narratives, perform tricks for their own sake. His actions have the specific purpose of preventing the killing of particular animals. He does not seek to interfere with hunting in general; his interest is only in protecting his special creatures, chiefly the eland, the hartebeest, the gemsbok, the quagga and the springbok. He is said not to love people when they kill these animals. |Kaggen, it must be emphasised, is also closely associated with these animals in the stories of the First Times. He creates the eland and gives the antelope their different colours by feeding them different kinds of honey (D. Bleek 1923: 10). |Kaggen's actions as the protector of certain big game animals in the present order are consistent with his actions in the stories of the First Times that concern these particular animals[10] — one of the indications, in my view, that the divide between the First Times and the present should not be exaggerated. It is a discursive rather than temporal division, and the two orders intersect in different and complex ways. |Kaggen is one of these intertextual crossing points.

|Kaggen, in his role as protector of particular animals, was ever present in |Xam everyday life. Rituals had to be performed to ensure success in the hunt in the face of |Kaggen's opposition (Hewitt 1986: 125). |Kaggen would do his best to protect certain antelope. He might, for instance, assume the form of a snake in order to startle hunters and alert the prey animals to their presence. He might also take the form of a hare so that the hunters would concentrate on shooting him and miss the presence of other animals nearby. His most telling interventions occurred after an eland, a hartebeest or gemsbok had been shot, in the period between the time the arrow struck and the animal's death from the effects of the arrow poison. During this time, a sympathetic bond was established between the hunter and the animal. The condition of the hunter paralleled that of the dying animal. |Kaggen exploited this relationship in order to enable the animal to fight off the effects of the poison and recover. He might, for example, become a louse and bite the hunter. As the hunter fidgeted and scratched, the eland would become more active and regain its life force. Or he might startle the hunter by becoming a puff adder. The shot animal would feel the infusion of energy as the hunter reacted to the snake's presence (Hewitt 1986: 127). If a hunter shot a gemsbok, |Kaggen became a hare and placed himself in the way of the hunter. If the hunter shot the hare, the gemsbok would recover (126). The man who had shot an eland had to return home as if wounded himself. He was then confined to a special hut, where he lay in agony while the old man who looked after him made a fire to drive |Kaggen away. The other men would track the dying eland and bring the meat home (126–27). To a considerable degree, the hunter and his wounded prey became a single organism.

|Kaggen is of undeniable importance in |Xam culture: he appears in too many places in the narratives and in too dominant a role to deny this. He is central to a whole cycle and genre of stories. Nor can his significance in the observances surrounding hunting be doubted. Yet it is also true, I would argue, that the beliefs, practices and experiences surrounding him exist in a wider discursive and cultural context, of which he is but an element, albeit a complex and recurrent one. |Kaggen is often central,

sometimes peripheral and sometimes absent, even from the signifying field that includes the hunting observances. 'ǀKaggen' is, I would argue, a signifier that operates through its juxtaposition with other signifiers, rather than a transcendental signified, an archetypal trickster. By locating him as the central operational principle in the narratives in which he appears, as Hewitt (1986: 183) does, or as a trickster or supernatural being, to whom the other elements of a narrative or practice are entirely subordinate — a common tendency in the analysis of the ǀXam texts — it is easy to miss the simultaneous independence and interrelatedness of these elements. They are not, I would argue, embellishments of an underlying structure or simply the subordinate appurtenances of the representation of a trickster figure. Rather, meaning is generated through the relationships among all the elements in the texts.

I have described how ǀKaggen attempts to produce a reaction in a hunter's body after an antelope, such as an eland or hartebeest, has been shot that will reproduce itself in the dying animal's body and lead to its rejuvenation. In so doing, he makes use of a network of signifying relationships that have a wider reach than hunting or the figure of ǀKaggen himself. The relationship between a person's body and the environment, in general, is a wide field in ǀXam discourse. It can also be described as intertextual, denoting, as it does the 'transposition' of one system of signs into another (Kristeva 1986: 111), i.e. those linked with the internal system of the body and those linked with the external world outside the body. It includes, is included in and intersects with the field that constitutes the experiences and stories surrounding ǀKaggen and hunting, but is, I would contend, far from confined to it. Broadly speaking, the materials present the body as a discursive space in its own right, one that is continuous with the world rather than separate from it. We have just seen how the body of the hunter and that of the shot eland are intimately linked, even when they are physically apart: 'the emphasis was always on the hunter as a medium through which messages might be transmitted to the game' (Hewitt 1986: 125). People are purported to receive information through their bodies: ǁKabbo uses an explicitly textual image to describe this means of acquiring information. It is the Bushman equivalent of books or letters, since 'tappings' in the body 'take a message or an account of what happens in another place' (Bleek & Lloyd 1911: 331). Bushman letters 'speak, they move, they make their (the Bushmen's) bodies move' (Bleek & Lloyd 1911: 331). The knowledge or information gained from tappings in the body is said to be reliable, unlike dream material, 'which deceives'.

A great variety of information is gained from tappings in the body. People know when other people are coming (L.II.28:2533). They know about the presence in a particular place of springbok (2537). Like books and letters, this information is borne in signs that require a certain literacy in their deciphering. A man knows his father is arriving, for he feels a tapping in a place on his body that corresponds to an old wound on the older man's body (2535). A tapping in the ribs signals the presence of springbok, since it correlates with the black hair on the side of the antelope. A man knows he will kill a springbok when he feels a sensation in his calves that corresponds to the feeling of blood dripping down his legs when he carries a slain springbok (2540). A reaction is felt in the feet when the springbok come and another in the head when absent hunters are severing springbok horns. When an ostrich scratches its neck, a Bushman might feel a tapping in his own neck (2533'). A man knows his wife is returning home when he feels a sensation on his shoulder at the very place where the 'riem' in which she carries her child rubs against her shoulder (2534').

The individual's body, then, is the site of a 'writing' that can be transcribed onto another person's or animal's body. This somatic field of signs belongs to a social domain that crosses species. |Kaggen exploits it in order to rescue certain game animals by eliciting a reaction in the man's body, which, in turn, elicits a reaction in the animal's poisoned body. But this discourse of the body can exist without him. It does not originate with him, unless we accept the often-repeated contention that 'Cagn [sic] made all things' (Orpen 1874: 2).[11] The link between the body and absent events (absent, that is, from the immediate locale of the body) is central to the narratives and the hunting observances involving |Kaggen, but is not confined to them. Nor does the complex of hunting observances itself always involve |Kaggen. A variety of elements are interwoven in particular ways to produce a discursive fabric within the site of |Xam praxis. The conjoining of these elements rather than the presence of |Kaggen as a trickster or supernatural being is the necessary condition, I would maintain, for |Xam signification. These elements are not simply supplementary to the presentation of a universal type. It is they themselves that generate the multiple meanings found in the ǀXam texts, including those that feature ǀKaggen. I shall proceed, in the remainder of this chapter, to supply further examples from the materials in order to support this contention.

We have already seen that ǀKaggen is particularly associated with eland, hartebeest and gemsbok in both the hunting observances and the stories. However, not only ǀKaggen is linked to specific animals in this way. Other phenomena and entities, including !Khwa, are associated with different creatures. The consequence, for instance, of unmarried women eating tortoises is the wrath of the rain. The thunder will search for those who breach this taboo (L.VIII.26:8303–9). If the children kill a locust bird, ǀKaunu (either a living sorcerer or spirit of the dead, depending on the interpretation of a translated term [see Solomon 2007: 157]), who caused the appearance of the edible locusts in the first place, will make them disappear (L.VIII.31:8754–58).

An intricate web of sympathetic relationships can impede or facilitate hunting. I have already described ǀKaggen's role in this complex. Many of these relationships do not, however, directly involve him. Looking at the moon after shooting an animal is ill-advised: 'the moon is not a good person, if we look at him ... when we have shot game' (L.V.21:5644–45). Beasts of prey eat the wounded animal as a consequence. Looking at the stars is also counterproductive, because the stars arouse the animal's heart and it will want to 'walk about like that which as the stars do' (L.V.21:5682). Children sneezing near a man who has shot an animal results in the poisoned animal's jumping up (L.V.21:5655). Hunters call to a wounded springbok in a certain way in order to prevent clotted blood from obstructing the action of the poison in the animal's body (Bank 2006: 360). A hunter's acting as if ill and weak is just one of the means of indirect communication connected to hunting. Hunters never directly announce that they have shot game: their actions tell the group that they have done so (L.V.21:5685–86). A man might refuse food (L.V.21:5688), for example, or simply say that he has seen spoor (L.V.21:5694). This applies to all game and not simply to the animals protected by ǀKaggen. Nor do all the observances involving the animals associated with ǀKaggen necessarily include him. A story is told, for example, in connection with arrow-making about a gemsbok that turned into a lion when it saw the hunter who was stalking it. The hunter in his fright stands on the arrow he himself has tipped with poison and dies (L.VIII.31:8775–82). In one account, !Khwa turns into an eland — that quintessentially ǀKaggen animal. When the men cut up the meat of an eland they have shot, it turns into water and evaporates. The men are then turned into frogs. The eland turns out to have really been the rain (L.VIII.16:7461–72).

A whole set of *nanna-sse* (hunting observances) that involve the disposal of bones appear to have little direct relationship with ǀKaggen. If bones are not placed on the correct heap, the hunters miss their aim. A shoulder blade, however, should be placed in the hut, because if the dogs eat it, the hunters will also miss their aim. Even worse consequences can follow from the wrong person's eating a particular part of an animal or from children playing disrespectfully with animal bones. The men will not only miss their aim if women eat the shoulder blade of a springbok, they will be shot with the springbok's invisible arrows and become sick. Extremely precise procedures relate to the apportioning of game. Only particular categories of people should eat particular parts (L.VIII.14:7257; 7260-75), and the consequences of infringing these rules are dire. Hunting bows must be treated in certain ways after being used to shoot baboons, or the curse of the baboons will live on in the bow (L.V.24:5911–16).

The observances are not always a question of avoiding obstructions in order to engage in successful hunting, as is the case with procedures connected with ǀKaggen and eland hunting. The observance of taboos and the following of procedures can help procure game as well, and the web of sympathetic relationships can be deliberately exploited in order to facilitate the success of hunting. A girl could, for example, chew meat killed by one of her father's dogs, mix this with dirt from her knee, spit the mixture into the dog's mouth, pat the dog and say 'la sa, sa, sa, sa!' to it. This ensures that the dog will never look away from game it has seen (L.V.20:5594–98).

These examples are chosen at random. There are hundreds more in the materials that could be used to demonstrate the ubiquity of sympathetic bonds in the context of hunting, only some of which involve ǀKaggen. But even this is misleading if it suggests that sympathetic relationships are peculiar to hunting; they operate in every sphere of life. I have already mentioned the corporeal 'messages' that presage a particular person's arrival. Once again, numerous examples could be used to illustrate the point. I will mention just one: the association between a dying person's heart and a shooting star (L.V.22:5776). There is a correspondence between the trajectory of a falling star and the manner in which the heart 'falls down' at the moment of death.

The meanings these materials offer the commentator shift and slide, as the angle with which they are looked at shifts. When |Kaggen is placed at the centre of the analysis, the observances and sympathetic relationships appear as elements in a |Kaggen complex; but, as we have seen, these sympathetic relationships between the body and the world are ubiquitous in |Xam experience. If hunting observances themselves become the focal point, |Kaggen recedes to an element — albeit a very important one — in a much wider complex. But again, this is an illusion, a partial view, for his field is much broader than this: he appears, of course, outside the sphere of hunting observances as well. Even this statement needs to be qualified, however. It is virtually impossible to determine in this kaleidoscoping interpenetration of shifting perspectives what is outside what. The more closely the materials are scrutinised, the more they 'render', in Baudrillard's words (2001: 275), 'the world as it was given to us – unintelligible': both their world and the world from which we attempt to apprehend them.

The stories and the materials, then, encompass a wide range of intersecting fields. They both emerge out of a wider discourse and help to constitute it. It is difficult to isolate what is central to a narrative or discourse and determine what is peripheral, for each element in a narrative, when investigated in terms of its location within the whole terrain of |Xam signifying practice, offers new vistas of meaning. Bregin (1998: 98) notes of the |Xam narratives that 'in their entirety, they form a vastly complex web of linked strands and recurring motifs, replete with esoteric ciphers, allusive references and coded axioms, that make them, to cultural outsiders, by no means easy to fathom'.

I will reiterate, in conclusion, that |Kaggen should be located within |Xam discursive practice and not situated within an idealist architectonics of universal types. None of the other elements in the narratives involving |Kaggen is merely fortuitous. All these elements derive their power to generate meaning from the intertextual relationships formed within |Xam signifying practice itself. These relationships, which include the interaction of the sign 'Kaggen' with a multitude of other signs, remain elusive to the critic, even though they reside in the open, on the outside of the stories. This elusiveness is not simply a question of the inaccessibility of another culture and its signifying systems; it is intrinsic to discourse itself. I would argue for an analytical strategy that reads the |Xam narratives that feature |Kaggen in a way that foregrounds these elements and their unintelligibility, rather than one that regards them as subordinate to a narrative of a trickster or a deity. Writers such as Hewitt (1986), Lewis-Williams (1996a; 1998a) and Guenther (1999) themselves all provide, at different points in their work, close readings of the texts that contain the seeds of a new approach to the |Xam materials, readings that, in my view, qualify their support for the view that |Kaggen is a trickster. In the next chapter, I will pursue this enquiry into the interpretation of the |Xam narratives in relation to Hewitt's work, which constitutes the most substantial body of analysis of the materials.

NOTES

1   See, for example, Schmidt (1996: 102–10); Brown (1998: 55), Lewis-Williams (2000: 8), James (2001: 157), Bennun (2005: 91–94) and Bank (2006: 182–83, 240).

2   Hynes and Doty (1993: 14) provide a brief history of the use of the term 'trickster'. Brinton's (1868) use of the term in relation to figures in Native American mythology was a crucial step in the incorporation of the concept of the trickster into the literature of the study of folklore and mythology. Monsma (1996) and Hultkrantz (1997) both provide useful information about this history.

3   Jung (1972: 200) regards this view of the trickster as unassailable: 'He [the trickster] is obviously a "psychologem", an archetypal psychic structure of extreme antiquity .... That this is how the trickster figure originated can hardly be contested if we look at it from the causal and historical angle'.

4   Jung employs the term 'primitive' without irony. He admires the primitive for having consigned less to the unconscious than has modern humankind. He has no doubt, however, that the primitive is lower on the rung of evolution. The higher archetypes appear in only rudimentary form in primitive cultures.

5   Somewhat patronisingly, Jung qualifies this position by asserting that for people like the Winnebago, the myth of the trickster is more than a stubbornly persistent 'remnant'. Trickster stories function as a source of amusement and 'undivided enjoyment' (Jung 1972: 200), but only if a people have not been 'spoiled by civilization' (201).

6   Popular culture, for Jung, seems to exist as a lower stratum of civilisation in which mental elements that are exorcised from higher consciousness continue to receive attention. It is a kind of sediment — the detritus of human evolution.

7 Unlike Jung, Lewis-Williams attributes |Kaggen's dual nature not so much to the difference between humans and animals (the lower and higher aspects of the human psyche) as to the |Xam propensity to inhabit a unified symbolic field in which the spiritual is not divorced from the everyday: 'This blending of the spirit world with the events of what many Westerners would see as ordinary, daily life is particularly clear in |Xam and other southern groups' concept of god. Known as the Mantis, the |Xam god was a trickster-deity. Although he created all things, he was capricious and often stupid' (Lewis-Williams 2000: 8).

8 Pelton (1980), writing about West African tricksters, and Guenther (1999), writing about |Kaggen and other Bushman tricksters, might disagree on this last point. Both seek to distance the religious view that includes the trickster from the monotheistic, humourless Judeo-Christian religious heritage.

9 This debate, they maintain, has taken several forms over the centuries, including the medieval battle between nominalists and scholastics and the 'nineteenth century controversies about idealism and realism' (Hynes & Doty 1993: 5). Historically, they argue, the natural sciences have been associated with the particular and the humanities with the general approach to knowledge. I locate the premises of the debate differently. As I will explain later in this chapter, I believe that the difference emerges from the contrast between an approach embedded in a metaphysics of presence and one that concedes to narrative its textuality and to language its materiality.

10 See particularly 'The Mantis Assumes the Form of a Hartebeest' in Bleek and Lloyd (1911: 3–17) or 'The Mantis Makes an Eland' in D. Bleek (1923: 1–9). His disrespectful attitude towards other animals in the stories provides a strong contrast with his solicitude for these particular animals.

11 This assertion occurs not in the Bleek and Lloyd Collection, but in Orpen's rendition of Qing's testimony in the Malutis, a document that echoes some of the Bleek and Lloyd materials, but which also differs markedly from them in many important respects, not least in the greater power it confers on |Kaggen: 'Cagn was the first being; he gave orders and caused all things to appear, and to be made, the sun, moon, stars, wind, mountains, and animals' (Orpen 1874: 3). Dorothea Bleek (1929: 305) notes that the Mantis 'is not worshipped, at least among the |kham; the Bushmen of the Malutis are said to have prayed to "Cagn"'. In the |Xam materials, |Kaggen is credited mainly with the creation of the moon and the eland, and the naming of places (Bank 2006: 285). Hewitt (1986: 138) says that at 'most it might be said that part of the present order of the world was believed to be caused by him'.

SECTION 2

Interpreting the ǀXam Narratives:
A Discussion of Three Books

CHAPTER 5

READING THE HARTEBEEST:

A Critical Appraisal of Roger Hewitt's Interpretation of the |Xam Narratives

ROGER HEWITT AND |XAM STUDIES

Roger Hewitt's work has been seminal in the field of the study of |Xam narratives. Despite its centrality, however, this work has not yet been critically analysed. The purpose of this chapter is to initiate such a critique. Hewitt's research is meticulous. As a result, his writing is a reliable source of ethnographic information about the |Xam and is regularly cited. I often rely on Hewitt as a source in this book myself. Although Hewitt is also a perceptive interpreter of the |Xam texts narratives, his readings, as one would expect, are informed and intelligent opinion rather than fact, and they are historically and theoretically circumscribed. It is my view that the unexamined repetition of many of Hewitt's statements about the narratives does not take this sufficiently into account.

The detailed nature of Hewitt's work deserves, I think, a detailed response. Accordingly, in this chapter I closely examine his claims about the materials and his approach to reading the texts. I also analyse their purchase on a specific story before going on to propose different ways of reading this narrative. In the course of my examination of his writing, I will argue that Hewitt's functionalist and structuralist treatment of the texts often misses their intertextual nature and their ability to generate multiple meanings. In earlier chapters, I mentioned the existence of competing tendencies in his work. In this chapter, I will discuss this phenomenon at much greater length. Hewitt, for example, sometimes emphasises the specific historical and biographical contexts of the narratives, but, at other times, particularly in his structuralist breakdown of the materials, reinforces the notion that the |Xam texts belong to a timeless realm of folklore in which the details of the stories are a decorative adjunct to core narrative structures.

Pippa Skotnes (2007: 43) writes that '[i]t took more than 70 years' from the appearance of Bleek and Lloyd's *Specimens of Bushman Folklore* in 1911

> for the publication of a second book that focused exclusively on the manuscript archive. This was the book version of the PhD dissertation by anthropologist Roger Hewitt, who was also responsible for bringing the collection to the attention of the library of the University of Cape Town (its curator) and recovering it from the obscurity in which it had languished since Dorothea Bleek's death in 1948.

The notebooks, as Skotnes observes, had disappeared from view after Dorothea Bleek's death. In the early 1970s, Hewitt, then a doctoral student who was conducting research in London, came across a reference to them in Otto Spohr's 1962 biography of Bleek and wrote to the University of Cape Town Library enquiring after the materials. He was told they were lost. Hewitt persisted, however. Eventually, some library assistants, paid by the hour by Hewitt, tracked them down in a forgotten corner of the University of Cape Town Library archives (Bank 2006: 390). Scholars clearly, then, have much for which to thank Hewitt, as his efforts made the |Xam archive directly available to researchers. *Structure, Meaning and Ritual in the Narratives of the Southern San* also provides, as I have already mentioned, both the most detailed analysis of the materials and the most comprehensive ethnographic context for them to date. It should be noted, however, as Skotnes remarks, that the book is based on Hewitt's 1976 PhD thesis, 'An examination of the Bleek and Lloyd Collection of |Xam narratives with special reference to the trickster |Kaggen'. Not surprisingly, therefore, Hewitt's theoretical framework in the book exhibits the influence of the theoretical climate of the early 1970s.

In a recent essay, Hewitt (2007: 164) himself refers to 'the glacial theoretical progress of folkloristics' at the time he conducted his research.

This essay suggests that Hewitt would read the stories differently today. It evinces, for instance, a stronger interest than his earlier work does in the political, historical and ideological context in which the archive was produced: 'The |xam creators of these texts came laden with their personal biographies and trajectories as well as an historical collective inheritance …. Their European partners came with the same. Wilhelm Bleek's freight was his immediate intellectual sphere' (163). Hewitt (166) proposes that the narratives could be seen as 'outcomes or even byproducts of the interactions at hand, between transcriber and transcribed'. While his earlier work emphasises the underlying structure of the narratives, he now foregrounds the role of the narrators, comparing their 'relationship to the pregiven, socially reproduced narrative' to 'the relationship jazz musicians have to the melody and chord structure on which they lean in various ways, sometimes incorporating just the barest of figures from the underlying score' (167). He also acknowledges that he 'uncritically' followed Bleek and Lloyd's division of the materials. These 'categorizations into legends, animal fables, myths and so on', he observes, 'may today legitimately be seen to be obstacles rather than aids to a fuller understanding and appreciation of the "collected", constructed texts' (164).

HEWITT'S STRUCTURALIST TREATMENT OF THE |KAGGEN MATERIALS

Hewitt (1986) divides the narratives into several kinds according to their content. He distinguishes among historical legends, the stories of !Khwa (a supernatural entity closely identified with the rain), animal narratives, sidereal narratives and the |Kaggen narratives, devoting separate sections of his book to each of them. By far the most extensive treatment is accorded the |Kaggen narratives. He identifies 21 separate stories concerning |Kaggen, many of which appear in several versions. He divides the stories into two broad groups, A and B, since 'so radical is the difference between the character of |Kaggen in each group, and so different is his role within the narratives, that it is necessary to treat them separately' (145). He also distinguishes between the individual stories according to the type of trick |Kaggen employs in them (154–58) and the type of opponent |Kaggen meets

(158–59). The narratives are articulated with topography: 'home (standing for safety, norms etc.); not-home (where a range of disordered events might occur); and an intermediary place, usually containing water (standing between home and not-home and importantly functioning as a condition for |Kaggen's return home)' (182). Most significantly, perhaps, Hewitt (180) breaks down the story plots into structural units, which, following Propp, he calls functions. These should not be confused with the function or purpose and role of the stories in |Xam society, which Hewitt also discusses in his book. The sequence of the units can change and some might be absent from particular stories, but the following broad outline remains the same for all the stories in group A in which he discerns this structure (180):

A. Protagonist departs from his house.
B. Protagonist incurs the hostility of another person or other people whom he meets.
C. Protagonist becomes involved in either actual or imminently threatening physical conflict with the person(s) he meets.
D. Protagonist triumphs over his adversaries.
E. Protagonist extricates himself by magical flight.
F. Protagonist soothes his wounds in the water near his house.
G. Protagonist returns home.
H. Protagonist is lectured by members of his family.

In the stories that follow this pattern, asserts Hewitt, the negation of social rules occurs away from home and the medium of water is involved in the renewal of life. This structure supplies the 'formal principles' for the generation of the narratives (Hewitt 1986: 181). It is the vehicle for 'dealing with the relationship between social order and its negation' (183). |Kaggen himself is the 'operational principle' that enables this fundamental theme to take the form of narrative. The stories, with their different events and characters, are ultimately only variations on this single theme. The individual narrators are bound to these forms and, by extension, to the articulation of an ideology of social cohesion. They are unable to generate meaning independently of this structure, but can only elaborate it 'at a "purely" entertainment level' (183).

Hewitt (1986: 183–84) also reduces another set of stories, the group B narratives, to their 'functions':

I. Non-member of central social group repeatedly kills members of that group.
J. ǀKaggen discovers this in a dream.
K. ǀKaggen informs members of the social group of his dream.
L. Member of the group, on the basis of ǀKaggen's information defeats threatening non-member.
M. Rebirth of the dead group members and/or survival of the instrumental group member.
N. Social endorsement of success by the group.

Hewitt identifies several differences between the two kinds of story. Although both sets follow a similar movement, from conflict to information (often gained by way of supernatural knowledge) and renewed conflict, and both include a phase of transformation before ultimately affirming social cohesion (Hewitt 1986: 185), the group B narratives deal primarily with life and death, while the chief focus of the plot A narratives is the social order and its negation. Another difference is that ǀKaggen is not necessarily the main protagonist of group B stories. Home is also differently located. In group B narratives, the household or one of its members is threatened by an outsider, while in group A narratives, home is the unassailable site of order and social rules, and breakdown occurs away from home. In group B narratives, ǀKaggen's 'family group is rarely mentioned and never has any bearing on the plots' (147). The chief disparity, however, is that the ǀKaggen of group B stories exchanges his anti-social characteristics for socially responsible ones. Accordingly, ǀKaggen in group B stories consistently acts with benign intent, whereas the results of his actions in group A stories are unintended consequences of actions bereft of benevolent motivation, even when these have benign outcomes. In group B narratives, the anti-social trickster of the group A narratives becomes a saviour and protector.

ǀKaggen, thus, displays very different characteristics in the two types of story. Hewitt's scheme invests him with two personae that scarcely intersect. Hewitt (1986: 185) does remark, however, that certain narratives display both plot structures. Presumably, |Kaggen would then combine the characteristics he displays in the two sets of narrative. Hewitt, as we have seen, attributes the structural difference between the two types of narrative to the exploration of different themes. According to this logic, we might have been able to expect a wider variety of |Kaggen personae and a greater range of plot structures if the |Xam had been concerned with more themes.

Besides the |Kaggen who appears in these two kinds of narratives, both set in the world of the First Times when animals were still people, Hewitt, as I pointed out towards the end of the last chapter, describes the existence of another |Kaggen, the protector of game who appears in the contemporary world of the |Xam, the world that succeeded that of the First Times and a world in which everything is mostly in its place. Hewitt presents the |Kaggen of the narratives, especially the group A ones, as a trickster and the |Kaggen of the hunting observances as a supernatural being.

HEWITT'S WORK AND THE STORY IN WHICH 'THE MANTIS ASSUMES THE FORM OF A HARTEBEEST'

I shall now turn from this broad discussion of Hewitt's work to a detailed treatment of his division and interpretation of the materials in relation to a single narrative, the story entitled 'The Mantis Assumes the Form of a Hartebeest'. This is the title given to the story in *Specimens of Bushman Folklore*, where it is the first story to appear. Bleek, who collected the story from ||Kabbo in 1873, calls it 'Mantis Turned into a Hartebeest' in his notebook. I have concentrated on this story for several reasons. I wanted to test Hewitt's framework without being overly selective in the choice of the narrative to which I would apply it. The story has also been commented on by other writers besides Hewitt, and, thus, offers an opportunity to discuss some of the different approaches that have been used to read the |Xam narratives.

For the purposes of this discussion, it will be necessary to first relate the story. I will use the version published in *Specimens of Bushman Folklore*, since it is more accessible to readers than the practically identical narrative in the notebooks. The story begins as follows:

The Mantis is one who cheated the children, by becoming a hartebeest, by resembling a dead hartebeest. He feigning death lay in front of the children, when the children went to seek gambro (|kūī, a sort of cucumber); because he thought (wished) that the children should cut him up with a stone knife, as these children did not possess metal knives.

The children perceived him, when he had laid himself stretched out, while his horns were turned backwards. The children then said to each other: 'It is a hartebeest that yonder lies; it is dead.' The children jumped for joy (saying), 'Our hartebeest! [W]e shall eat great meat.' They broke off stone knives by striking (one stone against another), they skinned the Mantis. The skin of the Mantis snatched itself quickly out of the children's hands. They say to each other: 'Hold thou strongly fast for me the hartebeest skin!' Another child said: 'The hartebeest skin pulled at me.'

Her elder sister said: 'It does seem that the hartebeest has not a wound from the people who shot it; for, the hartebeest appears to have died of itself. Although the hartebeest is fat, (yet) the hartebeest has no shooting wound' (Bleek & Lloyd 1911: 3, brackets as in the original).

Apparently undeterred by the movements of the 'dead' animal and the strangeness of finding an intact hartebeest that has not been killed, but has simply dropped dead, the girls quickly proceed with the task of cutting up the animal so that they can carry it home. Even when the separate hartebeest pieces move to more comfortable positions after they have been placed on a bush, the girls continue to apportion the parts of the hartebeest they will carry home. The biggest girl receives the animal's back as her load (Bleek & Lloyd 1911: 5). The youngest girl, the one who earlier experienced the antelope's pulling at her, is given the head to carry, but it is so heavy that the other girls have to lift it onto her (Bleek & Lloyd 1911: 7). As the girl walks, the head moves towards the ground since 'the Mantis's head wishes to stand on the ground'. The girl heaves it back onto her shoulders. Then, more alarmingly, the head begins whispering, asking her to remove the thong across its eye. When she looks back, the head winks at her. She begins to whimper. The other girls accuse her of lying when she tells them that the head winked. The procession continues, and the hartebeest's head goes on winking at the girl. Finally, she unties the thong and the head falls to the ground. The Mantis scolds the girl: 'Oh! oh! my head! Oh! bad little person! hurting me in my head' (Bleek & Lloyd 1911: 9). All the girls now drop their loads. The parts of the hartebeest rapidly assemble themselves into the 'human' body of the Mantis:

> The flesh of the Mantis sprang together, it quickly joined itself to the lower part of the Mantis's back .... The neck of the Mantis quickly joined (itself) upon the upper part of the Mantis's spine .... The thigh of the Mantis sprang forward, it joined itself to the Mantis's back. His other thigh ran forward, racing it joined itself to the other side of the Mantis's back (Bleek & Lloyd 1911: 9, brackets as in original).

The children flee. |Kaggen rises from the ground and pursues them in human form: 'while he felt that he was a man. Therefore, he was stepping along with (his) shoes, while he jogged with his shoulder blade' (Bleek & Lloyd 1911: 11, brackets as in original). When the children reach home, |Kaggen turns back, still running and carrying his shoulder blade. The Mantis runs along the riverbed, making a noise as he steps in the sand. He runs into his own house and then, after emerging from 'a different side of the house' (Bleek & Lloyd 1911: 11), runs back and passes the children's house again.

Now begins a lengthy recounting of the action to the girls' father. The children tell most of the tale in unison, but the youngest girl relates her own experience, enjoining her father to believe her: 'O papa! Dost thou seem to think that the hartebeest's head did not talk to me?' (Bleek & Lloyd 1911: 11). Her father, however, appears to understand exactly what has happened: 'Have you been and cut up the old man, the Mantis, while he lay pretending to be dead in front of you?' (Bleek & Lloyd 1911: 13). In response, the children emphasise that it was impossible to tell that the hartebeest was Mantis. They describe how the pieces of the hartebeest carcass reconstituted themselves as a man and chased them. Their description of the Mantis's running around the house is even more graphic than the initial description offered by the narrator:

> 'Therefore, the hartebeest ran forward, while his body was red, when he had no hair (that coat of hair in which he had been lying down), as he ran, swinging his arms like a man.

'And when he saw that we reached the house, he whisked round. He ran, kicking up his heels (showing the white soles of his shoes), while he running went before the wind, while the sun shone upon his feet's face (soles), while he ran with all his might into the little river (bed), that he might pass behind the back of the hill lying yonder' (Bleek & Lloyd 1911: 13, brackets as in original).

Both their parents, not just the father as before, now tell them that they have cut up the old man called 'Tinderbox-owner', another appellation for the Mantis. The girls respond with yet another account of their adventure.

I shall begin this discussion of Hewitt's work in relation to the story entitled 'The Mantis Assumes the Form of a Hartebeest' by considering the story's position in terms of his structural breakdown of the ǀKaggen materials. Clearly, this is not a group B narrative in which ǀKaggen saves his community from an external danger that he has been alerted to in a dream. In any case, Hewitt (1986: 146) himself lists it as a group A narrative. The story, however, appears to exhibit only a few of the features that he identifies with group A narratives. While admitting that it is anomalous in many respects, Hewitt employs ingenious arguments in order to show that it does indeed conform to the group A structure. The price of doing so, I would argue, includes the subordination of many of the singular elements of the narrative that enable it to generate meaning in particular ways.

According to Hewitt (1986: 180), function B in a group A narrative involves the protagonist, ǀKaggen, incurring 'the hostility of another person or other people whom he meets'. ǀKaggen usually initiates conflict with a non-family member whom he should either avoid altogether or in relation to whom he should follow certain rules of protocol. Hewitt maintains that this motif is still present in this story, but that the roles are reversed, since ǀKaggen 'is found in the position of the non-family member for whom the family employ rules of avoidance' (186).

Most of the other group A features have similarly to be stretched in order to accommodate this narrative. Function E, for example, involves a magical flight in which ǀKaggen extricates himself from a tight situation by flying away and commanding his things to follow him.[1] In this story, argues Hewitt (1986: 186), this motif becomes 'merely an escape without magic because it is performed not by ǀKaggen but by the girls whom ǀKaggen has frightened'. According to Hewitt, this does not matter structurally, since the magical element is still present in the story when |Kaggen transforms himself into a hartebeest and later 'reassembles the parts of the body of the dead hartebeest into the form of a man' (186).

In most of the stories, maintains Hewitt, |Kaggen contradicts socially sanctioned behaviour. In this story, he does not do this directly, but instead tricks 'others into doing so' (Hewitt 1986: 162). He accomplishes this aim by employing a type of trick not usually employed in 'a weakly stratified society' (158), the strategic trick 'involving a move which anticipates a response of which he intends to, and does, take advantage' (154). Hewitt's procedure here is adroit and contributes, no doubt, to achieving some understanding of the way narratives are constructed in terms of plot. It is also, to my mind, another example of the structuralist propensity to force heterogeneous materials into a unified framework.

The protagonist's leaving home is the first function that Hewitt accords group A narratives. Home, maintains Hewitt (1986: 181), is one of several 'structural co-ordinates which may have been culturally significant'. It is the zone of rules and stability, and it must be vacated in order for conflict to occur. To leave home is to leave behind the security of the social order and to enter a world devoid of rules. The girls leave home, and conflict inevitably follows in the unruly space of the wilderness, |Kaggen's true stage, before home is regained. The social order can then be reasserted in the socialised space of the homestead. But |Kaggen in this narrative is not pictured as leaving home; it is the girls who do so. In terms of Hewitt's delineation of the narrative functions, this should make them the protagonists of the story. The story, however, is located by Hewitt (146) as belonging to group A, and all the stories in this group, he asserts, feature |Kaggen as the protagonist.

Apart from the fleeting reference to |Kaggen's running through his house (Bleek & Lloyd 1911: 11), he is encountered outside the context of the home altogether. Unusually, for the narratives that Hewitt designates as group A stories, |Kaggen is not situated within his domestic group either. He is a mysterious figure who falls outside the human compass. He is last pictured disappearing into the wilderness behind the hill (Bleek & Lloyd 1911: 13). Although |Kaggen is critical to the narrative, he is not present in the same way as a character that he is in most of the other group A stories. In many ways, |Kaggen operates in this story, I would argue, more as the |Kaggen of the hunting observances than as the trickster with the extended family of Hewitt's plot A and B narratives. This kind of hybridity, a story that possesses elements of the First Times and the present order, cannot easily be accommodated in terms of Hewitt's structural breakdown of the materials.

Much of the difficulty Hewitt experiences in fitting this story into his framework arises from its narrative perspective. Although it has several narrative viewpoints, they all preclude the perspective common to many of the stories in which the narrator tracks the actions of |Kaggen and is able to comment on his intentions and motivations. While the |Kaggen of this story resembles the |Kaggen of the stories of the First Times insofar as he wears shoes, is still a person and lives in a house, none of the intimacy with which he is dealt with in many of the other stories attends his figuring here. Not only is |Kaggen's family absent from the story, but so is the narrative voice through which they might enter it. Hewitt (1986: 147) remarks as I have mentioned, that in group B narratives, |Kaggen's 'family group is rarely mentioned and never has any bearing on the plots'. This story, however, does not exhibit any of the other features that Hewitt attributes to group B narratives. Hewitt himself, as we have seen, insists that it is a group A narrative.

I shall now turn from the story's structural features to a consideration of it in terms of the social role that Hewitt imputes to |Kaggen narratives. Hewitt accords the family lecture a central ideological function in the narratives. The admonitions of |Kaggen's family articulate the social values of stability and order. The group A narratives are the vehicle for the enunciation and reinforcement of these values. Hewitt (1986: 162) states that in this story 'no reprimand is given by the parents and no direct statement is made to the effect that the girls had been doing anything wrong by cutting up the animal'. Nevertheless, he argues, the narrative does emphasise the discrepancy between their intention 'to collect *veldkos*' and 'what actually happened' (Hewitt 1986: 162). The message here articulated, then, by both the external narrator and the parents concerns the relationship between |Kaggen and the hartebeest and the wisdom of avoiding an apparently dead but mysteriously intact hartebeest. |Kaggen in the form of a hartebeest should never be mistaken for a real hartebeest

(Bleek & Lloyd 1911: 13). The message is delivered in an informative key, however, and not the normative key that Hewitt imputes to group A narratives. Nor does it conclude the narrative (Hewitt 1986: 162). Hewitt concedes that the story is not overtly didactic, although he does suggest that it might be delivering a message about the confusion that results from reversing gender roles. The cutting up of meat in the veld is generally performed by men (Hewitt 1986: 163).[2] It could also be argued that the story contains a message that is more consistent with hunting observances and practices than with the world of Hewitt's group A narratives. A hunter had to be able to distinguish between real animals and spirit animals. Dia!kwain's wife loses her life as a result of her husband's shooting the wrong kind of springbok (L.V.9:4653–88).

The other functions Hewitt gives the stories at various points in his text do not, in my view, fit the story altogether comfortably either. It is difficult, for instance, to see how the story functions as a safety valve for anti-social emotions through inviting identification with the Mantis. |Kaggen's strangeness and remoteness is one of the story's distinguishing features. This distance follows, as I have already pointed out, from a narrating perspective that is focused on the girls' experience of him as an unknown and frightening figure. Nor is the story aetiological in an obvious sense. It might, however, describe the origin of a taboo on women collecting meat (hunting) on their own, for instance. To prove such a point, however, on the evidence of both the narrative and ethnographic information available is difficult. Hewitt (1986: 171) himself notes that it was probably not 'tabu for women to handle meat in this way'. When Hewitt employs his function-alist explanations, he tends to encourage a reading of the stories as closed texts that culminate in the reinforcement of a message. The functions he lends the stories reflect also, in my opinion, some of the logocentric concerns that Jacques Derrida identifies in Western thought: the quest for presence and wholeness (social cohesion), the nostalgia for origins (aetiology), and the fall (the secret identification of the auditors with |Kaggen and his wildness). This story clearly, in important respects, eludes these frameworks.

The narrative, in my view, calls both Hewitt's structuralist division and functionalist explanations of the materials into question. It refuses to conform readily to the categories to which he assigns the materials. Instead, it exhibits qualities associated with both the observances and the stories. In doing so, it appears to span the divide between the First Times and the present order of things. From this it follows that it also participates simultaneously in two discursive orders, which Hewitt separates — the orders of narrative and the hunting observances, respectively.

Brown (1998: 54) notes that stylistically it is 'difficult to tell a narrative of recent events from one dealing with the Early Race'. The difficulty of positioning the story in which 'The Mantis Assumes the Form of a Hartebeest' results, however, as much from its thematic and discursive features as from its style. Hewitt, as I observed in the previous chapter, treats the narratives and the observances as different species of |Xam discourse and practice, but also argues for a continuity between them. He separates them by locating them in different orders of |Xam existence — the order of the present and the order of the First Times — and then brings them together again by finding deep structural and conceptual templates that unite them. In all the discourses involving him, maintains Hewitt (1986: 131), |Kaggen is consistently on the side of the animal world against the world of men. |Kaggen's opposition to the world of men in the group A First Times stories, however, does not take the form of directly protecting animals from hunters. Instead, he brings calamity to the group by ignoring common sense and social strictures. The consequences of his actions are largely unintended. |Kaggen's intervention in hunting in the present order, on the other hand, is intentional and direct. In terms of this difference, the story seems to conform more to the observances connected with |Kaggen than to the narratives. It could be read as an example of |Kaggen directly protecting one of his animals, at least from future attack. The results of his actions are intentional and he does not ignore common sense or warnings.

The continuity Hewitt discovers between the narratives and the hunting observances is an ideological and thematic correspondence rather than a generic one. The two types of discourse, in his scheme, are divided not only by time, belonging to mythological and 'real' time, respectively, but are different in kind. The group A narratives, it may be said, are fiction or literature, while the hunting observances belong to practice, entering discourse in a great variety of modalities: stricture, received wisdom, informal comment, instruction, biography and autobiography. |Kaggen appears in the observances as an impeding instrument in relation to the hunting of the big game animals that fall under his aegis. While many of the group A stories involve hunting, it is not their chief theme.

Hewitt (1986: 195–211) discusses the continuity of |Kaggen the trickster figure of the narratives with |Kaggen the supernatural being of belief and ritual in considerable detail. In the narratives, he has a creative aspect that consciously or incidentally benefits humans, depending on whether he appears in a group A or B narrative (195). In the beliefs surrounding hunting, he obstructs the actions of humans, but protects the animals he has created. He is, therefore, consistently 'for life even if the order which humans attempt to place on life is anathema to him'. Once again, his role in this story seems more consistent with the beliefs surrounding hunting. It could be argued that he is protecting an animal, but it would be difficult to suggest that his actions in the story benefit humans, either directly, as in the group B narratives, or indirectly, as in the group A narratives.

Hewitt (1986: 207–8) does argue for a structural correspondence between 'the narratives of group A and the belief structure informing the hunters' eland rites'. In both narratives and beliefs, |Kaggen employs tricks and occupies a liminal position between the normative human order and nature, on the one hand, and 'between amenable and unamenable nature', on the other (195). Nature, we might note, occupies a different position in these two sets of binaries. In the first instance, it is the pole that offsets culture; in the second, it takes the place that culture occupies in the first binary. It is positioned against unruly internal forces that threaten to overwhelm its own order. |Kaggen occupies the pole associated with nature in the case of the narratives and the pole associated with unamenable nature in the case of the eland rites. Structurally, they are interchangeable, argues Hewitt (196), since both 'moral autonomy and the autonomous wildness of game involve that which is non-social and irrational — that which is beyond the power of normal human strategies to control'. Despite Hewitt's conflation of the two structures, it is apparent that his location of the story entitled 'The Mantis Assumes the Form of a Hartebeest' as a group A narrative has to be questioned in terms of his own system of binaries. The story more readily fits the structure of the hunting observances, since |Kaggen's actions in the story figure the intractable and unpredictable aspects of nature. He occupies, therefore, the second pole of the binary of the observances rather than the second pole of the group A stories.

The relationship between the First and present orders is complex. It has important implications for reading ǀKaggen, who appears in both of them. The question remains as to how this complex web of convergence and difference should be named in terms of its temporality and its embedment in praxis. Later in this chapter, I will provide more evidence for my contention that 'The Mantis Assumes the Form of a Hartebeest' calls into question the clear division that Hewitt establishes between the First and present orders. But first, I will consider Mathias Guenther's sexual interpretation of the story, an interpretation that is shared by Sigrid Schmidt and, to some degree, by Hewitt himself (Hewitt 1986: 162–63). This reading qualifies my reading of the story as relating chiefly to hunting observances without, I would argue, foreclosing such a reading. Just as the story cannot be confined to Hewitt's structures or functions or to the mythical past or the practical present, so too, I would argue, it evades any single interpretation.

Guenther, as befits his comparative and general approach, links the story with others in the southern African Khoisan cultural area, a strategy also adopted by Schmidt (1996: 104–5). While Hewitt keeps to the sphere of ǀXam narrative practice when discussing the meaning of the story, Guenther elucidates the story on the basis of his knowledge of stories outside it. Both, however, appeal to structural correspondences and relationships rather than attempting to examine the details of the story itself. In the final part of this chapter, I will also investigate relationships that extend beyond the story. I will not seek, however, to reduce the story to a type, as Guenther, Schmidt and Hewitt do. Rather, I will attempt to foreground its protean multivocality and demonstrate something of the intertextual fluidity of its signifiers in relation to their appearance elsewhere in the ǀXam texts.

Guenther asks whether the ǀXam version of it has not been irreparably distorted by the need to divest it of sexual elements for its Victorian audience. He locates the tale within a widespread genre of lascivious !Xun, Dama and Nama stories that all involve a trickster figure who places himself in the path of girls in the form of a dead antelope.

The girls, excited about this windfall of delectable meat, proceed to cut up the carcass and either prepare it for cooking or walk off with it carrying away parts of the antelope-Trickster. The latter now starts to have his fun with the girls and, eventually his way, as certain of the severed parts enter the girls (Guenther 1996: 90).

Such a reading of the story might support some of the functionalist elements that Hewitt attributes to the stories. The description of the running Mantis does indeed seem to carry a suggestion of masculine sexual triumph, a characteristic of the story that emerges from Guenther's comparative approach to it. This might invite the sort of vicarious identification, at least from men, that Hewitt asserts acts as a social safety valve whereby potentially dangerous impulses are transferred from the realm of practice to the realm of fantasy. One could argue also, on the basis of Guenther's reading, that the story possesses aetiological implications involving the sexual sphere. The girls conclude their account with the statement that '[t]his fatigue, it is that which we are feeling; and our hearts burnt on account of it. Therefore, we shall not hunt (for food), for we shall altogether remain at home' (Bleek & Lloyd 1911: 17). This might literally refer to a temporary condition of fatigue from which they will recover and continue with their food-gathering activities. It might, however, also refer to hunting specifically and assert a division of labour in which hunting remains the preserve of men. In terms of Guenther's reading, it could be interpreted as a statement that reinforces or even inaugurates certain gender roles in the domain of sexuality. Hewitt (1986: 162) also detects such a possibility in the story, noting that 'the threat behind |Kaggen's actions' might have been sexual and concluding that, at the very least, 'the boundaries between male and female are ... undermined at a symbolic level behind the overt drama of the plot' (163). It is very likely that hunting antelope and sex are sometimes symbolically conjoined in the narratives. Biesele (1993) has shown how there is an identification between male sexuality and hunting, on the one hand, and between female sexuality and meat, on the other in Jul'hoan narrative. Parkington (1996; 2002) has detected a similar symbolic complex in the paintings and narratives of the Cape Bushmen.

The comparative approach of Guenther and Schmidt is invaluable in showing correspondences among stories collected over a wide area.[3] Their introduction of sexuality into a consideration of this story, which results from this broad approach, offers fruitful possibilities, such as those to which I have just referred. I would insist, however, that the particular elements of an individual story such as this are at least as critical to the way it produces meaning as are the broader relationships pointed out by Guenther and Schmidt. I will show in the next section of this chapter that the fact that the antelope is a hartebeest introduces into its interpretation a chain of significations that would be absent if it were another species of antelope, as it is in the other stories to which Guenther refers. The presence of |Kaggen rather than a !Xun or Nharo 'trickster', for instance, also brings with it a complex of signifying elements peculiar to |Xam discursive practice. Even when structural similarities can be found with other |Xam materials, as, for example, in the case of the correspondence between this story and an incident in which !Khwa (the rain) resembles an eland and is cut up by hunters (L.VIII.16:7461–72), the significance of the deployment within a narrative of specific signifiers needs to be carefully investigated.

One can agree with Guenther that the overtly sexual elements in the story have been suppressed, but also note that the story seems to display an integrity that does not point to hasty revision and censorship on the part of the narrators in order to protect the sensibilities of Victorian scholars,[4] a point conceded by Sigrid Schmidt (1996: 105). In addition, while it must be admitted, in the light of the comparative material provided by Guenther, that a reading of the story as primarily sexual cannot be discounted, evidence can also be assembled, as I have been suggesting and as I will attempt to show in the rest of this chapter, to support a link between the story and |Kaggen's propensity to protect certain large game animals. I would certainly disagree with Schmidt (1996: 104) when she argues that without the overt sexual element that characterises similar Nama, Damara and !Kung stories, '|Kaggen just tricks the girls for no obvious reason'. Hewitt, as we saw in the last section, maintains that the link between |Kaggen and the protection of certain game animals characterises the relationship between the narratives and the observances in general. This link is obvious in this story. In my view, both these readings — the sexual one and the one that foregrounds protection of game animals, as well as others that suggest themselves when considering the text — need to be allowed to coexist, a position that Guenther himself advocates (1999: 227–28). At the same time, it must be emphasised that the story signifies quite readily without the support of any of these sorts of explanation. Meaning is available on its surface even as it eludes easy explication. As a simple story, without reference to gender or hunting observances or any wider symbolic structure, the text readily yields meaning.

'THE MANTIS ASSUMES THE FORM OF A HARTEBEEST': A different approach

The story can be read, I would suggest, in such a way that the questions surrounding it multiply rather than get neatly, but artificially, answered. This occurs when elements within it are located within the context of their wider references within the singularity and practice of |Xam signification. In this way, the layers of possible meaning are increased and expanded, and the possibility of a final reading is always postponed.

Hewitt strips the story down to its structural functions; Guenther reduces it to its Khoisan type. Both read the narrative as predominantly a trickster tale, and in both their readings, many of the elements of the story become incidental. I would propose, instead, that the story be read in terms of its detail and as the site of an intersecting web of signifiers. While the signifier '|Kaggen' is clearly part of an intricate set of relationships that span narratives, other elements in the story apart from |Kaggen can be tracked as well in order to reveal chain upon chain of signifiers, capable of countless configurations and sequences. While a universalising approach surveys the materials with a panoramic gaze, a critical practice that is fascinated by the singularity of |Xam discursive practice can discover multiple networks of meaning in the detail.

'The richness of the San narrative tradition', observes Solomon (n.d.: 57) 'lies … in its differences' rather than in its relationship to a '"pan-San cosmology" which if it exists, does so at the most general (and in some ways, banal) level'.

When assembling the references from the materials that relate to one of the elements in a story, it should be borne in mind that these references are circumscribed for interpreters as they would not have been for |Xam auditors by the limited range of the materials available and by unfamiliarity with |Xam language and praxis. Such a procedure can never do more than hint at the levels of meaning that every signifier would have generated for a |Xam participant, meanings that would have continually shifted according to an individual's location in |Xam history. In addition, single |Xam words often have multiple meanings. Nineteen different words for hartebeest are included in Dorothea Bleek's, *A Bushman Dictionary* (1956: 723), and most of these words themselves have multiple significations. What this approach can do is point to the modalities of |Xam textual practice, which themselves create and generate meaning rather than reflect palely the meanings that emanate from an extra-linguistic origin.

I shall concentrate on the figure of the hartebeest from the story because of its overt links with the signifier '|Kaggen'. I will explore the ways in which the hartebeest is linked to |Kaggen, as well as to other signifiers whose contributions to the overall signification of the story are elusive, but important. In addition, I will argue that the term 'hartebeest' is itself an unstable sign. It is not simply a single term attached to a set number of signifieds, but can signify directly or through metaphorical association or metonymic extension. It can also refer to a particular animal or to a generic form.

In the story, we encounter not a real hartebeest, but |Kaggen disguised as a hartebeest. Lucy Lloyd's title already emphasises this point: 'The Mantis Assumes the Form of a Hartebeest.' This observation is duplicated in the page heading that accompanies the story for 14 pages: 'The Mantis in form of a hartebeest.' Even Lloyd's intervention in naming the story entails an interpretation that cannot go altogether untested, for, in a sense, as we shall see, the Mantis and the hartebeest already — and always — share a form. But let us assume for now that we have before us, as did the girls, a hartebeest that we, but not the girls, know to be |Kaggen. This creature is both more and less than a hartebeest. It possesses an uncanny wholeness and an uncanny capacity to elude the children's hands, to shrink from their grasp and to evade the status of object. This is a hartebeest only through the eyes and voices of the girls: 'The children perceived him, when he had laid himself stretched out … then said to each other: "It is a hartebeest that yonder lies"' (Bleek & Lloyd 1911: 3). We know, through our privileged relationship with the narrative voice, that this whole, intact hartebeest lying so enticingly in the way of the girls is really the Mantis who 'cheated the children, by becoming a hartebeest, by resembling a dead hartebeest'. |Kaggen does not merely pretend to be a hartebeest; he really becomes one. To do this, all he has to do is resemble one, a quality that is intrinsic to him, since the Mantis and the hartebeest possess the same head shape (Hewitt 1986: 128). What he does pretend, though, is to be dead: 'He feigning death lay in front of the children' (Bleek & Lloyd 1911: 3). |Kaggen wants the children to cut him up with a stone knife. These children, it is mentioned, do not possess metal knives. The |Xam, too, it would appear, retain a Stone Age!

The references to hartebeest in the Bleek and Lloyd Collection are not as extensive as those pertaining to springbok or eland, for instance. Nevertheless, an exploration of these references rapidly discloses a wider referential context for the story and reveals the exuberance of the signifier itself. The hartebeest is one of the Mantis's special animals, and is one of the buck endowed by the Mantis with colour. He fed the gemsbok, the hartebeest, the quagga and the springbok different kinds of honey, which resulted in their attaining different colours. The 'Hartebeest is red, because the comb of young bees which he ate was red. So he became like the comb of young bees' (D. Bleek 1923: 10). The Mantis not only creates the eland and the hartebeest, but endows them with colour by feeding them different kinds of honey. Colour is not simply descriptive: it signifies identity; it gives these animals their particularity. The hartebeest, as well as the other buck that |Kaggen invests with colour, are signifiers, then, of difference. While all the signifiers in the narratives participate in a play of difference, signifiers such as 'hartebeest' make this play explicit.

It is important to note in passing that in the scheme that Hewitt (1986: 116–19) applies to the materials, identity confusion prevails during the First Times until the anteater lays down the laws of the species and confers separate identities on them. If |Kaggen's endowing of the antelope with identity through feeding them different kinds of honey is also taken into consideration, then it must be admitted that the |Xam materials do not contain a single account of the division of the Early Race into creatures with separate identities; they contain instead many intersecting versions that are only contradictory for so long as they are read with a view to extracting from them an authorised version of the |Xam myth of origin.

The order of things in the narratives does not obey this logic or fulfil this expectation. It is possible for both the anteater and |Kaggen to parcel out identity at different times and in different ways.

No mention of eland appears in this narrative, and yet hartebeest and eland are always inextricably linked. The whole symbolic order in which the eland participates is present, I would maintain, in the story through a web of intertexuality. Eland would always have been a silent, but signifying presence in a telling of 'The Mantis Assumes the Form of a Hartebeest'. Guenther and Schmidt, as we have seen, link the story with sexuality. Parkington (1996: 282) emphasises the sexual significance of eland: 'The eland has a quite specific connotation related to the parallels seen by hunter-gatherer people between hunting and sex, and the roles these activities play in defining social roles.' An intertextual relationship between the two antelope is established by the sexual connotations they share as signs. But sexual signification is not the only link between them.

The notebooks contain several extended sequences in which the relationships between |Kaggen and the hartebeest and |Kaggen and the eland are explored together.[5] The eland and the hartebeest are joined through their relationship with |Kaggen. The information about the relationship between |Kaggen and the hartebeest that occurs in these pieces has an obvious and immediate relevance to a consideration of 'The Mantis Assumes the Form of a Hartebeest'. It is notable that the Mantis's relationship with the hartebeest parallels his relationship with the eland. According to Dia!kwain:

> The hartebeest and the eland belong to the Mantis. The hartebeest and the eland are the things of the Mantis. Therefore, they have magic power, on account of it. The Mantis is used to be with the hartebeest, when the hartebeest walks about. (Our) mothers were used to say, that, the Mantis sits in the middle between the eland's horns (L.V.6:4411–12).

|Han#kass'o explores the theme further, stating that the hartebeest and the eland are conjoined in the heart of the Mantis:

> The people say that he first made the eland, the hartebeest was the one whom he presently made (after the death of his eland). Therefore, he did

not a little love the eland and the hartebeest, for, he made his heart of the eland and the hartebeest (that is, he loves them very dearly); he does not a little love the eland (L.VIII.23:8036).'

|Kaggen loves the gemsbok, too, but not as deeply as he loves the eland and the hartebeest:

> The Gemsbok was the one whom he did not love nicely. He does love the gemsbok; for, hares are these which we are in the habit of seeing, when we shoot a gemsbok, those hares, they are those which do not stir (they seem tame) because they wish that we may tame kill them, we look at them; because we feel that his hares they are. He desires that we may kill the hare, in order that the gemsbok may live. And the gemsbok lives (ie. recovers) on account of it, if we kill the hare, which the gemsbok feels, that he (the Mantis) is the one whom we kill. He (the Mantis) is the one who becomes a hare because he wishes that we may kill him, in order that the gemsbok may live for him; while he feels that he formerly did so. He became a wounded hartebeest, because he intended the people to cut him up (L.VIII.23:8036'–38').

And so we return, by another route, to 'The Mantis Assumes the Form of a Hartebeest', embedded in a discourse that also features the eland, the hare and the gemsbok. Situated in this way, the story can be seen to participate in and expand the theme of the special relationship between the hartebeest and the Mantis, which is also the subject of the extract. In the extract, 'The Mantis Assumes the Form of a Hartebeest' is posited as history, something the Mantis did in the past. Although the story is set in the period of the First Times, |Kaggen's actions in it are seen as of the same order as his ongoing and 'present' protection of certain game animals. The common context of the story and the excerpt illustrates that there is a continuity between the order of the everyday and story time. But the grammar also signals their separation. The two orders are placed within a single discourse at the same time as they are separated by shifts in tense: 'He (the Mantis) is the one who becomes a hare because he wishes that we may kill him' and 'He became a wounded hartebeest, because he intended the people to cut him up.'

The Mantis's transformation into a hartebeest in the story is paralleled by his turning into a hare to assist the recovery of wounded gemsbok. The actions of the Mantis in the First Times and those of the Mantis of the present times are seen to directly correlate in |Han#kass'o's exposition. This interpretation accords with Hewitt's view of the correspondence between the trickster of the story time and the actions of the supernatural being of the present order context of hunting. He attributes the concordance, however, not to a direct parallel, as is presented in the extract about the hartebeest and the eland, but to a correspondence of outcomes. The social order, according to Hewitt, is reaffirmed in both the stories and the hunting observances, but in very different ways. In the former, the actions of the Mantis, who is a maverick part of the community, provides an opportunity for the articulation of social values. In the latter, certain collective behaviours become necessary as a result of |Kaggen's actions in protecting the game.

The hartebeest feels so strongly that it 'belongs' to the Mantis that this identification takes physical form. Their resemblance is the consequence, not the cause of the association of the hartebeest and the Mantis:

> (Our) parents used to say to us about it, did we not see that the hartebeest's head resembles the mantis ('s head?); while it felt that it was the thing of the mantis. This is why its head resembles the mantis (L.V.6:4414').

Lucy Lloyd, the translator, is uncertain as to whether the hartebeest's head resembles the Mantis's head or the whole Mantis. Whatever the extent of the resemblance, the correspondence is a product of love. The Mantis's heart is made, in part, from the hartebeest; the hartebeest, in turn, feels that it belongs to the Mantis. From this knowledge comes the physical correspondence between the insect and the antelope. The hartebeest's feeling for the Mantis is reciprocated, and |Kaggen goes with the hartebeest wherever it goes. In a sense, they are not separate beings, since they are so closely united. But neither are they a single being; they are not identical. To be in the presence of the hartebeest is also to be in the presence of the Mantis. To be in the presence of the Mantis does not necessarily entail being in the presence of the hartebeest, however. Neither the Mantis nor the hartebeest is a stable presence. Since they are overdetermined signs, they are always both more and less than themselves. The hartebeest is a metonymic signifier, standing in for a realm that is both more extraordinary and more mundane than itself. At the same time, its relationship with the Mantis is also partly a matter of metaphor or analogy, of resemblance.

The hartebeest is, in a sense, as in the story, always absent, always in the process of signifying. It never rests in a signified. But whether the term 'hartebeest' refers to the 'Platonic' type of the stories or to the hartebeest that one might encounter in the field (which also might not be a hartebeest after all), whether the mode is magical or economic, whether the context is the First Times or hunting practices, the relationship between |Kaggen and the hartebeest remains consistent. The bond is more than symbolic: it belongs to the elusive order of reality. It is manifested outwardly in the resemblance between the head of the insect and the head of the antelope, a resemblance that is interpellated for children by the employment of the negative form of the interrogative: '(Our) parents used to say to us about it, did we not see that the hartebeest's head resembled the mantis?' (L.V.6:4414'). In a sense, the girls of the story are not tricked by the Mantis. They fail to notice the obvious resemblance between the hartebeest and the Mantis and so cheat themselves.

As I pointed out earlier, not only is the hartebeest like |Kaggen, it is also, and as the result of a different relationship that also involves |Kaggen, but on another axis, similar to the eland. The two antelope are not linked by likeness or physical contiguity, as are |Kaggen and the hartebeest. They are joined, rather, through their being 'things of the Mantis' and sharing, as a result, magical power. They are both creations of |Kaggen, denizens of a common history, a history that involves human hunters and death. The tragic knowledge of this relationship with humans is carried by |Kaggen, whose heart is made from the eland and the hartebeest, the result, in part, of a primal murder, eternally replayed.[6]

|Kaggen accompanies both the hartebeest and the eland. He 'sits in the middle between the eland's horns' (L.V.6:4412) and does all he can to protect the eland from hunters. 'The mantis', as Han#kass'o puts it, 'does not love us, if we kill an eland' (L.VIII.23:8033). Since the eland and the hartebeest cohabit the Mantis's heart (L.VIII.23:8036'), it follows that killing a hartebeest elicits a similar reaction from |Kaggen. 'The Mantis

Assumes the Form of a Hartebeest' can then be read as a pre-emptive strategy of |Kaggen's, a way of protecting real hartebeest from future attacks. |Kaggen is impelled by his love for these animals, a love that is incorporated in his body and so exists as a force different from usual love, of which he is also profoundly capable. He cares, for example, for the gemsbok, even going so far, when a gemsbok has been shot, as to turn into a hare so as to tempt the hunters to kill him. In this way, he takes the energy of dying away from the gemsbok and transfers it to himself: 'He (the Mantis) is the one who becomes a hare, because he wishes that we may kill him, in order that the gemsbok may live for him' (L.VIII.23:8037'–38'). In relation to the hartebeest and eland, however, '[t]he gemsbok was the one whom he did not love nicely' (L.VIII.23:8036').

Dia!kwain (L.V.6:4415'–18') refers also to the danger that eating the flesh of the hartebeest constitutes for women with young children:

A Bushman woman who has a little child must not all eat portions of the flesh of the hartebeest, nor must she jump over its head: for fear of harm to her child. She must make a charm to hang upon her child of a part of a hartebeest's foot. A woman who has a child which is small, she does not eat the hartebeest, she also does not spring over the hartebeest's head; for the Mantis would press down her child's head's hollow place, the child would die, while it felt that its head's hollow place, that was that which the Mantis had pressed down. These things they were those which it died on account of them. Therefore, (our) parents were used to instruct women who had children which (were) little, that they might the thing above the hartebeest's between the toes, that they should cut it out, that they should thread it upon a sinew, that they should make a charm that they should put it in, that they should put it on the little child. For, things, which the Mantis sits on are those that his scent it might ascend from the little child, and the Mantis might smell the things scent upon the child, and he should not press the child's head on account of it.

The common approach to the interpretation of folklore or myth, as we have seen, seeks to discover the pattern that lies beneath the appearance of the text. In this case, it is tempting to discover the logic that links the eating of hartebeest to |Kaggen and to children's heads. |Kaggen and the hartebeest have the same head. It is, therefore, also a part of |Kaggen's body — his head — that is being violated when a hartebeest is eaten. Accordingly, |Kaggen exacts revenge by violating the heads of the most vulnerable humans — babies. But this is to treat such materials as riddles to be deciphered rather than accepted. There is no deeper truth or logic to be excavated, perhaps, only an appearance to be made more apparent. The logic of the transference of danger away from a child through the foregoing of one sort of use of the body of the hartebeest and the ritual embrace of another is here juxtaposed with eland hunting (the two texts exist side by side in the notebooks). In Han#kass'o's piece, as we saw earlier, eland hunting is linked to 'The Mantis Assumes the Form of a Hartebeest'. Hartebeest, hunting, children, women and |Kaggen occur directly in both the extract and the story. The story, then, has to be explored in terms of these relationships, the exact nature of which, however, it seems to me, is impossible to reconstruct in its entirety. This is partly because of the absence of the wider context of the |Xam discursive field as this might have been embodied in culturally situated |Xam auditors. It is also, however, an ineluctable consequence of the elusive nature of discourse itself.

A long piece delivered by Dia!kwain (L.V.17.5257–300) and published under the title 'The Mantis Tries to Save the Hartebeest' in Lewis-Williams's *Stories that Float from Afar* (2000: 229–32) provides a sense of the scope of the intertextual field in which the sign hartebeest participates. The extract describes the steps |Kaggen takes to rescue a wounded hartebeest. When a man has shot a hartebeest, the Mantis enters his hut and stands on his quiver. The women know then that a hartebeest has been shot: 'For this thing is showing us. It really knows that one of our men is shooting a hartebeest. The Mantis is a thing which is a hartebeest's thing. He is with the hartebeest' (Lewis-Williams 2000: 229). |Kaggen does not come into the hut simply to convey this information, however. He wants to provoke the women into catching him and expelling him from the hut or chasing him away with stones (230). He then flies to the wounded hartebeest and encourages it to recover. It is wise not to chase away the Mantis when he comes to a hut in this way or even to refer to his presence directly. Standing on the hunter's quiver is not |Kaggen's only option.

He can pinch the sleeping child of the man who has shot the hartebeest. When the child cries, the man will stand up and the dying hartebeest, with whom the man is sympathetically conjoined, will receive the strength to stand up too. The women are quick to give a crying child the breast before it can disturb its father. I would argue that the information in Dia!kwain's piece is directly pertinent to 'The Mantis Assumes the Form of a Hartebeest', even though the two texts belong to different orders in the scheme that Hewitt has applied to the materials. The close identification between |Kaggen and the hartebeest, evident in his steps to prevent the hunting of the hartebeest in the extract, is unquestionably a field of signification that intersects with the story.

There is yet another recurring connection between |Kaggen and the hartebeest, although it does not occur in this narrative in which they are physically conflated. |Kaggen, generally in the stories, goes out accompanied by his hartebeest things. This term refers chiefly to his bag. It is made from hartebeest calves and is addressed, accordingly, as 'Hartebeest children' (D. Bleek 1923: 17, 19, 23, 31). Whenever |Kaggen needs to extricate himself from a tight situation, he summons his hartebeest children, his kaross, his shoes and his quiver and they fly with him to a water hole where he recovers from his wounds (Hewitt 1986: 180). The ability of the 'hartebeest' in this story to reconstitute itself is paralleled in the ability of the hartebeest children to participate in |Kaggen's escapes and regeneration.

There are still more references to the hartebeest scattered about the materials, all of which, by participating in the intertextual web I have been exploring, expand the layers of meaning present in 'The Mantis Assumes the Form of a Hartebeest.' The Mantis, it seems, is not alone in its ability to turn itself into a hartebeest. 'A lion', according to |Han#kass'o (L.VIII.23:8075), 'turns itself into another thing; it becomes a hartebeest, becomes like a hartebeest.' The hunters lie in wait for the hartebeest, but it suddenly becomes a lion. As in the story, the position of prey and hunted is now inverted by a transformation: 'we see that a lion is that which walks coming up to us, and we have nothing with which we can do anything … if it perceives us; for, it slays us' (L.VIII.23:8077). This brief extract suggests that all the chains of signification in the materials that are linked to the signifier 'lion' would also have to be explored in order to deliver a fuller exposition of the narrative. And it does not stop there. Many creatures and entities in the materials become different creatures and beings for different reasons in a variety of contexts. I have already referred to the case of the rain turning into an eland. The materials are replete with such examples. This whole fabric of transformation, dissolution and reconstitution is linked with the narrative I have been discussing in ways that still require detailed investigation.

Following the tracks of a signifier such as 'hartebeest' is, to a significant degree, a question of guesswork. Apart from our linguistic, cultural and discursive remoteness from it, it is a sign that, within the context of the materials themselves, is unstable and unreliable. The hartebeest is not only dear to |Kaggen, it is also, to some degree, as we have just seen, part of him — his heart. The hartebeest is larger than life, a hyper-real entity. But hartebeest are also one of the most prized sources of meat. The term 'hartebeest' can signify a flesh-and-blood game animal that can be hunted and eaten; a 'mythological' denizen of the First Times and the generic hartebeest of the observances. 'Hartebeest' is not an individual animal, it exhibits no gender or personal characteristics, and yet, equally, is not a collective noun, as in a discourse, for example, that might describe the habits and movements of hartebeest. This multivocal sign is accorded relatively little space in the Bleek and Lloyd Collection. Nevertheless, the references to the hartebeest in the materials that I have explored here give some idea of the wide range of its field of signification. All the elements in the stories, including |Kaggen, can, in my view, be read as protean signifiers within a |Xam symbolic order that is never a closed system. Within this symbolic order, the hartebeest, |Kaggen, people and a great many other signifiers intersect in intricate ways. Hewitt, as we have seen, focuses on the structural components of the stories, imputes a conservative function to them, and regards |Kaggen as a trickster and narrative operational principle. This approach cannot, in my view, properly account for the discursive capacity of a signifier like the 'hartebeest' in this story. Nor can Guenther's comparative approach. As we saw earlier in this chapter, the species of the antelope discovered by the girls is incidental to his reading of the narrative.

In some — or even all — of its details, a commentary such as this may err. Inevitably, certain meanings have eluded the analysis and others have been found where they do not exist. The point is, however, not to unlock the meaning of the text, but to gain some idea of the intricacy of its workings and to indicate that the materials signify within a wider economy of difference rather than in relation to an underlying narrative structure or to a universal archetype, the trickster. Nor do the details in the story merely lessen the tedium of a didactic lesson or sugar-coat a moral.

While I would argue that 'external' readings often say more about their own location in an episteme than they do about their 'object', I do not wish to suggest that an analysis of the story is only possible from within |Xam discourse. Nor do I wish to imply that there exists somewhere a pure |Xam interpretation of the story that might be reclaimable were it not for the inadequacies of linguistics, history and ethnology. |Xam discourse was not a closed system, consistent with a timeless anthropological space of cultural purity. Discourse is always dialogic in the Bakhtinian sense, a lived practice, rather than a Platonic medium. The |Xam also interacted in complex ways with other languages and cultures. The intertextuality of their discourse stretched beyond the open confines of anything that might be described as intrinsically |Xam discursive practice. At the time of the recording of the materials, for instance, the informants spoke Afrikaans as well as |Xam. Each teller and listener would him-/herself have embodied different and unstable sites of textuality that would have interacted unpredictably with the stories. In the next chapter, these observations are explored further with particular reference to the work of the other major interpreter of the |Xam texts, Mathias Guenther.

NOTES

1   'Things' is the term that is frequently used in the narratives to refer to |Kaggen's possessions: quiver, kaross, shoes, cap and bag.

2   The plant food collected by women was consumed by individual families, while the meat hunted by men had to be carefully distributed among all the members of the band in the prescribed fashion (Hewitt 1986: 36). Hewitt surmises that this particular 'hartebeest meat' would have presented difficulties when it came to distribution, the preserve usually of either the hunter or the man who owned the arrow with which the animal had been shot. This was no small matter. 'The distribution of food was the cornerstone of |Xam life' (115), and it helped ensure not only survival, but social equality. Thus, the ideology connected to the practice involved the basis of social organisation.

3   The sort of comparative approach Guenther employs with this story was particularly popular among oral literary scholars in the 1950s and 1960s, when many of them were concerned with 'the geographical spread of particular motifs' (Hofmeyr 1993: 8). By 'the early 1970s, it was issues of performance and structuralism that came to predominate'. Hewitt's study, conducted as it was in the 1970s, although only published in book form in 1986, can be seen, in the light of this statement, to be a product of its time.

4   Wilhelm Bleek, to whom this story was narrated, was actually particularly interested in Bushman sexuality. Bleek elicited the 'IXam terms for sexually explicit vocabulary', but translated them into Latin rather than English in 'the only Latin recorded in the notebooks' — evidence of the particular reticence that was attached to sexuality at the time (Bank 2006: 98).

5   The first piece quoted below was narrated by Dia!kwain (L.V.6:4411–34) and was called 'The Hartebeest and the Eland Belong to the Mantis' by Lloyd. More information about the Mantis and the hartebeest is supplied by Dia!kwain on the reverse pages. Lloyd separates this information into two pieces: 'The Hartebeest Resembles the Mantis' and 'A Mother's Prohibition with Regard to the Hartebeest and Her Child' (4414'–18'). The longest extract in the notebooks about the hartebeest and the Mantis — apart, of course, from IIKabbo's story itself — was also narrated by Dia!kwain. Lloyd entitled this piece, 'The Coming of the Mantis [the mantis] to Sit upon the Quiver of the Bushman Father at Home Foretells the Shooting of a Hartebeest' (L.V.17:5257–300). The piece is reproduced in contemporary English in Lewis-Williams (2000: 229–32). Another extract from the notebooks that concerns the hartebeest occurs as additional material that accompanies an account narrated by IHan#kass'o of the ways in which the Mantis tries to rescue an eland that has been wounded with a poisoned arrow (L.VIII.23:8033–39). It concerns the Mantis's relations with the eland, hartebeest and gemsbok.

6   IKaggen clandestinely makes an eland from his son-in-law's shoe and raises it on honey. His family kill the eland after they discover what IKaggen does with the honey that he fails to bring home. IKaggen then restores it to life (L.V.1:3608–83).

CHAPTER 6

FORAGING, TALKING AND TRICKSTERS:
An Examination of the Contribution of Mathias Guenther's Tricksters and Trancers to Reading the |Xam Narratives

The only person to have written as extensively about the |Xam narratives as Roger Hewitt has done is anthropologist Mathias Guenther. As I have noted often in this book, the writing that does contain analysis of the |Xam texts, including that produced by Guenther and Hewitt, has not itself been subjected to close critical scrutiny. An important exception, I will argue in this chapter, is Guenther's own criticism of functionalist and structuralist approaches to the narratives in *Tricksters and Trancers: Bushman Religion and Society*, the book that forms the chief focus of this chapter.

GUENTHER'S VIEW OF THE |XAM 'TRICKSTER', CONTRASTED WITH HEWITT'S

Hewitt, as we saw in the previous chapter, divides the |Kaggen materials into two main groups and separates these from other materials such as animal and sidereal stories.[1] When the overriding concern is classification and grouping, the details of individual stories, with some notable exceptions, become of secondary importance. While Guenther also chooses not to concentrate on the textual details of the stories, he is not preoccupied with ordering the materials so much as with pan-Bushman comparison. He emphasises the fluidity and openness of the texts and the ambiguity, variability and protean nature of |Kaggen, matching this reading of |Kaggen with the requirements of a foraging economy in which socialisation tends towards adaptability and a high degree of individual autonomy. He locates the figure of the trickster within a foraging ideology, which, he argues, characterises all Bushman societies, as well as other hunter-gathering cultures worldwide. Guenther also stresses the material's multivocality, attributing this feature to the ambiguity of the protagonist, |Kaggen, and to the nature of hunter-gatherer orality.

Although Hewitt employs a structuralist approach and Guenther positions himself as an anti-structuralist, even though he consciously employs a structuralist analysis at times, they both attribute characteristics of the universal figure of the trickster to |Kaggen. They also both acknowledge his uniqueness among trickster figures and attribute this to the extraordinary and incompatible range of his characteristics. However, they interpret the coexistence of these contradictory elements differently. Hewitt, as we have seen, regards the trickster of what he terms the group A narratives as functioning primarily as an opportunity for the articulation of socially conservative messages or as a safety valve for the transference and disposal of anti-social impulses. Group B stories, on the other hand, feature a more serious, saviour kind of |Kaggen. Hewitt delineates the structures in which the two kinds of |Kaggen appear and relates these to the separate treatment of the two dominant themes of |Xam society, life and death, on the one hand, and the social order and its negation, on the other. He suggests that particular narrators might demonstrate a predilection for one or other of these themes and, thus, for one or other version of the trickster. Guenther, by contrast, attributes |Kaggen's paradoxical qualities, which include the coexistence of divine and absurd character traits, to his trickster nature rather than to his presence in different narrative types. The contradictions that lead Hewitt to identify two different types of |Kaggen are, in Guenther's view, essential properties of a trickster. His interpretation of |Kaggen, therefore, does not seek to resolve these differences, but to accentuate them.

Tricksters and Trancers: Bushman Religion and Society explicitly takes issue with structuralist and functionalist readings of the trickster, readings that, in terms of the Bleek and Lloyd materials, are most extensively and obviously represented by Hewitt's work. Guenther, we might note, does not mention Hewitt's work directly, although he does cite it frequently. It is fair to assume, however, that most of his criticism is levelled at Hewitt's work, since the only other writer to have examined IXam stories in some detail when Guenther published his book was Lewis-Williams (1996a; 1998a), whose analysis follows Hewitt's structuralist analysis of the stories, but adds a shamanistic interpretation to it. Unusually, Guenther opposes functionalist and structuralist interpretations through himself delivering an analysis that is functionalist and structuralist and noting its limitations: 'I took a double-barreled functionalist-structuralist shot at a couple of features of Bushman myth in chapters 5 and 6, and concluded that the analysis it allowed, while arguably elegant, obscured as much as it explained' (Guenther 244). The structuralist or functionalist analysis to which academicians are bound, he claims, gives the impression that Bushmen 'beliefs and myths are logically consistent and symbolically integrated'. In fact, argues Guenther (244), the '"wonderful muddle" that is Bushman religion contains every conceivable trait and pattern'. At its centre is a god who is simultaneously 'destructive and creative' (227).[2] The ambiguous blend of 'the numinous' and 'the ludicrous' (227) that characterises Bushman religion is difficult for Western scholars to understand: 'For deep-seated epistemological reasons we anthropological-academicians cannot tolerate ambiguity' (227).

Bushman religion, within which Guenther positions Bushman myth, is related to a life strategy required by a hunter-gathering economy: 'Bushman belief can be regarded as an ideology consistent with the mobility, openness, fluidity, flexibility, adaptability and unpredictability 'of the forager's life .... Foraging, as argued earlier, is an ideology, a basic ethos, which interacts dialectically with social organization' (Guenther 1999: 246). Bushmen only resort to structure in time of crisis, 'the reverse of the more familiar lapse into disorder undergone by ordered societies in like times' (246–47).[3]

Where Hewitt (1986) reads IKaggen as the operational principle of narratives that enable the articulation of social values and normative discourse, Guenther situates him in relation to the kind of formation of the self required of a foraging economy. IKaggen's character, in Guenther's view, is consistent with the opportunistic individual qualities required by such an economy. For Hewitt, by contrast, IKaggen's character provides an example to people of what they should not imitate. While Hewitt regards IXam society as conservative — a necessary quality, given the difficulties of surviving in a harsh physical environment — Guenther (1999: 135) maintains that 'Bushman expressive and mental culture, lie at a far remove from the conservative pole'.

Guenther (1999: 228) accuses both functionalists and structuralists, as well as anthropologists and academics in general (with their 'entrenched rationalism'), of bringing to their interpretations the 'a priori assumption' that 'there must be' structure. Functionalists, he claims, regard all religion and the myths through which religion is articulated as the 'grease and glue of tribal society, its core institution' (Guenther 1999: 228). Quoting Malinowski (1948: 101), the 'high priest' of the functionalist paradigm, Guenther (1999: 228) asserts that functionalism views myth as a 'hardworked active force' and a 'pragmatic charter of primitive faith and moral wisdom'. This does indeed seem an accurate description of Hewitt's functionalist explanations in which the |Kaggen narratives function to reinforce social cohesion and articulate social values and knowledge. The structuralist version of this tendency, argues Guenther, is based on the view that a 'deep-seated rationality within belief and ritual' exists. Accordingly myth 'is treated as a culture's "meta-theory", containing logical components that are based on binary oppositions and that operate through complex, chainlike metaphorical transformations and inversions' (Guenther 1999: 228). This, of course, is a neat summary of Lévi-Strauss's structuralism. And, as I pointed out in the last chapter, Hewitt's reading of the stories in terms of a nature–culture, raw–cooked, clothed–naked set of oppositions is inspired to a considerable degree by the work of Lévi-Strauss.[4]

In Guenther's view (1999: 229), both functionalism and structuralism assume that an order lies beneath the surface of myths waiting to be excavated and logically re-presented. This results in a two-pronged approach to myths: 'one concerns the selection of elements to include in the core, the other the treatment of those elements that lie outside it' (Guenther 1999: 230). Personal variation in the way in which storytellers present their materials as well as other 'peripheral phenomena' are often downplayed in this process. Guenther is referring directly to the comparative approach of Barnard (1992), Schmidt (1996) and himself (1989), but his analysis would apply also to Hewitt, for whom 'narrative forms' can only be 'elaborated at a "purely" entertainment level by individual performers' (Hewitt 1986: 183).

Guenther goes on to identify some of the work in the field of Bushman studies that for him employs the way of thinking he is criticising. Laurens van der Post, claims Guenther (1999: 231), exhibits the tendency to project categories onto the materials when he writes about the mantis as the god of the Bushmen and as an 'archetype of renewal and redemption'.[5] Yet another school of researchers, he claims, insists on regarding the Bushmen as proto-scientists. Then there is Lewis-Williams's "trance hypothesis" and Megan Biesele's work 'in which the theme of the equality and complementarity of men and women is seen to be the dominant symbol of Bushman cosmology and ritual' (Guenther 1999: 232).[6] Whatever the paradigm, argues Guenther (1999: 232), whether 'theistic, sidereal, animistic, prosaic, shamanic, gender–symbolic', none 'encompasses the field in its entirety, despite the claims to the contrary'.

Guenther contrasts the rationalist interpretive tendencies listed above with Bushman discourse itself, symbolised by the figure of the trickster, |Kaggen. This discourse is characterised by contradiction, ambiguity and fluidity. It is anti-structural (Guenther 1999: 235), open-ended, indirect and allusive (236). Guenther, as already indicated, links Bushman discourse directly to the particular constitution of self required by the demands of a foraging economy. In accordance with the exigencies of hunter-gathering, Bushman communities consist of small groupings of 'autonomous individuals rather than norm-governed social personae' (237). Unlike the cooperative activities of more pastoral or agricultural economies, many hunter-gathering activities, including types of hunting, are conducted by individuals and require the flexibility and opportunism displayed in the |Kaggen stories. Social groupings are mobile. Individuals or families can move from one band to another with comparative ease, in response to conflict or resource scarcity, for example. Only in times of threat, according to Guenther, would the Bushmen resort to structure. In their struggles with the settlers, for instance, they sometimes formed large social groups with centralised and hierarchical command structures. This is the exception, however — a temporary response to a crisis.[7] When the threat recedes, they break up into small bands again. These bands are characterised by egalitarianism, loose marital arrangements, and the absence of status and property.[8]

Foraging is subject to many variables and unpredictable circumstances such as rain, game movements and plant availability. It is a way of life that requires adaptability and a high level of opportunism from individuals, as well as a worldview that can accommodate contradiction. In the variable, topsy-turvy world of the forager, the trickster is a key 'meta-player' (Guenther 1999: 237–38). He embodies 'the ambiguity that pervades Bushman mythology and cosmology' (4). He injects 'ferment' and 'laughter', and he both affirms and derides values and beliefs (238). The mythological space of the First Order, with |Kaggen as its first citizen, is another critical component of this complex. It admits an 'extra dimensionality of existence' into the world that parallels the Bushman experience of the complexity and disorder of the everyday and provides another instance of the 'creative dissolution of the order of things' (238) that pervades foraging ideology. The mythic time and its exemplar, |Kaggen, are directly linked to the ontological requirements of a family-based foraging economy.

Guenther, then, contends that the stories of the First Order, with their ambiguous beings and dreamlike quality, accord, to a significant degree, with the ambiguity that characterises the present: 'To a certain extent, the ambiguity of the First Order, with its ontological fluidity, its trickster protagonists, were-beings, and meat-women, still persists in the present world' (Guenther 1999: 70). Hewitt, by contrast, considers the primal period as intrinsically separated from the present, a period of chaos that stands in contrast to the relatively stable condition of the everyday world.

Guenther (1999: 5) also questions the functionalist assumption, to which Hewitt subscribes, that religion and myth are always 'integrating' forces. This, he argues, is only true of more structured societies with hierarchically patterned distributions of power. Bushman social configurations, he maintains, are so loose that they may not even constitute a society (7). Accordingly, Guenther locates |Kaggen within a Bushman religion that, he argues, differs from most religions in that it does not legitimate a power structure. Many of the unusual qualities of |Kaggen and other Bushman tricksters can be attributed to their place in societies that are uniquely free of asymmetrical relations of power. Chief among these unusual qualities is that the Bushman trickster is both a protagonist 'of whimsical or outrageous tales' and a god, a figure of 'numinous power and portent' (6).[9] Nowhere else in the world does 'the figure's status as divinity appear to be defined as clearly as in Khoisan religion' (6). Hewitt (1986: 40), incidentally, does not identify

|Kaggen as a deity, arguing rather that the beliefs about him should 'be situated within the complex of beliefs concerning hunting'. The foraging ethos, maintains Guenther, requires equality and sharing, on the one hand, and self-reliance and individual autonomy, on the other. Altruism and communalism meet self-interest and individualism in a particular way in hunter-gathering economies (Guenther 1999: 48–49). An ambiguity, figured in the multifaceted trickster, arises from the tension between individual agency and collective values.

Where the Western tradition requires certainty and structure, Bushman religion, according to Guenther, is based on the premise that knowledge is uncertain. This follows from the relative absence of power in Bushman society. Since it is freed from its habitual role to legitimate power, myth can 'remain within its proper, mythic time, where order is inchoate and power absent' (Guenther 1999: 84). |Kaggen and other Bushman tricksters embody the uncertainty of knowledge and the fluidity of the Bushman mythico-religious complex: they are figures of 'profound ontological ambiguity and moral ambivalence' (98), attuned to a 'spirit of disorder and flux' (96).

Hewitt (1986: 19–20) insists that |Kaggen's role as trickster has to be understood within the local context of |Xam ethnography. Guenther (1999: 101), by contrast, regularly conflates |Kaggen and other Bushman tricksters with a global trickster: 'The Bushman protagonist, like his trickster colleagues all over the world, on the one hand, is a creator of beings and things, as well of rules and categories, and on the other, transforms, distorts and inverts what he has created or decreed.'

Hewitt situates |Kaggen firmly on the side of nature. Guenther quotes Lewis-Williams (1981: 124) who maintains that |Kaggen, the Mantis of both the |Xam and the Malutis, was 'a divinity who maintained the equilibrium between man and nature' (Guenther 1999: 112). The non-dualistic Bushman vision of life, argues Guenther, would not set nature against culture. The merging of contrary characteristics that are morally incompatible in one trickster God is a product of this non-dualism (Guenther 1999: 113), which, in turn, is a product of everyday experience. This, he notes, confuses interpreters schooled in various forms of European dualism. The Bushmen, in turn, with their non-dualism, misinterpret Christianity. They tend to regard Jesus as a trickster figure (Guenther 1999: 116), in spite of the fact that

Christianity, a religion of a God who does not laugh and who is an 'architect of order and structure' (Guenther 1999: 121), has little place for a figure who revels in self-contradiction and transgressing boundaries.

Guenther's work provides, I have argued so far in this chapter, a tacit but important critique of many of Hewitt's positions concerning the narratives and IKaggen. Hewitt's taxonomic organisation of the materials provides an example of what Guenther (1999: 227) identifies as a Western inability to 'tolerate ambiguity'. The materials, argues Guenther, are not susceptible to being located within a structuralist framework, since they are based on an anti-structural ideology. Guenther (161) also criticises the functionalist explanations of the type Hewitt offers. In everyday life, he maintains, the Bushmen are guided more 'by practical, rational, and secular considerations' than by 'their myths and tales'. He attributes the tendency by critics to inflate the didactic dimension of tales to too close an 'articulation between myth and social reality'. One should not overemphasise 'the normative influence of folklore on the behavior of people' or underestimate 'the ludic, recreational' aspects of myth (161).

A CRITIQUE OF GUENTHER'S *TRICKSTERS AND TRANCERS*

Guenther's criticism of the reductive nature of structuralist and functionalist interpretations of the IXam figure IKaggen is to be welcomed, in my view, as is his contention that the IKaggen narratives celebrate the ambiguity of experience. I would also agree with Guenther's contention that a fluid relationship exists between the period of the First Times, in which many of the narratives are set, and the present: 'Because the Second Order is both a continuation and an inversion of the First Order, the mythological past and primal time pervade the historical present and historical reality' (Guenther 1999: 66).[10] Nevertheless, I would maintain that Guenther himself exhibits a number of the tendencies that he criticises in the work of other, mostly unnamed, critics.

For a start, his insistence on considering IKaggen as a type of the universal figure of the trickster stems from the same generalising and rationalist impulse as the functionalist and structuralist readings of the narratives that he opposes, a point I argued at some length in chapter 4. It is revealing that Guenther (1999: 6) refers to Hynes and Doty's (1993) collection of essays on the trickster to support his contentions about ǀKaggen, while largely ignoring the essays by Tom Beidelman and Anne Doueihi in the same book that question both the ontological status of the category 'trickster' and the usefulness of the trickster term when applied to particular characters from specific traditions. Guenther (1999: 6) states near the beginning of *Tricksters and Trancers* that he wishes to make a contribution to trickster studies: 'I take delight in introducing this complex, unusual and highly interesting character to the world's rogues gallery of such figures.' At various points in his text he points out the ways in which ǀKaggen exhibits general trickster attributes.

Guenther, in fact, employs a more essentialist version of the trickster than most of the writers who use the term. Hynes and Doty (1993) themselves are careful to qualify their use of the trickster term and to distance their use of it from the metaphysical and archetypal version of the trickster posited by Radin and Jung (1972). Guenther describes Radin's book *The Trickster: A Study in American Indian Mythology* (1956ǀ1972), to which Jung, as I noted in chapter 4, contributes an influential essay, as the 'key work that conceptualized this figure in the study of world mythology and comparative religion' (Guenther 1999: 254). In an essay that appeared a few years after *Tricksters and Trancers*, he (2002: 13–15) explicitly aligns his pan-Bushman trickster with the Jungian trickster. He responds to Jung's complaint that 'the so-called civilized man has forgotten the trickster' (Jung 1972: 206, quoted in Guenther 2002: 13) by undertaking, through a consideration of the Bushman trickster, to 'recall this virtually universal mythological and folkloric figure back to our civilized memory' (Guenther 2002: 13).

Bushman Folktales (1989: 115–51) contains a chapter, 'The trickster', in which Guenther identifies several figures in both ǀXam and Nharo narrative as tricksters. This project is extended in *Tricksters and Trancers*. In a chapter entitled 'The Bushman trickster', Guenther (1999: 95–125) conflates ǀKaggen with several other Khoisan trickster figures:

> He is ǀKaggen to the Cape ǀXam, Pate and Pisamboro (or ǁGawama) to the
> Nharo and Gǀwi of Botswana, Piisiǀkoagu to the ǁGana of the Central
> Kalahari Game Reserve, Kaoxa (or #Gao!na, !Gara, Hice, or Hoe) to the

Zhuǀ'hoansi of Botswana and Namibia, Jackal and Haiseb ... to the
Heiǁom, Nama, and Damara (Guenther 1999: 97).

In a note (Guenther 1999: 253), he states that the tricksters (the protagonist-
divinity figures) of the Khoi and the Bushmen 'are the same in form and
substance'. *Tricksters and Trancers* goes even further than identifying different
figures as representatives of the type of the trickster, as its central thesis is the
linking of the ǀXam trickster with the Kalahari trance practitioner.[11] The two
figures, for Guenther, are symbolically and structurally analogous. Both are
masters of the liminal and the ambiguous; both are metasignifiers in the
foraging ideology of the Bushman.

Guenther's pan-Bushman, comparative approach to the materials characterises, too, his treatment of actual narratives, both in *Bushman Folktales* and
in *Tricksters and Trancers*. Schmidt has also followed this strategy with regard
to the narratives (1989; 1996). It underlies, too, Alan Barnard's approach to
Khoisan ethnography and Lewis-Williams's shamanistic theory of rock art. In
this regard, it is significant that Lewis-Williams (1996a) also links the trickster
with trance in his interpretation of a ǀXam story that concerns ǀKaggen, which
I will discuss in chapter 11. Work such as Guenther's, Barnard's and Lewis-
Williams's that is based on a posited pan-Bushman or pan-Khoisan culture
necessarily ignores or glosses over differences and details and betrays a
tendency to dehistoricise. This is evident in Guenther's foraging ideology,
exemplified in the figure of the trickster, which downplays much of the
historical complexity of the economic and social position of the Bushmen.
Edwin Wilmsen (1989) explores this history in relation to the Kalahari in his
work, *Land Filled with Flies: A Political Economy of the Kalahari*. He argues
that for several hundred years at least, Bushmen in the Kalahari have been
caught up in broader political and economic relationships than Guenther's
positing of a foraging ideology would suggest. It is perhaps consistent with the
essentialising, ahistorical thrust of Guenther's work that he should have
argued so strongly against the historical and materialist position of a writer
such as Wilmsen (see, for example, Lee & Guenther 1993).

ǀXam contact and conflict with both Korana groups and white settlers is
documented in the Bleek and Lloyd notebooks. One of the informants,
#Kasin, was himself half Korana, a fact that Bleek might have tried to

suppress, since he failed to 'record a genealogical diagram for #Kasin, yet he did for all his other informants' (Bank 2006: 205–7). This, conjectures Bank (207), was because Bleek's 'ethnographic enquiries were also shaped in terms of race'. The |Xam traded with whites (152) and with the Tswana to the north (93). 'There were Xhosa migrant communities living not too far from Dia!kwain's home area' (253), as well as a little to the south of ||Kabbo's home at the Bitterpits (141). All the chief informants spoke Afrikaans and worked on white farms at some point in their lives. In the period during which the informants lived, at least, and perhaps before this as well, |Xam individuals and groups would, it seems reasonable to conclude, not have consistently required the traits that Guenther argues were inculcated by the foraging ideology that is figured in |Kaggen. At other times, different life-coping strategies would have been required. Of course, Guenther's foraging ideology is premised on flexibility, but this flexibility is based on the notion that the |Xam's primary and essential way of life was foraging, and that deviations from foraging were temporary.

As I have noted, Guenther does not usually engage with the textual elements in individual narratives. His introductions to the narratives in *Bushman Folktales* concentrate on identifying common elements in the stories of the |Xam and the Nharo. Brown (1998: 36–37) observes with regard to the work of Guenther and Megan Biesele that 'anthropologists generally offer little discussion of thematic intricacy'. Guenther's statements follow from a broad consideration of the narratives and pan-Bushman culture in general rather than from the sort of close reading of the texts that might point to some of their discursive strategies and signifying practices. While celebrating the Bushman proclivity towards uncertainty of knowledge, figured in the ambiguous trickster protagonist, Guenther himself, for the most part, does not explore the play of signifiers in Bushman texts that might offer this sort of uncertainty, but instead submits the texts to generalised claims. His remarks, for instance, about the story 'The Mantis Assumes the Form of a Hartebeest', which I discussed in the previous chapter, concern the universal ability of the trickster to regenerate himself (Guenther 1999: 105). Guenther (1996) avoids the question as to why the antelope in this |Xam story is a 'hartebeest' and not another antelope, as is the case in the other stories with which he identifies it.

Although Guenther criticises the academic impulse to submit materials to an overarching paradigm, this tendency is exemplified in his own Platonic approach to the IXam narratives. Individual stories are repeatedly identified with their types in an ideal realm of Khoisan narrative. His theory of a foraging ideology works also as an overarching paradigm into which the narratives can be fitted. His reading of the IKaggen of the narratives is predetermined by this thesis, it seems to me, and by his position regarding the role of the trickster in world mythology.

Guenther's yoking of a rigid social structure and the intellectual tradition of structuralism can be questioned, too. He implies that structuralism itself originates in tightly structured societies. Only an 'anti-structural' social configuration like the IXam band could have at its ideological centre a figure as anarchic and unpredictable as IKaggen. There is in Guenther's work a correlation between highly organised social formations with centralised authority structures and rationalist intellectual tendencies, a contention that an examination of intellectual movements in the West would have difficulty in establishing. It would be hard to prove that the twentieth-century intellectual phenomenon of structuralism originated always in the most tightly structured sites of European society. This link appears more metaphorical than historical. Guenther, in my opinion, too loosely conflates philosophical or linguistic structuralism with social structure.

Guenther's attitude to power in Bushman social formations also needs to be examined more closely. The foraging ideology he attributes to Bushmen is based on individual flexibility and the avoidance of structure whenever possible, an ideology figured in the character of IKaggen, with his irreverent attitude to power and authority and his predilection for opportunism. Guenther's (1999: 5) contention that societies like the IXam are 'free of hierarchy and power structures' stems, I argued in chapter 2, at least in part, from a romantic philosophy of the noble savage that Derrida links with a nostalgia for a lost origin. It rests also on a narrow understanding of power that Foucault's work especially, I maintained in chapter 1, has rendered redundant. Guenther (49) himself comes close to a more sophisticated version of the analysis of power pioneered by Foucault when he observes that individuals in such small groups are continually under surveillance. At different points in his text he also acknowledges that

Bushmen do experience social conflict (44–45) and that Bushman societies exhibit unequal gender relations. The male activity of hunting, in particular, claims an unequal 'share of social, political and religious significance, if not power' (148). Despite these qualifications, the overall thrust of Guenther's work is to downplay the existence of power relations in |Xam society. In the statement just quoted, he seeks to distance the exercise of power to some degree from an unequal 'share of social, political and religious 'significance'. He fails to acknowledge that power can be exercised through such phenomena as tradition, precedent and the pressure of the group as much as through formal power relations. Guenther (34) describes the presence of a mechanism of 'reverse-dominance' that takes the form of deflation of anyone who appears to be getting above him-|herself, which is displayed in the narratives whenever |Kaggen overreaches himself. This mechanism, he claims, is symptomatic of the relative absence of power relations in Bushman culture. It seems to me, however, that this mechanism could just as easily be read as indicative of the existence of the tensions of power within |Xam bands, tensions that might even be exacerbated by the absence of formal power structures. 'Reverse-domination' could then be seen as a means whereby the group exercises power over the individual. Its presence registers the contestation of certain kinds of power, not the absence of power itself. Identities, even those such as the |Xam identities discerned by Guenther that are predicated on the freedom of the individual from the group, are formed within discursive and ideological systems, and these are sites of power.

The absence of power, at least in its institutionalised guise, is crucial to Guenther's positing of hunter-gathering society as fundamentally different from other kinds of economic and social formations. Religion in Bushman societies, he claims, for example, is freed from its usual role of legitimating power. This allows Bushman religion to concentrate instead on 'altered states'. 'Myth, too, is able to remain within its proper mythic time, where order is inchoate and power absent' (Guenther 1999: 84).

Guenther's position regarding power within Bushman communities parallels his statements concerning Bushman orality in both *Tricksters and Trancers* and in his essay '*N//àe* ("talking"): The oral and rhetorical base of San culture' (2006). As I indicated in chapter 2, Guenther consistently emphasises the radical difference between speech and writing. He writes, for example, that 'unlike the written style, which is fixed, orality, by its very nature, creates variation' (Guenther 1999: 85). In a discussion of the work of Megan Biesele (1993), he notes that 'oral texts evince a greater propensity for being metaphorical and oblique' (Guenther 1999: 85). Orality for Guenther is on the side of spontaneity, fluidity, ambiguity and an absence of power, while writing falls on the side of rigidity, structure and power. Rather curiously, considering his linkage with orality and variation, his avowed dislike of structuralist reductionism and his stress on ambiguity and uncertainty in both the narratives and in Bushman religion, Western familiarity with writing results, claims Guenther (1999: 85), in '[o]utsiders such as anthropologists and folklorists' overemphasising differences and gaining 'the impression that people's ideas and beliefs are much more varied in their meaning than is the case from the native perspective'. From this statement it follows, it would seem, that the variety that Guenther celebrates in the |Xam texts is decorative rather than substantial, a position that seems inconsistent with his linking of religious and narrative variety and ambiguity with important processes of socialisation.

Duncan Brown (2006) discusses an extract from the Bleek and Lloyd materials that is entitled '‖Kabbo's Intended Return Home' in *Specimens of Bushman Folklore*. He argues that ‖Kabbo's discourse shows a sophisticated ability to traverse the epistemological binaries of Western thought, such as modernity–pre-modernity and orality–writing, in order to assert a claim to his land and to a particular identity (Brown 2006: 19). Brown links this ability to ‖Kabbo's textual skills, arguing that the textual extends well beyond the realm of actual writing. It encompasses a variety of 'forms of cultural coding' (Brown 2006: 12) such as rock art, tracking and other activities that involve the interpretation and manipulation of signs. Guenther (2006) quotes and discusses part of the same piece by ‖Kabbo at the beginning of his article. Where Brown uses the extract to illustrate his point about the textual nature of |Xam discourse and other cultural practices, Guenther (2006) uses it to posit a radical difference between a way of life based on orality and other sorts of social configurations that depend on writing.

Although Guenther confesses his functionalist position at the beginning of his book — 'my framework is essentially sociological (or functionalist)'

(Guenther 1999: 3; brackets in original) — he consistently criticises the reductionism of functionalist interpretations. On the page after he identifies his analytical framework as functionalist, he writes that 'the paradigms based on these two notions, functionalism and structuralism, have severe limitations in the context of an analysis of Bushmen religion' (4). Since he links narratives to religion, it follows that these limitations apply also to the analysis of the lXam texts. That Guenther's critique of functionalism does not liberate his own text from functionalist explanations is to be expected in chapter 6 of *Tricksters and Trancers*, in which he deliberately invokes a functionalist reading in order to question it (146–63). Functionalist thinking underlies much of his argument in the rest of book as well, however. Its major thesis — the articulation of Bushman religion (which includes narratives and the figure of the trickster) with a foraging ideology that socialises individuals for flexibility — relies on a functionalist foundation. In this view, the lKaggen narratives function to reinforce a foraging ideology that produces particular kinds of individuals.

lKAGGEN IN THE STORY OF 'THE SON OF THE MANTIS'

After a reading of Hewitt and Guenther, we are left with two versions of lKaggen. In many ways, these versions compete. While Hewitt struggles at times to reconcile his reading of lKaggen as a trickster with his close reading of the lXam texts, Guenther, with his predilection for comparative mythology and Jungian archetypes, displays no such unease. It is my view that the sign 'lKaggen', as I argue in the previous two chapters, should be situated within lXam discursive practice itself rather than placed within an idealist framework of universal types, the 'world's rogues gallery' of tricksters (Guenther 1999: 6). I would disagree with Guenther (1999: 97) when he echoes Joseph Campbell (1959) and implies, in a heading, that lKaggen is one of the ' many faces' of a pan-Khoisan trickster. This is not to claim that lXam discourse is a closed system or that all comparisons between lKaggen and other figures from the discursive traditions in the area are unhelpful. Guenther's (1989) and Schmidt's (1989; 1996) comparative approach to the narratives has undoubtedly contributed to a deeper understanding of the range and interrelatedness of Khoisan traditions. As we saw in the previous chapter, Guenther's comparative method opens the way for a possible sexual interpretation of 'The Mantis Assumes the Form of a Hartebeest'. But an unfortunate side effect of the comparative approach, and one identified by Guenther himself (1999: 230), is that it tends to regard the actual details in the stories as incidental regional variation. This leads Guenther to ignore the special relationship that exists between |Kaggen and the hartebeest. I have insisted, by contrast, that none of the elements in the narratives, including those that feature |Kaggen, is adventitious. They all derive their ability to generate meaning from the intertextual relationships formed within |Xam signifying practice, to which they, in turn, contribute. The sign '|Kaggen' generates multiple layers of meaning as a result of its interactions with a multitude of other |Xam signs and its place within a |Xam order of things rather than as a consequence of its relationship with cultural figures in distant parts of the world or even in the southern African region. These meanings often remain elusive to the critic, not simply because of the relative inaccessibility of |Xam culture, but because, as Guenther himself emphasises throughout his book, multivocality is intrinsic to |Xam discourse itself. The |Xam narratives that feature |Kaggen, I have argued, should be approached in a way that foregrounds all the elements in them rather than in a manner that regards the details of particular narratives as subordinate to a universal narrative of the trickster, or to a foraging ideology, or to an imperative to reassert the social status quo. This contention is illustrated by the close examination of selected texts in different parts of this book. The remainder of this chapter contributes to this project by examining the story of 'The Son of the Mantis' in conjunction with some of the other texts that deal with baboons in the collection.[12]

|Kaggen sends his son to fetch a stick, which he apparently wishes to use against the baboons in a hostile manner (Bleek & Lloyd 1911: 21). The baboons discover |Kaggen's intent after questioning the boy, and the news is circulated among the troop. One of the baboon elders orders the other baboons to 'strike the child with [your] fists' (Bleek & Lloyd 1911: 23). The boy's eyeball falls out of his head after he has been struck. The baboons then begin to play a game of ball with the eyeball, singing a playful song as

they do so. |Kaggen finds out what is going on in a dream, and he proceeds to try and rescue his son. Armed with his quiver, he approaches the baboons. Hiding his tears from them, |Kaggen takes off his kaross and begins to play with the eyeball with a feather brush that he takes out of his bag. The startled baboons stop playing until |Kaggen encourages them to resume their game. |Kaggen anoints the eyeball with the sweat from his armpits, which enables the eye to ascend into the sky. The baboons search for the eyeball. After failing to find it in |Kaggen's bag, they turn on him and begin to beat him. |Kaggen fights back, but gets the worst of it. He extricates himself by flying away to a waterhole with his quiver and bag. He takes the eye out of his bag and puts it in the water, proclaiming that '[t]hou must grow out, that thou mayest become like that which thou hast been' (Bleek & Lloyd 1911: 31). He then returns home, where he is met by his grandson, the ichneumon, who asks him what has happened. |Kaggen relates his story. His son-in-law, Kwammang-a, tells the ichneumon to scold |Kaggen for mixing with strangers. He cannot do this himself, since a son-in-law may not directly address his father-in-law. Later, |Kaggen returns to the waterhole, approaching carefully so as not to frighten the child whom the water has resurrected. The child soon grows back to his former size. |Kaggen makes clothes for him, catches him when he lies in the sun, puts the clothes on him and anoints him with his scent. He reminds the boy of his identity and tells him that he, |Kaggen, is his father before they return home together. The ichneumon asks |Kaggen why he had told them that the boy was dead. |Kaggen relates how the boy had indeed been killed by the baboons, but was restored to life by the water in the pool.

|Kaggen is clearly a central figure in this narrative.[13] I would argue, however, as I did in the last two chapters, that the sign '|Kaggen' gains its power to generate meaning from its place within a wider signifying system. I would also maintain that this narrative contains a configuration of elements that are peculiar to |Xam narratives and that have not been derived from a universal genre of trickster stories or from a pan-Bushman belief system. A discussion of 'The Son of the Mantis' that investigates these elements would have to consider the signification of baboons, waterholes, sticks, body scent and eyes for a start. Many of the references to these signifiers in the notebooks as a whole are directly relevant to this story.

Even when these references do not seem linked to the narrative, a closer exploration of the web of signification in which they occur often reveals unsuspected resonances. Signifiers such as 'waterhole' occur as frequently in the materials and display a similar capacity to generate meaning as the signifier 'IKaggen'. While the consideration of the sign 'waterhole' and the others that appear in the text is essential to a comprehensive exploration of this story, I shall confine myself here only to some remarks about the sign 'baboon' in the materials, in order to support my contention that a reading of the narratives that focuses on IKaggen as a trickster downplays the web of IXam textuality from which narratives are constituted and which they, in turn, help constitute.

The story in which the baboons play with IKaggen's son's eyeball is not the only piece concerning baboons that appears in *Specimens of Bushman Folklore*. In another extract, a man named XabbitenIIXabbiten encounters a group of baboons on his way back from visiting some white men from whom he had procured flour (Bleek & Lloyd 1911: 255–59). The baboons see him coming and say, 'Uncle XabbitenIIXabbiten seems to be returning yonder; let us cross his path, that we may knock him down'. The man responds to the action of the baboons by teasing them about the steepness of their foreheads. This angers the baboons, who decide to beat him more. The baboon children ask for the man's head to play with. The man climbs up a krieboom and scares the baboons away by pretending to talk to a group of white men who have guns with which to shoot at the baboons.

This piece belongs to 'historical' time. Not only does it contain references to white men and guns, but it was told to the narrator, Dia!kwain, by XabbitenIIXabbiten himself (Bleek & Lloyd 1911: 254). It belongs, therefore, to a different order of discourse to the First Order narratives to which the story of IKaggen's son belongs. When IKaggen does feature in the present order, it is, we saw in the last chapter, as the supernatural protector of the game rather than as the character of the First Times who lives in a family group. Despite their belonging to different kinds of narrative, the two texts display several common features, consistent with their location within the broader field of IXam signifying practice. Trouble follows from engagement with baboons. In both extracts, the baboons either actually play with human parts or desire to play with them before they are outwitted by human or quasi-human ingenuity. As is evidenced by the second extract, these features do not depend on IKaggen's presence in the text.

Several other pieces in the materials provide further intertextual illumination of the relation between the people and baboons and the way that the sign 'baboon' signifies in IXam discourse. Many of these pieces were published by Dorothea Bleek in the journal *Bantu Studies* in the 1930s. Bleek actually chose to concentrate on baboons for her first set of selections for the journal. Jeremy Hollmann (2004: 2), who has assembled and edited Bleek's *Bantu Studies* pieces, points out that she published materials that exemplified IXam culture rather than recounted narratives. All the information assembled by Bleek regarding baboons was collected from Dia!kwain, the same narrator who describes the encounter of the man with the troop of baboons.

The first extract, entitled 'Baboons speak Bushman' (Hollmann 2004: 10–13), is drawn 'from three separate narratives from Dia!kwäin's twenty-fourth notebook'. It discusses the ability of baboons to speak IXam. It is therefore easy to mistake a group of baboons for humans when one hears them from a distance. Both the IXam and the baboons make use of a special plant. A baboon will hold a stick from the plant in its mouth that 'tells it about things which it does not know' (10). These sticks also protect baboons from pain and illness and warn them of danger. Not surprisingly, the Bushmen try to get hold of these sticks from the baboons (11). Men also kill baboons in order to procure some of their hair, which is used as a charm to protect children against illness.

According to Dia!kwain (Hollmann 2004: 14), baboons know the names of people whom they have not even met before. Although baboons can speak IXam, people should not speak to them (15–16), because the place in which the conversation occurs will be burnt. Talking to baboons on the morning of a hunt militates against success in the hunt. People should ignore baboons, therefore, and hunters only refer indirectly to them (15). People generally avoid using the IXam term for baboon so that the baboons do not know that they are being discussed (17). Many observances attend the hunting of baboons. Special marks are made on the bow after shooting a baboon so that, among other things, 'the baboon's eyehollow' would not remain in the bow. The 'baboon's death would live in our bows' (20).

Baboons were once men and react like men when they are being hunted (20–21). A baboon can shoot an arrow back at the hunter who has shot it. To prevent this, the hunter should tell it that it is a girl's arrow with which it has been shot. This makes it ashamed, and it accepts its death (22–23).

In the lXam stories of the First Times, as I have noted before, the divide between human and animal is blurred. As Dorothea Bleek (1929: 9) puts it: 'The whole animal world is very much alive to Bushmen, the border line between the powers of nature and animals is vague, that between animals and man more so.' In this story, the characters are animals who live like people and who display human characteristics. It should also be remembered, as has been pointed out by Hewitt, Guenther and Hollmann, that the sign 'baboon' most clearly signals the play of difference and similarity between people and animals in both the First Times narratives and the discourses of the present order that appear in the materials (Hewitt 1986: 38, 109–10; Guenther 1999: 74; Hollmann 2004: 7–9). Baboons and people share many traits, and baboons were people even before people existed (Hollmann 2004: 24). The baboons play a human game (Hollmann 2004: 24–28) and come to watch people play the same game. Guenther (1999: 74) observes that '[b]aboons have wives like humans; they have speech, as well as songs; and they understand the human language and call the Bushmen by their names'. This produces a high level of 'moral ambiguity' when it comes to killing baboons, which, it should be noted, are hunted for medicine and not for food.

Hewitt (1986: 109) claims that baboons 'represent the stereotype of undesirable in-laws. They are seen repeatedly as undesirable neighbours whom one would certainly not want one's daughter to marry.' A girl in one narrative discussed by Hewitt who marries a baboon begins to look more and more like it (L.VIII.18:7608–25). Hewitt (1986: 109) conjectures that this structure may reinforce the importance of marrying 'within one's own racial group'. The story, suggests Hewitt, carries resonances of the practice of Khoe-khoen men of stealing lXam women as wives. Hollmann (2004: 8) notes, in relation to the same story, that marriage was often a euphemism for sex, a point also made by Guenther (1996: 90). Hollmann also mentions that the girl in the story was menstruating. The baboon violated several taboos by seducing a girl in this condition. Such a girl was confined to her hut and could only be visited by a narrow category of old women at this time.

Hollmann (2004: 7) links the baboon materials with |Xam hunting observances, while also surmising that the need to distinguish between people and baboons might have had 'an ecological component', since the two species often subsisted on the same plants.

Even this brief overview of the intersecting web of signification carried by the sign baboon gives some idea of its place in some of the chief signifying fields of |Xam discourse and practice: hunting, menstruation, identity, marriage, death, sex and medicine. A story such as 'The Son of the Mantis' has, in my opinion, to be considered in terms of all these fields, as well as that of |Kaggen, the |Xam representative of Guenther's pan-Bushman 'trickster'. I will conclude this discussion by briefly offering some preliminary suggestions as to how this broad field is present in the story. I should reiterate, though, that other elements in the story besides baboons, such as sticks, sons, eyes, body parts and waterholes, would have to be followed in the same way if an analysis were to do justice to the intricacy of the narrative.

It is not clear from the narrative whether |Kaggen intended to hunt the baboons or to chase them away. Ecological competition might have provided him with a reason to chase the baboons. Equally, however, as Guenther suggests in relation to the |Kaggen materials generally, he could have been following his trickster nature by transgressing accepted codes of behaviour for its own sake. These codes commonly relate to relations with strangers. Kwammang-a's reprimand supports this: 'Why is it that grandfather continues to go among strangers [literally, people who are different]?' (Bleek & Lloyd 1911: 33, brackets in original). |Kaggen, however, refutes this. He implies that his actions were driven by love for his son: 'Thou dost appear to think that yearning was not that on account of which I went among the baboons' (33).[14]

If hunting and killing the baboons was |Kaggen's motive, then the question needs to be asked as to whether he was intending to eat the flesh of the baboon or to use it for medicine, the culturally sanctioned use. Given the nearness of human and baboon flesh, eating it would virtually constitute cannibalism, an act of identity transgression that in relation to baboons equals marrying them or having sex with them. Did |Kaggen violate the hunting observances connected to baboons? If he had used the name of the baboons directly while issuing his instructions to his son, he would have done so. His son certainly transgresses the observances by talking to the baboons. These questions, it could be noted, arise from the intertextual field in which the story is situated rather than directly from the story itself. They arise as soon as the interpenetrating web of signification is considered. |Kaggen might also, this discursive web suggests, have been attempting in some way to draw the baboons' power into the stick rather than hunting or chasing them — something that present-day Bushmen also try to do when they take the baboons' sticks away from them (Hollmann 2004: 10–11).

The question of identity is directly expressed in the story, especially in Kwammang-a's assertion that one should not go among strangers. The story, as well as the wider field that relates to people and baboons, suggests that identity requires both difference and similarity. Animals in general need to be separated from people and from other species of animal. This need, however, also emphasises the ontological closeness of humans and the various animals. Nowhere in the |Xam materials does it appear is if humans were both radically different from and superior to animals. Baboons, who share traits such as speech with people and whose flesh resembles human flesh, are especially close to humans. They have, therefore, to be distinguished even more rigorously than other animals from people, even if these people are only proto-people, as in the case of the story of 'The Son of the Mantis'. Hewitt, as we have seen, relates this structure to the need to identify suitable categories of people to marry, as well as to racial differentiation. Given Guenther's (1996: 90) contention that marriage sometimes stands for sex, it is possible that a story such as this alludes to an incest taboo or indirectly to sexual intercourse with a menstruating girl.

The story offers many more sorts of interpretation than those that I have offered here. These possible sorts of interpretation proliferate when the story is situated within the wider |Xam signifying field. The recurring references to baboons' playing with human body parts in the materials elicits intriguing questions. Can this phenomenon be related to identity and the fragility of its construction? Why do the baboons choose the eye in one case and the head in the other, and not some other body part? Why do they play with these parts rather than engage in some other activity with them? Why do people fear that the 'eyehollow' of a baboon might reside in a hunter's bow and not some other part of its anatomy? One would also want to know which parts of a baboon's body people would use for medicine.

The precise answers to these questions will remain elusive, a consequence of both our distance from the world of the materials and the multivocal and ambiguous nature of the texts themselves. Guenther would agree that the texts produce multiple meanings and display ambiguity. He attributes this, as we have seen, to the fact that the narratives participate in the '"wonderful muddle" that is Bushman religion' (Guenther 1999: 244). This makes them, he maintains, amenable to a variety of hermeneutic strategies. I would support Guenther's celebration of the ambiguity of the texts and their amenability to multiple modes of interpretation. I would attribute these qualities primarily to the ideological and discursive nature of all textual production, written and oral, however, rather than to the nature of Bushman religion and orality. In my opinion, the application of this insight to |Xam discursive practice in a manner that is both self-reflexive and detailed offers fresh possibilities for reading the materials contained in the Bleek and Lloyd Collection. In the process of this sort of reading, it is likely that the |Xam texts themselves will expose some of the limitations of the hermeneutics that seek to engage with them and that the historical and local nature of an analytical tradition with universalist epistemological ambitions will become more apparent.

Guenther's book, I have tried to show in this chapter, goes some way towards indicating the limitations of functionalist and structuralist readings of the materials. However, as I have also tried to show, its comparative approach and reliance on universal figures such as the trickster and the trancer, as well as its positing of a radical, essential divide between written and oral production, extends the kind of universalist thinking that underpins functionalism and structuralism even as it seeks to challenge it. Nor does Guenther's analysis of individual stories, with some exceptions, attempt to engage with their textuality. This engagement is, I have argued, critical if progress is to be made in the analysis of the |Xam texts. The historical work of Andrew Bank on the Bleek and Lloyd Collection, I will argue in the following chapter, provides further justification for an approach to the materials that treats them as discourse, belonging to a signifying field that is open to history and its vagaries rather than to an eternal and universal realm of mythology, even when this realm is located within a specific region and set of economic practices, as is the case with Guenther's work. Bank's writing, in my view, corroborates Roland Barthes' (1986: 110) contention that myth 'is a type of speech chosen by history: it cannot possibly evolve from the "nature" of things'.

NOTES

1 Hewitt, of course, is not alone in separating the materials in this way. The published collections, from Bleek and Lloyd (1911) to Lewis-Williams (2000), including Guenther (1989), all order the materials in various ways. Hewitt's interest in constructing structural typologies, however, means that his ordering of the materials is more systematic and forms an integral part of his understanding of them.

2 Like Barnard (1992), Guenther posits a pan-Khoisan deity with multiple and ambiguous qualities. In my view, this deity is attributed to the |Xam chiefly as a result of their identification as a Khoisan people, and there is little evidence in the Bleek and Lloyd Collection to support it (D. Bleek 1929: 305; Hewitt 1986: 40).

3 Guenther and Pelton (1980) both emphasise the fluidity of a worldview that contains the trickster. Guenther though, relates this fluidity to economic practice, while Pelton reads it as primarily a philosophical and theological orientation. Lewis Hyde (1998) links the trickster with hunting in a similar manner to the way in which Guenther links him to hunting and gathering. The difference is that Hyde operates within a biological evolutionary framework, according to which the trickster has his roots in hunting and the development of the intellect that accompanied it. He transcends his origins, however, and flourishes in all cultural contexts. Guenther's Bushman trickster is more firmly located within a hunting-gathering economy. This does not prevent him from linking the Bushman trickster elsewhere, however, to a great many other figures from around the world, including the devil and Bugs Bunny (Guenther 2002: 12–13).

4 Hewitt (1986: 264) lists several of Lévi-Strauss's texts in his bibliography, although he only refers to his work once in the body of the text (Hewitt 1986: 102).

5 Rather surprisingly, given his own employment of the trickster motif, Guenther does not extend his critique of Van der Post's use of the language of Jungian archetypes to a consideration of the use of the trickster term itself. In an article on the Bushman trickster, Guenther (2002) endorses Jung's Platonic, dehistoricised version of the trickster.

6   Hewitt is conspicuous by his absence from this list, even though, as I have already
    mentioned, his work contains the most extensive treatment of the narratives and
    exemplifies many of the positions Guenther wishes to criticise.

7   Hewitt (1986: 30) notes that 'children were explicitly encouraged to be self-support-
    ing and learn to gather, catch and cook food as an insurance for themselves against
    the sudden loss of both or either parent'. Although Hewitt is discussing the vicissitudes
    of hunter-gathering in a difficult environment here, the evidence of the notebooks
    and the narrators' biographies make clear that settler violence was a chief cause of
    adult mortality. The genocidal context in which the narrators were raised underlies
    the statement of one of Lucy Lloyd's chief informants, Dia!kwain, that being an
    orphan was not a 'light thing' but 'a great thing it is' (L.V.6:4411'). The encouragement
    of self-reliance might, then, be seen as a response to crisis. Guenther's thesis, however,
    contends that cooperation superseded individualism in times of crisis.

8   As I pointed out in chapter 2, Guenther's representation of simple traditional
    societies corresponds in many respects to that of Lévi-Strauss. Guenther's emphasis
    on the fluidity and flexibility of Bushman belief and social organisation is quite
    different, however, from Lévi-Strauss's depiction of the unchanging impulse of
    cold societies.

9   This contention, it seems to me, is no different in kind from Van der Post's contention,
    criticised by Guenther (see above), that the mantis is the god of the Bushmen and an
    'archetype of renewal and redemption'. Other figures, too, despite Guenther's asser-
    tion of |Kaggen's uniqueness, have commonly been accorded the attributes of trick-
    ster and deity in the literature on the trickster. An example would be the Yoruba figure
    Esu (Gates 1988: 52). Jung (1972: 195) also attributes a dual nature to tricksters that
    includes the divine.

10 It seems to me that Guenther's earlier book about the |Xam narratives (1989: 86–88)
    establishes a firmer division between the two orders than *Tricksters and Trancers* does
    (Guenther 1999: 30–31, 49).

11 The linking of |Kaggen and |Xam culture generally to shamanism and the practice of
    trance has also been central to Lewis-Williams's trance hypothesis of rock art (Lewis-
    Williams & Dowson 1989). It is not certain, however, that the trance dance was ever
    practised by the |Xam, and there is no unambiguous evidence of trance dancing in the
    Bleek and Lloyd Collection (Solomon 1997; 2008; n.d.). The rock art debate has been
    accompanied by another heated exchange in Bushman studies, one in which
    Guenther has directly participated, which concerns the category of the Bushman
    'hunter-gatherer' itself (Lee & Guenther 1993). In contrast to Guenther, Mac Ricketts
    (1993: 105) separates the shaman and the trickster, maintaining that the shaman rep-
    resents the impulse to transcend 'the weakness of the human condition', while the
    trickster helps people endure 'the absurdity of human existence'.

12 The story is called '*!gaunu tsaxau* (the Son of the Mantis), the Baboons, and the
    Mantis' in Bleek and Lloyd (1911: 16). I will use, for the sake of conciseness, the
    heading that appears at the top of each page in Bleek and Lloyd (16–36), 'The Son of
    the Mantis'.

13 Hewitt (1986: 205) though, identifies |Kaggen's son as the protagonist of the story.

14 The two motives attributed to ǀKaggen belong, according to Hewitt's division of the stories, to group A and group B stories, respectively. Group A stories involve ǀKaggen the trickster, while group B stories depict him as a hero and saviour. Once again, as with the narrative that I explored in the last chapter, the narrative seems to resist Hewitt's classification of it in many respects.

CHAPTER 7

HISTORY AND INTERPRETATION:
Some of the Implications of Andrew Bank's *Bushmen in a Victorian World: The Remarkable Story of the Bleek-Lloyd Collection of Bushman Folklore* for Reading the |Xam Narratives

THE ROLE AND IDEOLOGY OF THE COLLECTORS

It has increasingly been recognised that the |Xam materials are a product of both the intellectual milieu of Victorian Cape Town and of |Xam culture itself. A growing body of literature has over the years attempted to explore this context, beginning, it might be said, with Otto Spohr's (1962) *Wilhelm H.I. Bleek: A Bibliographical Sketch*. Robert Thornton's (1983b) paper, "'This dying out race": W.H.I. Bleek's approach to the languages of Southern Africa', however, marked the beginning of the critical reappraisal of Bleek's work. This process has culminated, at the time of writing, with Shane Moran's (2009) *Representing Bushmen: South Africa and the Origin of Language*, a detailed analysis of some of Bleek's major texts. Moran emphasises Bleek's role as a producer of colonial ideology. Andrew Bank's (2006) history, *Bushmen in a Victorian World: The Remarkable Story of the Bleek-Lloyd Collection of Bushman Folklore* includes an investigation of Bleek's thought and its links with the nineteenth-century intellectual world. It also presents the most thorough account of the genesis of the Bleek and Lloyd project to date. Bank places the project in its historical environment in Cape Town and in the frontier zone of the northern Cape Colony. He also provides biographies of the major players. This work, together with some of Bank's papers (1999; 2002), has, in my view, certain far-reaching implications for the interpretation of the narratives. This chapter sets out to explore some of these.

Bank (1999) details the celebratory manner in which Bleek and Lloyd and their project have generally been represented by scholars. Lewis-Williams depicts Bleek as a visionary: 'Bleek saw down the decades and realised that San rock art very possibly constituted the most powerful argument against those who believed the San authors of these paintings to be simple, primitive and distasteful' (Bank 1999: 2, quoting Lewis-Williams 1996b: 307–8). Deacon and Dowson (1996) present Bleek and Lloyd as far-sighted and courageous pioneers whose prescience and endurance led to the linguistic preservation of an extinct language and the transcription of one of the largest bodies in the world of oral literature from a single culture. Bleek and Lloyd transcended the narrow racial prejudices of their era in admitting the lXam informants to their household and recognised the value of the lXam tradition at a time when the prevailing attitude was that the primitive Bushman should be extirpated. Their project, in this view, entailed a miraculous interracial partnership in the context of nineteenth-century South Africa (Bank 1999: 6). Even today, argue Deacon and Dowson (1996: 3), Bleek and Lloyd's work 'provides much fuel for challenging the racial stereotypes and perceptions held about the San of southern Africa'.

Even those writers who have adopted a more critical stance towards the lXam project, Bank suggests, celebrate Bleek's contribution in a way that tends to ignore some of what, from a contemporary perspective, are the less acceptable aspects of both Bleek's theoretical position and his ethnological practice. Although Michael Godby (1996), for example, notes the ambiguous origins of anthropology and the complicity between science and colonial domination, he regards the relationship between Bleek and Lloyd and their informants as exceptional. Pippa Skotnes (1999: 18) contrasts the respectful relationship between European and Bushmen that prevailed in the Bleek household with the genocidal racism that generally characterised colonial attitudes towards Bushmen at the time.

Bank sets out to present a fuller picture of Bleek's position in the intellectual milieu of the mid-nineteenth century. Bleek was not only the leading scholar in the Cape at the time, part of 'a tight colonial intellectual network which included Bishop Colenso and Governor George Grey', but also corresponded regularly with 'the leading evolutionists and scientists of his day, Charles Darwin and his disciples, the German zoologist Ernst

Haeckel, the British anthropologist Thomas Huxley, and the British geologist Charles Lyell' (Bank 1999: 2). Thornton (1983b), notes Bank (1999: 2), emphasises the "liberal universalism" shared by Bleek and Grey, as well as Bleek's 'Carlylean romanticism' and 'religiously inspired monogenism' (the idea that people had a common origin). Although Grey has subsequently been exposed by the historian Jeff Peires (1989) as a ruthless imperialist, Bleek, maintains Bank, continues to enjoy good academic press. Martin Hall (1996: 146), for example, favourably compares the enlightened philologist with his autocratic friend, Grey.

Bank (1999: 7) himself offers a more critical view of Bleek and his Bushman project, arguing that Bleek was 'South Africa's first systematic theorist of racial difference ... the figure who marks the transition from the hardened racial stereotyping of the early mid-nineteenth century to the intellectual racism of the twentieth century'. He demonstrates his thesis by examining Bleek's extensive oeuvre. These include Bleek's private correspondence, his 1869 treatise *On the Origin of Language*, his *Comparative Grammar of Southern African Languages* (1862) and his articles in the *Cape Monthly Magazine* (1858; 1873a; 1874a; 1874b). Bank describes Bleek's championing of an evolutionary philology in which languages and cultures are located within a hierarchical structure that is closely articulated with race.[1] Within this scheme, Bleek situates Bushman languages close to the 'communication of primates' (Bank 1999: 9). Bleek was especially interested 'in comparing the Bushman languages with sounds produced by apes' (Bank 1999: 13), since he believed that such a study might help to corroborate the evidence for the evolution of humans from apes. He saw |Xam as a language that represented an intermediate stage of an uninterrupted progression from apes to modern Europeans (Bank 1999: 15). In a letter to Grey in 1871, Bleek describes the speech of ||Kabbo and |A!kungta as 'monkey like' (Bank 1999: 15).

Bleek's interest lay in human origins and the history of the asymmetrical linguistic and cultural evolution of different peoples. Understanding this history required a comparison of 'the conditions of those peoples which have stopt [sic] short at the lowest phases of development' with those of the 'most cultured nations' (Bleek 1869: 36–37, quoted by Bank 1999: 11). Long before he arrived in the region, Bleek had studied southern African languages with a view to better understanding the development of Indo-European languages (Bank 1999: 15). He considered South Africa particularly suitable for the sort of comparative studies he wished to pursue, because the region was home to two of the

> distinct varieties of the human species ... the Hottentots and the tribes of the Kafir kindred. And the very primitive stages in which both nations have remained render them peculiarly fit to serve as safe bases for ample comparative ethnological and philological researches (Bleek 1858: 23–24, quoted by Bank 1999: 17).

It was important to study the Bushmen because their primitive state afforded insights into earlier phases of humankind's history. This would contribute towards an understanding of 'the most primitive methods of structural arrangement and modes of thought' (Bleek 1857, quoted by Bank 1999: 19).

The studies of mythology and language were the keys to understanding the primitive mentality. Bleek posited a correlation among belief systems, mythological complexes and language structure. Only certain language structures permitted higher modes of thought and creativity. Bleek believed that the Bushmen possessed a greater aptitude for myth-making than did Africans. This, in his view, meant that they were more closely related than were Africans to Europeans, despite their lower degree of 'civilisation', a position that explains, to a large degree, his particular interest in Bushman mythology (Bank 1999: 22).[2]

The close correspondence that Bleek believed existed between race and language also helps explain his interest in anthropometric photography. Anthropometric photographs, Bleek hoped, might provide proof that racial type could be linked to linguistics in an evolutionary framework. Photographs enjoyed at the time 'an unprecedented (and often unquestioned) credibility' as evidence due to their 'apparent veracity' (Webster 2000: 1; brackets in the original). They were central to the colonial project of the period:

> As a form of representation of external reality the photograph in its colonial context played a powerful role in helping to establish concepts of order and

interpretations of an alien environment ... it could provide the means to place
an alien world in a comprehensible European context (Webster 2000: 1).

The anthropometric project was initiated in 1869 by Thomas Huxley, who
prescribed exact criteria for the photographic recording of anthropological
subjects, and was introduced at the Cape by Bleek. Among the subjects
photographed and measured in conformance with Huxley's criteria was
||Kabbo. Ten sets of the photographs that Bleek commissioned are housed
in Oxford's Pitt Rivers Museum, in which exhibits were 'organised along
typological and evolutionary lines' (Bank 1999: 26).

Bleek emphasised the need to preserve the language and mythology of a
people who were facing extinction. He did not, however, explicitly analyse the
reasons for the disappearance of the Bushmen. Bank (1999: 30) argues,
however, that Bleek regarded natural selection and the survival of the fittest as
inevitable processes in human history. Bleek influenced and participated in
'the discourse of dying races' (32) that inspired much of the intellectual
interest in the 'aboriginal inhabitants' (39) of the Cape Colony in the last
quarter of the nineteenth century. The progress of 'civilisation' was considered
inevitable and so were its consequences for the more 'primitive races'.[3]

Bushmen in a Victorian World retains much of Bank's earlier appraisal of
Bleek's theoretical positions. It also, in my opinion, significantly qualifies
some of his earlier views of the Bleek and Lloyd project. On the basis of an
exhaustive examination of the notebooks and other sources, Bank
demonstrates that Bleek revised some of his attitudes towards the Bushmen
and their culture once he became better acquainted with the informants
and their narratives. Initially, as we have seen, the speech of his informants
reminded him of chattering monkeys. Soon, though, Bleek came to view
the |Xam informants as 'part "of the most interesting nation in South
Africa"', and he describes their stories as 'wonderful' (Bank 2006: 165).
Bleek refers respectfully in some of his correspondence to ||Kabbo as his
teacher. He hung a portrait of ||Kabbo in his study, the dignity of which
contrasts starkly with the anthropometric photographs of ||Kabbo the
prisoner that Bleek had earlier commissioned (185).[4] It is above all,
however, his investigation of the collaboration between the informants and
Lucy Lloyd that leads Bank (397) to characterise the project as 'an

extraordinary tale not only of survival and resilience, but of hope and creative possibility'.

Bank recreates the life history of each of the informants in considerable detail and closely articulates these histories with their stay in the Bleek-Lloyd household and the nature of the materials they delivered. The informants emerge as agents who exercised choices and showed resilience and adaptability, even in the harsh conditions imposed on them by the expansion of the colonial frontier into their areas in the decades preceding their incarceration in the Breakwater Prison. Despite their subordinate position in the Bleek household, they continued to display these qualities, in various ways and according to their individual histories and temperaments, in their interactions with members of the family and in the ways in which they transmitted the materials that were recorded in the notebooks.

Bank shows how Lloyd, especially, developed close relationships with the informants and became fluent in |Xam. He also shows that her role should be separated from that of Wilhelm Bleek in many respects. She was not bound by his theoretical preconceptions (Bank 2006: 158) and, especially after his death, moved away from a narrow concern with mythology to pursue an interest in |Xam culture generally. Nor was she involved in supervising the informants' domestic work (162). She also evinced anti-colonial and liberal views (341, 352–53).

Bank (2006: 157) argues that the informants invested emotionally and creatively in the project. They were truly collaborators, especially in their work with Lloyd (161). The result is 'our only (and a remarkably rich) point of access to the cultural life and history of an entire people' (397). Concludes Bank (397): 'Without romanticising the motivations of the researchers or the life histories of the informants, we can recognise that their ability to sustain a decade of dialogue is without precedent in the history of this country and perhaps that of the world.'

Bank's work suggests that discussions about the genesis, historical context and nature of the Bleek and Lloyd project need to become more complex. His earlier work demonstrates that Bleek did not transcend the ideological and racial categories of the period. Bank's book, however, suggests that the characterisation of the project by some of the commentators, whom I will discuss in the section that follows, as one of colonial appropriation in which the collectors exercised power over subordinate informants, a situation exemplified for these commentators by the hegemonic acts of transcription and translation of an oral tradition, might also be an oversimplification of a complex process and set of relationships.

Bank's work shows that generalised statements about both the collectors and the informants invite inaccuracy. The informants were people with varied histories and experiences. They belonged to different generations, and the extent and nature of their exposure to both settlers and African or other Khoisan groups on the fluid frontier differed. The informants pursued different strategies of survival at different times, strategies that included hunter-gathering, farm work, illegal hunting and cattle theft. Bank demonstrates how this history is present in the kinds of materials they delivered, as well as in the relationships they enjoyed with the collectors and the amount of agency they were able to exercise in the situation in which the |Xam archive was assembled.

The collectors, too, were subject to different and often contradictory ideological and personal impulses. They were quite capable of evincing different positions in different contexts. Their reports to parliament (Bleek, 1873b; 1875b; Lloyd, 1889), official correspondence and the preface by Theal that Lloyd, surmises Bank (2006: 382), felt it politic to include in *Specimens of Bushman Folklore* often exhibit different attitudes from those contained in private correspondence or in comments in the notebooks. Crucially, as pointed out earlier, Bank demonstrates that the collectors' positions changed with time and that Lloyd, especially, moved far from the sort of intellectual and ideological stance exhibited by Bleek at the beginning of the project. All this suggests that the ambiguity of the texts themselves, noted by those who have tried to interpret them, is replicated in the historical and ideological milieu in which they came into existence.

It is notable that Bank's understanding of the project has emerged gradually from a process of engagement with a wide range of primary materials, including the notebooks themselves, rather than from theoretical preconceptions. His writing over the years reflects significant changes in his thinking. The same could not be said of all the work in the field. Bleek's own work, as we have seen, was predetermined in many ways by his theories of human evolution. I have already described in earlier chapters some of the ways in which inherited frameworks of interpretation have framed the way in which the narratives have been read. In Moran's (2009) view, the claim to a common, all-encompassing humanity has predisposed white South African scholars to largely ignore Bleek's racist attitude to Bushmen. Preconceived ideas have also informed the uncritical enthusiasm for the Bleek and Lloyd project that Bank (1999) describes. Moran attributes some of this enthusiasm to the desire to create a new South African literary canon. He notes, in this regard that the

> conclusion of such a literary historical route is usually the insertion of a representative (here the Bushmen) into the place reserved for the authentic South African voice that, as the aboriginal embodiment of national unity, can serve as the proper origin of national identity (Moran 1995: 31).

This desire can be situated within the context of an even deeper desire for 'democratic nationhood and an all-inclusive citizenry' in which the intellectual can finally expunge his settler origins (Moran 2009: 117). It is important, Moran insists, to remember 'Tony Voss's warning that the "desire to identify with the San represents an ideological claim to status other than intruder"' (Moran 2009: 117, quoting Voss 1990: 60).

Colonial guilt and the urge to 'restitutively acknowledge the injustices of the colonial past' (Moran 2009: 116) inform, no doubt, much of the idealisation of hunter-gatherers and small-scale societies that I have referred to in previous chapters. Political readings of Bleek's work as colonial texts are an important antidote to the tendency that viewed the Bleek and Lloyd project as a humanist response to racist colonialism. I have argued also for a conscious engagement with the politics of interpretation. This book itself aims to produce a critique of the interpretation of materials such as those that are contained in the |Xam archive, as well as readings of the narratives that are more theoretically self-reflexive and politically orientated. But political readings themselves can produce distortions and inaccuracies. Moran (2009: 117) observes how 'Bleek's texts are now valued for the prescient postcoloniality', a move that has sometimes been accompanied by the screening out of the racial ideology that underpins them. Anne Solomon (2009) has provided a good example of some of the dangers that might attend reading the materials through the lens of a contemporary political outlook. A post-colonial interest in detecting anti-colonial elements in the texts has led several commentators to interpret Dia!kwain's well-known extract about the broken string as a metaphor for land dispossession and subsequent cultural alienation. The evidence of the text itself, however, and its relationship to the |Xam cosmology and beliefs that can be discerned by the careful reader in the rest of the Bleek and Lloyd archive suggests that the broken string relates primarily to '[t]he severed connection between Dia!kwain's father and the *spirit*-rainmaker with whom he enjoyed a special relationship' (Solomon 2009: 35–36; original emphasis). The imposition of a contemporary anti-colonial reading on the materials could ironically itself constitute an enactment of a new kind of intellectual colonialism. Bank's work on the Bleek and Lloyd Collection shows that the project has to be understood in a nuanced way. I would argue for a similar caution when interpreting the materials in the archive.

THE STATUS OF THE BLEEK AND LLOYD MATERIALS AS ORAL LITERATURE

The unusual circumstances of the process of transcription of the materials in the Bleek and Lloyd Collection and the effect this would have had on the narrative mode itself have been explored in some detail by scholars.[5] In much of the commentary on the transcription and translation processes, reference is made to the artifice that accompanies writing. Oral literature, it is implied, loses its spontaneity and authenticity when it is written down. Stephen Watson (1991: 19), for example, notes that the narratives were collected in 'artificial circumstances'. Helize van Vuuren (1994: 65) notes that we can only get a second-hand idea of |Xam oral literature from the transcribed and translated texts in the Bleek and Lloyd Collection.

Mathias Guenther (1996: 77–99) also emphasises the differences between 'true' oral literature and the Bleek and Lloyd materials. He emphasises the role of audience interaction in storytelling. In the context in which the Bleek and Lloyd materials were collected, the audience consisted of a single interviewer. Particular norms of interaction were prescribed by the context, which would also have affected both narrative style and content. The |Xam narratives, notes Guenther (83), were collected not through storytelling so much 'as story-*dictation*'. Nor were the |Xam informants narrating their materials to a 'high context group', with whom they could have shared a language that was more culture-specific in its use of metaphorical and connotative features (81).

While commending Guenther's critique of the collecting process and noting its influence on his own work, Bank (2006: 157) argues that Guenther's position underestimates both the dynamism of the storytelling context in Mowbray and the complexities of the relationships between the informants and the collectors. Storytelling was often not a 'one-to-one' procedure. Gesture and other performative techniques also formed part of the process (Bank 2006: 168, 364–65), a point also made by Lewis-Williams (2000: 31–32). Bleek's children, Edith and Dorothea, recalled, for example, that |Han#kass'o 'was "great in storytelling", allowing them to "feel more than know what was happening". They remembered his "eloquent gestures" and dramatic re-enactments, and the notebooks are filled with evidence of this' (Bank 2006: 364). While the dictation was slow and awkward initially, especially since the only language Lloyd and the informants had in common at first was Afrikaans, a language in which Lloyd had limited competency, it later became more relaxed and natural (Bank 2006: 179).[6] Lloyd became fluent in |Xam and developed easy-going relationships with several of the informants (Bank 2006: 161). Her dealings with the informants, as noted in the previous section, was less characterised by the master–servant relationship, to which Guenther alludes, than was Bleek's. Less burdened than Bleek, too, by theoretical expectations, she increasingly allowed the narrators to lead the way in the sessions and became as interested in general |Xam culture as in myths (Bank 2006: 158). Bleek, on the other hand, employed a more formal approach, often using leading questions to elicit materials of a mythological character in accordance with his emphasis on the religious importance to the Bushman of the sun, moon and stars and the figure of |Kaggen (Bank 2006: 159). Lloyd's approach to translation was 'often highly collaborative'. It was usually 'a complex negotiated interaction, the researcher "working out" the meaning of the |Xam text with the assistance of the informants' (Bank 2006: 157–58).

In my view, the discussion of the authenticity of the Bleek and Lloyd Collection as oral literature often reproduces the notion of a clear division between speech and writing that, as I noted in chapter 2, forms the basis of the Western metaphysics of presence (Derrida 1976). Speech, in this tradition, is linked to reality, presence and truth, while writing is considered supplementary and artificial. Although Bank himself does not enter the debate, his reconstruction of the narrating context has important consequences for the way in which discussions about the relationship of the written materials to oral performance are conducted in the future.

One of the implications of Bank's work, I would argue, is that the notebooks should be seen to possess the properties of a hybrid genre that displays features of both writing and oral performance. Bank's work suggests that the |Xam texts should not be seen as a sort of debased oral literature. This would be true even if the notebooks contained only 'traditional narratives', instead of the eclectic blend of history, biography, cultural information and narrative that they do. The |Xam texts are writing, but writing that is heavily influenced by |Xam oral technique. As Bank demonstrates, the process of recording the materials included a significant degree of performance, traces of which are evident in the text themselves. Oral literature and writing are not, of course, mutually exclusive. It is important to remember, in this regard, Derrida's (1976) insistence that speech and writing both always require the elements usually associated with the other in order to generate meaning.

INTERPRETATION OF THE |XAM NARRATIVES

Bank's discussion of the stories themselves contributes to filling in some of the gaps in the existing research that I identified at the beginning of this book. By identifying Bleek and Lloyd as interpreters and critics, Bank also enlarges the scope of what should be understood as constituting the critical literature that exists in relation to the materials. Subsequent interpreters of the texts have to take into account, too, that they are already dealing, in some sense, with interpretations and not some kind of hypothetical 'original' Bushman literature.

Bank (2006: 184) points out that Bleek and Lloyd did not only transcribe the materials, but imposed their own understanding on them.

The act of translation of the texts into |Xam was itself a form of reading them, a point made earlier by Watson (1991: 10). While they did not engage in close and systematic exegesis of the texts they collected, analysis and interpretation underlay Bleek and Lloyd's project. Since they enjoyed direct access to the informants, they were able to deepen their understanding of the materials by making direct use of indigenous exegesis, an advantage not enjoyed by later commentators. The analytical aspect of Bleek and Lloyd's work appears in many forms, apart from the translated texts themselves. These include asides and notes in the notebooks, correspondence, reports to parliament, magazine articles and prefaces.[7]

Bleek's interpretations were coloured by the theoretical positions outlined earlier in this chapter. These positions probably led him to try and elicit particular kinds of materials. It is likely that his theory that the Bushmen were 'sidereal worshippers', for example, prompted him to concentrate on materials that involved the sun, moon and stars (Bank 2006: 189).[8] Bleek was also particularly interested in the figure of |Kaggen, the Mantis, and accordingly encouraged the informants to narrate materials that featured him (200). Much of Bleek's reading of mythology and folklore as it appears in his writing was of a comparative nature, since comparison was a necessary part of his hierarchical theory of human cultural and linguistic evolution. Lloyd, too, engaged in comparative analysis, pasting cuttings from newspapers and journals into the notebooks that pointed to a parallel between |Xam beliefs and those of peoples from other parts of the world such as Japan, Russia and India (352). She also identifies |Kaggen with the !Xun figure |Xue (373).

A consideration of Bank's work, I would argue, shows that Bleek and Lloyd were not only interpreters of the texts, as Bank suggests, but were also, to a considerable degree, the producers of them. In a sense, the |Xam collection is as much nineteenth-century European literature as it is Bushman mythology. It is clear from Bank's account of the genesis of the Bleek and Lloyd Collection, as well as from Moran's critique of Bleek's theory of language, that the collection, transcription, translation and categorisation of folklore and mythology in the second half of the nineteenth century was a consequence of a complex and far from consistent blend of European ideological, philosophical and aesthetic motivations. Something comparable to the orientalism identified by Edward Said (1991) (the complicit relationship between anthropology and colonialism has often been noted), as well as Social Darwinism and other ideological and intellectual currents, underpinned the collection, classification and study of folklore and mythology. The process of the collection of oral materials such as those of the |Xam and their presentation in translation as mythology or folklore are as much a representation and invention of a tradition as they are a recording of pre-existing materials. Bleek and Lloyd were writers, it could be argued, as much as they were collectors, transcribers and ethnographers.

Can one make too much of this position? The relationship of the translations from the |Xam in *Specimens of Bushman* to the materials related by the narrators 40 years earlier is not the same as the overtly aesthetic relationship between Edward Fitzgerald's 'The Rubaiyat of Omar Khayyam' and the Persian, for example. As Watson (2005: 53) argues in his criticism of Antjie Krog's versions in poetry of some of the |Xam materials, Lloyd was not trying to produce literature of her own (and, therefore, of the European nineteenth century), but accurate translations of the materials she had collected from the |Xam informants. He is probably right. But, at the same time, it is clear from an examination of the texts that her translations do add a degree of exoticism to the narratives that has a literary effect, even if this effect is unintended. This is partly due to the transportation of some of the techniques of oral literature into writing: multiple forms of repetition, mixing of genres, digression, the interplay of narrative voice, ellipsis. However, Lloyd also contributes a kind of language herself that is less a product of |Xam oral literature than of nineteenth-century conventions for the presentation of folklore and mythology. She presents and reconstructs the materials as discourse of a certain type. The texts frequently contain archaic expressions, for example. Roger Hewitt (2007: 167) notes that the translated texts employ

a language that seems to be frequently infused with epistemic verbs — the continuous embeddedness of belief, feeling and thought that Bleek and especially Lloyd rendered through a quasi-Elizabethan or Jacobean English that, in the rigour of its attempted faithfulness to the |xam, is not

embarrassed to pile up awkwardnesses and to achieve, by a kind of
accident, a luminous poetry of its own. … it's hard to tell quite what we are
receiving, a Lucy Lloyd ǀxam trance dance of words or a chimerical ǀxam
core working its way through the medium of Lucy Lloyd.

Lloyd's acts of writing are accompanied by editorial interventions, for
example decisions as to what constitutes a story, such as where it begins
and ends; the giving of titles; and the classification of the materials into
myths, legends, animal fables, customs and superstitions, and so on.

The materials in the collection might, then, be described as both ǀXam
oral literature and nineteenth-century literature, not only because they
were transcribed in the nineteenth century, but also because they belong to
a European nineteenth-century intellectual project that sought to
construct a universal literature consisting of traditional mythology and
folklore that lent itself to comparative classification and analysis. In their
translation and presentation, the ǀXam materials exhibit many of the
characteristic literary, rhetorical and discursive conventions that accompanied the presentation of 'traditional' lore during the last quarter of the
nineteenth century in the Victorian world of Bank's title.

Although Bank's book (2006) is predominantly history and biography, it
also contains direct interpretation of materials from the notebooks. His
commentary on the stories provides an important historical context for the
narratives, showing in considerable detail how individual narratives reflect
the interests of the collectors, the life experiences of the informants, and the
relationship between an informant and a collector. ǀHan#kass'o, for
example, gives richer 'descriptions of groups on the boundaries of his world'
than the other informants, a phenomenon that Bank (286) attributes partly
to 'Lloyd's increasing knowledge of his language and her warm and easy
relationship with him, which can be read between the lines of her
notebooks' and partly to the proximity of ǀHan#kass'o's childhood home to
the Korana. He is the only informant to relate detailed stories about the
Korana. He heard these stories from his maternal grandfather, Tsatsi, and
from his mother, ǀXabbi-an (287–90). In addition, the recounting of these
stories to Lloyd coincided with a 'British campaign to subdue the Korana'
(287). Events in the Bleek-Lloyd household itself also often influenced the

narratives, maintains Bank. Dia!kwain's extensive discourses on death were delivered around the time of Bleek's death, for example (258).

Bank's historical approach to interpretation forms a valuable antidote to analytical strategies that tend to view the materials as timeless myths, an assumption that particularly underlies comparative approaches such as Guenther's (1989) and Schmidt's (1989). The historicity of the |Xam materials is also underestimated by structuralist and functionalist reading strategies. The breakdown of the materials into narrative units, for example, cannot easily accommodate the historical influences that Bank shows are present in the narratives. The elements of the narratives that Hewitt dismisses as surface detail emerge, in Bank's account, as central to the discursive strategies of particular narrators. Hewitt also imputes a conservative social function to the narratives by means of which they reinforce social codes. Bank's approach suggests that multiple and diverse motives, as well as contemporary historical and political factors, might influence a narrator's choice and presentation of materials. Although Bank does not engage in close textual analysis himself, his reconstruction of the historical context of individual narratives can only enrich and inform such analysis. It is this task — the analysis of individual narratives — to which I will turn in the chapters that follow.

NOTES

1 A good example of the sort of thinking that was influenced by Bleek's position with regard to race and evolution would be George McCall Theal's introduction to Bleek and Lloyd (1911: XL), in which he writes that '[t]he myths indicate a people in the condition of early childhood, but from the language it is evident that in the great chain of human life on this earth the pygmy savages represented a link much closer to the modern European end than to that of the first beings worthy of the name of men'. Lucy Lloyd's views, Bank (2006: 382) maintains, were very different from those evinced by Theal in his introduction. Bank surmises that Lloyd was forced to include Theal's piece in *Specimens of Bushman Folklore* in order to ensure publication of the manuscript. Theal was by then a well-known writer and an important patron.

2 Moran (2001: 50) observes that Bleek's assertion about the relative closeness of Bushmen to Europeans occurs at a time when '" Bushmen" [had been] pacified to the point of extinction' and settler expansion in southern Africa was chiefly contested by Nguni speakers. 'The "Bushmen" can be safely idealised since they provide no threat

to the evolving settler polity'. The contemporary interest in Bushmen, he conjectures, might similarly be driven by the identification that marginalised white academics feel with 'a victimised non-Nguni minority'. The historian Saul Dubow, as described by Bank, links the idealisation of the Bushmen, evinced by the rock art copyist George Stow, to 'his defence of the rights of white settlers to the land of Bantu-speakers. If the Bushmen were Africa's original inhabitants, the underlying logic ran, the black tribes had no greater claim to the land than the white settlers' (Bank 2006: 312).

3   Bleek's view that the Bushmen were destined for extinction does not survive close scrutiny. Nigel Penn (1996: 81–91) surveys the history that led to the 'perishing' of the Bushmen, including the |Xam of Bushmanland, in the nineteenth century. Penn (1996: 83) concludes that the Bushmen 'perished not because it was so fated but because of the legacy of violence inherited from the eighteenth century frontier'. In other words, they were defeated not because they were destined to perish, but because of 'the murderous and unchanging ideas of their foes' (Penn 1996: 91). In Mklós Szalay's (1995) view, the Bushmen did not become extinct at all. For the most part, they were incorporated into the colonial labouring population, where they became part of a heterogeneous rural proletariat.

4   Two anthropometric photographs of ||Kabbo are reproduced in Bennun (2005: plate 6). These are contrasted with a later portrait of ||Kabbo by William Schroeder (Bennun 2005: plate 14). Bennun's text accompaniment to the portrait states: 'In plate 6 he was photographed as an anthropological specimen, in circumstances that allowed him little dignity; this portrait suggests the esteem in which he was held during his time in the Bleek and Lloyd household.' Bennun compares Bleek's enlightened attitudes with brutal colonial photographic practices, but disingenuously omits to mention the fact that the prisoners were photographed as anthropological specimens at Bleek's instigation.

5   See, for example, Hewitt (1986: 235), Brown (1998: 9–14, 42–43) and Guenther (1996: 77–79).

6   Bleek himself did not need Afrikaans as an intermediary language. He was able to translate the narratives directly from |Xam into English from the beginning (Bank 2006: 181). He never attained the fluency in |Xam that Lloyd was to develop, however (394).

7   See W. Bleek (1873a; 1873b; 1874a; 1874b; 1875a; 1875b), Lloyd (1889), and Bleek and Lloyd (1911).

8   An example of this bias would be his commissioning of 'Lloyd to compile a fuller record of |Xam stories about stars' (Bank 2006: 190).

SECTION 3

Reading the Narratives

CHAPTER 8

HARE'S LIP AND CROWS' NECKS:
The Question of Origins and Versions in the IXam Stories

VERSIONS AND ORIGINS

Claude Lévi-Strauss, as we saw in chapter 1, posits a close relationship among myths that might appear quite different at the level of manifest content. Hewitt, following Propp, regards the 'verbal surface' as subordinate to a narrative's underlying structure. While Lévi-Strauss's mythemes recur across a wide geographical and cultural spread, Hewitt confines himself to the common features of groups of IXam narratives. In Hewitt's view (1986: 71), not only the differences among versions of a story, but the differences among stories that display the same plot patterns are a matter of aesthetic embellishment rather than substance. Since Lévi-Strauss regards myths with different content as virtually identical at a structural level, we might assume that he does not regard the differences among versions of the same story as especially significant either. Although he is interested in the process of transformation of stories, his main concern is the way in which the basic structure that underlies them survives change. Guenther, too, is more concerned with the elements that narratives have in common than the differences among them. He goes so far as to suggest that gaps in the narratives of one tradition might be filled with details from the 'corresponding' tale in another tradition (Guenther 1989: 49).

I have argued in the course of this book for a strategy of interpretation that concerns itself with the play of signifiers that occur on the 'verbal surface' of the narratives. In this chapter I will contend, using two stories as case studies, that the differences between what appear as versions of the same narrative represent a critical site of the production and contestation of meaning in the narratives. I would disagree with the notion that this level of signification is only incidental to another, hidden structure of meaning. The question of versions is one of two areas of concern in this chapter. The other is one that is related to it: the question of aetiology in the narratives. When the narratives are read as creation stories, then their account of the origin of things is foregrounded and their textual detail is largely ignored. Stories become versions rather than discourse in their own right, since they all attempt to describe the same creation event. I will argue that the texts are more than vehicles for aetiological explanations. Both the question of versions and of aetiology accord with the overriding concern in this book with the matter of origins. If the stories are versions, what are they versions of? Is there an original or core version of a story? In Lévi-Strauss's view, there is no original version of a myth, but the myth itself can be understood as a composite of all its variations. Only the critic or reader, then, can be in possession of the myth itself. The common elements in myth originate in the common structure of the human mind. By contrast, Guenther's and Schmidt's interest in the occurrence of versions of the same narrative across the region presupposes some sort of geographical or cultural origin of a story, which is then spread and changed through a process of diffusion. A clear example is Schmidt's (2001: 334) contention that a story that occurs in the Caprivi originated with slaves in the Cape and even further back to the places in Asia from which the slaves came. Malinowski ascribes the origin of a myth not to the structure of the mind or to geographical diffusion, but to the practical requirements of individual societies. The content of a myth is a correlative of its role 'to strengthen tradition and endow it with a greater value and prestige by tracing it back to a higher, better, more supernatural reality of initial events' (Malinowski 1926: 125). Aetiology, or the explanation as to how things came to be as they are, is therefore central to the role of myths in Malinowski's view. The function of a story of origin is not so much explanation, however, as legitimation. Differences among versions signal a shift in power and the sanctification of a new status quo (Malinowski 1926: 77–78).

I will pursue this discussion of versions and aetiology in the IXam narratives in this chapter in relation to two sets of narrative. The first concerns the well-known story of the moon and the hare, commonly interpreted as the story of the origin of death, which gives it its title. This story occurs in more versions in the Bleek and Lloyd Collection than any other. My discussion of the story looks forward to the next two chapters, which also concern narratives of the sun, moon and stars. These sorts of narrative are usually considered to be major myths of origin. The second narrative that I investigate in this chapter, 'The Dasse's and the Crow's Story', features |Kaggen. The discussion of this story contributes to the examination of this figure that has occupied several of the preceding chapters of this book. The story is also present in the collection in several versions. 'The Dasse's and the Crow's Story' is not concerned with a major creation event as such, although all the |Kaggen stories are generally described as creation tales. It does, however, describe how the different species of crows came to have different coloured necks. This discussion of the questions of aetiology and versions in relation to two different sorts of |Xam narrative will lead to the identification of some of the recurring theoretical issues that concern the interpretation of the |Xam narratives in general and to an exploration of the textuality of both stories.

The Bleek and Lloyd project was concerned from its inception with origins. As we have seen, the study of Bushman language and mythology, in Bleek's view, could shed light on the evolution of the languages and cultures generally. As the title of his book on the study of Khoisan languages, *The Origin of Language*, suggests, he situates people such as the |Xam at the origins of humankind. The connection between a concern with origins and the Bleek and Lloyd project continues, in my view, to exhibit itself in a variety of ways in the literature that has been produced in relation to the |Xam materials. This chapter, as I have indicated, concentrates on two examples: the treatment of stories as versions of an original or prototypical story and the treatment of stories as myths of origin.

The designation of the |Xam stories as 'myths of origin' has rarely been questioned.[1] Roger Hewitt (1986: 48) emphasises the 'formative' nature of the 'fictive early period' in which many of the narratives are set. He claims that '[t]he narratives which deal with the sun, moon and stars are, with few exceptions, entirely aetiological constructions' (Hewitt 1986: 93). Mathias Guenther (1989: 36) considers the 'major concerns of Bushman mythology' to be 'creation, primal times and the trickster'. In his collection of |Xam and Nharo folktales, he places 'all the myths about the sun, moon and stars into the category of creation' (Guenther 1989: 37). In Anne Solomon's (n.d.: 4) opinion, all the narratives that are set in the First Times are 'creation tales' or 'creation stories'. If critics accept that the |Xam sidereal stories are predominantly aetiological, it is not surprising that they are more interested in the function of the stories than in attending to their textual details, a dominant feature of the analysis of the |Xam stories that has been noted by Brown (1998: 36). If the narratives are myths of origin, they clearly have a predominantly explanatory function. They also provide a sanction for features of the social system that carries a cosmogonic authority. While a reading of the narratives as aetiological can be said to invite functionalist pronouncements about them, it is equally true that reading the stories as primarily aetiological in the first place can be attributed, at least in part, to a functionalist analytical predisposition. Whatever the sequence of cause and effect, however, the resulting designation of the narratives as chiefly myths of origin that fulfil a social function encourages, in my view, the erasure from critical analysis of the play of signifiers in |Xam discourse. The textual details of the stories become subordinate to their role and the differences among stories or among versions of stories are dismissed as decorative.

The next section of this chapter will examine some of the implications of the view that the story of the hare and the moon, 'The Origin of Death', is predominantly a myth of origin. I will argue also that the existence of different versions of the story is not simply a question of extraneous detail that has been added to or subtracted from a stable core narrative about how death came into the world. Nor is the existence of multiple versions attri-butable only to the poor memories or creative enthusiasms of individual narrators. Rather, the versions point to the interdiscursivity of the |Xam materials. Variation among narratives is itself part of the way in which the texts are set up to invite exegesis and discussion (Barber 1999: 28).

While I problematise the idea of the creation myth in relation to the story, I do not, of course, deny that it possesses a strong aetiological component. The great majority of the narratives that concern the sun, the moon or the stars indisputably contain accounts of how things in the celestial realm came to be as they are now. Some boys threw an old man with the sun under his arm into the sky. Since then, the days have been lit up by the sun. The Milky Way was formed after a girl threw ashes into the sky. |Kaggen, the Mantis, threw a shoe into the sky and made the moon. The aetiological aspect of these stories does not, however, I would argue, constitute their raison d'être. Several features of the narratives suggest that they are not primarily intended as accounts of creation. For a start, the stories often contain different and contradictory explanations for the same event. Nor is it possible to discover a consistent sequence of creation events when all the stories are taken together.[2] Often the aetiological element in a story is only an incidental detail in a complex narrative.

In this chapter I intend to explore the consequences for interpretation when a story such as this is read as part of |Xam discourse rather than as a creation myth. I will both criticise and build on the interpretation of the sidereal materials by other writers. Their readings of the narratives are in any case, I would argue, often at odds with their stress on the tales' aetiological character. Hewitt's detailed and suggestive analysis of the story of 'The Wife of the Dawn's Heart Star' in his chapter on the sidereal narratives belies his own contention that these materials are 'entirely aetiological constructions', since his analysis focuses on elements in the story that are not aetiological at all (Hewitt 1986: 91–104). Guenther (1989) emphasises the aetiological nature of 'The Origin of Death' in his book *Bushman Folktales*, which brings together Nharo and |Xam materials in a comparative format. He follows Bleek and Lloyd (1911) in calling it 'The Origin of Death' and includes several versions of it in a chapter that he entitles 'Creation' (Guenther 1989: 50–75). In his later discussion of the story in *Tricksters and Trancers*, however, he offers an altogether different sort of approach to it, one that highlights its performative and textual features rather than its aetiological character (Guenther 1999: 126–45).

'THE ORIGIN OF DEATH'

Wilhelm Bleek, as we saw in the last chapter, was not working in an intellectual vacuum when he set out to study the language and mythology of the |Xam Bushmen. Among Bleek's intellectual contacts was fellow philologist Max Müller (Bank 2006: 41), a proponent of comparative mythology who believed, as Bleek did, that the combined study of language and mythology was the key to decoding the primitive mentality from which the sophisticated mind of modern humans had emerged. Müller's linguistic study of mythology led him to conclude that all myths were based on observations about the sun, moon and stars (Okpewho 1983: 3; Csapo 2005: 19–30). Bleek himself believed that the |Xam worshipped the celestial bodies (Bleek & Lloyd 1911: 435). It has been suggested, as I mentioned in the previous chapter, that these ideas influenced him to elicit more sidereal narratives from the |Xam informants than was justified by the importance the |Xam themselves would have attached to these materials (Hewitt 1986: 91–92; Guenther 1996: 89; Bank 2006: 155). Be that as it may, the very first story that ||Kabbo related to Bleek at the outset of the project in September 1871 concerned the creation of the moon by |Kaggen (Bank 2006: 155). Shortly thereafter, in October, ||Kabbo related the story of the moon and the hare ('The Origin of Death') to Lucy Lloyd.

The |Xam story of the 'The Origin of Death', as its title indicates, is generally interpreted as an explanation for the presence of death in the world. There are several versions of this story in the collection;[3] I shall concentrate on only two of them. In the first, told by Dia!kwain to Lucy Lloyd in August 1875 and published in *Specimens of Bushman Folklore* (Bleek & Lloyd 1911: 57–65), the baby hare is punished for crying for its apparently dead mother.[4] The moon strikes him on the lip and condemns him to be chased by dogs. The moon then decides that people shall 'altogether die' (Bleek & Lloyd 1911: 63). In the second version, narrated by #Kasin and published in Lewis-Williams (2000: 253), the hare mischievously reverses the message of eternal life that he is sent by the moon to deliver to humans.

The story is very widespread. All Khoisan peoples, apparently, possess a version of it (Guenther 1999: 127), and about 70 versions have been collected over the last two hundred years (28). The people of southern Africa who speak African languages also often possess variants of the story. The common features of these stories are usually emphasised, an emphasis that accords, I would argue, with the interpretation of them as chiefly accounts of the origin of mortality. When these diverse texts are considered as discourse rather than as a single myth of origin, I will argue, their differences and variations assume a new importance, and fresh layers of meaning begin to emerge from the texts.

Both the |Xam versions that I will discuss involve the hare. In the first version, the baby hare refuses to stop crying for its seemingly dead mother. It will not believe the moon's assurances that the mother hare will return to life, just as the moon himself dies and lives again. Interestingly, the baby hare already possesses knowledge of death, although death has not yet been introduced into the world. The baby hare's lack of faith results in the moon's decreeing as follows:

> And they who are men, they shall altogether dying go away, when they die. For, he was not willing to agree with me, when I told him about it, that he should not cry for his mother; for, his mother would again live; he said to me, that, his mother would not again living return. Therefore, he shall altogether become a hare. And the people, they shall altogether die (Bleek & Lloyd 1911: 59–61).

A logic is signalled here by the syntax, at least in translation. There is an inevitable progression between incidents. But what is the nature of this logic? From what elements is it produced and what are its premises? It can also be asked how the moon comes to possess the power to impose such a logic on both discourse and the world. What, ultimately, is the source of the moon's power to console, punish and condemn to death?

There is, of course, something very familiar about this story: it is the narrative of a fall. The consequence of the hare's lack of faith (disobedience of a sort) is a fall from immortality. Placed, however, in the wider context of the narratives of the First Times, this fall corresponds with how things should be. It forms part of the realisation of a better order rather than contributing to a fallen world. Even if it is accepted that this world is not ideal (which is likely, given the influence of malign spirits in it), it is never presented as fallen. The fall into mortality is a fall towards rather than out of presence. It inaugurates the realm of spirits. The advent of death is linked in the story to that other event that commentators place as central to the transition to the establishment of the present order: the separation of species — the hare shall 'altogether become a hare'. There is also the curious suggestion in the story that people have always died. The difference now is that they will go away when they die. In a sense, the story concerns the revelation or formation of a realm of spirits more than it concerns dying itself.

Guenther (1999) emphasises the theme of separation in the story. This theme takes several different forms in the narratives as it charts the division of the 'mythological past from historic present, life from death, child from parent, man from boy' (145). He notes the binary elements that

> permeate the story, giving the theme of separation pervasive lateral roots: night (moon) and day (people's villages), and this opposition's incumbent polarities of dark and light, above and below, and cool and warm; solitariness (moon) and community (village); wisdom and maturity (moon); and folly and childishness (hare) (145).

The presence of this binary structure reinforces his assertion that the story concerns 'the division of what was once whole' (Guenther 1999: 145). Almost immediately, however, he refers to elements in the story such as the presence of human flesh in 'today's hare-animal' that qualify such an analysis. He intentionally casts 'doubt on the binary features this brief structuralist foray into the symbolic meaning of the tale has revealed' (145) in order to cross-examine the efficacy of a structuralist reading of Bushman mythology.

While Guenther questions the structuralist technique of discovering binary structures in the narratives, Roger Hewitt's (1986) analysis of many of the lXam stories relies, as we have seen, on reading them in terms of a nature–culture binary. It is interesting to note in passing the questions that can be elicited from this story when this binary is applied to it. Does the institution of death, with its accompanying separation of species — the process by which substance and form become coterminous — signal a drift towards or out of culture? Alternatively, does the establishment of a code of difference and likeness among groups, as well as the introduction of categories of the familiar and the strange, constitute a move in or out of nature? A natural order is accomplished that requires an unnatural or cultural mechanism of separation. Is death, then, the necessary displacement in which culture arises? Can culture only exist in a space circumscribed by death? The hare's becoming altogether a hare is also nature fulfilled, an expression of the assertion of nature, the reclamation of the natural order of things from a state of relative identity that belongs to culture and the play of fluid social relations that does not exist directly in nature.[5]

In the first version of the story, the moon decrees death, or at least a world of spirits where people go when they die rather than, as before, returning to the realm of the living, as the mother hare was going to do before her child contested the moon's claims concerning the resurrection of the body. It might even be asserted that the moon is recruiting for its own realm during one of its cyclical absences from it. In the second version, however, the hare rather than the moon acts as death's protagonist: 'The moon, it was the one who ordered the hare, that the hare should to go tell the people, that a man who is ill, he shall rise up, like himself, for, he who is the moon, when he dies, he comes again, living comes' (Lewis-Williams 2000: 253). The hare goes on his errand, but deliberately turns the message around:

> The hare it went, it told turning round the story, it said that a man who dies shall not arise; for, it ordered that a man who dies, he shall altogether dying be finished. Therefore, people do not rise up, people who die, do not arise; for, they dying are finished. Therefore, people who die, do not living come, for, they, altogether dying are finished. They do not arise, for, they are truly finished (Lewis-Williams 2000: 253).

Although some of the differences might be attributable to translation, it is notable that in this version, death signals an annihilation, whereas in the first version, in which death is introduced by the moon, a being who himself exists in the two realms of the living and the dead, the dead go away in order to exist somewhere else.

These clearly are two closely related stories, variations of one narrative; but their differences are striking and significant. The role and motives of the moon differ markedly in the two accounts. In the first version, immortality is part of the dispensation, and the moon introduces mortality as a consequence of the baby hare's disbelief and ingratitude. In the other version, immortality is a gift that the moon wishes to bestow on a world in which it is only an unconscious state of affairs, i.e. it is the *knowledge* of immortality he wishes to grant rather than immortality itself. It is interesting to note that in both versions, knowledge affirms immortality, whereas in Genesis it leads to mortality.

In the first story, the hare seems at first sight to be pathetic, a victim of its youth and emotional dependence on its mother. The punishment meted out by the moon appears harshly disproportionate to the hare's offence. But the hare's ignorance here is not a matter of a lack of knowledge. He obdurately rejects the opportunity to relinquish his ignorance. It is this refusal to accept knowledge that results in the introduction of death. The story departs from the story in Genesis, in which knowledge is proscribed. The hare's punishment, however, is linked to a notion of collective guilt that should seem familiar from the long play of original sin in Western thinking.

In this first version, it appears that mortality is a departure rather than an annihilation, a moving to another place, presumably the world of spirits. The deliberate exercise of lunar agency results in the creation of this other place or dimension. It could more accurately be said, perhaps, that the moon initiates the living into the place to which he himself disappears and from which he reappears. Its decree might then be read not as punishment, but as an empirical demonstration to the disbelieving hare of the ultimate nature of the illusion of life and death. In the second story, by contrast, the consequence of mortality follows inevitably from the hare's malicious or mischievous disobedience when he deliberately turns the moon's message around. Death is not a journey to another place, but an end.

In the second version, the hare proves an unreliable intermediary between the moon and men. Henry Gates (1988: 5) emphasises the intermediary role of the Yoruba figure Esu-Elegbara, who 'interprets the will of the gods to man' and conveys 'the desires of man to the gods' (6). Gates compares Esu's role to that of the Greek messenger of the gods, Hermes, from whom the term 'hermeneutics' is derived (8). Esu is 'the god of interpretation' and a 'metaphor for the uncertainties of explication' (21). It is tempting, then, to read the unreliability of the hare in this version of the story as illustrative of the uncertainty of interpretation!

These stories offer two significantly different accounts of death. They do, however, agree on the origin of the hare's split lip (i.e. cleft palate). Schmidt (2001: 249) does not attach much significance to this aspect of the narrative: 'The secondary aetiology is a more or less playful coda not necessary for the story itself.' It could even be argued, however, that the two versions of the story are more concerned with the origin of the hare's split lip than with the origin of death. The stories display a hierarchy of significance that is not erected on the foundation of a fall from presence. Zygmunt Bauman (1997: 169–70) asserts that organised religions manufacture the big questions 'of the purpose of life' in order to create the need for an answer to them. This is necessary, since most people, he maintains, are too concerned with mundane exigencies to ask big, metaphysical questions. The |Xam seem as interested in the lips of the hares they encounter in their daily activities as in mortality. Is this attributable to their focus on the everyday realities of survival or did they have such a surplus of time that they realised that the little questions are as important as the big ones?

The questions elicited by the story effortlessly proliferate. The moon dies; the moon lives once more. Where does the moon go when it dies? Does it visit the world of the dead? Where is this other world? What are its contours, its nature? Is it a psychological zone or a narrative and textual one? Is it an extra-physical space that is, nevertheless, susceptible to empirical investigation and experience? Is it only the categorising, universalising mind and the mechanism of translation from diverse languages into a common one that makes it seem as though different cultures refer to the same phenomenon when they speak of the realms of spirits or the place of the dead? Do these categories exist for the enquirer only through the foreclosure of other categories? If this is indeed a story of a fall, does it describe a happy landing in the arms of grace or a descent into death and disfigurement? Once again, this narrative can be shown to be working both ways, against and with the grain of the dominant frame of interpretation, which contends that the movement in the stories is from disorder and lack towards order and plenitude. The story simultaneously describes a fall into and out of grace.[6]

Things in the world are more suitably and properly ordered than they were in the First Times. People and animals are not as stupid or foolish as the hybrid beings of the Early Race. On the other hand, the living become susceptible to the ambiguous world of spirits. The story speaks not only of mortality, but also about the separation of nature from the human. Henceforth, people have the sole claim on being human. Animals such as the hare that were once included in the human are now excluded. They will be completely themselves. But it also indicates the porosity and fragility of these boundaries: the hare possesses human flesh; its lip is part of the human history of mortality.

One could also ask where the moon's power comes from. Is it derived from the power of |Kaggen, which itself is of mysterious provenance? The moon, after all, began its existence as his shoe.[7] It possesses some of his properties: it rises again from near death; its nature is ambiguous and manifold. Once again, however, origin is probably an explanatory red herring. The moon signifies differently in different contexts: it is not consistently a Mantis thing. Could its power reside in its unique nature — its dying and coming to life again, the gift of death to life that it signifies? But even its ability to participate in life and death plays differently in different narratives. In this story, this attribute resides within the moon's selfhood; it invests the moon with special power. In the next chapter, however, I will consider a story in which the sun attacks the moon and reduces it to a sliver from which it grows again. In this story, the moon's cyclical character is a function of the sun's violence and mercy, and signals the moon's weakness in relation to the sun.

This discussion of the two versions of 'The Origin of Death' has produced more questions than it has supplied answers. Some of this uncertainty is attributable, no doubt, to a distance from the world described in the texts. More importantly, however, I would argue that the narratives themselves produce ambiguity and openness and invite interpretation; these are properties of their discursiveness. As literature, they do not provide information about the world so much as direct attention to the signifying systems that produce 'truths' about the world. Nor does the text contain ready-made viewpoints; it is in the production and reception of the text that viewpoints proliferate. 'The text itself says more than it knows; it generates "surplus"' (Barber 1991: 3). Reading this story as simply an explanation of death ignores its multivocality, a quality that exploring the differences between the versions quickly makes apparent.

'THE DASSE'S AND THE CROW'S STORY'

The story entitled 'The Dasse's and the Crow's Story' (D. Bleek 1923: 47–50) does not describe a major creation event such as the inauguration of death. The aetiological element that occurs in it is more of the order of the origin of the hare's split lip. It might be argued that the question of the difference between species of crow was a big one for |Xam people. It would not follow, however, that the incident in which two different species of crow get their different coloured necks is a critical part of this particular narrative, for it only appears in the story at all because Dorothea Bleek decides to include it in the version that appears in *The Mantis and His Friends*.

I will begin this section by extending the discussion that has been running through this chapter about the phenomenon of versions, before exploring the story's situatedness within |Xam discourse. This will lead me to conclude that the different versions of stories can be regarded as discursive sites in which meaning is generated through the temporary juxtaposition of signifiers rather than as variations on a single narrative that preserve a core plot, structure or function.

The story, as it appears in Dorothea Bleek's *The Mantis and His Friends* (1923: 47), begins as follows:

> Kwammang-a once went visiting. They were two, he and the Mantis, and they went to the Bee's house, when the Dasses lived with the Bees.
>
> Then a young Bee offered Kwammang-a his ostrich egg-shell, out of which Kwammang-a drank; while a young Dasse offered the Mantis his ostrich egg-shell, into which he had put dirty water. So the Mantis drank out of the Dasse's egg-shell. When he tasted the Dasse's dirty water, he cursed the young Dasse.
>
> Then the Mother Dasse, who was on the hunting-ground, sneezed, and drops of blood came from her nostrils. Therefore stones rolled. The stones said 'V v v v v v,' because stones which had stood fast were falling.
>
> Then the young Bee spoke to his Grandfather Kwammang-a; he said: 'You should go to this gambro (a sort of cucumber); mother has made a hole in it. You get into it, for the Mantis was really with you, that man who has been teasing. Therefore hard things are falling upon you; for the Mantis who has been teasing was really with you.'

Then Kwammang-a arose, he went quietly along, and quietly reached the hole in the gambro; he went to sit in it, while the Mantis was outside, because he had come later. He was covered up fast; the stones fell covering him up fast, while Kwammang-a lay loose.

The women (at home) said: 'What can be the matter? You ought to send the ring-necked Crow, that it may go and see where the people are.' And the ring-necked Crow went; it had on its neck a little piece of fat which was very small. It went and ate up the fat half-way and it turned back.

I have deliberately chosen to use Dorothea Bleek's text rather than the notebooks themselves, for it offers me the opportunity to problematise the question of versions even further. Bleek has intervened in particular ways in the story. Her version contains more incidents than the notebook versions by |Han#kass'o from which she derives her text, but also contains less repetition: '[s]ome I have shortened by leaving out wearisome repetition' (D. Bleek 1923:V).[8] She considerably underplays the scale of her manipulation of the texts. She does not, as she rather disingenuously suggests, simply provide a selection from the materials in the notebooks with needless repetition removed, but rewrites the language, in many instances. Her headings, as in the case of the narrative about the dasse and the crow, direct attention to particular aspects of a narrative. In addition, and much more controversially, she actually combines different texts to make new texts. In effect, she takes it on herself to improve the narratives as they were presented by the informants: to make them better-written literature, texts for readers rather than listeners. Her failure to signal her own part in the rewriting of the |Xam texts in the Bleek and Lloyd Collection (already themselves a writing and a rewriting — a transcription of a verbal account that has been translated) could be seen as self-effacing. Dorothea Bleek is simply the editor, according to the title page, of a selection of Bushman folklore collected by Bleek and Lloyd. Her 'editing' could also be considered in a harsher light, of course: it is an example, perhaps, of a hegemonic ethnographic power to present and represent subjugated people for external consumption, a milder version of the brutal appropriation of their land and bodies by colonial forces.

Bleek's versions, one could say at the very least, should be treated with caution, since they misrepresent the narratives in the notebooks to varying degrees. I should like here to offer a partial defence of them, however, not in order to defend Bleek's editorial procedures as such, but to support the proposition that a |Xam narrative should not be read in isolation from other narratives and from |Xam discourse in general. In forming a story from different texts in the collection, Bleek is following, not necessarily deliberately, the |Xam practice in which narrators continually rearrange themes and plots into narratives that are both new and also recognisably reinterpretations of other stories. The narratives, then, are not versions of a core or original story so much as examples of the operation of |Xam discourse in action. This discourse works according to its own logic, a logic that does not necessarily concern itself with the replication of stories as such. Bleek's text exhibits some of this logic, I would argue, even though she herself is trying merely to present a better story — the story the narrators might have presented themselves had they possessed her insights into the literary sensibilities of European readers.

The two texts from which Bleek chiefly draws in order to create this version of the story are contiguous in the notebooks and are clearly related. The first (L.VIII.2:6146–64) contains the aetiological section that occurs in Bleek's text about the ring-necked crow going out to look for the men who have been covered over by stones. On the way, it eats most of the sheep fat that was placed on its neck in order to sustain it on its journey. It fails to find the men, as does a second ring-necked crow, which also eats most of the fat that has been hung around its neck. The ring-necked crow has today only a thin band of white around its neck as a consequence of this primal event. A pied crow is then sent out. It finds Kwammang-a and the others covered by the pile of stones and leads the rescuers to them, but does not touch the fat around its neck. The result of this restraint is that the pied crow today has a large band of white around its neck and on its chest. Bleek's introduction of the piece about the crows' necks might be seen as proof of the importance that she attaches to aetiological features in the materials, or it might merely signal an attempt to bring more variety to the narrative. However, it is also, I hope to show, an intervention that is consistent with the intertextual logic of the materials.

The second major source for Bleek's version of the narrative, also by |Han#kass'o, recounts the incident, some of which I include in the quote earlier in this section, in which |Kaggen and Kwammang-a visit the bees. Kwammang-a enjoys the sweet honeyed water that the young bee gives him, but |Kaggen curses the young dasse (generally spelt 'dassie' nowadays) for giving him dirty water to drink (L.VIII.2:6165–236). The dasse's mother, who is out on the hunting ground, responds to her child's being cursed by sneezing drops of blood. These turn to stones that roll on |Kaggen and Kwammang-a and cover them. This narrative excludes the section about the crows altogether. It proceeds instead to describe how Kauru, who is both the dassie and the Mantis's wife (not to be confused with the mother in the story, spelt 'Dasse' by Bleek), together with his adopted daughter, the porcupine, are accompanied by the giraffe, elephant and rhinoceros to the hunting ground where they remove Kwammang-a and the Mantis from under the pile of stones. Importuned by the porcupine, the 'people' first extricate Kwammang-a as gently as possible so as not to hurt him. They are tempted to leave |Kaggen under the stones, since he has caused the trouble in the first place. |Kaggen's wife begs them to rescue him: he is her husband, after all, and his childlike nature means that he is not really responsible for his actions. They do rescue him, but pull him out roughly. They soften a bit on the way home and anoint his wounds so that they begin to heal. |Kaggen's sister, the blue crane, is especially distressed to see his wounds when he reaches home.

Finally, |Kaggen is subjected to a series of admonitory lectures. His grandson, the ichneumon, scolds him on behalf of Kwammang-a who, as |Kaggen's son-in-law, may not address him directly. |Kaggen had especially violated the rules of visiting and interacting with strangers by complaining about the water he was given to drink. In so doing, he puts not only his own safety in danger, but also that of Kwammang-a. |Kaggen has been warned about this sort of infraction countless times before, but always fails to listen.

|Han#kass'o's discourse about the crows from which Bleek draws for her composite narrative is itself a hybrid text that moves between fiction and non-fiction, the First Times and the present, aetiology and cultural information; while it also straddles narrative and the presentation of knowledge. It begins by supplying information about the naming of birds. The crow story follows on directly from a piece about why the secretary bird is called 'carry-feathers' (L.VIII.2:6146–64). Much of the information

about crows is located in the First Times, since it deals with the origin of the appearance of the different crow species and also mentions the discovery by the pied crow of Kwammang-a under the stones, an event that occurs in the same First Time story of the Mantis, |Kwammang-a, the dasse and the bees that forms the backbone of Bleek's integrated version. Bleek can thus be seen to be following |Han#kass'o in integrating the two narratives, since he links them in his first piece, even though it is only in passing, and he omits the crow incident in the second. |Han#kass'o's discourse about the crows also goes on to relate crows to springbok hunting in the context of present hunting practice. Bleek does not include any of this material in her narrative.

This generic hybridity is common in the |Xam materials and presents particular difficulties for those would like to place the |Xam materials into categories — mythology, narrative, cultural information, etc. It also, of course, makes the quest for 'pure' versions of a narrative more difficult. This hybridity is no doubt partly attributable to the |Xam informants' not drawing the same rigid distinctions between fact and fiction, past and present, and the real and the imaginary as their commentators do, but also, and crucially for interpretation, to the fact that they were relating their narratives to an audience who were not steeped in |Xam culture and interdiscursivity and who consequently required a great deal of background explanation. In effect, as I argue in chapter 3, the |Xam informants delivered a commentary on the narratives they recounted. Thus, the reference to the crow's finding Kwammang-a and |Kaggen that Bleek includes as a central incident in her version of the story (even using it in the title) is accompanied by a long discourse on the role of crows as messengers and intermediaries in |Xam hunting practice. We can ourselves augment this direct explanatory material by exploring the other references to crows in the collection. In this way, a sense of the intertextuality that a |Xam auditor experienced can to some extent be obtained. This procedure might be regarded as the opposite of one that seeks to extrapolate versions of core narratives from the materials. It does not strip away incidental verbal material in order to leave behind a coherent narrative that is recognisably and essentially the same as others, the sort of univocal procedure that Doueihi (1993) criticises in relation to the way in which narratives that contain a trickster figure are treated. Rather, it concerns itself with the verbal surface and its play of signifiers.

There are two extended disquisitions on the role of the pied crow as instrumental in the finding of missing men in the |Xam archive; both display the same sort of mixing of genres and of 'fiction' and 'non-fiction' that characterises |Han#kass'o's text about the crows. !Kweiten-ta-||ken's piece (L.VI.2: 3975–3996) relates directly to husbands who have gone missing while hunting, and, like |Han#kass'o's, goes on to give intricate detail about children, crows and springbok hunting. Her discourse also contains a reference to stones falling on men and to fluids connected with bees and dasses, in this case their urine. Dia!kwain's discourse (B.XXVI:2473–86) brings many of the same elements together with a piece of near-contemporary history. Once again, two different kinds of crow are sent out to look for husbands who have not returned from the hunting grounds. The women put sheep fat around a /xuru (ring-necked) crow's neck. When it returns without finding the men, they transfer the meat to a /kagen (pied) crow's neck. It finds vultures devouring the corpses of the men, who had been murdered by boers (Dutch-speaking farmers).

These texts are directly and obviously linked to the events in the narratives. There are also other references to crows in the materials, however, that could be investigated, especially relating to the more sinister and ambiguous figure of the black crow, often accused of spying for lions (Hollmann 2004: 41–44), but also sometimes providing a warning of the latter's presence, a role that can in some ways be contrasted with the ring-necked crow's neutral stance towards humans and the pied crow's benign one.

So what do we make of the signifier 'crow' in this story? I can only give some indications here. Perhaps to a comparitist, the first and most obvious point to note would be the correspondence between the roles of crows in the story and the roles of crows in other literature. The story of the crow as messenger in the biblical story of Noah's Ark comes to mind, for a start. It is one with which, incidentally, the |Xam narrators might well have been familiar. It is not surprising that widespread and general patterns of meaning that relate to crows exist if we take into account their wide distribution and certain obvious characteristics about them: their cawing, their predilection for coming close to people, and the divide they span as carrion eaters between the living and the dead. The position of the crow in the regional literature is another stratum of investigation that would provide further indications as to the way that the sign 'crow' might be signifying in the story. Most importantly, however, in my opinion is a detailed investigation of the signifier in the |Xam interdiscursive field itself. We are not only dealing with the universal sign 'crow', after all, but with particular species of crows in a specific environment. In the same way, we need to investigate how the signifier 'crow' (and there are several terms in the materials for the three different species) generates meaning in |Xam discourse itself.

This picture becomes especially complex when we consider the field of signifiers that are interconnected with these signs and the intertextual links that they in turn provoke. In this story we have links with fat, missing husbands and submersion by stones. When we consider the piece by !Kweiten-ta-||ken, we have in addition a recurrent association with dasses and bees that also corroborates Bleek's bringing of her two texts together. The web of connotations that link fat, bees and honey in the archive is enormous. For a start, each of these signifiers is heavily linked to relations between the sexes and to female sexuality. Although the signifier 'springbok' does not appear in Bleek's text, it occurs in both |Han#kass'o's and !Kweiten-ta-||ken's discourse about the crows. Even if not directly present in a particular narrative, it would have still continued to signify through its association with crows. It is a potent multivocal sign, as I will show in chapter 10.

Had Bleek omitted the crow materials, as she might easily have done without any damage to the story, then the detailed investigation of the crow signifier would not, it might be assumed, have been necessary. It is quite likely, however, that the sign 'crow' would still have emerged as one to be considered in the course of the examination of some the other signifiers in the story, just as the signifier 'springbok', as I remark in the previous paragraph, soon emerges when the intertextual field is explored. A search connected to submersion by stones, for example, would immediately lead to the linking of crows with the events in the story. 'Crow' as an absent signifier would, in all likelihood, have been present for a |Xam auditor through a familiar web of interdiscursivity. Bleek, it could be argued, makes explicit for non-|Xam readers what was implicit for |Xam auditors.

A consideration of this wider discursive field also points to its consistency across the categories into which commentators have placed the |Xam materials. The piece with the crows used by Bleek, as I have already mentioned, moves from 'mythological' time (the submersion of the First Times character Kwammang-a with stones) to springbok hunting in the 'present' (the everyday world of the |Xam before the arrival of the settlers into their territory in the mid-nineteenth century). !Kweiten-ta-||ken's piece also refers to the mythological dasse and bee characters in the same discourse as looking for lost husbands and springbok hunting. We cannot, in any event, easily separate the cultural information from the obviously literary materials. Did |Xam women really capture crows, tie sheep fat around their necks and send them out to find lost husbands, a motif that recurs in Dia!kwain's account of a boer massacre? Surely this invites a literary interpretation as much as do the events in the First Times narrative in which 'Kwammang-a Is Found by Crows'?

An investigation of the whole Bleek and Lloyd corpus provides, then, a wider context for the reference in the story to the crows. It is this wider context that in my view provides the best resource for interpreters who wish to investigate the |Xam texts more closely. I have here only discussed a small part of the story. To do justice to this text would require a much broader investigation of its signifiers. The characters that appear in it such as Kwammang-a, |Kaggen, the porcupine and the blue crane feature in many narratives, and their roles in this narrative have to be related to this wider context. But the most detailed work concerns the investigation of the signifiers in the story. The list is very long. It includes fat, honey, blood, sneezing, stones, the elephant and the giraffe. The work of Hewitt (1986), Lewis-Williams (1996a; 1998a; 2000), Parkington (2002), Hollmann (2004) and James (2001), among others, provides very useful leads about how some of these signs signify in |Xam discourse, although the main resource remains, in the absence of living |Xam informants, the notebooks themselves. It is often on the margins of stories, its seemingly incidental elements such as the crow episode in this story, that the web of signifiers becomes foregrounded.

This chapter has explored the question of versions of a narrative in this chapter. I argued in relation to 'The Origin of Death' that the differences that appear between versions of the same story are crucial indexes of the literariness of the materials and point to the way in which they invite interpretation and offer multiple meaning. In my discussion of 'The Dasse's and the Crow's Story' I tried to expose something of the discursive field that feeds into narratives and produces what have been described as different versions of the same narrative. I chose to use Dorothea Bleek's story, since it might be called a version of other stories, but it is also clearly a new story, for it contains elements that do not occur together in those stories. But the narrative also, in a sense, pre-exists in the materials, as my exploration of its web of signifiers shows. Even though Bleek is a writer and the narrators were oral performers, I would suggest that something of the same sort of textual procedure as Bleek employs would have informed their storytelling. The aetiological elements in the narratives, which have led to their being called creation tales, I have argued in this chapter, are also part of this sort of textuality. This assertion reverses the claim that the texts are primarily vehicles for explanations of origins or the legitimation of the status quo through investing it with a sacred origin, as functionalist approaches in the tradition of Malinowski might suggest. The next chapter pursues this enquiry further, choosing as its subject another of the narratives that, like 'The Origin of Death', tells of a major creation event, the story in which 'The Children Are Sent to Throw the Sleeping Sun into the Sky'. This story also exists in two major versions.

NOTES

1   The view that the stories are creation tales is sometimes qualified, however. Parkington (1996: 284) observes of some of the narratives that they are 'clearly not simple creation stories because a wide range of animals (porcupine, dassie, blue crane, baboon, meerkat, springbok) already exist and participate in these early events. The real creation is that of the category, hunter, or more generally the relationship between a hunter and his prey'. Solomon (n.d.: 31) notes that the narratives are more concerned with the 'social significance' of 'objects or entities' than with their origin.

2   An example of the different sequences of creation events that can be extracted from the stories concerns the sun and the moon. According to a narrative that will be discussed in the next chapter, the moon preceded the sun. Before the sun is thrown into the sky and hacks at the moon's stomach, the moon is always full. In 'The Mantis and the Eland', however, in which the moon is created, sunlight already exists

(D. Bleek 1923: 1–9). The Mantis creates the moon from his shoe in order to provide light only when the contents of the burst eland gall darken the sky.

3   See B.XV:1403–82; B.XXV:2361–64; L.II.6:664–70; L.IV.4:3882–89; L.IV.4:3890–900; L.V.15:5159–68; L.V.16:5169–98).

4   Dialkwain's narrative occurs in L.V.15:5159–68 and L.V.16:5169–95, and #Kasin's in L.IV.4:3890–900.

5   In his essay, 'From bystander to actor', Bauman (2002: 209–10) claims that the distinction between the animal and human worlds, so important in the epoch of solid modernity now replaced by the liquid era of capitalism, no longer holds: 'Culture and morality are no longer seen as the exclusive property of *homo sapiens* and the boundary-mark of humanity. This is not so much a matter of the scientific discovery of facts as of an "attitudinal shift": a sudden willingness to see what previously went unnoticed, and to dismiss as of secondary or no importance what previously was put right at the centre of the world picture.' Bauman considers various reasons for this seminal shift. He conjectures, for example, that 'insisting on the uniqueness of *homo sapiens* lost its function once the need and the urge to differentiate the 'degrees of humanity' (and so also of 'bestiality') of the superior and inferior ('civilized' and 'retarded') members of the human race fizzled out, having lost its pragmatic urgency and political usefulness' (210). Suddenly the distinctions between the human and non-human, as well as nature and culture, begin to be understood, from the vantage point of the postmodern, as the specific product of a particular history rather than as inherent in the world. Readings (such as Hewitt's analysis of the |Xam narratives) of other cultural products that turn on the tension between nature and culture more and more begin to seem as though they emanate from the context of the analysis rather than from the materials themselves.

6   In an interview I conducted with her in June 2003, anthropologist Megan Biesele described the template of the Bushman narratives of the Early Race as a 'fall into grace'.

7 |Kaggen throws his shoe into the sky in order to provide a source of light after the gall of the eland he has made bursts and plunges the world into darkness. 'That is why the moon shines at night. That is why the moon is cold, because it is a shoe, it is leather. It is red, because it has earth on it, the dust in which the Mantis had walked' (D. Bleek 1923: 5).

8   By removing the 'wearisome repetition', she also transposes the story even more firmly into writing. Repetition with its dramatic opportunities is a distinguishing feature of |Xam oral narrative. Bleek herself included excerpts from this narrative in one of her *Bantu Studies* articles in order to illustrate the |Xam use of particular types of speech for certain animals, a technique that would have been much enhanced by repetition and one that disappears in translation (Hollmann 2004: 349–55).

CHAPTER 9

THE STORY IN WHICH 'THE CHILDREN ARE SENT TO THROW THE SLEEPING SUN INTO THE SKY':

Power, Identity and Difference in a ǀXam Narrative

The ǀXam texts, I have argued in this book, owe their signifying capacity to their place within ǀXam discourse rather than to a location within a universalising narrative of generic types. In this chapter, I will discuss the multivocality of the ǀXam texts in greater detail, a quality that, to my mind, resists attempts to reduce them to structural skeletons or to assign them a social function. The basis for this discussion will consist of an examination of the story entitled 'The Children Are Sent to Throw the Sleeping Sun into the Sky'. I will use two similar versions of the narrative that occur in the Bleek and Lloyd materials. Both versions were related to Lucy Lloyd by ‖Kabbo. The first version (L.II.15:487–99) was published in *Specimens of Bushman Folklore* (Bleek & Lloyd 1911: 44–57). The second and longer version, on which I have mostly relied, is to be found in the unpublished notebooks (L.II.35:3150–59 & 3165–236), as well as in Guenther (1989: 75–81). These texts are consistent, on the whole. I will not explore the differences between them, as I did with the story of 'The Origin of Death' in the last chapter, but assume instead that taken together they provide a fuller account than if each were to be taken on its own. Lucy Lloyd, it should be noted, has already expanded the narrative before including it in *Specimens of Bushman Folklore* by incorporating a section that was recorded on the reverse side of Bleek's notebook pages (Bleek & Lloyd 1911: 45–51). This piece is a narrative in itself, but it also augments and helps interpret the wider narrative within which Lloyd has embedded it.

Much of the story consists of the recounting of the same events by different actors, a feature of ‖Kabbo's narratives (Hewitt 1986: 240). The plot is thus quite easily summarised if these repetitive elements are left out. The result appears scanty, however. This is perhaps one of the reasons why Roger Hewitt (91) observes that the plots of such stories are undeveloped. In my opinion, however, the story's real interest resides in its textual elements rather than in its plot. The narrative's repetitive features, I will argue, are integral to its rhetorical effect.

THE STORY

Two women of the Early Race instruct the sons of the younger woman (the older woman is childless) to creep up on the old man who has the warmth and light of the sun under his armpit[1]. The boys should toss him into the sky and instruct him to follow the path designated as his: 'Ye shall say to the old man, that, his path must truly be yonder … Oh children! Ye must give directions (orders) strongly to the old man, that the old man may not forget; for the old man alone is the one who is warm' (L.II.35:3168–69). The boys are to creep up on him quietly, 'For, a man who (is) very cunning, he (the sun) also is' (L.II.35:3157). Not only should they caution the younger children not to laugh while the old man is sleeping, lest he awakens, but when they 'presently go stealthily to lift him up … ye shall not go laughing' (L.II.35:3166). If they manage to contain their laughter, he will only be 'startled awake' while he is ascending.

The women instruct the boys as to what they should say:

> The old woman said to the children, 'O children going yonder! ye must speak to him, when ye throw him up … ye must tell him, that, he must altogether become the Sun, that he may go forward, while he feels that he is altogether the Sun, which is hot; therefore, the Bushman rice becomes dry' (Bleek & Lloyd 1911: 47). [2]

The children faithfully carry out these instructions and then eagerly await the first dawn: 'They sleep; the day breaks, the children first, they awake, they look at the darkness, they say, "The Darkness does yonder go …

Darkness goes out from the daybreak's side; the Darkness goes towards the evening's side"' (L.II.35:3213–14). They are praised by the women for having listened well and for having acted with resolution. The boys' grandmother (an older woman who is not necessarily their biological grandmother) especially congratulates them: 'Yes, my grandsons, I wished that ye should do thus for me, to the old man, that I might be able to be warm'(L.II.35:3219). The acclaim earned through this action is extended to all the First Bushmen: 'For, we are the earliest Bushmen, we are those who work well.'

The story does not end there. On the morning after his unexpected elevation into the sky, the sun discovers that he is not alone. Just as he is setting at dusk, the moon comes out. This angers the sun, who attacks the moon with a knife. He does not completely destroy the moon, however, but leaves the moon's backbone behind for the sake of the moon's children. This enables the moon gradually to recover his full size, at which point the sun attacks him again and the cycle is repeated (Bleek & Lloyd 1911: 51–55).

INTERPRETATION AND THE QUESTION OF ORIGINS

Stories invite different interpretive strategies; this particular story is no exception. A structuralist reading might gloss over the details and seek the underlying pattern in the narrative that links it to others of its type. Hewitt, however, finds the sidereal narratives generally unsuitable for the kind of structuralist analysis he applies to the IKaggen stories. These stories, he asserts, do not 'warrant much attention as verbal art'. They 'are very undeveloped as narratives' because 'there is little or no attempt to build up the narrative in any way, and no plotting of events' (Hewitt 1986: 91, 94). This makes them structurally uninteresting. Despite this contention, 'The Children Are Sent to Throw the Sleeping Sun into the Sky' is amenable, I think, to the sort of structuralist treatment, pivoting on the nature–culture binary, that Hewitt regularly employs in his readings. The story could, for instance, be read as one in which the sun (nature) is separated from and subordinated to culture (the economic practices of the Bushmen). The sun is forcibly placed in its proper sphere within nature, ejected from, and repositioned in relation to, the cultural field. The story could also, in this sort of analysis, be located within the liminal zone between nature and culture. Bushman rice is a natural product — the larvae of ants — that is cooked by nature in the form of the sun rather than on the cooking fire (a part of culture), but which is transformed, nevertheless, into a cultural product, cooked larvae. But the nature–culture binary in such stories could as easily posit a contrary logic: the recognition of the interpenetration of nature and culture. Both formulations — the separation of culture from nature, and the interdependence of nature and culture — presuppose a nature–culture binary that is universal rather than the product of a specific intellectual history. In my view, however, neither forms part of the direct enunciating strategy of the text itself.

Different ideological interpretations also offer themselves. The very fact that the story is capable of mobilising different perspectives supports Karin Barber's (1991: 3) observations about the ideological nature of oral texts. The story's ideological ambiguity stems not only from differences in interpretation, but also from the ideological and dialogical nature of the texts themselves. The sun's ejection into heaven could reflect either power differentials in Bushman social systems or a non-hierarchical ecological interdependence. The manner in which women and children together determine the position of the sun could be cited as evidence of an egalitarian ethos that is blind to age and gender. Conversely, it could be read as a compensatory mechanism whereby old women and children are granted a role in stories that they lack in ordinary daily life. Another option, of course — and the one that I choose in this chapter — is to allow these possibilities to coexist, so that none of the meanings generated by the text is foreclosed.

Most commentators, as I noted in the previous chapter, read the |Xam narratives as origin stories about a creation time when things were still coming into being. This particular story lends itself more readily to this designation than many of the others, since it obviously deals with a major inaugural event, and its aetiological import is explicit. The narrative explains how the sun came to be in the sky, which is convenient and practical for the |Xam: the rice is dried and the women can leave the warmth of the fire and go out and collect food. Humans have taken the chance to adjust the cosmos to their satisfaction. Even if the narrative is read as a myth of origin in this way, however, it must be conceded that it is not an account, along the lines of the first part of Genesis, of the beginning of everything. The sun already exists as an old man living in a Bushman band. The story concerns not his creation, but his elevation into the sky. The focus is as much on the activity of the boys and the initiatory role of the women as it is on the sun. Nowhere in the stories related by the lXam informants is an attempt made to explicate ultimate origins. Barnard (1992: 83) ascribes the absence of an account of ultimate origins in Khoisan stories to a double creation framework in which a deity brings a world into being and then leaves other agents to finish off the details.[3] Be this as it may, in this story the sun already exists in the armpit of the old man. How this state of affairs arises in the first place is a question the story does not attempt to explore.

Even if the story is considered to be primarily aetiological, it is surely important to examine both the particular anatomy of the aetiological explanations it offers and the ordering of the discursive elements within it. The sun is depicted as selfish, jealous, violent and bad-tempered, and he is expelled from human society. A dualistic identity politics is enacted in which his difference and distance from the human community is asserted. By the end of the story, however, the sun is praised for 'having worked well' and is seen to possess a sense of service, invoked when he is celebrated for shining so that the people may be warm and the rice may dry. His sense of compassion and 'humanity' is appealed to when he is asked, for the sake of the children, not to completely destroy the moon after he attacks it with a knife. The sun is not given a one-dimensional, archetypal nature. Does it follow, then, that the story provides evidence of a non-dualistic ideology in which good and evil are not essentialised? The one figure in the lXam stories who seems to lack mitigating qualities and who thus might be interpreted in terms of essential evil, the all-devourer, is said to have been borrowed from African sources (Hewitt 1986: 225). Anne Solomon (1997: 5), however, links !Khwa, a lXam figure who is closely identified with the rain, with !Kaonta 'a death-giving or evil being' from the central Kalahari. Whether or not the danger posed by these figures is a function of a particular relational or temporal structure, or the result of their essentially evil nature is a question that requires further investigation. To what extent, one could also ask, is a secularised form of the Manichaeism that runs through Western thought responsible for the detection in materials such as

the |Xam narratives of dualistic categories like good and evil, raw and
cooked, nature and culture? Conversely, does the attribution of an absence
of categories of good and evil among people such as the |Xam rest on a
Utopian desire to recover a sense of unalienated wholeness?

The sun is represented as an old man who can speak and be addressed
as a person.[4] In the time of the stories, human and non-human are not
clearly differentiated. The attribution of human form or personality to
animals, gods and cosmic entities like the sun is a form of anthropomorphism, as Guenther (1999: 73, 161) points out.[5] The sun, moon and
animals mostly speak as humans do only during the time of the First
Order. In Guenther's (1999: 73) view, these 'symbolic acts of anthropo-
morphization link the wild animals of today more closely to the human-
animals of the first order; thus, echoes from the mythological past resound
through the world of animals of the present'. This is surely true, too, of the
sun, moon and stars, which continue to be present as emissaries of other
realms, including those of the narratives of the First Times. In terms of the
|Xam discursive order, cosmic entities are crucial signifiers in the
intertextual field that encompasses not only discourse and the body, but
also the wider physical world. They operate at the threshold of several |Xam
sign systems, marking the cross-pollination and interpenetration of, as well
as the difference among, these systems. Their territory is the 'passage from
one sign-system to another' (Kristeva 1986: 111; original emphasis).

Some kinds of theory offer a critique of language itself as a form of
anthropomorphism, a projection of human categories onto the always
elusive 'other'. Language is the medium through which the always deferred
human subject hails the haunting absence of the extra-human world and
takes the echo of its own address as an object, which always remains a
source of desire, since it is never attained: 'the order of the signified is never
contemporary' (Derrida 1976: 18). This narrative, in which the sun is
invested with human attributes, as well as the many others that employ this
technique, could be said to be making visible this language of desire. It is
also possible that the anthropomorphism that operates in regard to the sun
and other mixed beings of the narratives demonstrates a |Xam under-
standing of the phenomenon Buddhists term *sunatta*, or emptiness, in
which there is no independent arising and nothing exists apart from its

interrelatedness with other things and beings. The sun's separation from
the human world in the story is, paradoxically, the necessary condition for
the proper expression of this interrelatedness. But whatever the precise
anatomy of this complex in the |Xam materials, it has always to be borne in
mind that the identification of anthropomorphism in them, as well as the
delineation of a temporality in which mythological time is divided from
the present, might in the end say more about modern rationalism's performance of the erasure of certain forms of experience and signification
from its own discourses than it does about the narratives themselves.

We have seen that it is often maintained that myth shapes, reinforces or
reflects in some way the ethos of a community by referring to the possibility
of infraction and imaginatively previewing the consequences of selfishness
or disobedience. This lends myth a moral ambiguity that, it could be argued,
undermines the ethical thrust imputed to it. In the |Kaggen stories, for
example, the verve and swagger of the protagonist outweighs the moral force
of the reproofs from family members that follow his escapades. His 'bad'
motives, after all, usually have beneficial consequences. On one level, this
story of the sun sanctions the sharing ethos and condemns the withholding
of the individual's power from the communal energy grid. One suspects,
however, that the moral message is incidental — that it is less about the sun's
not sharing than about how others have to devise a strategy to acquire his
warmth. It is at least as much, then, about being successful as it is about being
'good'. The narrative, in my view, is not primarily ethical or didactic, just as
it is not chiefly aetiological. Nor is its meaning likely to be inferred from the
consideration of a combination of ethical, aetiological and other factors. The
story's nature also refuses to emerge through a process of the elimination of
possible readings, a kind of negative theology of criticism. What, then, is its
nature? How does it speak to us, its untutored listeners? It does not hide
beneath its surface: it possesses no mystery; anyone can understand it. And
yet it does not easily allow metastatements to adhere to it.

THE CHAIN OF SPEAKING

'The Children Are Sent to Throw the Sleeping Sun into the Sky' starts with
a chain of speaking. We are placed immediately within discourse and its

materiality. Barnard (1992: 83), as I have mentioned, attributes the absence of an account of an ultimate origin in Khoisan stories to a double creation framework in which a deity, like a Florentine master, leaves the details of his incomplete canvas to the apprentices to complete. The apprentices here are the old women and their boys, whose chief instrument of artifice is speaking. A chain of speaking is established in which the speakers change, but the speaking itself never ceases. This chain involves the old women telling the older children to tell the younger children not to laugh. The old women then tell the older boys what to tell the sun. The older children in turn tell the women what they have told the sun, and then the women tell (themselves? the world?) what the older children have told them, and so on.

At the point in the story when the children report back to the women, the narrative voice switches from the women to the boys, who continue to articulate their experience until the women join them in watching the first sunrise.[6] In between, the narrator himself either directly describes the action or reports on what the women or boys are saying in the third person.[7] The rapid switching of narrative voice characterises the |Xam stories in general, and this is a technique that affords obvious opportunities for commentary, dramatisation and characterisation.[8] In many of the stories, the technique of shifting narrative voice allows for multiple versions of the same event (Hewitt 1986: 54–55). This is particularly noticeable in a lengthy story, included in Lewis-Williams (2000: 52–77), concerning a death on the hunting ground. The narrative, also by ||Kabbo, is built up almost entirely of different accounts of the same event. In the story of the sun, the boys' voices are an extension of the women's voices. The presence of different narrative voices does not, in this instance, betoken a multiplicity of contending perspectives, but an aggregation of discursive power. There is a unity of forces, a balance between old and young, male and female, as the human community directs its energies towards procuring a reliable source of energy.

In the |Xam materials, the power of speaking to bring about or cancel events is continuously reiterated.[9] Representation makes things happen. Here, the chain of signification begins with an injunction to the boys to tell the young children not to laugh at the old man sleeping. In order for an even greater state of plenitude to ensue, laughter must be suspended. A completely contrary state of affairs does not prevail prior to the events related in the story: there is no formless void waiting to be filled, only an unsatisfactory situation requiring improvement. The story occurs in a setting of domestic congeniality characterised by the excessive gaiety of children. The sun himself is represented as a grumpy, selfish old man rather than as a figure who engenders fear, even in small children.

It is not only the young children who have to still their laughter; the older boys, too, are cautioned to go stealthily. What is the nature of this laughter? Is it a nervous laughter, 'a laughter that does not laugh' (Bakhtin 1968: 45)? The children do not appear to fear the old man unduly, however. Is it ribaldry? A mode of speaking or a mode of forgetting? Is it a species of hilarity peculiar to the nature of children? Does it participate in the 'undestroyable ... eternal laughter of the gods' (70)? The women make no appeal to the boys' courage and masculinity. They impress upon the boys, rather, the requirement for success of temporarily repressing their hilarity. We enter a comic modality. Why does this old man, who does not himself laugh, elicit this laughter? Is it merely a response to his isolation and anti-social nature, or does it derive from some other source?

Ironically, the old man's social alienation leads to his performance of a benign social function. His self-assumed isolation precipitates his ejection from the community, the necessary prelude to his provision of the required solar services. Ironically, too, he follows his own path by a decree of others, a victim, ultimately, of the power-speaking of women.[10] The sun's presence in the skies will be an enduring testimony to the force of the integration of the energies of old females and young males — of anima and animus, if one wishes to accede to the unfashionable inducement, but only in passing, of a Jungian interpretation. The process could also be described in terms of interpellation. The sun knows himself and his function as 'natural' when hailed by the authoritative speaking of the boys. His self-knowledge, which is coeval with his social function, is summonsed.[11] This identity has been there all along. It only has to be activated, acknowledged, the call answered again and again. The use of the imperative by the boys has less of the force of a command than a revelation. The sun should assent to their talking not because they tell him to, but because the order of things requires it.

This order of things is already known to the women. In this, the women are unlike many of the other first Bushmen in the stories, who are often ignorant of even the most basic sorts of readily acquired empirical knowledge. A man, for instance, cuts his pregnant wife's stomach open in order to gain access to a share of the meat he believes her to have eaten. The man does not know that cutting her open will kill her. Poignantly, he holds the corpse up on a stick, hoping that his wife will live again and lamenting, 'My wife! My wife! My wife!' He has to be told by the other people 'that a woman is one who always used to seem as if filled (with food) when she is pregnant' (L.VI.2:4064–68). The events in the story are foreknown to the women, but are not preordained; the order is predetermined, but not predestined. The boys must faithfully follow the steps laid out by the women if humans participating intentionally in the correct ordering of things are to succeed in their objectives. They must go stealthily, matching the old man's cunning. They must speak strongly if their use of language as an instrument of power is to be effective. The old man has to be brought within the compass of their discourse and become part of their knowledge system. In this way, a correlation between knowledge and practice is established. The man becomes subject to culture and the linguistic field, the verbal !xoe.[12] But he is also ejected from culture, the community and the !xoe. This results partly from his lack of culture (attending to his own needs only). In the process, two possibilities of venerability are contrasted: the wise women closely connected to the children and the frozen solipsism of the old man who has severed his ties with the life-giving forces that make fructifying relations possible.

As I mentioned earlier, the old man, in structuralist terms, is thrown into nature — the sky — where he again becomes part of culture when he turns the raw (the ant larvae) into the cooked (by drying the eggs). But even as a division is being instituted between nature and culture, it is being collapsed, since the process of bringing the sun into human economic activity is as much a movement of locating the natural within culture as it is of accepting the limits of culture and recognising its dependence on nature.

The boys should speak strongly to the old man so that he does not forget. Speech has the power to resist the extinction that follows forgetting — or, rather, it has the power to replace a certain type of remembering with another. The old man should forget his self-containment — his state outside memory — and begin with a recollection from which the coercive origin of his social role has been replaced by the knowledge of his identity as the sun. In this way, the agenda and values of the society become naturalised in him. Memory acquiesces in this process. It is domesticated — the condition of remembrance. The power of one sort of forgetting, which is simultaneously a remembering of another sort, will maintain the sun in his revolutions. His new knowledge must become habitual and embodied. This involves a constant retracing of the beaten path rather than a quest across new horizons. Through the old women and the boys, the sun is produced by the social world; he is removed from his state of static self-sufficiency and inducted into social categories of thought. His role in the world will now appear self-evident to him, since his self has become an artefact of the world. It is not the contents of the boys' speech alone, but the materiality of words strongly asserted, words as objects rather than signifieds, that will inscribe upon the mind of the sun the course he will subsequently tread through the sky, a path that is both physically and psychologically located. The sun's assumption of his self, which is also his role, is his path.

The sun assents to his position in the new geopolitical order the boys establish through their practice and naming. The boys, then, engage in self-panegyrics, a mode of speaking in which signifier and signified are conjoined. The women extend the praise to all the doings of the First Bushmen. This, in the mouths of the storytellers, might be read as ancestral praise. More often than not, however, the First Bushmen are figures of ridicule rather than eulogy (Hewitt 1986: 48), and their actions do not always have salubrious results. Nor are the First Bushmen the direct ancestors of the |Xam.[13]

The first part of the story concerning the sun ends with an inaugural sunrise and more speaking. The boys do not immediately see the fruits of their exertions; they have to wait until the next day: 'They sleep; the day breaks, the children first, they awake, they look at the Darkness, they say, "The Darkness does yonder go ... Darkness goes out from the daybreak's side, the Darkness goes towards the evening's side"' (L.II.35:3213–14). The awe with which the children witness the first light of dawn is dramatically expressed. The women then awake and deliver a commentary, one that affirms their foreknowledge. Here is James's (2001: 33) version of this moment in poetry:

look there and you will see the old man's rays
that come up first to give some light in that part of the sky,
and the sun will follow as he comes from behind the hill,
and he will soon become white,
and he will stand above the head of the hill.

This commentary is repeated by the children and the women, in turn, several times.

But even now, the chain of signification does not stop. The children remark on what they witness. The women verbally pre-empt the next event in the sequence. The children then validate the women's predictions with their observations as events unfold in the manner the women have foreseen they will. The children have praised their own actions. The women have praised the cleverness of the First Bushmen. Now, in the course of their witnessing, the children praise the sun and invest him with agency:

the sun is now coming to stand above the hill's head:
it seems he has really worked well since yesterday
when he started travelling along his road in the sky
... the sun has worked well
for he is white and will travel above us (James 2001: 33–34).

IDENTITY

The boys are told to throw the old man into the sky and instruct him to follow the path designated as his: 'Ye shall say to the old man, that, his path must truly be yonder' (L.II.35:3168). By the end of the story, the sun travels this path day after day. The connection between journeying and ontology occurs regularly in the Bleek and Lloyd materials. Being and movement are inseparable. Death is seen as the erasure of a person's footprints by the wind and rain that attend her death, the effacement of the inscription of her movement.[14] The sun's path and his journeys along it are not merely metaphors: a path is matter made social. The enactment of the self involves 'going along in one's way'. The sun cannot be the sun while he remains still. Identity requires fluidity, movement, action, praxis, discourse. It is not a static state of being, but a mode of acting in the world.

228

The force with which the children imprint upon the old man's mind the path he is to follow mobilises another critical aspect of identity, one I have already invoked — memory. Memory and identity are closely linked. The ego discovers itself, who it really is, through the activation of 'correct' memory. The self can now proceed along its path. The social participates in the individual: it is the necessary factor in the potentiation of individuality. But the individual also participates in the social: the properties of the individual illuminate the world of the social, facilitating its activities. The individual, thus, forms part of a social ecology that embraces nature and culture.

The sun is in the sky so that the rice may be dried and the women may be warm when they set about gathering food. This social and economic ecology is embedded in discursive practice. It is also installed in the sun's memory in the form of a knowledge of the path he is to follow. The social, economic and ecological purchase of identity is proclaimed: 'O children going yonder! ye must speak to him, when ye throw him up ... ye must tell him, that, he must altogether become the Sun, that he may go forward, while he feels that he is altogether the Sun, which is hot; therefore, the Bushman rice becomes dry' (Bleek & Lloyd 1911: 47). More than an inscription of the women's will upon the sun's memory occurs, however. The activation of the circuits that the sun must describe each day also goes beyond learned behaviour. Particular values, norms and codes become such an integral part of individual being that their practice is unthinking and embodied. They become part of the individual's structure of feeling and constitute his/her body. Bourdieu's notion of 'habitus' comes to mind.[15] The sun's new behaviour will be embedded in his new body. He possesses a man's body before the boys throw him up. Once he is in the sky, he loses this body; he becomes round and shines.

This is, of course, to read the story from a position in which identity is understood as the confluence of the social and self-consciousness — the mechanism whereby the social order (and its truth regime) is naturalised within the site of the individual. The story of the sun does concern one unique individual: there is only one sun. In most of the stories of the First Order, however, identity is located, rather, in individuals who typify groups (the different species) and is represented either as a process of becoming or as a sudden initiation through crisis into an individuation that embraces the species and goes beyond the individual — part of the emergence of the natural order of things from the creative disjunctions of the First Order.

The story can be enlisted as an illustration of the social manufacture and incorporation of self-identity. A particular conception of self is asserted in relation to a group identity. The manner in which the sun is practised upon by speech (the process of his textualisation), the meeting of power and knowledge in discourse, the naturalisation of learned behaviour, the acknowledgement of the instrumentality of identity, and the recognition of its economic utility (the sun in the sky can dry the rice and enable the women to gather plant foods) all point to the constructed nature of identity. But it is equally possible to discover in the story support for a different notion of identity, one in which identity becomes something waiting to be uncovered. Although there is indeed a false identity that results from conditioning, there is somewhere a true identity that is not a construct or the result of a positioning within discourse. The discovery of this authentic self becomes a matter of stripping away or of a sudden conversion, such as occurs when the sun is tossed into sky.

TWO MYTHS OF ORIGIN

Jacques Derrida, as we have seen, contends that Western thought is based on a myth of origin that involves a fall away from presence. Although I have argued that the |Xam narratives are far from simple aetiology, I shall presuppose, for purposes of discussion and comparison in this section, that both traditions (Western and |Xam) are grounded in myths of origin, and shall take the story of Genesis as the representative Western myth of origin. One evident starting point for comparison is the contrast between the depiction of woman as responsible for the fall in Genesis and the depiction of women as the source of creative activity in the story of the sleeping sun. Women, in the |Xam materials, appear unquestioningly to accept that their economic role consists of collecting plant food. There is no suggestion anywhere that women feel that there is an unequal division of labour in a |Xam band. They will not, however, accept a man's not fulfilling his role as hunter. A man who does not provide meat is scorned. Similarly, the sun's failure to provide light and warmth is unacceptable. A strong picture of female agency and initiative is presented in the story; unlike Eve's agency, which results in the expulsion of humankind from paradise, theirs has beneficial consequences.

In the |Xam narrative, there is a congruence between discourse and event and a correspondence between power and knowledge. The sun is inserted into discourse, an insertion that is conditional on the women's foreknowledge of the sun's path. The result is a particular relationship of power between people and the sun. It is not a question, however, of a pyramid of hierarchically structured relationships so much as a creative tension of forces. People eject the sun into the sky, but subsequently ask it for 'warmth and light' (Hewitt 1986: 92). In the period of becoming, people enjoy some influence with natural forces. Through their relationship with spirits who control the rain and the movement of game, for example, they continue to do so in the world of everyday living (Solomon 1997: 7). But people are also subject to power exerted the other way. The moon introduces death; spirits of illness harm people; the biblical myth of origin establishes humankind's dominion over nature. In the |Xam narratives, we seem to be in the presence of another sort of complex altogether, one that includes interdependent and ecological features and one in which power flows in different directions simultaneously.

Identity in the stories usually concerns categories, but the sun, moon and certain stars are unusual in that their categories consist of only one member. It is in the interests of the overall order of things that each category should discover its identity and incorporate all its members. Each species, for example, should behave in accordance with its latent identity. One could, then, ask the theological question of the |Xam narratives that is asked of Genesis about determinism and free will. Here, however, one would not be interrogating the story in order to problematise the origin of evil, but to explore the strange dynamics of a space of becoming. In this space, identity appears to be fluid and plastic, with species cross-dressing and coexisting in a problematic, but common humanity/animality. Simultaneously, however, it is subject to a design that will inevitably be realised. Genesis concerns a fall away from perfection, while the |Xam story represents a movement towards the way things ought to be (even if this state is imperfect), an unfolding revelation in the comic rather than the portentous mode of the first myth. One mythical complex results in a teleology and the other does not. The |Xam stories, instead, celebrate a process of becoming that is open-ended. In the story of the sun, it is in the interests of the general community that the sun follows his path in the skies. The women help to precipitate this event. There is a sense of creation unfurling through the medium of a tapestry of agents rather than through the brute commands of a dictatorial creator. The biblical story, by contrast, is centred on a single transcendental agent; it continually plays itself out in history and turns on an experience of lack and desire.

At the beginning of the narrative, the women describe how 'the sun lies (in his own sun)'.[16] The sun sleeps in himself, complete — an unsatisfactory situation. Here again the Western and |Xam mythical structures diverge. In the Gnostic tradition, the loss of unity results in the descent into matter and the confusion of dualism, while in Genesis the creation leads directly to division and the introduction of good and evil. But in the |Xam story, the movement towards emanation is encouraged and the condition of unity condemned. Narcissistic, self-contained withdrawal is rejected. Attributes should not remain locked within ideal substance, but should reach out and nourish life. Only when the sun's rays radiate into the world can the women leave the space that is circumscribed by the reach of the fire's warmth and go out and collect food, the life-giving principle that in turn generates fresh life.

THE SUN AND THE MOON

Soon after the sun has been thrown into the sky, he discovers that he is not alone in his circuits. Already jealous of his unsolicited position, the sight of the moon on the opposite horizon, red and round, enrages him. He attacks the moon:

> He resembles fire which blazes (burns) up, as he comes out, he does resemble which burns up a great tree, as he comes from behind the mountain top, he red above standing comes. Therefore the sun is angry with him. Therefore the sun says that the sun soon shall pierce/break him with the sun's assegai/spear (B.IV:559–61).

Whenever the sun and moon are both in the sky, the moon is red and full. The moon most resembles the sun at this time, which the sun considers a provocation. The sun is also angered by the moon's ability to resurrect itself: 'I was angry with him because he living did come again. Therefore, I piercing broke him, when he did not know, that I should piercing break him. Therefore, he was startled, as his body stood streaming with blood' (B.IV:569–70).

'All societies', Zygmunt Bauman (1997: 17) asserts, 'produce strangers; but each kind of society produces its own kind of strangers, and produces them in its own inimitable way'. The sun is made strange when he is ejected into the sky from the band of the familiar.[17] This movement, however, is simultaneously — and paradoxically — a movement towards domesticity and socialisation, since it is the mechanism whereby the sun's labour becomes part of culture. As we have seen, his solipsistic state of self-completion is forcibly rendered social. Yet in his first voluntary act in his new position, he asserts his isolation. The sun discovers another man, like himself, red and bright (it would take more science than he possesses to realise that these lunar attributes are his own reflection) on the opposite horizon, in his new domain and directly in his path. He could perhaps embrace his double as himself. But the double, by its proximity and its bearing of a likeness that threatens to nullify the markers of identity, elicits his rage.[18] Complete in himself, the old man cannot embrace an equal. The similar must be attacked, almost destroyed, and then only allowed continued existence if it signifies in a key of otherness, as a stranger. Difference here oscillates between the poles of the same and the other. Although the sun allows the moon to live in a reduced form, he is incensed that even 'the putrid can emit light'. His alternation between anger and mercy is continually replayed: the inevitable cycle provoked by the stranger who is the same but other, or other but the same.

In the process of making strange, of differentiation, the sun and moon are relegated to their own spheres: the sun to the day and the moon to the night.[19] At the same time, their difference can only be invoked through bringing them together, forcing them into the tension of the proximate and the similar. In the First Times, all beings, including the sun and moon, are people who become separated into various categories in the course of the stories. This history, in the case of the sun and moon, extends to the present.[20] These cosmic bodies can be addressed now in the language of people, although they can no longer reply in this language.[21] They remain partly things of the First Times, carried over into the present, because they are not subject to mortality (although the moon is and is not).

The sun is always alone. In the days of his association with the band, he keeps to himself. Now, he will not countenance company in the sky and behaves like a lone male animal, jealous of its territory. The moon, on the other hand, is figured as a family person. The moon's role in the naratives is ambiguous, however, as it both gives and takes away. The moon brings light and betokens regeneration, but, as we saw in the previous chapter, is also responsible, in some sense, for the presence of death. This ambiguity is replicated in its ambiguous gender identity in ||Kabbo's version of the story. In this narrative, which he told to Lloyd, the moon changes gender at different points in its cycle. The full moon is female:

> [T]he moon mounts the sky yes, for the moon is the great moon, the moon with her stomach .... [T]he day breaks, while the moon stands there (in the west), the sun he comes out, while the moon stands, the sun pierces her, with the sun's knife (L.II.1.285–87).

The moon ('she is a moon which talks') asks the sun to spare her life for the sake of her children. At this point in the story, the moon, greatly diminished by the attacks of the sun, begins to be referred to as a male. He asks the sun to allow his (the moon's) children to see him again. The sun relents and puts his knife back in his bag. The state of fullness, repletion and being fat is associated with femaleness. The moon becomes a man (here, less than a woman) when it is reduced by the sun's attacks to an exiguous crescent. In another version of this first encounter between the sun and the moon recounted by ||Kabbo, the wounded moon is described returning home: 'his wife said to her children, "Father does slowly come, the sun did cut him, therefore he there slowly comes"' (B. IV.534). The changes wrought by the violence of the sun are immediately reproduced in the moon's family. The moon changes from mother to husband and father, and is simultaneously supplied with a wife.

Although the sun, too, is imbued with the power of speaking and first-person consciousness, the moon's ability to speak is especially emphasised by the narrator, for the moon was created from |Kaggen's shoe, and the things of |Kaggen speak (Hewitt 1986: 239).[22] The moon uses this facility to plead with the sun to spare its backbone, for the sake of the children. In the story of the moon and the hare ('The Origin of Death'), the moon decreed that there shall be death in the world in order to punish a baby hare who will not believe the moon's assurances that the hare's mother will awaken. In the story under consideration here, the moon is only rescued from his own institution — death — by the sun's tempering his aggression and acceding to the moon's request to leave him his backbone: 'Therefore, the Sun says that the Sun will leave the backbone for the children ....
Therefore, he becomes a new moon'(Bleek & Lloyd 1911: 51–53). The sun's mercy is only temporary; his aggressive territoriality is endlessly reiterated. On the moon's return, '[t]he sun shall perceive him, this night, for he did come in the dark. The sun shall perceive him, as he stands there'. Once again, the round moon is attacked and survives only as a rotten remnant of meat clinging to its own backbone. The new moon is a wounded man with an empty net, a rotten thing.[23] In this form, the moon is an unlikely figure of hope or new life, as a more familiar juxtaposition of discursive objects might lead one to expect. With the sun's permission and for the sake of the children, however, the moon still emits light, the sign that it will return to full life. Bleek's translation conveys this message with a biblical resonance, although the actual words undermine the biblical deity's claim to a monopoly of power and glory: 'the putrid shall make light' (B.IV:518).

The vestige of light that the sun out of consideration for the children allows the moon to retain enables the moon to grow to full size again. In another text, the moon's capacity to regenerate is directly linked to the dead:

> [T]he cavity in any new moon which had the appearance of horns was the 'catching place' for people who had recently died. As the moon grew full by this means, the corpses inside were revived by the 'moon water.' When no more room was left, the people were tipped out onto the earth and lived again until they died again when the whole process was repeated (Hewitt 1986: 42).

The belief in reincarnation evinced here is not repeated in other accounts of death in the notebooks. In this extract, the moon resurrects people, but in several versions of the story of the moon and the hare he is responsible for their deaths. There is only a contradiction, however, if the materials are seen as transparent windows onto a unified ǀXam belief system rather than as multivocal discourse.

CONCLUSION

As I noted in the last chapter, Bauman (1997: 165–85) claims that identity is a new phenomenon, a response to postmodern humankind's unprecedented loss of socially sanctioned certainty. Individuals are now condemned to find/make their own way in the world. One of the consequences of this is that people no longer have time for the 'fundamental' questions that, Bauman maintains, religions once produced in order to monopolise the answers that people then required. Once again, let us ask the question: 'Did the ǀXam have time for these big questions?' This story of the sun and the moon is generally interpreted as an explanation of the big question about why the moon waxes and wanes, just as the story of the moon and the hare is generally understood as an answer to the even bigger question about the origin of death (Guenther 1999: 144). The presence of different and often contradictory versions of the same story, as well as conflicting explanations of natural events, already suggests, however, that the narratives are not simply explanations of puzzling phenomena or primarily answers to the big questions. But let us accept for the moment that this story provides an explanation of how the moon's cycles originated. The question still arises of what is to be made of the particular anatomy of this particular aetiological explanation. Why does this explanation assume this form and consist of precisely these details? What is the significance of the display of violence from a protagonist whose presence is so necessary to the perpetuation and pursuit of life? Bank (2006: 163) observes that the 'language, often visceral and violent, as in so many of ǁKabbo's stories, is of hunter and prey'. What is the link between power and origin? Would it not be more productive to think of the solar and lunar narratives in terms of power rather than of origin? The boys throw the sun into the sky (exerting a form of power over him), the sun wounds the moon (asserting his power over him|/her), the moon institutes death (displaying power over the living), and so on. Power is circular, diffuse.

In the story of the sleeping sun, meaning results from the relationships between the different elements that occur within it, including relationships between thinness and maleness, fullness and femininity, moon and death/immortality. But the story is only one instance of the ordering of these elements, which assume their signifying power not within the compass of a single narrative, but in relation to a far wider web of elements, the archive of possible statements available to |Xam narrative at a particular time in history.

I have argued here for a criticism that emphasises both the capacity of the |Xam texts to generate multiple meanings and the multivocality that the narratives would have contained for |Xam participants themselves. The precise composition of the structure of meaning and feeling generated for psychologically and historically situated |Xam auditors by such narratives, however, will ultimately always elude a contemporary reader. But even for a |Xam auditor, a story's meaning would never have been fixed and transparent. Rather, its telling would have provided an opportunity for the experience and processing of a variety of ideas and feelings (Scheub 1998: 22). The story would also always have been an invitation to exegesis that could not be turned down. The next chapter continues this discussion. It also discusses a sidereal narrative that has obvious aetiological import. Its chief argument is that the narrative's multivocality is related to its web of intertextuality.

NOTES

1 The old man is generally referred to in the story as the sun. This seems to be an accurate rendition of the logic of the story here. Generally, the logic of the stories is often strange and unfamiliar.

2 'Bushman rice' refers to the ant larvae that formed an important component of the |Xam diet.

3 See also Guenther (1989: 31).

4 As I noted in chapter 3, the Bleek and Lloyd notebooks contain valuable insider commentary on the stories, often on the reverse sides of the pages of the notebooks. ||Kabbo delivers such a commentary on this story: 'the Sun was a man; but, *not* one of the early

race of people who preceded the Flat Bushmen in their country. He only gave forth brightness for a space around his own dwelling. Before the children threw him up, he had not been in the sky, but, had lived at his own house, on Earth. As his shining had been confined to a certain space at, and round his own dwelling, the rest of the country seemed as if the sky were very cloudy; as it looks now, when the Sun is behind thick clouds. The sky was black (dark?). The shining came from one of the Sun's armpits, as he lay with one arm lifted up. When he put down his arm, darkness fell everywhere; when he lifted it up again, it was as if day came. In the day, the Sun's light used to be white; but, at night, it was red, like a fire. When the Sun was thrown up into the sky it became round, and never was a man afterwards' (Bleek & Lloyd 1911: 54–55).

5 Moran (2009: 38–42, 44–47) shows how anthropomorphism, like mythology, was an important category in Wilhelm Bleek's ethnocentric theory of developmentalism. 'Anthropomorphism, the projection of subjective properties onto nature, presumes the perception of the equivalence that makes dissimilar things comparable' (40). This representing capacity of the 'reproductive imagination' is an essential component of 'the progress of self-consciousness', the journey to 'rational objectification' (40–41). It has, however, to be overcome and subjugated if civilisation's goals are to be attained.

6 'The children returned. Then, the children came (and) said: "(Our) companion who is here, he took hold of him, I also was taking hold of him; my younger brother was taking hold of him, my other younger brother was also taking hold of him; (our) companion who is here, his other younger brother was also taking hold of him." I said: "Ye must grasp him firmly." I, in this manner, spoke; I said: "Throw ye him up!" Then, the children threw him up. I said to the children: "Grasp ye the old man firmly!" I said to the children: "Throw ye up the old man!" Then, the children threw up the old man; that old man, the Sun; while they felt that the old woman was the one who spoke' (Bleek & Lloyd 1911: 49).

7 The narrator presents the action directly: 'They arose, going on, they stealthily approached him, they stood still, they looked at him, they went forward; they stealthily reached him, they took hold of him, they all took hold of him together, lifted him up, they raised him, while he felt hot' (Bleek & Lloyd 1911: 49). The narrator also presents the action through reported speech: 'The other old woman said to the other, that, the other one's children should approach gently to lift up the Sun-armpit, that they should throw up the Sun-armpit, that the Bushman rice might become dry for them, that the Sun might make bright the whole place' (45). The action is sometimes presented directly through the speaking of the women; usually this takes the form of their addressing the boys: '"Ye must go to sit down, when ye have looked at him, (to see) whether he lies looking; ye must go to sit down, while ye wait for him"' (47). Finally, the action is presented through the voices of the boys: 'They came to speak, the youth spoke, the youth talked to his grandmother: "O my grandmother! we threw him up, we told him, that, he should altogether become the Sun, which is hot; for, we are cold. We said: 'O my grandfather, Sun-armpit! Remain (at that) place; become thou the Sun which is hot ...' (51). To this chain of speaking could be added ||Kabbo's commentary on the story (45, 54–57).

8 It was but one of the rhetorical devices that storytellers had at hand. Others included accents and registers and a wide repertoire of expression and gesture. Storytellers

employed a specialised vocabulary for different animal characters, as well as specialised forms of enunciation based on the shape of the animal's mouth (Hewitt 1986:
51–53).

9   James (2001: 149) writes: 'The people of the early race were, it is suggested, able to
intervene to re-order their world partly because they were in command of a powerful "First Bushman's language" (LII.35:3197). This could be used like a potent, perhaps
magical, formula to bring about a desired result: so that "the thing should assent to
their talking (discourse)", ||Kabbo explained: the word as creative word'.

10 That is, women's ability to effect transformations by speaking.

11 'I shall then suggest that ideology "acts" or "functions" in such a way that it "recruits"
subjects among the individuals (it recruits them all), or "transforms" the individuals
into subjects (it transforms them all) by that very precise operation which I have
called *interpellation* or hailing' (Althusser 1971: 163).

12 The *!xoe* constitutes the territory of a |Xam band (Hewitt 1986: 27).

13 When the first Bushmen had passed away, the Flat Bushmen inhabited their ground.
Therefore, the Flat Bushmen taught their children about the stories of the First
Bushmen' (Bleek & Lloyd 1911: 57). According to |Han#kass'o, the |Xam are descen-
dants of springbok: 'We who are Bushmen, were once springbucks, and the Mantis
shot us, and we really cried (like a little child). Then the Mantis said, we should
become a person, become people, because we really cried' (L.VIII.4:6365'). Such a
momentous event, from an anthropocentric perspective at any rate, is recorded in the
Bleek and Lloyd Collection only as a brief explanatory aside in a long story about ele-
phants stealing a child.

14 See L.V.15:5147 and L.VIII.28:8465.

15 For Bourdieu, social practices and structures do not exist, other than as intellectual
abstractions, unless they are 'embodied, absorbed into the sense making apparatus of
the individual in order to constitute the practical reason of the habitus' (Webb,
Schirato & Danaher 2002: 116).

16 '[F]or we always are warming ourselves here, while we do not go seeking food; that
we might eat; while we do frightened sit, on account of the cold, while the sun is the
one who afar lies in the sun (his own sun)' (L.II.35:3170).

17 He was already a stranger in the band, not a First Bushman like the others, according to
||Kabbo's note to the story (Bleek & Lloyd 1911: 54). He thus becomes doubly a
stranger.

18 In a similar way, baboons, as we saw in chapter 6, have to be marked off from humans
because of their resemblance to them. They are shown to make the most undesirable
in-laws in the narratives (Hewitt 1986: 109–10).

19 The moon's origin is as a thing in the dark, something that lights the dark, as when
the Mantis's shoe is thrown up to become the moon and light the darkness caused by
the burst gall bladder of the baby eland; see D. Bleek (1923: 4).

20 In a sense, this is true of all the beings of the First Times. After they died, they continued to live in the spirit world and interact with this world. The sun and moon,
however, have never died and gone away. In this sense, they are supernatural.

21 According to ||Kabbo, the sun and moon can no longer speak as they could in the First
Times: 'The Sun had been a man, he talked; they all talked, also the other one, the

Moon. Therefore, they used to live upon the earth; while they felt that they spoke. They do not talk, now that they live in the sky' (Bleek & Lloyd 1911: 57).

22 |A!kungta elaborates on the moon's speech in a discourse delivered to Bleek. He explains why the moon speaks like a shoe: 'He is the Mantis's foot's shoe, and he feels that it was the Mantis who called his name, he will act like a shoe' (Hollmann 2004: 368).

23 Elsewhere, the full moon is described as looking like a man carrying food in a net. This is a good moon (L.V.16:5206–57).

CHAPTER 10

THE STORY OF 'THE GIRL OF THE EARLY RACE WHO MADE STARS':

The Discursive Character of the |Xam Texts

INTRODUCTION

This chapter, like the last, consists of a reading of a single narrative from the notebooks. The story, which also concerns a primal creation event, is called 'The Girl of the Early Race Who Made Stars'.[1] My aim once again is not to provide a definitive interpretation of the story, but to demonstrate instead something of the ability of the |Xam texts to generate meaning as soon as attention is given to their details. Two major versions of the narrative occur in the collection. Together they offer, in my view, a significantly wider range of meanings than a single version would. This is not because they augment one another, however, as was the case with the versions of the narrative about the sun and the boys that I explored in the last chapter. Rather, like the versions of the moon and hare story that I discussed in chapter 8, their differences elicit questions and excite exegesis. In |Han#kass'o's version, the girl's actions follow directly from anger at her mother and, by extension, the social order (L.VIII.10:6879–84). As Belinda Jeursen (1995: 40–54) has emphasised, it is the ritual restrictions on her movements and diet at the time of menarche, enforced by her mother and other closely related older women, that elicit the girl's ire and leads her to throw ashes and roots into the sky.[2] In ||Kabbo's longer version (L.II.28:2505–24; Bleek & Lloyd 1911: 72–79), the girl's actions are driven not only by anger, but by a calculated intent that contains benevolent elements.

The existence of different versions of the story stimulates the same sort of questions that I explored in chapter 8. Even if it is accepted that individual stories and their variants illustrate deep |Xam, Khoisan or universal structures, the question remains as to why the differences between stories and versions take particular forms. Is this variety indicative only of unconscious and hopeless struggles against the rigid determinism of the structure? Or is it chiefly a question of the preferences of different narrators, as Hewitt (1986: 235–46) implies? It is probably no coincidence that the complementary versions of the story in the last chapter were both related by ‖Kabbo, while the divergent accounts of ‘The Origin of Death’ that were discussed in chapter 8 were supplied by different narrators. Could the differences rather be seen as celebrating the radical plurality of experience, life and the world? Is it possible that the structure is as subservient to the surface elements as are the keys of a piano to the sonata played upon them? Do these elements themselves locate the sites where new meanings are generated and realms of signification opened?

Texts such as these, as I have noted frequently in this book, have elicited both structuralist and functionalist treatment. Both approaches have downplayed difference. All the menarcheal stories, from a functionalist perspective, become cautionary tales designed to inculcate the puberty rites: ‘there is no doubt’, writes Hewitt (1986: 76), ‘that these narratives functioned primarily to support the [menarcheal] practices outlined above.’ In the discussion that follows, I aim to show that ‘The Girl of the Early Race Who Made Stars’ is more productive of multiple interpretation than this statement might suggest.

THE EARTHLY ORIGIN OF THE STARS

In both versions of the story, the girl creates the Milky Way by throwing the ashes of !huin roots into the sky. Red and white stars form from the different coloured !huin roots that she also throws into the sky. It is instructive to submit briefly to the impulse to detect general patterns and enumerate the things of heaven that have their origins here on earth in the various narratives: the moon (a shoe, a dust-impregnated thing of animal skin), the sun (an old man asleep on the ground in a hut of branches), the

Milky Way (the ashes of burnt roots) and the stars (roots, things sunk in the earth). In each case, something is thrown into the sky: the sun by boys, the shoe that will become the moon by ǀKaggen, and, in this story, the ashes thrown by the girl of the Early Race that become the stars. In each case, the agents act with deliberate and calculated intent. The least premeditated of these acts is ǀKaggen's throwing of his shoe into the sky. Even this act, a spur-of-the-moment solution to a particular predicament, has intended and foreknown results.[3] In each case, the presence of light is the sought-after and realised consequence of the act. In each case, the radiant properties of an object or person that remain latent on earth are released by the elevation of that object or person into the sky.

Elevation does not in itself produce light. The agent of transformation has to instruct the cosmic body as to its role and direct it to the path that it must follow in perpetuity. A new discourse must be put into circulation. The girl in this story addresses the Milky Way, which appears from the ashes she has cast into the sky: 'The Milky Way must go round with the stars; because the Milky Way feels that the Milky Way lies turning round; while the stars sailing go' (L.II.28:2506–7).

The source is the earth: the stars originate in things sunk into the earth. They first enter into discourse through the actions and speech of a menstruating girl in a hut who lifts herself up off the earth floor on which she is lying in order to throw the ashes of roots into the sky. The girl's feet are planted firmly on a small piece of earth, from which she may not move for the duration of the period of her menarcheal confinement. The sky exists in relation to the earth; its luminaries are intended to illuminate the earth.

In the book of Genesis, creation occurs outside the earth, somewhere else. This has contributed, as Derrida emphasises, to the existence of an intellectual complex that is predicated on an origin that is always absent. The inescapable distance from the origin elicits a longing for absolute presence that can never be satisfied. In the ǀXam account of the making of the Milky Way, roots — things of the earth that draw their potency from its mineral embrace[4] — become, through the medium of a menstruating girl, celestial lights. This betokens a very different ideological complex to the one Derrida describes in Western intellectual practice, in which a whole history of the isolation and privileging of a particular type of reason are linked to a structure in which matter originates in spirit and represents a fall or separation from it (this separation is sometimes intended, as in God's acts of creation, and sometimes unintended, as a consequence of angelic or human disobedience, for instance). Could another, altogether different, way of experiencing and knowing be expected to follow from the earth-to-heaven movement discernible in these |Xam stories? The answer, no doubt, is 'yes'. The exact anatomy of this structure of reason, imagination and feeling, however, remains elusive to interpreters who are schooled in a very different tradition of thought.

It has been claimed that the idea of an extraterrestrial creative source is a universal one that originates in what was once a ubiquitous human tendency to venerate the stars, moon and sun.[5] Without wishing to offer the |Xam and their stories as primal evidence to the contrary — i.e. without wishing to situate the |Xam as representative of the earliest stratum of humankind (among whom veneration of celestial bodies might have been universal; but we will never know) — the absence of this sort of veneration from the |Xam stories and practice should at least caution one against this kind of universal claim.

'THE GIRL OF THE EARLY RACE WHO MADE STARS'

'[T]he girl arose, she put her hands into the wood ashes; she threw up the wood ashes into the sky; she said to the wood ashes: "The wood ashes which are here, they shall altogether become the Milky Way"' (L.II.28:2505). She then gives detailed and precise instructions as to how the Milky Way, the stars and sun should arrange themselves relative to each other, spatially and temporally:

> They [the wood ashes] must white lie along the sky, that the stars may stand outside the Milky Way. … The Milky Way must go round with the stars … the stars are those which go along. While they feel that they sail … they did sailing along, follow their footprints. They become white, when the Sun comes out. The Sun sets, they stand around above; while they feel that they did turn following the Sun (L.II.28:2506; L.II.28:2512–13).

This order is linked to the needs of people by the girl's intention and to the Milky Way's affective knowledge of this intention:

> The Milky Way gently glows; while it feels that it is wood ashes. Therefore, it gently glows. While it feels that the girl was the one who said that the Milky Way must glow for the people; that the people might return home by night, in the middle of the night. For, the earth would not have glowed had the Milky Way not been there. That and the stars (L.II.28:2515–16).

All the girl's actions are presented as considered: 'The girl thought, that, she would throw up above the roots of the *!huin*, so that the *!huin* roots might become stars' (L.II.28:2516). The creation of the Milky Way is the necessary prelude to the creation of the stars: 'She first laying along threw the wood ashes, into the sky; that she might afterwards throw up the *!huin* roots' (L.II.28:2517). The results of this second action can be seen at night: 'The darkness comes out; they become red, while they were at first white. They feel that they stand visible around' (L.II.28:2513–14).

With her act of defiant creation, the girl overcomes the limitations of her confinement and of the materials available to her, i.e. the roots she was given to eat during the period of her first menstruation. This root, ‖Kabbo explains, is a fragrant one eaten by Bushmen. The girl makes the red stars from the old *!huin* and the white ones from the young roots. She does not stop at star-making, he adds in a note, but also makes locusts, a prized but infrequent source of nutrition, from another edible root that she is given to eat (L.II.28:2516').

In the space of a single sentence, in the midst of ‖Kabbo's narrative, an abrupt shift occurs. The girl throws the ashes into the sky 'while she felt that she was angry with her mother, because her mother gave her not many *!huin* roots; so that she might eat abundantly; for, she was in the hut' (L.II.28:2517–18). The girl's anger is foregrounded in |Han#kass'o's version. In a fit of petulance, she throws the ashes and roots into the sky and, in what reads as an unintended consequence, they become the Milky Way and stars (L.VIII.10:6879–84).

‖Kabbo's version reads as at least two main narratives: one of celestial aetiology and the other of menarcheal taboos. But there are other narrative possibilities present in the story as well. Far from being a closed text, the story is a textual site where diverse discursive, symbolic and ideological strands converge to form a narrative. In the course of the story, an unravelling already commences. The language is restless; it wants to move along and form other narratives. This might be why the narratives, in the form in which they appear in the Bleek and Lloyd Collection, often only possess artificial endings, products of the process of their recording rather than of an internal narrative dynamic.

Some of the story's elements accord with its usual designation as a story of origin.[6] The stars originated as roots thrown into the air by a menstruating girl of the Early Race. If the story does explain how the stars originated, however, it has to be recognised that there are multiple, sometimes contradictory, accounts in the Bleek and Lloyd materials of how the stars were formed. Specific stars have particular origins. Some stars are 'said to have been animals; there are Elands, Hartebeests, Steenboks, and Tortoises' (D. Bleek 1929: 304). The two lions, Bel and Mat, for instance, become the pointers of the Southern Cross (D. Bleek 1929: 304; Hewitt 1986: 107). A group of people who are sitting eating a rock rabbit are turned into the constellation Corona Australis when a menstruating girl looks at them (L.II.37:3333–43). Certain stars were once young men who were trans-formed into stars after being seen by a menarcheal girl (Hewitt 1986: 79). In some stories, a menarcheal girl's disobedience leads to 'whole families becoming groups of stars' (Hewitt 1986: 58–59). The precise mechanics of this transformation of person into star and the power that is at work remain unstated. The ontological status of the wrath provoked is not established. Nor is it explained why this wrath should take the form of turning people into stars, although it is probable that death and the spirits of the dead are part of the connection. A star, after all, is said to fall at the time of a person's death (James 2001: 245). It is also said that '[w]hen a sorcerer dies, his heart comes out in the sky and becomes a star' (Hollmann 2004: 240).

Some of the stars actually feature as characters in the narratives. The Dawn's Heart Star lives in a curious community of people, hyenas, cranes and crows. Another star, |Gauna, named the stars, thereby bringing them within the circuits of signification (James 2001: 156). This diverse stellar narrative context, with all its ambiguities, should once more alert us to the fact that the stories do not work as simple aetiological explanations. Hewitt contradicts his own statement that narratives dealing with the stars are, 'with few exceptions, entirely aetiological constructions' (Hewitt 1986: 93) when he contends that the stories connected to menstruating girls and stars exist primarily to emphasise the message that 'menstruating girls are an extreme source of danger to society and need to behave in strict accordance with the rules laid down for their behaviour if disaster is to be averted' (Hewitt 1986: 93). According to the logic of his statements, the star stories are at the very least both aetiological and cautionary tales. But I would argue that the star stories are more implicated with the business of generating multiple layers of meaning through the way they order discursive elements than they are with explaining origins or with underlining social norms.

The girl makes the stars by throwing roots into the sky. Her motives, in ||Kabbo's version, seem to be humane: she wishes to provide light for people at night, specifically for the young men out hunting. At first reading (but not, I suspect, at first hearing for a nineteenth-century |Xam auditor), the anger she displays towards her mother and the other women appears as an adjunct to this central narrative.[7] Closer consideration, however, suggests that the anger might be a critical component of the narrative. Interestingly, Jeursen (1995: 41) attributes this anger not to tension between individuals, but to 'opposition in a ritual context ... between an individual and gender-biased traditions'. This reading, it should be noted, is unlikely to be acceptable to those commentators who emphasise the high levels of gender equality that characterise Bushman bands.

Whatever its source, the precise character of the girl's anger remains elusive. She does not throw up the few roots that remain for her to eat in a fit of thoughtless pique. If there is a causal link that the critical mind can scavenge in the story, it is that the girl's anger with her mother leads her, through some mysterious process not elucidated in the narrative, to consider the problems people experience in finding their way at night and to calmly discover and execute a plan that provides a solution to that problem. She throws the ashes 'gently' (L.II.28:2518). One possible explanation, but not one the story wishes to offer directly, is that her lighting up the night defiantly links her with the social group from whom she is ritually most excluded: the young men. It is their nocturnal hunting excursions that especially require this light. Another is that she contests her state of deprivation and immobilisation by an act that leads to conditions conducive to abundance and movement. She counteracts the circum-scribed interior space to which she is reduced with a sky full of stars and the sweep of the Milky Way. Whatever its precise motivation, and however beneficial its results, it is the rebellious nature of her act that in all likelihood leads to the narrator's criticism of her. Lloyd notes that the girl is said 'to have acted ill' (L.II.23:2505').

The logic of the linkage between the two elements of the narrative appears elusive and strange, but this is so only because the ordering of the elements in the story is unfamiliar. All accounts link the girl's confinement with the appearance of the stars. The Bleek and Lloyd Collection contains a great deal of material pertaining to menarcheal confinement, the chief ritual feature of a society not overburdened with formal ritual. The violation of the seclusion rules by a menarcheal girl is always represented as being attended by the gravest consequences. Menstruating girls should, in any event, be avoided by young men. Hewitt surmises that the danger they represented was connected to the liminal nature of physical emissions. He quotes Mary Douglas: 'We should expect orifices of the body to symbolise its specially vulnerable points. Matter issuing from them is marginal stuff of the most obvious kind' (Hewitt 1986: 190–91, quoting Douglas 1966: 145). A menarcheal girl not only inhabits the liminal space that menstruation represents, but also the margin between girlhood and womanhood. The danger she embodies is, thus, especially potent.

In several stories, the wrath of !Khwa, the rain 'god', is provoked by a girl's violation of the seclusion rules. !Khwa, as we have seen, is particularly associated with the destructive power of male rain and with death (Solomon 1997: 5). !Khwa is death personified in many ways. The consequences of inviting his anger are always extremely serious. Everyone in the band might be turned into frogs or killed by lightning, for example. But !Khwa's rage is complicated by, or perhaps explained by, the sexual passion that the smell of a menstruating girl or woman arouses in him. He is also drawn by the smell of blood. Between menarche and marriage, unmarried girls should avoid the rain even when they are not menstruating (Hewitt 1986: 282).

In one story, the rain smells a woman in her hut and comes to her as mist. She experiences the sweetness of his fragrance. He abducts her, carrying her off on his back. She manages to escape when the rain falls asleep after she rubs his forehead with the aromatic herb *buchu*. She has also to disguise her own scent with *buchu* so that the rain cannot find her again (L.VIII.16:7434–48). The narrator, |Han#kass'o, adds in a note that the young woman's 'understanding was that with which she worked the rain nicely; and this was why all the people lived, who would have been all dead; all would have become frogs' (L.VIII.16:7447'). A direct refusal to comply with the rain's wish to take her would have resulted in the gravest consequences: the death of the community in human form and their transmogrification into frogs. The resistance of the rain's desire leads to forcible incorporation within the order of the rain's things.

!Khwa is not mentioned in this story of the girl and the stars. The threat he represents at this time would almost certainly have been implicit to a |Xam auditor, however, in the associations elicited by other elements mentioned in the story. Menstrual blood, for example, was also known as !Khwa (Hewitt 1986: 284). However, it is also possible, as Solomon's work suggests, that the threat of death that !Khwa represents was not yet present at the time of the story, since it occurs in the First Times, before the introduction of mortality.

Whatever the nature of the danger surrounding her, it must be emphasised that the girl does not actually violate the restrictions, and in fact observes them scrupulously. The anger she evinces as a result of the women's not supplying her with sufficient food is not unusual in the rites of passage of menarche, in which withholding of food is a deliberate and essential part of the initiation. Everyone in the band is linked to a confined girl by a web of sympathetic relations. If she were to eat a lot of food, then everyone would have to eat more food than usual. This would often have been impossible in the arid north-western part of the nineteenth-century Cape Colony. A girl's frustration at her confinement and state of ritual semi-starvation becomes a necessary part of her transition to womanhood. While her frustration is an expression of her powerlessness, it is also an inescapable consequence of her power.

In this story, the girl's frustration has fruitful results. She is angry, but her actions are calm and calculated, and they have a creative intention.

Nevertheless, she is said to have 'acted ill', even though she does not actually violate the taboos.[8] Nor is it her anger itself that is reprehensible. Despite its beneficial consequences, it is her act of creation that is condemned. Why should this be so? |Kaggen's creative acts do not elicit disapproval. Acts of aetiological import are not in themselves blameworthy. It could be that she is a girl of the Early Race, and all the people of the Early Race and their actions are considered foolish and reprehensible. She might then be guilty simply by her location within the First Times and the Early Race, although the boys and women in 'The Children Are Sent to Throw the Sleeping Sun into the Sky' are similarly positioned and do not receive the same sort of criticism. Other explanations offer themselves when the different elements in the story are carefully considered. When the aetiological aspects of the story are foregrounded at the expense of these other elements, which are dismissed as merely adventitious and decorative, the order of things established in the narrative is suppressed and so are many interpretive possibilities.

There are different ways of disobeying the menarcheal injunctions. One of the most common is when a new maiden (i.e. a girl who is experiencing menarche) visits a waterhole. This is not the case in this story. Another common infringement involves a new maiden looking at young men. This girl does not look at young men, but the taboo she is mentioned as observing does, however, concern them. The story emphasises that the consequences for the young men and their hunting would have been dire if the girl had eaten meat that they had hunted. The story also makes it clear that she avoids this meat. Instead, 'she ate the game of her father, who was an old man. While she thinks that, the young men's hands would become cool. Then, the arrow would become cool' (L.II.28:2522). The girl realises the danger of eating their meat and only eats game killed by her father, as decreed. But, somehow, the link between the girl's creation of the stars and her confinement is established through her relations with the young men of the band. Even though these relations are not explicitly mentioned in the story and have to be divined from the information supplied by the narrator in the notes that accompany the story, they generate, in my opinion, many of the story's meanings.

The young men are the group from which the girl's sexual partners will come. For this period, however, she is potentially a source of the gravest danger to them, for she can render their hunting activities ineffectual.

‖Kabbo states that if she looks at the game, it will become 'wild'.[9] The consequences of new maidens looking at men are detailed in many places. In one story, a man is turned into a tree by the glance of a new maiden, who cannot resist the attraction of the music he plays on his *goura* (L.II.2:295–305).

Generally, the status of menstruating women is ambiguous. They have the potential to harm, but also to bestow benefits. 'Menstruating women were simultaneously a positive and negative source of energy ... The power of women during menstruation was both confined and en-hanced [sic]' (Jeursen 1995: 44). Elsewhere, menstruating girls are described as being invested with 'rain's magic power', for they have the power by their actions to either keep away or provoke the rain's wrath (L.V.13:4989).

In this story, the girl's creation of the Milky Way is intended to assist the hunters by lighting their way at night, i.e. her act helps them. She might, however, be said to be defying the terms of her separation from the men whose meat she may not touch by performing an act that links her with their hunting. In other words, she abides by the letter of the rules of menarcheal confinement, but defies their spirit. Although she cannot eat the springbok flesh that the young men bring in, she nevertheless assists them in their hunting of springbok, as she provides the light by which they can see their prey.

A story like this cannot be confined to its own narrative circuit, and it is situated within a much broader signifying system. As I observed in chapter 5, hunting and sexuality are linked in the general symbolic order. Megan Biesele's book *Women Like Meat* concerns the linking of game and women, female sexuality and fat, and the pursuit of love and the pursuit of game by the Jul'hoansi of the central Kalahari. A similar complex, whose exact contours are extremely difficult to distinguish, occurs in the |Xam narratives, most explicitly perhaps in 'The Story of the #*Nutu ru*', a horned insect (probably a species of weevil) that entertains the children when the adults are away. On their return, the #*nutu ru* removes her horns and presents a visage of irresistible beauty to the men, who feed her fat and springbok breasts, while their wives have to be content with the lean meat. The men are described as feeling as if they were married to the #*nutu ru* (L.VIII.9:6786–857).

A menarcheal girl possesses a unique status. She exists in a liminal zone, 'a conceptual Noman's-Land (sic)' (Hewitt 1986: 88). She is neither adult nor child. She is in danger from !Khwa, but also derives a power from him that endangers others. In a symbolic sense, she participates in a reversal of gender roles. Generally, women are identified with antelope as prey or meat. The menarcheal girl, on the brink of sexual availability, attains in her liminal state the status of hunter, and the men endure the peril that attends their inverted position as prey. That menarcheal girls and hunters were symbolically conflated is supported by Hewitt's observation that the observances of hunters who have shot an eland and menarcheal girls were almost identical (131–32).[10]

Success in the hunt is critical to gender harmony. Women, I pointed out in the previous chapter, would not consider staying with a man who did not bring home meat. When men return with nothing from the hunt the women round on them:

> They spare the men nothing: reproaches, insults, threats. They want a separation, they want to leave these husbands without courage and go and find others who would be able to feed their wives and children (Glenn 1996: 43, quoting Le Vaillant 1790, II: 197–98).

#Kasin recounts how he was seriously injured by a leopard he was trying to hunt. Instead of receiving his family's sympathy, he was scolded for his lack of judgement in pursuing the leopard in the first place and consequent failure to return home with food (Bank 2006: 218). This reaction is not related simply to need, for the meat brought by the men comprised a much smaller portion of the daily diet than did the food collected by the women. Hunting not only supplies meat, it also feeds an intricate discursive complex, which involves a web of interactions with spirits, the environment and other people. It is central to economic practice and it is equally critical to the social and symbolic orders.

SPRINGBOK AND THE ORDER OF THINGS

The discursive order overdetermines the meanings present in a story such as this. I shall illustrate this contention by tracking one of the elements in the story: 'springbok'. My choice of this signifier does not imply that it is more significant than the others in the narrative. In fact, I choose to explore the sign 'springbok' because springbok are mentioned only in passing. I hope, by showing that the allusion to springbok in the story is not merely adventitious, to add weight to my argument for the examination of the textual details of the narratives. I will claim that springbok themselves constitute an expansive realm of practices, beliefs and discursive possibilities. Although the exact nature of the signifying power of 'springbok' is impossible to delineate, the narratives and statements about 'springbok' in the materials can, however, be identified and elaborated — a process that in itself illustrates the protean character of this sign.

The signifier 'springbok' occurs in the story solely in relation to the girl's avoidance of the young men's game. She can only eat game killed by her father, an old man (L.II.28:2521–22). This girl — the first girl to experience menarche — is presented as knowing of her own accord, and not as the result of special instruction (as would later be the case), that her eating of the young men's game would render their hunting ineffectual: 'While she thinks that the young men's hands would become cool' (L.II.28:2522). The game is only once identified as springbok, and that towards the end of the section on avoidance of the young men's meat that terminates the story: 'While the girl thinks of her saliva, which, she eating, puts into the springbok's flesh; her saliva goes with the bow, the inside of the bow becomes cool' (L.II.28:2523). Another reference to springbok occurs in an explanatory note: 'She must not when in retreat look at the springbok, or they become wild' (L.II.28:2521). This note occurs for the instruction of the interviewer and would have been unnecessary for |Xam listeners. Nevertheless, despite the single — and delayed — presence of the signifier itself, I suspect that for a |Xam auditor, the signified 'springbok' would have pervaded the story, as would other elements that might seem to be marginal to the central narrative themes.

It is possible, of course, that springbok merely serve as an example of the sort of species hunted as game by the young men. It was the most abundant species in the area, after all. But the girl makes stars so that people 'might return home by night, in the middle of the night' (L.II.28:2515–16). Although the story does not directly mention the fact, it was springbok, especially, that were hunted at night (L.II.14:1374–76; L.VIII.14:7221–35).

The girl's motive for providing starlight could have been to facilitate the young men's hunting of the springbok by night. She might even be said to have initiated this activity by making it possible. Stars and springbok hunting are brought together in several other places in the |Xam texts. Eustacia Riley (2007: 306) notes that the |Xam 'name the stars in Orion's Belt according to springbok-hunting — the stars and the game are thought to travel together, the game imitating the movements of the stars above them'. Dorothea Bleek (1929: 307) maintains that the |Xam ask 'certain stars' for 'certain food'. This food, on the evidence of the notebooks, is springbok. |Han#kass'o (L.VIII.28:8447–58) describes how the |Xam ask the stars to exchange their hearts for the hearts of the hungry |Xam: 'For the star is not small; the star seems as if it posseses food.' The stars effect this exchange practically by cursing the springbok's eyes so that they can be easily hunted. He relates also how his grandfather asked Canopus to exchange arms with him so that he would not miss shooting springbok.

It should not be forgotten, in addition, that the girl in the story was the first to attain sexual maturity. I have already alluded to the link between meat and women, and between hunting and sex. Springbok in the narratives are frequently associated with reproduction, fatness and female sexuality. In 'The Story of the #Nutu ru', referred to in the last section, it is springbok flesh that the hunters divide unfairly among the women, giving the #nutu ru the fat breasts and their wives the lean meat. Might then 'The Girl of the Early Race Who Made Stars' be primarily aetiological after all? But might it be a story not of the origin of stars, but of sex? Through enabling springbok hunting by night, the girl might be said to symbolically initiate sex, substituting springbok for herself, or even, through her newly acquired sexual potency, actually becoming a hunter herself? The presence of starlight introduces another sort of 'springbok hunting': courtship and sexual relations.

This possibility should not be allowed to foreclose others. The proliferation and richness of meaning generated by the signifier 'springbok' in the stories is extraordinary. Sexuality is only one of the interlocking spheres of meaning it covers. Others include identity, maternity, the rain, interaction with spirits and knowledge. Many of these meanings can be claimed for this story in the way that I have claimed sex for it, despite the paucity of direct references to springbok. A story such as this, I would insist, does not owe its signifying power to its relations with other stories from around the world that share its deep structure. But nor does it form a hermetically enclosed world of its own. It is situated in a world of IXam stories embedded, in turn, in a wider IXam discursive field, which at the time of the stories' transcription, was located in intricate ways within the wider society of the north-western nineteenth-century Cape Colony. Each signifier in a story is linked to an elaborate and interrelated system of signifieds in all the other stories and in IXam discursive practice generally.

In several extended narratives, the female young of the springbok are coveted by other animals, and they are kidnapped and raised by mothers of another species. In one story, for example, a she-elephant substitutes her own child for a baby female springbok (L.VI.1:3881–194). The baby in these stories is always female, and the illicit coveting always maternal. Overweening maternal desire occurs, it is interesting to note, in the narratives more frequently than does illicit sexual desire, although the latter may be more coded; a possibility that, as we have just seen, may be present in 'The Girl of the Early Race Who Made the Stars' itself.

In both IIKabbo's (L.II.2:323–46; L.II.3:383–93, 429–41) and IHan# kass'o's versions (L.VIII.29:8561–602) of another story featuring a kidnapped springbok child, an anteater offers to hold a baby springbok while its mother fills a bag with Bushmen's rice. The anteater takes the child into its hole and refuses to return her to her weeping mother. The anteater raises the child. Eventually, the girl escapes with the help of the lynx whose assistance the springbok's mother elicits. The lynx first reveals the springbok girl's true identity to her. The lynx's motives, however, are far from disinterested. He lies next to the springbok child because she is a 'maiden'. The anteater covets the springbok girl as a daughter, while the lynx wants her as a wife. In the end, the anteater, who fails to retrieve the springbok girl after a desperate underground pursuit, begins to proclaim the rules of species differentiation. Each species should marry its own kind and eat particular foodstuffs. The springbok is the first to be fixed with its identity, fittingly in this context, with one that places it in an adversarial relationship with the lynx: 'Then the anteater says, "springbok stand! The Lynx kills thee, the Lynx kills thee, for thou art a Springbok, for thou art really art a springbok, a springbok which grass eats"' (L.II.2:336–37).

This story does not seem at first sight to link directly with that of the girl and the stars, but it is possible to establish connections. For a start, there occurs a subtextual sexual element in both narratives, and this is intimately related to the presence of the signifier and motif 'springbok'. Then the themes of identity and motherhood occur in both stories as well and could be explored in various ways. I am not trying to provide a comprehensive map of these links here so much as trying to demonstrate something of the common textual fabric that the narratives share, so that even a single reference to 'springbok', as in the star story, alludes to many other narratives and the meanings that the term 'springbok' generates in all of them.

The reference to the springbok in the story of the girl and the stars occurs in the context of hunting. The information relating to hunting springbok in the collection is varied and extensive. In the story, it is stated that a menarcheal girl's saliva coming into contact with the flesh of springbok killed by young men harms their hunting. This is only one of many situations in which the process of hunting springbok can be obstructed. When a springbok has been hit by an arrow, it takes an especially long time to die. The hunters call gently to the dying animal. Its blood would otherwise congeal and stop running out of its body, allowing it to recover. The relationship between the hunter and the hunted animal leads to the death of the animal when correctly conducted. This relationship is disturbed, as we have seen, when a new maiden eats the flesh of springbok killed by the young men from whom she is ritually separated for the duration of her menarcheal confinement. Her saliva, entering the flesh of the springbok, is the medium for the 'bewitchment' of the springbok that the young men will unsuccessfully attempt to hunt. The animals become wild and unapproachable. In a similar way, the girl in her confinement is unapproachable, particularly by the young men. Her condition could be said to render her 'wild'. She is positioned outside the sphere of the social, which for the |Xam appears to extend beyond the human world to encompass the general ordering of things — the following by the different species, including stars, of the paths set out for them.

Once again, this conjunction of elements is not peculiar to this story. The death of a man's hunting companion will cause him to miss his aim and the springbok will not die (L.VIII.14:7281–86). This phenomenon is particularly linked to springbok, a signifier with manifold signifieds, but in this case, women do not bring down the curse. Instead, the mediation of women and the medium of their saliva provide the mechanism through which the 'spell' is lifted and the springbok are returned to the sphere of the 'tame'. They first smoke the man's arrows with *buchu*. Then they make cuts in his shoulders with the arrows, suck out some of his blood and spit it into a springbok horn. When the horn is full of blood, they burn *buchu*. To ensure that the springbok come straight to the man, the women shave a path through his hair. The springbok will now once again lie down and die when the man shoots them. The power of women here to rectify the situation regarding springbok contrasts with the destructive power the new maiden can exert on hunting — a paradoxical product of her 'spiritual' intimacy with the hunters during the time of her confinement, in which she is prohibited from having any physical contact with them.

Hunters enter into a relationship with the springbok that they have shot in which every action becomes significant. The arrow is not only an instrument of death, but an 'artefact of mind' (Deacon 1992: 1); it establishes a connection between the consciousness of the hunter and the wounded animal. His attitudes and actions become critical in determining whether the shot springbok will die or recover. The confined girl exists in a similar sympathetic relationship to the young men and their hunting. Her actions affect their well-being and their hunting success intimately. Although separated from them, she is powerfully joined to them. She becomes involved in the relationship between the hunter and his prey, a connection that symbolically parallels the sexual relationship between men and women. The other women, those with the power to restore the hunting powers of a man whose companion has died, stand outside this 'hunting' relationship. In a similar way, the old women who supply the girl with food and water and her father whose meat she can eat stand, to some extent, outside the realm of power and danger surrounding a new maiden, protected, it seems, by the distance age or consanguinity has given them from the girl's sexual and reproductive potency.

Although no mention is made of the rain in this story, rain, as noted earlier in this chapter, is usually present in narratives concerning the confinement of new maidens (Hewitt 1986: 75–88). The new maiden is hidden because her condition can be smelled by the rain that comes to take her. This rain can also enter a hunter's hut and wet his bowstrings so that he cannot shoot springbok. His wife then has to turn the hut around (L.VIII.14:7221–23). Springbok are particularly associated with rain: they come after the sorcerers have made rain. Solomon (1997: 7–8) maintains that these sorcerers are actually spirits of the dead with whom certain people intercede for rain. This sort of rain would not be the angry rain associated with !Khwa, however, but the female rain that brings the grass. When the rain has come, the men make a wind that helps them and wait for the springbok (L.VIII.8:6725–27). Unusually, the women participate in this hunting (L.VIII.8:6753). Once again, this has echoes in the story: the girl makes the stars to facilitate night-time activity. This kind of springbok hunting is one of the most important |Xam nocturnal activities. The involvement of women in the hunting of springbok is particularly notable, as it does not often occur in relation to other animals. Their participation is not only practical, however. Women participate as signs in the signifying field relating to springbok and to springbok hunting. The story of the girl and the stars contributes and belongs, in part, to this field, even though springbok apparently appear only in passing in the story.

In the present order — the world that interacts with that of the spirits of the dead — springbok are associated not only with abundance and sexuality, but also with death, as their presence at certain times and places signifies the death of a human. Interestingly, in the context of this star story, a falling star possesses the same signification (L.V.19:5478–505). Dia!kwain describes his own experience of the interrelatedness of springbok and death (L.V.9:4653–88). He shoots a springbok, breaking its leg. It looks up at him, bleats and then runs off. He chases and kills it. When he returns home, his wife tells him he should have left the animal alone, since it was giving him a message.[11] The next day, the gemsbok he is hunting mysteriously know he is present and avoid him. He consults a 'healer' named Snore-White-Lying who tells him that the 'wildness' of the gemsbok is related to the springbok he had killed the day before. He returns home to find his wife dying. After fetching his niece to suckle the baby, he buries his wife.

[A]nd the springbok … that night upon which we were sleeping, the springbok came, the springbok came to sleep at the place at which we had buried my wife. And Snore-White-Lying spoke, he said to me about it, 'Look! Why is it that the springbok come to a place to which the springbok have not been used to come? ... These things they are those about which we now shall not speak; for, we will remain silent' (L.V.9:4684–88).

Snore-White-Lying tells Dia!kwain that now he can see the results of the actions of the springbok he had shot.

Springbok, then, are connected not only with identity, fecundity, motherhood and sexuality, as we have seen, but also with death. This link is reiterated often in the texts, and it is a link that is shared with stars, which are also closely identified with death and the spirits of the dead. A dead person's heart or soul, observes Solomon (1997: 7), is believed to become a star. By creating stars, the girl could be said to be participating in the creation of a realm of spirits of the dead. Whatever the anatomy of this structure and the significations it mobilises, it is clear that the new maiden, in her liminal position, is identified with death and the spirits of the dead.

The signifier 'springbok' is linked to death in manifold ways. A springbok wounded by a poisoned arrow will bleat in order to attract lions to the scene and endanger the hunter. It also tries to lead the hunters away from home to places where their safety is less assured. Springbok, it is said, wish for the men who have shot them to die as they die. Any wounded springbok behaving in a strange manner should be left alone: 'For a springbok which takes us to our death, it is' (L.V.9:4635). Game in general, but springbok in particular, are said to know when a person is about to die — they can smell death. Springbok are thought of as being endowed with a special type of knowledge: 'For a thing which smells it is ... it knows it, that which we do not know' (L.V.9:4647). It follows, presumably, that springbok, through their intimacy with human death, can be considered as being closely connected to the spirits of the dead. As I have just argued, this is also a property of new maidens, who are connected to !Khwa and to the watery and stellar realms of the spirits.

The more the meanings surrounding springbok are examined, the less the identification of the meat hunted by the young men as springbok meat appears as accidental. Both springbok and new maidens carry a signification that is linked, at the very least, in intricate ways to fertility, sexuality, maternity, identity and death.

INTERPRETATION AND THE STORY: Some observations

This exploration, prompted by the single appearance of the signifier 'springbok' in the narrative, demonstrates — I hope — how a seemingly simple story evades easy interpretation, for it inhabits a world in which meaning is generated through an order of things whose scope lies well beyond individual stories. Nor is this order fixed. It consists of constantly changing relationships among countless signifiers.

A hasty reading of the story might be content with a description of it as aetiological. Apart from its reductiveness and failure to acknowledge the narrative's discursive qualities, such a description leaves unanswered many of the questions arising from a consideration of the ordering of the elements that appear in this story and in the materials as a whole. How does one account, for example, for the association of menarcheal girls and stars, which occurs in a different form elsewhere (for example, L.II.37:3333–43), if this story simply explains the origin of the stars? A functionalist interpretation might be satisfied with an account that finds evidence for the reinforcement of the social order in the narrative.[12] In many stories, violation of the social order through the breaking of the taboos surrounding new maidens results in people becoming frogs and other water things or girls becoming stars. Such a sequence easily invites a functionalist explanation. But it must be remembered that the girl in this story does not violate taboos, nor do her actions immediately elicit the harmful consequences that violation of the menstrual observances generally do.

In the story, the girl's actions assume a superhuman dimension. Her power derives in part, at least, from her position as an Early Race person and as a menstruating girl. She is, as it happens, the first girl to menstruate. This, for Dia!kwain, makes her 'the first girl'. She is not, however, according to ‖Kabbo, a ǀXam heroine:

> This girl is said to have been one of the !khw -th -ssh -!k'a ('People of the Early Race') and the 'first' girl; and to have acted ill; she was finally shot by her husband. These (Early Race people) are said to have been stupid, and not to have understood things well (L.II.28:2504').

Despite being the first girl to attain both biological womanhood and, through her confinement, symbolic womanhood, despite the solicitude she displays towards the young men, and despite her creation of spectacular cosmic entities, she is still condemned by the narrator. This |Xam 'Eve' receives no better historical press than does the Eve of Genesis.

This discussion of 'The Girl of the Early Race Who Made the Stars' is intended to indicate something of the multivocality of the |Xam stories. As I have argued frequently in this book, this aspect of the narratives has been suppressed in many of the interpretations of the materials from the Bleek and Lloyd Collection. For the most part, these readings have ignored the discursive and intertextual nature of the |Xam texts and instead concentrated on making comparative, structural and functionalist statements about them. The textual details in a narrative such as this deserve far more extensive and particular treatment than they have hitherto been accorded. In this chapter, I have attempted to consider a single aspect of a single narrative in some detail. This endeavour should be understood as a contribution to an open-ended and ongoing discourse generated by the narrative rather than as an exhaustive analysis of it. The focus of the rest of this book switches from the interpretation of particular narratives to an examination of two of the controversies that have emerged in |Xam studies over the years. However, this examination is framed in terms of the questions that I have asked about interpretation so far in this book.

NOTES

1   This is the title of the story in Bleek and Lloyd (1911: 72–79), which is drawn from L.II.28:2505–24.

2   Hewitt (1986: 76) provides the ethnographic background: 'At the onset of her menses a young girl was segregated from the band and placed in a small hut ... There she would remain in isolation until a new moon appeared. The hut was so small that she was forced to lie prone. Her food and water supply was restricted, and she was forbidden to leave the hut for anything except defecation.'

3   Calculated intent is not an aspect of the great majority of aetiological events in the materials, however. The 'raw and hairless buttocks' of baboons, for instance, are said to be a consequence of their sitting on hot stones (Hewitt 1986: 109). Greed and restraint, respectively, result in the crows' obtaining different coloured necks rather than the desire for a certain look on their part (Bleek, D. 1923: 47–48).

4   In the arid north-western part of the nineteenth-century Cape Colony, this power is triune: the power to nourish (food), heal (medicine) and slake thirst (water).

5   See, for example, Campion (1994, ch. 1).

6   See, for example, Hewitt (1986: 93).

7   These women, the girl's *xoakengu* or 'mothers', were also 'responsible for the instruction of the girl in those rites which she had to perform to protect the band from !Khwa' (Hewitt 1986: 76). The consequences of her violating the conditions of her confinement were usually first visited on these women and the girl's immediate family (79–80).

8   There is, it should be noted, some ambiguity as to whether the observation that she 'acted ill' refers to her actions in the story or to her behaviour in general. In either case, her creation of the Milky Way and stars does not make her a heroine.

9   'Wildness' here signifies a state beyond the merely non-domestic; a state of the extreme unapproachability of game animals. For the |Xam, it would seem, 'wild' is a state that occurs on the other side of the natural order of things in which game can be approached by humans; it is a condition in which game animals are possessed of a knowledge that places them outside the compass of men and their arrows. It is not simply a state outside culture, but a state outside nature.

10 Eland hunters and menarcheal girls were both isolated and treated as if they were ill. Both avoided particular kinds of food and were cared for by older members of their sex. Hewitt's (1986: 132) explanation for this correspondence avoids the question of gender and invokes, as his explanations often do, an oppositional relationship between nature and culture: 'Both the hunter and the girl had the capacity to harm the band by causing nature to follow its own course beyond the influence of men and against the interests of the land.'

11 An animal might not be what it seemed. Spirits of the dead sometimes visited in the guise of beasts of prey. An ancestral spirit might assist hunters by sending a spirit springbok to lead a springbok herd into the hands of hunters (Solomon n.d.: 77–79). Dia!kwain's father shot such a springbok by mistake (L.V.10:4707–43).

12 Hewitt (1986: 87, 94) provides just such an explanation. It is perhaps not surprising, therefore, that he finds the story 'undeveloped' and of little interest as a narrative.

SECTION 4

Controversies

CHAPTER 11

RELIGION IN A |XAM NARRATIVE

|XAM RELIGION

According to the Breakwater Prison records, the Bushmen convicts had no religion. People of the bush and considered to be almost wild animals, they were purported to display few human characteristics such as religion. Wilhelm Bleek would not have concurred. He observed of Bushman rock art, for example, that it represented an 'attempt, however imperfect, at a truly artistic conception of the ideas which most deeply moved the Bushman mind, and filled it with religious feelings' (Bleek 1874b: 13). As I noted in chapter 8, Bleek believed also, as a matter of science rather than religion, no doubt, that, like all Khoisan peoples (Hottentots in his vocabulary), the |Xam worshipped the moon. Guenther (1996: 89) has suggested that Bleek's view of Bushman religion was predetermined by the influence on his thought of reading the work of Max Müller, who saw evidence of sun worship behind every traditional tale. Guenther himself, in his books and articles on the |Xam narratives (1989; 1996; 1999; 2002; 2006), concentrates on delineating the true features of |Xam religion and tracking its presence in Bushman mythology, identifying especially the trickster deity, |Kaggen, and the figure of the trance practitioner as central components of this religion. Lewis-Williams (1996a; 1998a; 2000) is another writer whose interpretation of the |Xam narratives concentrate on what we might call their 'religious' features. His influential and controversial trance theory of rock art interpretation informs his approach to the reading of the narratives. This chapter will provide a discussion of this approach as it is presented in his essay, "'A visit to the lion's house": The structures, metaphors and sociopolitical significance of a nineteenth-century Bushman myth' (Lewis-Williams 1996a).

The prison authorities, Bleek and contemporary writers such as Guenther and Lewis-Williams hold different positions with regard to |Xam religion. These views correspond, for the most part, to those that have been held in regard to Khoisan religion generally in the colonial and post-colonial periods of South African history. David Chidester (1996a; 1996b: 51–59) describes how the attribution or denial of religion to the indigenous population fluctuated in relation to the situation on the frontier. The prevailing attitude in the period of early European contacts with the people of the Cape was that the local people exhibited no trace of religion (Chidester 1996b: 52). This view continued after the Dutch occupation of the Cape and was linked to the contention that people who had no religion were close to beasts and, consequently, had no right to land. Descriptions of Khoisan religion only became common around 1700, a time when 'Khoisan resistance had been largely subdued' (Chidester 1996b: 53). Its main characteristics differed from writer to writer, but moon worship and 'the notorious "Pissing Ceremony", which required a male elder to urinate on all participants in rituals for birth, marriage and death' (Chidester 1996b: 53), were some of the recurrent features identified by writers at the time. The idea that the Khoisan had no religion — and, consequently, no right to land or humane treatment — again predominated during the period of the genocidal attacks on Bushmen in the 1780s.

The Sotho, Tswana, Zulu and Xhosa people were also said to have no religion during periods of settler conflict with them. When they were subjugated and mostly confined to designated tribal areas in the latter part of the nineteenth century, the description of their different religious systems became part of the project of defining and entrenching ethnic divisions. The position with regard to Bushman religion in this period, however, was somewhat different. Their extinction was considered an evolutionary inevitability, and Bushman religion was discussed in the context of a discourse of displacement. The historian George Theal, who wrote the introduction to *Specimens of Bushman Folklore*, surmised that the

Bushmen had originated in the Malaysian peninsula, since their religion exhibited the same kind of childish mentality as that of the Philippine, Andamanese and Semang peoples of that region (Chidester 1996b: 57). This 'conceptual removal' of the Bushman from South Africa's past was accompanied by their displacement from southern Africa's future (58). The primitive level of the Bushmen, as evidenced by their religion, meant that they 'were destined to be removed from southern Africa in order "to satisfy God's law of progress" ... the religious system of the Bushmen appeared to certify their disappearance' (58).

More recently, interest in Bushman religion has formed part of a re-examination of the categories of religion itself. It is 'emerging as a new frame of reference for recognising what counts as religion' (Chidester 1996b: 59). Bushman religion is described as lacking the organisational and institutional features that are commonly attributed to religion. 'Rather than constituting a "system", Bushman religion appears as a cultural repertoire of discourses and practices for negotiating the meaning and power of being human' (59). Several writers in the field of Bushman studies discuss the features of Bushman religion in these terms. In the remainder of this chapter, I will examine some of this writing, concentrating, as I have mentioned, on Lewis-Williams's reading of a single |Xam narrative. I will argue that some of the enthusiasm that attends the project to which Chidester refers has resulted in the narratives being read in ways that are not always supported by the |Xam materials themselves.

Roger Hewitt (1986: 40–43) identifies several phenomena with regard to |Xam religion. He asserts that the |Xam did not believe in deities. He would have disagreed, therefore, with Lewis-Williams and Guenther's reading of |Kaggen as a trickster-deity and also with Alan Barnard's (1992) view that the Khoisan belief in a dual divinity was ubiquitous.[1] Instead, he refers to |Kaggen and !Khwa (the figure associated with the power of the rain) as supernatural beings. He notes, importantly I think, that 'the powers of |Kaggen and !Khwa were discrete and concerned only with specific areas of activity' (Hewitt 1986: 41), such as hunting observances and menarcheal practices. This accords with |Xam beliefs about the supernatural generally 'in which different things are credited with various powers which might be tapped or avoided depending on their nature' (Hewitt 1986: 41). The materials provide evidence, too, of a wind or rain that is connected with each person, as well as with certain animals and stars: 'What kind of wind and rain a man had, might influence his deployment in the hunt or whether or not he could address !Khwa.' The |Xam themselves, Hewitt (1992: 42) points out, did not regard this force as 'magical or supernatural', an astute observation with several consequences for the way in which |Xam religion is delineated.

Hewitt mentions the role in |Xam religion of the *!giten*, the figure that Lewis-Williams and Guenther regard as central to Bushman religion.[2] Hewitt refers in an appendix to the *!giten* as a shaman, who could cure the sick, make rain or influence the hunt. A malignant *!giten* could make people sick or kill them. Hewitt concludes his examination of the features of |Xam religion with a discussion of the beliefs regarding the afterlife. In one account, a spirit of a dead person 'travelled along an underground path leading from the grave to a vast hole where it then lived' (Hewitt 1986: 42). According to another informant, the spirits of the dead reside in the hollow of the new moon. Those spirits who were reluctant to leave the company of friends and relatives lingered near the living for a while (Hewitt 1986: 43).

Guenther, as I noted in chapter 2 and discussed at length in chapter 6, has written extensively about the |Xam narratives and Bushman religion. He argues that small, loosely constituted Bushman bands are largely free of politics and organised religion. This is a good thing in his view, since the absence of formal institutional features from Bushman religion allows it to concentrate on spiritual rather than political matters. Crucially, for discussions of |Xam narrative, Bushman mythology, part of Bushman religion in Guenther's view (1999: 84), is similarly relieved of the burden of sanctioning power. It is the lack of the very organisational factors that traditionally were said to constitute religion that give Bushman religion its distinctive features. This religion is authentically religious, for it deals with real spiritual experience. In this it differs radically with what passes for religion in complex societies, which, according to Guenther, is really a mask for power politics. Bushman religion is an ideology, but not one that naturalises power. Instead, it socialises individuals for life in a changeable foraging economy.

As I have already observed in earlier chapters, several aspects of Guenther's characterisation of Bushman religion recall the properties commonly accorded authentic spirituality in particular Western traditions of thought. In the thinking of the Romantics, for example, as well as in several versions of post-Christian forms of Western spirituality, the view has prevailed that the complexity of contemporary industrial and urban life results in an alienation from both nature and the life of the spirit. Only those peoples who remain close to the earth and the simple life retain ready access to spiritual life. A quintessential practitioner of the natural life, the Bushman according to this view is therefore practically spirituality incarnate. Bushmen are not weighed down by everything that separates modern humankind from the sphere of the spiritual: materialism, reason, politics and organised religion. Proof of this can be seen in their mystical identification with the animals that they hunt, their shamanism and trance skills, and the sacred character of their rock art and mythology.

How does one sift through these ideas? What do terms like 'spirituality' and 'religion' mean in the context of |Xam culture as it appears to us through the medium of the materials in the Bleek and Lloyd Collection? Émile Durkheim (2001) famously located the distinction between the sacred and profane at the root of religious thought and experience, and saw the sacred as the site of authenticity and truth. How did |Xam people distinguish between the sacred and profane? Answers to these questions first require, of course, some clarification of terms. It is frequently asserted that religion, as opposed to spirituality, entails institutions, priesthoods, dogma and organisation. Guenther has argued, using the Bushmen as an example, that this view is inadequate. They have religion, but no religious institutions. Another hoary anthropological distinction involves the separation of religion — the sphere of worship and belief — from magic — the sphere of the manipulation of matter and events by practitioners such as medicine men and shamans. Once again, this distinction raises a host of questions when applied to the |Xam. As we shall see later in this chapter, there is some dispute as to whether the |Xam consistently practised magical techniques that produced particular results, in the manner of the shaman, or whether they were more often supplicants, pleading with the spirits of the dead to make the rain fall, facilitate hunting and heal the sick.

It is my view that the investigation of the question of spirituality and religion in relation to the |Xam can best be conducted in the course of a close examination of the |Xam texts. Such an enquiry must begin with the analysis of individual narratives, if general and, often, self-fulfilling statements about Bushman spirituality are to be evaded. This approach accords, in my view, to some degree with the aims of post-colonial analysis, which attempts to interrogate Western categories of thought while also allowing the categories of indigenous thought and exegesis to emerge at the margins.[3]

LEWIS-WILLIAMS'S ANALYSIS OF THE STORY OF 'A VISIT TO THE LION'S HOUSE'

One of the few scholars, I pointed out earlier, who has closely analysed individual stories is Lewis-Williams (1996a; 1998a). Along with Guenther, he probably is the writer, also, who most consistently emphasises the spiritual character of Bushman narrative. In the remainder of this chapter I will describe and critically discuss his analysis of the story of 'A Visit to the Lion's House' in order to continue the investigation of his work that I began in chapter 3 and advance at the same time this enquiry into |Xam religion and spirituality. The title of his essay, '"A Visit to the Lion's House": The structure, metaphors and sociopolitical significance of a nineteenth-century Bushman myth', establishes certain expectations. The major study of the |Xam narratives, Hewitt's *Structure, Meaning and Ritual in the Narrative of the Southern San*, has a similar metrical ring to it. Lewis-Williams, as we shall see, echoes Hewitt's reading of the narratives with regard to their structure. Although he omits the term 'ritual' from his title, he pays more attention to this aspect of the stories than Hewitt himself does. This accords with his contention that both San rock art and narrative consistently depict ritually induced trance experience. Lewis-William's title also indicates that a political dimension will be included in his discussion, something that Hewitt's more formalistic approach to analysis does not invite.[4] He calls the narrative a myth, a term that in its anthropological context often suggests a traditional sacred narrative of timeless significance. But he also locates it in historical time: it belongs to the nineteenth century. While this designation raises interesting questions, Lewis-Williams does not indicate in the course of his analysis whether he is suggesting that |Xam stories should be periodicised, and, by extension, that myth is a type of discourse that is historically situated, or whether he is referring to the colonial context in which the story was collected. The title indicates that several kinds of interpretation — structural, symbolic and political — will coexist in his reading of the narrative. Religion itself is absent in the title apart from a whiff of the spiritual in the use of the term 'myth', which, as I indicated in chapter 3, often betokens the sphere of the sacred.

In the story analysed by Lewis-Williams, |Kaggen's son-in-law, Kwammang-a, reports that his relatives, the lions, have killed a quagga. He intends to visit them with his son, the ichneumon, and share in the feast, a prerogative of relatives. |Kaggen, generally referred to as the Mantis by Lewis-Williams, insists on accompanying them, even though they remind him that he is terrified of the lions. The party sets off. They find the lions at the end of a trail of quagga blood. The predictably terrified |Kaggen hides in the ichneumon's bag. A young lion spots him, however and thinks that he is a hare. |Kaggen whispers to the lion and winks at him. Three times the lion cries and tells his mother about the thing in the bag. Finally, the angry lioness stamps on the bag. |Kaggen escapes by flying into the air and commanding his belongings to follow him. He dives into a waterhole and washes his things before returning to the camp. He then deceives his wife, the dassie, and step-daughter, the porcupine, by telling them that Kwammang-a and the ichneumon have been devoured by the lions. The two soon return, however, very much alive and laden with quagga meat. The narrative ends with the ichneumon admonishing his grandfather to behave better in future.

This story forms part of a much longer narrative recounted by ||Kabbo to Lucy Lloyd over a period of almost a month in late 1871. Dorothea Bleek (1923), Lewis-Williams notes, broke the longer narrative into four parts. Each of these narratives, argues Lewis-Williams in his introductory remarks, can stand on its own and displays a ternary structure that derives 'from the |Xam world-view and from a set of metaphors that came out of the most profound experience open to the |Xam' (Lewis-Williams 1996a: 122). The story also possesses 'two interlocking cosmological axes' (Lewis-Williams 1996a: 124). The extreme poles of the horizontal axis are the camp and the hunting ground. The camp stands for familiar relationships, cooperation and safety, while the hunting ground constitutes an opposing complex; it is dangerous, anti-social and associated with strangers. The waterhole is located between the two poles: it is a place of social interaction, but also of ambivalence; an intermediary place, associated with positive and negative transformation.

Less known, and unavailable also to ordinary |Xam people, is the vertical axis along which 'shamans' travel between the sky and the subterranean realm (Lewis-Williams 1996a: 125). The regions below the surface of the earth were associated with the spirits of the dead. In Lewis-Williams's view (1996a: 126), incidentally, these beliefs were not 'well developed or formalised', a contrast, as we have seen at various points in this book, with the views of fellow rock art interpreter Anne Solomon (1997; 1999; 2007; 2008). The 'moon, the sky — the realm above — was associated with spirits, shamans and the Mantis', the prototypical shaman (Lewis-Williams 1996a: 126). The waterhole is once again the intermediary point, this time between sky and earth. Water wells up from the earth and also falls from the sky.

Lewis-Williams proceeds to analyse the story of 'A Visit to the Lion's House' in terms of both this axial structure and the ternary episodic structure that he asserts is internal to all |Xam narratives. The initial episode occurs in the safe, normal space of the camp. The central episode breaks the pattern of the established order that is apparent in the first episode before order is restored in the final episode. |Kaggen is the agent of this disruption. He offends the lions and escapes by supernatural means. Hewitt, according to Lewis-Williams, reads this as a magical event, but Lewis-Williams himself insists that it is more than this. It belongs primarily to the area of shamanic experience. There are several elements of the central episode, he argues, that seem nonsensical at face value, an unmistakable indicator that deeper meanings are concealed in them.

Lewis-Williams proceeds to disinter these meanings. |Kaggen's conceal-ment of himself in the ichneumon's bag only makes sense, he argues, when interpreted in the context of shamanism. An artefact always retains something of the identity and nature of its raw materials. Climbing into a bag is tantamount to climbing into the animal from whose skin it has been made (Lewis-Williams 1996a: 128). This, in turn, is equivalent to entering a state of trance and the spirit world. 'A |Xam shaman possessed, or owned, the potency of a specific animal or two' (128). Antelope, such as the hartebeest out of which the bag was made, conferred a particular potency, a potency that was primarily transferred by scent. By climbing into the bag and immersing himself in the animal's power and scent, |Kaggen was enacting 'the first stage of effecting his entry into the spirit world of trance experience' (129). This reading is reinforced, in Lewis-Williams's view, by the fact that the ichneumon places another antelope skin product, a kaross, over |Kaggen. Karosses, he asserts, are closely associated with shamans in the rock paintings across the region that depict the partial transformation of men into antelope.

Lewis-Williams (1996a: 129–31) reads |Kaggen's interaction with the baby lion in terms of shamanism also. 'Whispering', 'hares' and 'winking' are all elements that belong in a complex that is associated with trance. This is corroborated, he argues, by other references to these motifs in the materials. The term 'winking', for example — in his view an unsatisfactory rendering of the |Xam word *dabba*, which in the *Bushman Dictionary* (D. Bleek 1956) includes opening and closing the eyes and blinking — occurs elsewhere in the collection in connection 'with dying, causing rain to fall (or foretelling it) and "bewitching"' (Lewis-Williams 1996a: 131). This observation leads him to conclude 'that the "winking" incident ties in with the other four elements of the central episode, getting into a bag, covering with a kaross, "whispering" (conspiring) and transformation into a hare, in that it too is in some way associated with shamanism' (Lewis-Williams 1996a: 131).

The lions, argues Lewis-Williams, are feline shamans. |Kaggen's conflict with them represents a common feature of |Xam shamanistic practice: 'conflict in the spirit realm' between good and evil shamans. A |Xam shaman would sometimes grow lion's hair, in other words, become a lion or hostile shaman in trance (Lewis-Williams 1996a: 132). By trying to poke out the young lion's eyes, |Kaggen was not only attempting to physically harm him, but to impair his 'shamanistic ability to "see" into the future and to far away places' (132). This explains the ferocity of the lioness's response. |Kaggen's escape by flight and his descent into the water are both metaphors for trance. |Kaggen's escape involves a movement from the horizontal axis of the camp and hunting ground to the vertical axis of shamanistic experience.

The final episode describes |Kaggen's returning alone to the camp and telling the women that the lions have killed Kwammang-a and the ichneumon. The women's distress is soon relieved, though, by the arrival of the father and son. Not only are they alive, but they arrive carrying quagga meat. The ichneumon scolds |Kaggen for his behaviour at the lion's house. Lewis-Williams (1996a: 133–34) partly exonerates |Kaggen's attempt to deceive the women by explaining that after a successful hunt, the men pretended that they were returning empty-handed.

Lewis-Williams goes on to explicate the overall story in terms of both its ternary structure and its two levels of meaning. On the horizontal axis, the action moves from the order of the camp to the disorder at the lion's camp, through the transitional point of the waterhole, and back to the order of the camp. This level directly affirms meat sharing and, by extension, the kinship relations that meat sharing symbolises. Lewis-Williams (1996a: 134–36) then discusses the story in terms of its structure and meaning, two of the three terms that appear in Hewitt's (1986) title. Lewis-Williams echoes Hewitt in his discussion of the horizontal axis and also follows Lévi-Strauss in stating that 'the myth presents both a denial and an assertion of affinal relationships and concomitant responsibilities' (Lewis-Williams 1996a: 134). |Kaggen's actions entail a denial of these relationships, while Kwammang-a affirms them 'by bringing the (symbolic) meat back to the Mantis's camp'. A dilemma of the sort 'created by the need to share scarce resources with affines, cannot be resolved; it is inherent in Bushman social structure and economy. But it can be mitigated' (Lewis-Williams 1996a: 134). Lewis-Williams passes quite quickly over these sorts of meaning, it should be noted. The socio-political investigation that the title promises is not provided in any detail. He is clearly more interested in exploring the story in terms of trance and shamanic motifs, the vertical axis of meaning. His examination of social tensions is subordinated to his discussion of the role that trance plays in mediating them.

The story presents, in Lewis-Williams's reading of it, a |Xam instance of 'universal shamanistic experiences' (Lewis-Williams 1996a: 135). This experience, he indicates, has been most clearly elucidated by Mircea Eliade (1972), who identifies three 'cosmic zones' — the sky, the earth and the underworld. These zones are linked by a central axis and accessed by passing through a hole of some sort. Lewis-Williams links the waterhole in the story with this hole. The |Xam entered the spiritual dimension chiefly through trance, which, in his view, played as an important part in mediating social tensions in |Xam society as it does among present-day Bushmen living in the Kalahari. Meat sharing and relations with affines would have been two of the most common sources of social tension. These tensions, which |Kaggen brings to the surface through his anti-social actions, can only be resolved on the vertical or shamanic plane of trance experience.

A CRITICAL RESPONSE TO LEWIS-WILLIAMS'S READING OF 'A VISIT TO THE LION'S HOUSE'

The first point to consider about Lewis-Williams's reading of the story is his focus on the figure of the shaman and on trance experience and, therefore, on |Xam religion and spirituality. Lewis-Williams does not explicitly use the term 'religion' in his essay. It is clear, however, from his analysis of this narrative, and even more so from his writing on the interpretation of rock art, that he situates both Bushman narrative and rock art in a religious context. This is made explicit in some of his other writing. In a more recent piece on the Bleek and Lloyd Collection (Lewis-Williams 2007: 181), for example, he argues that 'religion must include beliefs in a supernatural realm and in rituals that make contact with that realm'. The rock paintings, he emphasises, 'were among the vehicles that made San religion real ... [t]he people lived in places embellished with symbols derived from their religious system'. We could reasonably extend this logic to his discussion of the story of the visit to the lions and conclude that Bushman mythology provides a similar, if non-material, setting and that metaphor works in the same way in the narratives as symbol does in the paintings.

Lewis-Williams's identification of socio-political tensions in Bushman society acknowledges that hunter-gathering societies are political. For Guenther, by contrast, as I mentioned earlier, the absence of politics in |Xam society makes the practice of true religion possible and allows for myth to remain properly in its own sphere, since it is freed from the obligation to sanction power. However, the socio-political significance of the story that is promised in Lewis-Williams's title is, as I have already pointed out, subordinated to the religious dimension, in which socio-political conflicts are resolved. The power accorded trance experience and its centrality in Bushman life that is evident in this story becomes more and more pronounced over the years in Lewis-Williams's rock art interpretation (1981; Lewis-Williams & Dowson 1989; Lewis-Williams & Pearce 2004; 2005). In this piece, he concedes that further work on the narrative is required in order 'to uncover further "meanings", such as gender relations and the range of other tensions in Bushman social structure' (Lewis-Williams 1996a: 137). Nevertheless, it is reasonable to conclude from the thrust of his arguments that the primary significance of the narrative, embedded in its ternary structure, resides in its relationship with

> the experience of profoundly altered consciousness. Such experiences start in the normal world, move into a world of fantasy and hallucination that is some sense on a different axis and to which different rules and limitations apply, and finally return to normality (Lewis-Williams 1996a: 137).

In his discussion of the story of 'A Visit to the Lion's House', Lewis-Williams uses examples from rock art and from contemporary Kalahari ethnology to support his contentions about the story. In his extensive writing about Bushman rock art, he often employs the |Xam materials in the Bleek and Lloyd Collection to buttress his interpretation of the paintings. Lewis-Williams's theory of rock art is based on the same set of premises as those that inform his reading of the stories (1996a; 1998a). It follows that a critique of his reading of the narratives will inevitably question some of the assumptions that characterise the rock art theory and echo some of the criticisms that have been levelled against that theory. Anne Solomon (1997; 1999; 2007; 2008; 2009; n.d.), in my opinion, has delivered the most sustained critique of Lewis-Williams's rock art theory to date. These criticisms apply directly to his interpretation of the narratives. Solomon maintains that Lewis-Williams's position assumes that a pan-Bushman cultural reality exists whereby only surface differences separate the narrative and rock art traditions of different groups. Beyond this lies a universal order, the result of a common neuropsychological structure, in which shamanism as practised in Eliade's Siberia, for example, is virtually identical with healing and trance practices in southern Africa.[5] Solomon considers this reductive. She argues, in addition, that the paintings do not merely reflect another sphere of cultural or religious experience, but themselves constitute a primary site of the production of signification. They are capable of producing multiple meanings and were produced for different reasons in a range of contexts.

Solomon (n.d.) re-excavates the Bleek and Lloyd materials and decides, on the basis of a close examination of them, that the term *!giten*, translated as 'sorcerer' by Lloyd but referred to as 'shaman' by subsequent researchers, only sometimes refers to living healers. For the most part, it refers to spirits of the dead. Nor do the |Xam appear to have practised trance dancing. There is only one reference in the whole 12 000 pages that could be directly interpreted as a reference to trance dancing, and that is not unequivocal, a point also made by Pippa Skotnes (1996b: 238). The |Xam instead practised sucking out illness through the nose or snoring, a practice that is clearly described in the notebooks.

Skotnes (1996b: 234) notes that 'the testimony of the Bleek and Lloyd informants' does not support 'the current trend to search for uniformity, generic similarities and common purpose in the paintings'. She actually discusses the role of the lion in the same volume of essays that Lewis-Williams's analysis of 'A Visit to the Lion's House' appears in so as to illustrate this point. She decides after examining the references to the lions in the collection that:

> [l]ions, often interpreted within the framework of the trance hypothesis as transformed malevolent shamans, when depicted in the paintings may thus quite reasonably be depicted as lions behaving as lions, as benevolent or as malevolent transformed shamans, as wild cats wreaking vengeance on hunters who kill them (L.VIII–23 8080-8083), or as … lions behaving as men (Skotnes 1996b: 239).

Like Solomon, Skotnes (1996b: 234–44) contends that art does not only reflect another reality; it helps produce reality. She emphasises that content cannot be divorced from form. Greater attention to formal technique, the placing of the paintings and even the composition of paint (some ingredients seem to have been added for purposes that were not entirely practical) would yield more meanings from the art. In the sphere of narrative, I would argue, these contentions might take the form of a call for greater attention to be given to the ways that meanings are produced in the context of performances. In addition, and this is more central to my argument in this book, attention needs to be given to the narratives in terms of their status as discourse. They are not merely reflections of other aspects of |Xam life, such as ritual and trance experience, but themselves comprise a resource for the production of meaning. Discourse, including that from which narratives are produced, is a constitutive rather than reflective medium. It does not mirror in a coded way an underlying universal reality so much as generate an ideological and aesthetic space in which multiple meanings can be circulated or contested. It is a rhetorical realm that relies on cultural and discursive conventions, as well as specific and indigenous techniques of exegesis, rather than a Platonic one that points to an unchanging, cross-cultural, ahistorical reality, such as a universal shamanistic trance experience.

Certain work on oral narratives, as I have noted, suggests that they are set up to be interpreted in various ways (see Barber 1991; 1999). The manner in which people understand their own texts must be an essential component of an analysis. In Lewis-Williams's approach, much of the way the story works is unknown to the storytellers themselves. They are unaware of both its deeper structure and, probably, its underlying meaning. This would, in any case, only have been available to a shaman, since ordinary |Xam people only had access to the horizontal level of meaning. In the case of the |Xam, we have no contemporary |Xam commentators on the texts. The Bleek and Lloyd informants did, however, as we have seen, deliver commentaries and explanations of the materials in the form of what were recorded as explanatory notes and also in the form of informative digressions within the narratives themselves, which probably would have been omitted in a 'traditional', indigenous storytelling context. In my opinion, these explanations should be taken at face value. It has been my contention in this book, too, that an exploration of individual signifiers across the archive has the potential to produce an intertextual network in which the texts illuminate each other in a way that is internal to a |Xam discursive economy. Lewis-Williams himself pioneers such an approach in both the essay under discussion at present and the article that I discussed in chapter 3, one of the chief reasons, in my view, for the importance of these pieces. He shows how intertextual links across the materials illuminate specific pieces of text. A good example in this essay is the way in which he links 'winking', 'hares' and 'whispering'. I would argue, however, as I did in chapter 3 in relation to the signifier 'shoe', that he does not take this procedure far enough. He employs it only insofar as it strengthens his contention that the story is an extended metaphor for shamanistic transformation.[6] An intertextual approach can, however, as I have shown in previous chapters and will attempt to show in the rest of this one, be used in a more open-ended way, a way that treats the stories as sites in which multiple and often contradictory meanings are produced rather than as texts whose surface detail conceals a hidden, univocal meaning or one in which there is a clear and recurrent hierarchy of signifiers.

'A VISIT TO THE LIONS' HOUSE': An intertextual approach

I can only in the limited space of this chapter give another short example of the sort of procedure I am proposing and hope that in this process a dialogue with Lewis-Williams's analysis will emerge. I do not wish to exclude Lewis-Williams's analysis, only to demonstrate the possibility of other readings, a procedure with which he himself would concur (Lewis-Williams 1996a: 137). Nor do I wish to pretend that my analysis will be something other than a product of Western hermeneutics with its history of epistemological domination. At best, it intends to be a reading that enlists a |Xam perspective to some degree.

All the signifiers in the narrative could be explored, as could those in the wider narrative from which this one has been excerpted, in a similar way to which I followed the web of signification connected to 'springbok' in the last chapter. I shall choose only one here, the potent signifier 'lion'. My discussion of this term will rely partly on its appearance in the materials and partly on the commentary of other critics, Lewis-Williams included. By the end of this experiment, I shall see to what extent Lewis-Williams's reading, a reading that foregrounds its religious or spiritual import, is supported by it and which other readings emerge as well. This will, in turn, lead to further reflections on the religious and spiritual status of the narrative.

The signifier 'lion' appears frequently in both the collection and in the commentaries on it. What is evident from even a quick survey of the references to lions in the materials is that it is a protean sign that occurs in an astonishing variety of contexts. Dorothea Bleek published a lot of the materials that appear in the Bleek and Lloyd Collection on lions. Some of the references clearly have a supernatural import, and many involve transformations that could be linked to shamanism. In a number of cases, lions clearly represent spirits. Some curers sprout lion's hair in the course of their possession by a lion spirit. It should be noted that the narrators themselves, however, often offer alternative explanations for these meta-morphoses. One of the most common reasons is that the lion wishes to trick a person and then attack or eat them.

The lion has an ability to turn into other animals, and even people. In the period of the First Times, a man is sewn up in a mouse's skin. He turns into a lion and later attacks and kills his brother's wife (Lewis-Williams 2000: 209–10). Lions sometimes turn themselves into people in order to drive vultures away from a springbok (L.VIII.18:7630'; Hollmann 2004: 59). An attack on a girl is described in which a lion tries to trick the girl into pulling him up onto the rock on which she is hiding by speaking like a person (Hollmann 2004: 37–40). |Han#kass'o describes, too, how a lion can turn into a hartebeest in order to trick people into hunting it. The hunters become the prey when the animal reverts to its true form (L.VIII.23:8075–77; Hollmann 2004: 62). Apart from the lion's ability to turn into other animals, different animals can turn into lions. |Han#kass'o's grandfather, Tsatsi, told him how some wildcats they had killed in the daytime turned themselves into lions after dark and attacked the people who had hunted them (L.VIII.23:8080–83, 8082'; Hollmann 2004: 60). In another account (L.VIII.31:8775–88), a gemsbok that is being stalked by a man turns into a lion. The man is so surprised that he stands on his own poisoned arrow.

Many references to lions simply relate to the danger that a man-eating carnivore represents. Lions not only provide competition for game, but are also an ever-present threat to human life. Lions, according to ||Kabbo (L.II.10:1053–56), will kill and eat all animals, humans included. Humans have to be vigilant and constantly interpret the signs that might indicate danger. Certain behaviour by owls and crows represents forewarnings of danger from a lion (Hollmann 2004: 41–44). Humans have to move away from the area where the threat could be expected and keep the fire blazing. This will fool the lion into believing that men are awake who will shoot it if it approaches.

Apart from the steps that need to be taken when a lion is planning an attack, there are certain precautions that have always to be taken in order to prevent a lion attack in the first place. These precautions possess, for a contemporary reader, supernatural elements. We should remember, however, that this was not necessarily so for the |Xam themselves. To return to a point made by Hewitt (1986: 41–42), a force that might be considered 'supernatural or magical' by us, might 'have been thought of more as a physical attribute than a spiritual one'. A torn water bag might be the work of an invisible lion that will turn into a tangible one and lie in wait for his victims at the waterhole (Hollmann 2004: 53–55). People, especially children, should avoid using the word 'lion' in case the flies hear what they are saying about the lion and report it to him. He would then be angry and attack at night. Children should mention lions indirectly and only when they have to, such as when they spot lion prints in the vicinity of the camp, for example. Several expressions can replace the term 'lion'. These include 'hair' (Hollmann 2004: 51). It is not only flies that inform a lion when people have been carelessly using his name. His dreams are another source of disclosure, and a lion can learn in a dream that people have seen his prints or used his name (Hollmann 2004: 47). People should never take the whole of a lion kill if they come across one, but leave the head and the backbone. The meat they find should not be cut up in view of the lion. A lion that was left no part of its kill would consider that it had been treated without consideration and track and harm the men who had taken all its meat.

Part of the danger of lions derives from their similarity to people, with whom they stand in a relationship of identity and difference. They think like people; they also share a number of habits. Both people and lions are predators capable of killing big game such as eland, gemsbok and, as in this story, quagga. Neither predator consumes its prey at the place it killed it (Hewitt 1986: 47). Lions and men both bury the contents of their victim's stomach.

A story that describes how a man of the Early Race pretended that a young lion he found was a dog (Lewis-Williams 2000: 174–205) introduces the sphere of the wild and the domestic. Lions have to be vigorously excluded from the environs of the camp. Fire is seen as a defence against lions — amenable nature, as Hewitt might put it, can be harnessed to act as a protection against uncontrollable nature.

This is a small sample of the materials that feature lions in the collection. The very predominance of the signifier points to its significance in |Xam life. It occurs with much greater frequency than the sign 'eland', for example, despite the importance that that sign enjoys in |Xam belief and practice. What are we to make of this? Does the prolixity of the sign result from its centrality to shamanic experience? Could it relate to the play of difference and sameness that characterises the definition of men and lions? Is it merely the result of the power of the animal itself? Lions were an everyday presence in the world of the |Xam, and most of the informants had direct or indirect experience of lion attacks. Do all the meanings that the term 'lion' generates coexist in a hierarchical order with the deeper shamanic one at the pinnacle, or should one meaning not be subordinated to the others? 'Lion' obviously is not a univocal sign, but what is the nature and source of its multivocality? Finally, does the sign gain its power to generate meaning from its relation to a universal archetypal or neuropsychological world, as Lewis-Williams's references to the universality of shamanism imply, or to the internal economy of |Xam discursive practice?

We might conclude that the signifier 'lion' refers in part to shamanic experience and trance techniques of conflict mediation, if we accept aspects of Lewis-Williams's analysis. In this sense, a religious interpretation is invited. A religious reading would also be appropriate if a link between a belief in spirits of the dead and the lions in the story could be established. This link is explicit elsewhere in the materials, but seems either tangential to or deeply coded in this story. A religious aspect of the narrative is also retained if it is understood as a myth, a sacred creation tale. In addition, |Kaggen himself, as we saw in chapters 4, 5 and 6, is often understood as a supernatural, religious or sacred figure, a trickster-deity. His ability to transform and regenerate himself perhaps invites recourse to a religious trope that is not unfamiliar to Christianity.

What happens if we take the story and the references to lions in the rest of the materials at face value; in other words, if we accept |Xam explanations for things rather than uncover layers of meaning closed to them in their own discourse? The result then is that the story seems to be primarily dealing with questions that we might today more usually characterise as secular than religious. Once again, however, this depends on what we mean by the religious and, even more to the point, what the |Xam might have considered as belonging to the sphere of the religious. This sphere has to be constructed by the interpreter. There is nothing in the materials that signals that one has entered the realm of the sacred and extraordinary and left that of the ordinary and profane. It is true, as I have already observed, that many of the events in the materials strike a contemporary reader as extraordinary, magical or supernatural. That this was the case for the |Xam themselves is not clear. Nor, we should note, is the ordinary always excluded from religion, as the example of Zen poetry, for instance, might suggest, or the dietary laws of Judaism, Islam and Hinduism. For now, though, I should like to set aside such considerations and discuss briefly the meanings that do emerge from a reading of the story when |Xam information about lions is taken into account.

Lewis-Williams is surely right when he links the story to relations with in-laws. Particular protocols attended this relationship, and their observance and violation are explored in this narrative. The sharing of meat with kin is an integral part of this relationship.

The story clearly concerns identity, as do most of the stories of the First Times in which people and the different kinds of animals had not yet been separated into their species. Lions, especially, need to be distinguished from people, because they are so similar. It is not so much a question, I would argue, of a nature–culture dichotomy or even of separating humans from animals, but of navigating the relations of difference and likeness between lions and people.

The story also quite simply alludes to the danger of lions. Lions, as we know from the personal histories in the collection, represented a real danger. This does not, of course, mean that they do not also represent spiritual danger and competition, as Lewis-Williams argues.

The story needs to be understood, too, in terms of |Xam hunting observances. I have concentrated on the signifier 'lion' in this discussion. A full enquiry into both the story and Lewis-Williams's reading of it would require a comprehensive consideration of several other signifiers in the story. I would argue that it is no mistake, for example, that the animal in question is a quagga. The quagga, along with the eland, hartebeest, gemsbok and springbok, is one of |Kaggen's special animals. He does everything he can to prevent the hunting of these animals. The quagga is an animal with whose hunting and consumption |Kaggen might be expected to interfere. The materials, as we have seen, frequently elaborate this complex, both in the general cultural information supplied by the informants and also in First Times stories such as this one.

One of Lewis-Williams's main assertions is that nonsensical events are a sure indicator that a story is referring to something that is not comprehensible on the literal plane or that contains concealed meanings. This, in the case of the |Kaggen stories, is a signal that the vertical access of shamanistic experience is about to be engaged. These 'non-sense events' include |Kaggen's climbing into the ichneumon's bag and his whispering to and winking at the baby lion. Lewis-Williams (1996a: 128) argues that 'it is the activities and experiences of shamans that explain the otherwise bizarre central section of the myth'. By climbing into the bag, |Kaggen enters the antelope from whose skin it has been made and takes on the power of the animal. Entering the antelope skin bag represents the beginning of his access to a state of trance. Leaving aside this interpretation for now, I should like to consider whether this part of the story is really bizarre and inexplicable. |Kaggen's decision to hide in the bag can, in my opinion, be quite easily explained in terms of the story itself. He was terrified of the lions. Neither the stark Kalahari terrain nor the other objects carried by the members of the party would have afforded him a better place to hide from them.

In many stories besides this one, |Kaggen escapes from trouble by taking flight. He commonly summons his belongings to follow him and regenerates in a waterhole. It is reasonable to assume that Lewis-Williams would interpret all of these events as describing an act of shamanic transformation. One might expect that the events that preceded these magical flights and transformations would be bizarre, but examination of these stories and the articulation of the elements within them with the recurrence of these elements in the collection as a whole does not, in my view, support such a supposition. The general pattern is that |Kaggen provokes a fight, begins to lose and escapes by flying off and summoning his belongings to follow him. He is a master of leaping away from tight situations: 'And the Mantis sprang aside and ran away, because he felt he could not bear it any longer. Then he called to the quiver and his shoes, that his things should follow him home' (D. Bleek 1923: 13). 'He said, as he went up into the sky: 'O shoes, you must come! O Hartbeest's children (to the bag), you must come. O quiver, you must come. O kaross, you must come! The cap must come!' (D. Bleek 1923: 16–17, brackets in the original). 'The Mantis quickly got feathers, he flew away. He called to the Hartebeest-skin bag: "O Hartebeest's children, leave here, we must fly"' (D. Bleek 1923: 19). It is not unreasonable to read these events as Hewitt reads them, simply as part of |Kaggen's stock in trade, his magical ability to extricate himself from dangerous situations. Nor, it could be mentioned in passing, do unexplained features in stories necessarily have to be explained in terms of hidden meanings, as Lewis-Williams contends. Italo Calvino (1996) relates such features to the quality of 'quickness', one of the literary attributes he admires in both folktales and literature generally. 'Quickness' in language results in logical leaps and in statements that defy explanation. The events in a narrative such as this move with extraordinary alacrity. There are at least four shifts of physical location. Characters move rapidly in and out of the action. The text abjures explanation and explication, any element that would detract from the pace of the action, and is characterised by a great 'economy of expression' (Calvino 1996: 37); it is pared to its bare essentials. In such narratives, 'meaning is conveyed through a verbal texture that seems weightless' (Calvino 1996: 16).

One of the elements that Lewis-Williams finds 'non-sensical' in the story is the young lion's mistaking |Kaggen for a hare. |Kaggen, it could be noted, turns into hares elsewhere in the |Xam materials in order to divert the hunters' attention from the gemsbok they are hunting. Such hares are referred to as |Kaggen's hares. This transformation occurs in the context of the hunting observances. It is not without relevance, as I have already suggested, that the animal whose flesh is being shared is a quagga, one of the animals that enjoy |Kaggen's protection. He would be expected to try to interrupt the consumption of the meat. I am not claiming that Lewis-Williams is incorrect in linking |Kaggen's association in the story with a hare to shamanism; I am merely arguing that the elements in the story that he finds bizarre, and that, therefore, in his view, must contain a hidden meaning such as shamanic transformation, occur in other contexts in the materials in which they make obvious sense. These contexts, moreover, sometimes seem to have links with this story and help to explicate it.

CONCLUSION

The centrality of shamanism in Lewis-Williams's reading of this story and in the story that I discussed in chapter 3 is replicated famously in his trance theory of rock art. The critics of this theory, as we have seen, have contended that it does not suitably account for the diversity in the rock art that their own research reveals. Lewis-Williams is aware, too, of diverse themes and layers of meaning in both rock painting and the |Xam narratives. He does not, however, accord different meanings equal weight. Instead, he subsumes diversity within a unified theory that elevates the spiritual experience of trance above other kinds of experience and activity. The material aspects of |Xam life become the raw ingredients for |Xam spiritual life. This accords with the temptation I mentioned earlier, and which several writers have noted in regard to the representation of Bushmen, to regard the Bushman as a spiritual person, the embodiment of authentic, natural humankind. The alternatives to a shamanistic interpretation of the |Xam stories do not, however, exclude spiritual and religious experiences or the realms of transformation and the supernatural. This particular story clearly contains supernatural and magical motifs. The fact that the prey is a quagga, as I have mentioned, links it with the complex of |Xam hunting observances and |Kaggen, a complex that is characterised by what seem, at least to a mind schooled in contemporary thought, to be extraordinary features. What is important, in my view, is an enquiry into how |Xam categories of the supernatural, the secular, the profane and sacred are produced and reproduced in the discursive field of the narratives.

This chapter and chapter 3 both include an examination of Lewis-Williams's shamanistic interpretation of |Xam narratives. These interpretations have not elicited much opposition among interpreters of the narratives, but this is not the case in the field of rock art interpretation, in which Lewis-Williams's shamanistic theories have generated considerable controversy. As I have mentioned before in this book, dissension has been peculiarly absent from discussions about the |Xam narratives. The obvious exception was the heated exchange that occurred when Stephen Watson accused Antjie Krog of plagiarism after she published a selection of |Xam narratives in the form of poems. I will examine this controversy in the next and final chapter of this book, using it also to reiterate many of the contentions about interpreting the |Xam materials that have emerged in the course of this book.

NOTES

1   Hewitt's views accord with those of Dorothea Bleek (1929: 305). Neither |Kaggen nor !Khwa should be seen as deities, in her view. Of |Kaggen, she writes: 'Nor is the term "God" correct, for the Mantis is not worshipped, at least among the |kham [sic]; the Bushmen of the Malutis are said to have prayed to "Cagn". But the impression given in the folklore I am dealing with is of a sort of Puck, a helper or mischief-maker, but not at all a deity' (305).

2   Although, Lewis-Williams is not mentioned in Hewitt's bibliography, his writing on the rock art clearly influenced Hewitt. Hewitt confirms this influence in the acknowledge-ments that appear in the new edition of his book (Hewitt 2008: ix): 'David Lewis-Williams was a fellow at Cambridge working on his earliest ideas concerning the San rock paintings he had been so meticulously recording and analysing when we some-how came into contact at the start of my doctoral research. We had many fascinating conversations and debates in London over the published Bleek and Lloyd materials at a time when it was hard to find a soul who even knew of their existence.'

3   This statement particularly describes an aspect of Spivak's work that has influenced my approach in this book. The post-colonial criticism of Homi Bhabha (1994) poses as one of its central problematics the Western humanist project of demarcating dis-crete cultures in the first place and accommodating them within a universal structure of cultural diversity.

4   Hewitt's study of |Xam narrative has several components, however. The more ethno-graphic parts of his book do not exclude what might be described as the political aspects of |Xam life.

5   Eliade (1972: 4) himself maintains that the term 'shaman' should be used with a degree of precision. The figure has a clearly defined role. While he is a healer and miracle worker, he is, above all, 'a psychopomp, and he may also be priest, mystic, and poet'. While the figure, according to Eliade (6), is not a universal phenomenon, he does cross regions and cultures. He is especially to be found in hunting or pastoral societies.

6   Bank (2006: 314, 335) argues that the tendency to use the |Xam materials to shore up his trance theory of rock art interpretation also characterises Lewis-Williams's selective use of the |Xam informants' comments on the examples of rock art that they were shown.

CHAPTER 12

ANTJIE KROG, STEPHEN WATSON AND THE METAPHYSICS OF PRESENCE

Stephen Watson provoked a furious debate, conducted for the most part on the Internet and in the newspapers, with his contentions in *New Contrast* (2005) that Antjie Krog's *The Stars Say 'Tsau'* (2004) constitutes a form of plagiarism. This tendency is not new in her work, avers Watson. Parts of Krog's *Country of My Skull* were borrowed, he claims, from Ted Hughes's 1976 essay 'Myth and education' (Watson 2005: 59–60). While conceding that Krog's work might not directly quote other writers' work without acknowledgement, it possesses, Watson (2005: 50) claims, a 'plagiaristic spirit'. In Watson's opinion (2005: 54–57), Krog's adaptations in poetry of the |Xam materials are so close to Bleek and Lloyd's prose originals, mostly as published in *Specimens of Bushman Folklore* (1911), that they represent an illegitimate instance of borrowing. The very 'conception' of *The Stars Say 'Tsau'*, argues Watson (2005: 49), too closely parallels his own *Return of the Moon* (1991). Nor, he asserts (2005: 49–50), can it be accidental that many of Krog's statements in her introduction resemble the statements in his introduction, or that more than a third of Krog's selection of extracts coincides with his own.

Watson appeals to a commonly accepted tradition of originality in scholarly and literary practice and the protocols that attend the use of sources. He distances himself, however, from a rigid and legalistic application of these principles (Watson 2005: 57–58). The critical question is whether the borrowing is 'derivative' or 'transformative'. In Krog's case,

Watson concludes (60), it is merely derivative and thus constitutes 'a blatant act of appropriation', especially of Lucy Lloyd's translations from the |Xam.

The reactions to Watson's article were immediate and strong. Apart from Krog's own responses (Krog 2006a; 2006b), a number of academics, journalists and publishers defended Krog's work. These defences rarely included a dispassionate consideration of the broader questions that Watson raised. Several writers remarked that Watson's failure to observe academic rules of engagement and his 'vituperative language' (Gray 2006) did not invite a measured and impartial response (Mason-Jones 2006; Johnson 2006; De Lange 2006). For the most part, they attacked the suspected motives behind Watson's allegations, reiterating, for instance, the criticisms levelled against Watson's own volume of |Xam verse and suggesting that he was still smarting from them.

Kwela Books and Random House, the publishers of *The Stars Say 'Tsau'* and *Country of My Skull*, respectively, both rejected the claims against their author. Eve Gray of Publishing Solutions and several academics examined the specific instances of plagiarism and borrowing that Watson identified in Krog's work and dismissed them as unreasonable and unfounded. Krog, they pronounced, had adequately acknowledged her sources. They pointed out that she had never claimed to be the author of the poems she presents, a feature of her book that is clearly signalled in the subtitle, which announces *The Stars Say 'Tsau'* as the */Xam Poetry of Dia!kwain, KweitenTa//Ken, /A!kunta, /Han#kass'o and //Kabbo*, while it is clearly indicated that they were selected and adapted by Antjie Krog. In any event, several poets and other writers had reworked the |Xam materials before Watson did so in *Return of the Moon*. It was unreasonable, therefore, for Watson to suggest that Krog had borrowed the idea for her project from his earlier one. They argued that most of the statements regarding the |Xam in her introduction were based on publicly available sources. Even if some of her statements were inaccurate, these inaccuracies did not constitute theft.

Only a few writers suggested, as Colin Bower (2006) did, that Watson's allegations might be valid or addressed the broader questions that the controversy raised. Annie Gagiano (2006), who had criticised several aspects of Watson's *Return of the Moon* (Gagiano 1992; 1999), was one of the first to allude to these questions. She (2006) stated that she did not wish to take sides in the controversy, but reminded everyone that 'appropriation (and its validity or otherwise) is a larger issue than plagiarism' and that 'underlying the present quarrel are deeper questions concerning cultural "ownership", cultural border crossings, cultural sharing'.[1]

An article on the dispute in the *Mail & Guardian* pointed to some of the other questions framing the controversy:

> It's tempting to see in this spat an example of the split between modernist and postmodernist aesthetics. The former places emphasis on personality, originality, style, on the transformative value of art; the latter can't see originality in much, and no virtue in style as such (De Waal 2006).

Barbara Adair (2006) identifies the main question that arises from the dispute as 'Can a writer ever do anything that is unique and original?' In this, the concluding, chapter of this book, I wish to concentrate on this question of originality. I will consider, especially, the different conceptions of originality that are evident in the two poets' approaches to their projects. I will also attempt to show that the questions elicited by the controversy are more complex and open than a partisan response would concede. Both Watson and Krog, in different ways in their respective volumes of |Xam verse, acknowledge their debt to the |Xam narrators and to the collectors, Wilhelm Bleek and Lucy Lloyd. Neither claims that his/her work is altogether original. How then, in Watson's view, does his own practice differ from Krog's and what is the nature of his claim that his versions are more original than are Krog's? Why does he regard his project as legitimate and hers as illegitimate?

Watson's charge of conceptual borrowing against Krog implies that his own volume was original in its conception. Krog (2006a) disputes this. Instead of directly levelling a counter-accusation of concept theft, however, she suggests that Watson's claim to originality is attributable to ignorance or laziness:

> Unlike Watson, I read the adapted versions of |Xam poetry in *The Penguin Book of South African Verse* (1968) by Jack Cope and Uys Krige during my high-school years; not to forget Alan James's impeccable versions in *The*

First Bushman's Path, published three years before my version appeared. (James also mentions A. Markowitz's 1956 poetic versions.)

Since Krog must know that it is unlikely that Watson would be unfamiliar with *The Penguin Book of South African Verse*, she is, in effect, accusing him of inflating the originality of his book by neglecting to mention his predecessors. She also accuses him of not mentioning his successors — clairvoyance, it seems, is a gift Krog expects of her adversaries. Watson, of course, could not have read James's volume, since it appeared ten years after his own *Return of the Moon*.

Krog's counter-accusation that Watson failed to acknowledge his debt to illustrious pioneers such as Marais (1959) and Jack Cope is itself a repetition of a point raised by Gagiano (1999: 164), who observes that Watson neglects to mention Cope as his predecessor in versifying the Bleek and Lloyd translations.[2] While Krog (2006a) claims that she is more aware than Watson is of her antecedents, it should be noted that Krog does not mention Marais, Markowitz, Cope or James in *The Stars Say 'Tsau'*. Krog's inclusion of Krige as one of the poets who produced versions of |Xam poems suggests, too, that she has not closely read either Cope and Krige's book or the review by Annie Gagiano (1992), to which she refers in her retort to Watson's criticisms (Krog 2006a). Gagiano (1992; 1999: 164) explicitly identifies Cope as the editor responsible for the Bushman poems that appear in the anthology. The anthology, for the most part, also makes this clear.[3] Crediting both Krige and Cope with the poems is, I think, an understandable oversight. Considering the importance that details assumed in the controversy between Watson and Krog, however, it is also an unfortunate one.

Whether or not Watson failed to properly acknowledge his predecessors, his poetic project was clearly different in scope and kind from the other work to which Krog (2006a) refers. Krog's own volume of verse much more closely resembles Watson's work than it does either Marais's or Cope's. Marais's *Dwaalstories* (1959) is written in the form of long prose poems and is based only in part on the Bleek and Lloyd Collection. Marais reworked his source materials to an extent that makes it difficult to distinguish between what he invented and what he derived from informants or published texts (Swart 2003: 96–97). Even though Watson does not supply his 'precise sources in the Bleek and Lloyd documents' (Gagiano 1999: 169), his versions of the materials do not often present this difficulty.[4] In contrast to Watson, Cope only reworked a relatively small number of extracts into verse, and these appear in a general anthology of South African poetry. Watson's project is perhaps closest to Arthur Markowitz's *With Uplifted Tongue* (1956). Their volumes are similar in length and often in content, and they also follow a similar method with regard to the materials. According to Alan James (2001: 20), who acknowledges Watson (1991) and Markowitz (1956), along with Gideon von Wielligh (1919–21), as his forerunners, Watson and Markowitz both aim 'to provide accessible and persuasive literary versions of the translation texts as products that are at the same time aesthetically instrumental and responsibly mediatorial of the texts from which they draw their life'.[5]

Gagiano (1999: 164) might be right for reprimanding Watson for not referring to Cope in his introduction. Markowitz (1956), as Krog suggests — on the basis, it should be said, of her reading of Alan James's introduction to *The First Bushman's Path* (2001) rather than of her own reading of Markowitz — is certainly another writer he could have mentioned. Nevertheless, as I have already remarked, Watson's project was clearly different in important respects. By working only with |Xam texts, his poetry (but not always his introduction) does not perpetuate the view that all Bushman belonged to a single culture. Cope, Markowitz and Marais indiscriminately included materials from different Bushman languages as though they all belonged to a homogeneous tradition. In addition, Watson was the first poet to supply notes to the poems that take into account the scholarship that relates to the materials. In any event, his predecessors could only have relied on Bleek and Lloyd themselves or on the work of Bleek's daughter, Dorothea, even if they had wished to provide a more extensive framework for their work. Roger Hewitt's pioneering study of the |Xam narratives only appeared in 1986. Most significantly, Watson was the first poet to work directly with the Bleek and Lloyd notebooks,[6] although relatively few of Watson's final pieces were actually based on previously unpublished material (Lewis-Williams 2000: 37).[7]

Central to the concerns of this chapter is Watson's criticism of the lack of originality of Krog's adaptations on the grounds that they entail little more than a literal recasting of the originals, i.e. that they are closer to typing than to writing (Watson 2005: 57). Krog's enterprise, in Watson's view, does not represent a creative advance on her sources. For the most part, he charges, she simply reproduces Lucy Lloyd's translations. Innovation is mostly limited to changes to punctuation and lineation, the latter intended, claims Watson (53), to make the words on the page at least look like poetry. His own |Xam poems, by contrast, are not merely derivative; they transform and breathe life into their sources.

Watson (1991: 11–12) maintains in the introduction to his volume of poems that he seeks to recover, to some extent, the vitality of the originals that had been obscured by the laboured Victorian translations. He is well aware of the delicacy of this project and that it can never altogether do justice to the original |Xam context for the narratives. This presumably, for Watson, was to be found in the performance of traditional narratives to a |Xam audience in a pre-colonial setting, a presumption that is supported both by the description in his introduction of the nature of |Xam mythology (Watson 2005: 19), which I will discuss later in this chapter, and by his characterisation of the genesis of the Bleek and Lloyd archive. The narratives, he states, were collected in a way that was, for narrators used to performing for 'their own people', 'bizarre' and 'artificial' (Watson 2005: 8). However, since Watson's volume also contains pieces that are clearly not rooted in |Xam mythology or oral literature, such as ||Kabbo's account of his capture and his request for sewing thread, which only ever existed in the Bleek-Lloyd archive, and by virtue of the relationships its development involved, Watson must also be referring to the |Xam language texts in the collection, the originals of Bleek and Lloyd's literal English translations.

Translating the |Xam materials, maintains Watson (1991: 11), entails a betrayal of the 'originals', the 'excuse' for which 'is to be found only in the type of end one seeks to achieve'. The end that justifies Watson's practice is the attempt to resurrect the materials, which are 'dead, doubly dead'. Not only are they locked away in an archive, where they are accessible only to scholars, but they are preserved in a language that is incapable of speaking to contemporary people (Watson 2005: 11). Watson (1991: 10) emphasises the peculiar difficulties that attend translation from a language that has no living practitioners who can monitor the accuracy of the translation:

any translator from the |Xam has always to set to work in the face of one corrosive certainty: he or she does not know, and knows it can never be known, whether an interpretation — and all translation is interpretation — is entirely faithful to the original, to the letter or the spirit.

Watson's characterisation of his project as translation is a feature of his introduction that has elicited criticism. In Annie Gagiano's view (1999: 169), Watson's claim to be a translator of the texts 'suppresses the extent to which his work rests on what Bleek and Lloyd achieved'. Lewis-Williams (2000: 36) argues, too, that Watson does not offer new translations; he has 'simply rearranged Bleek and Lloyd's translations'.[8] As a poet rather than a |Xam linguist, Watson (1991: 10) might reply that his 'translations' attend to the 'spirit' rather than to the 'letter' of the original.

While observing that 'the very fact of the |Xam's extinction would seem to demand an absolute measure of fidelity from any translator', Watson (1991: 11) forgoes this sort of fidelity by employing the 'periphrases, re-writings and re-structurings necessary to achieve' his goal of reanimating |Xam literary expression and helping it to live for a new audience. 'One could either remain close to Bleek and Lloyd's literal English version and produce a piece without poetic charge, fated to remain inured in the past; or one could re-work so as to bring the material into the present, living for those alive in the present' (Watson 1991: 12). Watson's rewriting of the materials, however, is not, he adds, 'dictated solely by poetic purposes' (Watson 1991: 13) or driven by guesswork. He directly incorporates the findings of Hewitt (1986) and Guenther (1989) — described in the acknowledgements as his 'indispensable guides' — in his versions. At the time that Watson produced his |Xam poems, Hewitt and Watson were the only contemporary scholars who had produced significant interpretations of the |Xam narratives. Krog, Watson (2005: 50–51) charges, has not followed his example of assiduously consulting the relevant scholarly literature.

Watson argues that the poetic form suits the treatment of excerpts from the materials. It enabled him

> to seek out the poetic — the possible 'poetic idea' — in any single piece and highlight it. Poetry, in short, enabled me to cast into relief certain features

which would almost certainly have been lost in even the best prose translation (Watson 1991: 16).[9]

This is not to suggest, he cautions, that 'the IXam were inhabitants of some
mythical-poetical Eden ... [who] spoke nothing but poetry' (Watson
2005: 16).

Krog's project follows a contrary strategy to Watson's, and she remains
close to Bleek and Lloyd's translations. This approach is followed by
Guenther (1989: 27) and by Lewis-Williams (2000: 38) in their prose
selections of materials from the collection and, to some degree, by James
(2001: 25). While James does not follow Watson in completely rewriting
the materials, he does intervene to a much greater degree than Krog does.
For a start, he modernises the language, while Krog sometimes — although
not as consistently as Watson's critique might suggest — preserves the
archaisms of the original, a strategy that Watson (2005: 53) attributes to
Krog's mistaken belief that archaisms are themselves poetic.

Krog, as Watson (2005: 57) points out, and as she herself acknowledges
(2004: 10), sometimes draws on Lewis-William's book for her selection.
Krog's acknowledgement of Lewis-Williams, it could be noted, does not
prevent her from ignoring his opposition to turning the IXam materials
into poetry, which, in his opinion, is a 'very real temptation' to resist since
it leads to a 'prettification' of the materials that belies 'the tragedy that
permeates the whole collection' (Lewis-Williams 2000: 38). James (2001:
21–23), by contrast, responds in some detail to Lewis-Williams's objections
to presenting the Bleek and Lloyd materials in verse.

Krog's introduction displays little of the sort of self-consciousness about
the ethics of the enterprise of reworking the materials into poems that
Watson's or James's introductions do. Accordingly, she does not attempt to
justify her project or defend her decision to recast the materials in the form
of poetry. By describing the narrators as the 'Bushman poets' — erroneously,
Watson (2005: 51) points out — she suggests that the materials are, in any
case, already poetry. She only briefly discusses her 'method' (Krog 2004: 10),
observing that some of the material lends itself peculiarly well to poetry:
'Often the text fell into verse. Nothing else was necessary: the poem was clear
and complete.' At other times, however, she intervenes more: 'I let myself be

guided more by what would work as a poem than by a faithful rendering of the original' (Krog 2004: 10). Krog attributes the lack of originality of which Watson accuses her to the fact that the original translations already work as poetry. Greater originality, on her part, would entail a loss of the authenticity of the originals and detract from their natural poetry. Only where necessary, asserts Krog, will she resort to the sort of interventions practised by Watson. Most of these cases concern the excising of 'the kind of repetition which works well in an oral context but smothers everything on a page' (Krog 2004: 10).[10] She describes this sort of intervention as adaptation. This accords with the aim of her book, which is to provide a selection from the |Xam poets, rather than her own original poetry. Krog's extensive use of the actual words of the Bleek and Lloyd materials is, therefore, partly attributable to her goal in compiling her selection — that of presenting the work of the |Xam 'poets'. A greater intervention on her part would have meant that the poems became hers rather than theirs. |Xam authorship of the materials is signalled by the adherence of her versions to the originals.

This, of course, ignores the fact that the |Xam narrators were not poets and the materials in the notebooks are not poetry. This is not to dispute the fact that the collection does contain many pieces, such as songs and prayers, that are presented in the form of poetry. Nor would one wish to deny that the |Xam texts are 'poetic', at least to a contemporary ear. This is partly due, I suggested in chapter 7, to nineteenth-century conventions of translating folklore. Krog (2004: 8) herself notes that the materials were 'translated into formal Victorian English'. One could go even further and argue that the |Xam materials are presented not so much in nineteenth-century English as in 'a quasi-Elizabethan or Jacobean English' (Hewitt 2007: 167).

Nevertheless, Krog's book does not literally reproduce the poetry of |Xam poets. It constructs a genre, as much as do the work of Bleek and Lloyd themselves and the 'versions' of Von Wielligh, Marais, Markowitz, Cope, Watson or James.[11] In this sense, she is being more innovative than she claims, although still not inventive enough to escape Watson's censure.

Krog's approach is consistent with her faith in the accuracy and authenticity of Bleek and Lloyd's translations. While several commentators, including Helize van Vuuren (1994) and Mathias Guenther (1996), have stressed the mediated and unsatisfactory aspects of these translations,

Krog describes the meticulous process in which the translations were made in collaboration with the informants, a position supported by Andrew Bank's (2006) study of the genesis of the collection, especially with regard to Lucy Lloyd's translation practice. It does not follow, of course, that the faithfulness of the translations means that the materials work automatically as literature or poetry. Watson himself acknowledges their accuracy, but argues that this detracts from their accessibility, a view held also by Markowitz (1956: 10) and James (2001: 18–20). Bleek and Lloyd 'were concerned, above all, with providing accurate *literal* translations' (Watson 2005: 53; original emphasis). The 'contortions' this linguistic enterprise often produced should not be mistaken for 'a form of poetry, only waiting to be rediscovered in the 21st century' (Watson 2005: 53).

In actual fact, for Krog, much of the authenticity of the texts is attributable not to the accuracy of the English translations, but to their preservation of an 'Afrikaans substructure', which makes it easy for Krog, the Afrikaans poet, 'to identify with the original voices' (Krog 2004: 10). Krog's (2006a) reply to Watson's criticisms especially emphasises the Afrikaans component of her project. The initial motivation for her book, Krog asserts, was 'to bring the lXam voices back into Afrikaans after so many years', adding to the body of Khoisan literature in Afrikaans and consciously following in Eugéne Marais's footsteps. Not only is she presenting the work of the lXam narrators, but she is doing so in a medium, Afrikaans, that is closer to their live speech rhythms than English is. Afrikaans, it is hinted, but not overtly stated, is also a language that is more genuinely South African than is English. It is closer to the indigenous voice and, perhaps, to the African soil as well.[12] Where Watson restores the materials to their original spirit — or something more proximate to it than Bleek and Lloyd's translations — through his poetic interventions, Krog brings them closer to their original form by recasting them in Afrikaans.

Krog (2004: 9–10) attributes 'the Afrikaans sub-structure' of the material in the Bleek and Lloyd Collection to the fact that 'Bleek and Lloyd had to make use of Cape Dutch as a means of communication with the lXam'. She implies that Afrikaans was always the chief medium of exchange between the interviewers and the informants in the storytelling/dictation process. Krog's view of the importance of Afrikaans is probably accurate with regard to the early materials in the notebooks (Traill 1996: 168–69; Bank 2006: 179–80). Bleek himself, however, was able to translate directly into English from the |Xam from quite early on in the process of collecting the narratives. Lloyd later became fluent in |Xam (Bank 2006: 262). Many of the materials reworked by Krog did not, in all likelihood, emerge into English from |Xam via Afrikaans. Watson (2005: 52) insists that the sentences offered by Krog as examples of the Afrikaans structure of the materials 'have nothing to do with Afrikaans syntax, and everything to do with the grammatical structure of the |Xam language'.

Whatever the merits of Krog's argument regarding the Afrikaans cadences in the Bleek and Lloyd translations, her claim that her Afrikaans ear enables her to judge the closeness of the Bleek and Lloyd materials to the |Xam originals and thus to sanction their authenticity is central to her |Xam poetry project and to her subsequent defence of it. The |Xam materials, to Krog's Afrikaans ear, are already alive, and there is no need to resurrect them. She is in a better position than Watson to discern this, for, '[u]nlike Watson, I know more than one South African language' (Krog 2006a).

As I have frequently maintained in this book, at least some of the scholarly and popular fascination that Bushmen elicit can be attributed to a nostalgia for 'the "naturalness" of small-scale societies as opposed to the "artificiality" of industrial society' (Wilmsen 1996: 186). Much of this interest (including, perhaps, the impulse to turn their materials into poetry) follows, in this analysis, from the Bushmen's symbolic status as archetypal representatives of the age of the childhood of humankind. This attitude is often explicit in the earlier writing on the Bushmen. Sandra Swart (2003) has tracked its influence in Eugéne Marais's Bushman tales, mentioned by Krog (2006a) as an inspiration. It dominates Laurens van der Post's books (1958; 1961), in which it is mixed with Jungian psychological evolutionism.[13] Cope and Krige (1968: 18) refer to 'our earliest poetry, the literally stone-age songs and recitals of the Bushmen and Hottentots'. Phillip Tobias (1956: 5) maintains that 'the Bushmen provide one of the rare surviving human links with the palaeolithic world'. George Theal (1911: xl) writes of 'a people in the condition of early childhood'.

I have argued throughout this book that the view of the Bushmen as close to original humans is still present in contemporary writing about them, although it is expressed differently. It is also true that not all interest in the Bushmen should be reduced to this fascination with origins. Helize van Vuuren (1996: 129) has observed, sensibly I think, that the scholarly attention that is given to the Bushmen can be attributed to multiple factors. Nevertheless, nostalgia for a lost origin is, undoubtedly, a consistent strain in both popular conceptions concerning Bushmen and in Bushman studies itself. It is instructive, therefore, to investigate its presence in Krog's and Watson's poetry projects and in the debates that have followed from Watson's critique of *The Stars Say 'Tsau'*. Both Krog and Watson appeal, after all, to an original state of |Xam orality. Krog purports to remain true to an original |Xam discourse that can be discerned in the Afrikaans substructure of the Bleek and Lloyd translations, while Watson seeks to reclaim something of the power and immediacy of the original |Xam oral literature through presenting the texts in the form of a poetry that is at once contemporary and true to the spirit of |Xam culture.

Watson's introduction shows a considerable degree of awareness of the complex of the lost origin and exhibits a desire to avoid some of its pitfalls. He does not wish, he writes, 'to suggest that the |Xam were inhabitants of some mythical-poetical Eden' (Watson 1991: 16), nor does he want to sentimentalise Bushmen or reinforce stereotypes of them (17). His most striking recognition of the nostalgia for a lost origin that characterises much of the literature on the Bushmen is contained in his observation that '[t]he conviction has long flourished that there is something like a spirit, an essence, or "soul of the Bushman", and that this embodies precisely those habits of mind not readily available to us, living in modern technological societies today' (18). While he does not dismiss the sentiment out of hand, he does state that it is a temptation to be resisted.

Despite his awareness of the temptation of the metaphysics of presence, some of Watson's statements in the introduction to *Return of the Moon* might be said to betray some of its influence. Although Watson insists that the |Xam were not part of a 'mythical-poetical Eden', several of his other statements tend to locate them in an ahistorical realm. He refers, for instance, to them as 'the oldest of all South African cultures'(1991: 7). While this might simply refer to the fact that the people whom scholars would later refer to as Bushmen preceded others within the boundaries of present-day South Africa, it also suggests that the |Xam possessed an unchanging, pure culture that was immune to history and the complex interactions it produces. Other cultures are newer, since they are more contaminated by history and are, thus, further from the origin and presence. Watson's statement also implies that all Bushman groups everywhere possessed the same culture. Elsewhere, Watson (1991: 10) refers to |Xam culture as having a 'continuous existence for something like five thousand years', a vague and imprecise figure in historical terms, but one that signifies timelessness and proximity to an origin.[14] It is only in the nineteenth century, implies Watson's introduction, that the |Xam enter history. |Xam culture proved tragically unable to adapt to the historical: 'the mythical being doomed to disintegrate and then vanish under the onslaught of historical forces' (Watson 1991: 16). |Xam literature, in this complex, belongs to myth, the realm of the archetypal and timeless, of speech. It escapes writing, the textual and the materiality of discourse. Moran (2001: 48) notes, in this regard, that in Watson's poems, '[t]he idiomatic and disjunctive form of *Specimens* is peeled away to reveal what Watson sees as the humane kernel, a mythic content that transcends cultures and time'.

Watson's (1991) project of reworking the Bleek and Lloyd texts follows from the differences between written and oral literature. Part of the reason that the Bleek and Lloyd texts do not work as written literature, in Watson's opinion, is that they are literal transcriptions of an oral form. His poetry is a form of writing that is necessarily different in kind from oral literature. Nevertheless, it is not altogether far-fetched to claim that part of Watson's attempt to resurrect the spirit of the original is based on an implied assumption that poetry is closer to the spoken word than is prose. Poetry, after all, is often written to be spoken and heard. The Bleek and Lloyd materials were spoken in order to be written. Watson is, in some sense, returning the texts to speech and investing them with presence. The artist as poet is well positioned to do this, for, as Moran (1995) points out, a close connection can be established between 'the teleology of meaning as return to origin' (19) and the idea that 'originality' is 'the genius of the sublime artist' (23). In Hegel's version of white mythology, for example, writes Moran (18), '[t]he telos of the fulfilment of man as the fulfilment of world history is the transformation of sensory presence into the self-presence of (self) consciousness — the propriety or property of subjectivity to and for itself that is the nature of man'. The |Xam, in this scheme, enjoy direct access to sensory presence, which infuses their oral narrative performances, but has been stifled in the Bleek and Lloyd texts. The poet, who has access to presence in the form of the self-presence available to the artistic genius, can reinfuse the materials with presence. I am not proposing, of course, that Watson subscribes to the ethnocentrism of this scheme, but am suggesting, rather, that some of the historical roots of the conception of the sort of artistic originality for which Watson argues in connection with the reworking of the |Xam materials can be located in the complex that Moran (1995; 2001) links with other writing on the |Xam.

Watson reproduces what Andrew Bank (2002) has identified as one of the most common misconceptions about the Bleek and Lloyd project when he writes that 'the |Xam informants lived in grass huts at the bottom of the garden of Bleek's home in Mowbray, Cape Town' (Watson 1991: 8). Bank (2002) suggests that the location of the informants in the garden rather than in the house, where they actually resided, strengthens the stereotype of the Bushmen as pure embodiments of natural humankind. Watson, however, it must be noted, mentions the grass huts in order to emphasise the 'dislocating' circumstances experienced by the |Xam informants in Mowbray rather than to signal Bushman proximity to nature.

Watson's introduction and his poetry might at times exhibit traces of the influence of the metaphysics of presence. As often, though, he demonstrates an explicit intention to elude it. A close reading of his article on Krog's |Xam poems suggests too that he has revised some of his earlier positions regarding the |Xam and their materials. It should also be remembered that Watson, writing 13 years before Krog, did not have access to much of the recent scholarship in which the sort of critique I have just delivered has become prevalent. His introduction to his poems could even be seen as a relatively early contribution to this scholarship, much of which is characterised by 'the frequency and range of expressions of cautionary criticism' (Gagiano 1999: 155).

Antjie Krog demonstrates none of the same self-reflexivity. Her statements about the |Xam in her introduction to her volume of poems and also in her foreword to Brown's *To Speak of This Land* (Krog 2006c) consistently situate her attitude towards the |Xam in the broader complex identified by Derrida, in which the spoken word, particularly that uttered by members of 'original', pre-literate people like the |Xam, is posited as possessing a peculiar sort of authenticity lacking from the written word and cultures that depend on it. This attitude informs, I have already suggested, her contention that the |Xam language is more accurately conveyed in Afrikaans than in English. It also colours her view that the |Xam were all poets and their utterances all natural poetry (Krog 2004: 7–8). Her 'fanciful' (Watson 2005: 51) picture of 'charming scenes of small people, clothed in skins, sitting in the study or on the veranda or in the garden' (Krog 2004: 8) exemplifies the characterisation of the |Xam informants as innocent Stone Age denizens of nature. Krog also succumbs, in this statement, to the temptation of what Watson (1991: 17) terms 'the little Bushman syndrome'.[15] The |Xam, writes Watson, 'do not deserve the posthumous charity of being sentimentalised as dwarfs'. Krog, it would seem, either disagrees with Watson or she has not read his introduction as closely as he claims she has.

The statement with which Krog (2006c) begins her foreword to Brown is extraordinarily revealing of her desire to position the |Xam as close to a presence-filled origin.[16] It is worth, therefore, investigating in some detail. She writes that '[o]ne of our country's earliest stories was told by ||Kabbo through Wilhelm Bleek and Lucy Lloyd' (Krog 2006c: xiii). The |Xam, it is implied, participate in a common South African national identity. They represent the earliest strata of a single history, precisely because they stand outside history.

The piece to which Krog refers was related to Bleek towards the end of ||Kabbo's stay in Mowbray in 1873. It is not, contrary to Krog's description of it, primarily a story at all, but an expression of ||Kabbo's will to return home. It contains ||Kabbo's request that Bleek supply him with the gun that he had promised him. The text includes observations about |Xam storytelling, and it tells of some of ||Kabbo's hunting experiences and other aspects of his personal history. Only part of this account is cast in the form of narrative.

While modern people, implies Krog, possess history, literary criticism and biography, the |Xam possess only stories. In terms of Derrida's analysis, they have speech, not writing. This reading is reinforced by Krog's contention that it is an early story. This statement would have been unsurprising had it been applied to one of the |Xam stories of the First Times, but her application of it to a text that is not a story of this type at all is characteristic, I would argue, of Krog's ideological immersion in the metaphysics of presence. The piece is only one of South Africa's earliest stories if one accepts that its teller, ||Kabbo, is one of South Africa's earliest people, even though he lived in the latter part of the nineteenth century. Once again, the |Xam and their utterances are located outside history in a primal time that is presence filled and proximate to the origin.

In this chapter, I have concentrated only on a single line of enquiry, one suggested by the work of Wilmsen (1996), Moran (1995; 2001), Van Vuuren (1994), Brown (1998) and others. Many other questions arise from the Krog–Watson dispute, including those identified by Gagiano (2006). The different expectations that are held of oral performers and published authors is another question that could be investigated. Such a study would require further consideration of the nature of the |Xam materials of the sort in which I engaged earlier in this book. Should they be seen as discourse or as timeless myths? Are they fluid texts produced by psychologically and historically located individuals, or are they local manifestations of a 'universal genre' that emerged whole and pure from the '"collective consciousness" of the tribe'? (Brown 1998: 17). Close textual analysis of the poetry that has been based on |Xam texts is another project that awaits a literary scholar.

I will conclude this chapter with a brief foray into yet another possible line of enquiry, one that follows from a strain in the work of writers such as Hewitt (1986: 192), Van Vuuren (1994: 63) and Brown (1998; 2006), all of whom, as I noted in chapter 3, allude in various ways to the presence of indigenous exegesis or literary theory in the |Xam materials. ||Kabbo, in a piece I have referred to in chapter 3, and which is also discussed by Krog (2006c), provides his own thoughts on the nature of |Xam narratives. They float from afar; he sits in the sun and listens for them. Stories come while one is sitting in the sun: 'that I might sit listening to the stories which afar come ... I shall perceive a story with them; while I feel that they sail out from afar; while the sun does feel a little warm' (L.II.32:2875–77). Stories are social and discursive products:

I do not hear stories, while I feel that I do not visit, that I might hear stories which sail along, while I feel that, another place's people are those which are here, those do not hear my stories. They do not talk my language; for, they do visit their fellows (L.II.32:2878–79).

What, one might ask, could one say about the 'IXam' poetry of Watson and Krog in terms of IXam 'literary theory'? Although the question is largely metaphorical, given the historical and discursive distance between the practice of a IXam storyteller and a contemporary literary practitioner, it is, I think, worth asking as part of a short, admittedly polemical and superficial, experiment with a type of criticism that allows the IXam materials to begin to interrogate the analytical frameworks that have been used to interrogate them (Brown 1998: 27).

Stories, according to IIKabbo, float from afar, but only if one visits people who are like oneself. Watson (1991: 10) laments the fact that 'there no longer exists a single person to whom one could go in order to clear up a cultural reference' or 'to gain clarity on the possible meanings of a IXam word'. Nevertheless, he has tried, he states, 'to hear the voice of Bleek and Lloyd's three main informants ... and create poems which work in the English language' (11). He has also visited his peers, the scholars whose work informs his poems (13). Watson's reliance on poetic judgement could be interpreted as a visit to the muses, a process comparable, perhaps, to receiving stories that float from afar. He accuses Krog of conducting the secret, illicit visits that constitute literary theft and not making the mandatory visits to either the scholars or the muses. The inaccuracies in her introduction, such as her belief that the materials were collected partly in the Breakwater Prison (Krog 2004: 8) or that narratives were not collected from !Xun informants (Krog 2004: 11) demonstrate that Krog's visits to the notebooks in the collection and the socondary literature were, at best, selective. Watson (2005: 52) quotes lines such as 'new moon being visible thither' to show that if Krog visited the muses, they were having an off day. Krog might maintain, in reply, that she never intended to go anywhere. She was simply playing the self-effacing hostess, bringing the reader and the IXam 'poets' together with as little intrusiveness and artifice as possible, so that, once again, stories might float from afar.

NOTES

1 These are, of course, recurring issues in debates about the scope and nature of South African literature; see, for example, the essays in Smit, Van Wyk and Wade (1996). In an essay in this volume, Helize van Vuuren (1996) examines the place of Bushman orality within a broader South African literature and the ways in which Bushmen and their narratives have been represented in and incorporated into Afrikaans literature.

2 Gagiano (1999: 164) prefers Cope's versions to Watson's; they are, in her view, better poems. She also likes the way that Cope supplies the name of each IXam narrator above his poems. Watson (1991: 74), by contrast, only refers to them in an index at the back of his book. Van Vuuren (1994: 68) goes so far as to accuse Watson of 'literally colonizing the translated IXam texts', because he conceals the narrators names at the back of the collection, before the footnotes'. Gagiano also criticises Watson for describing himself as a translator in the introduction to *Return of the Moon* (1999: 169). It is interesting, however, that she does not mention that Cope too presents himself, along with Wilhelm Bleek, as the translator of the IXam poems in *The Penguin Book of South African Verse*. In the light of the opposing claims to authenticity made by Krog and Watson and of Watson's stated intention of enabling the IXam poems to speak to contemporary readers, it is also interesting that Gagiano (1992; original emphasis) accuses Watson's poems of lacking a 'real *voice*'. Her appraisal of Cope's and Watson's versions of IXam poems appeals to authenticity. Cope's version of 'The broken string' exhibits, in Gagiano's (1999: 166) opinion, 'a more "authentic" irregularity ... than Watson's'. She concedes that this judgement is a matter of the 'essay-writer's — or any reader's —preferences'. Nevertheless, she contends — correctly, in my view — that the questions of 'authenticity' and 'authority' are 'large but necessary' ones.

3 The letter 'C' appended to the poems indicates that they were translated by Cope (Cope & Krige 1968: 190). Sometimes, however, only Wilhelm Bleek, and not Cope, is credited with the translation of the poem. The letter 'K', indicating Krige as the translator, does not appear after any of the Bushman poems.

4 Lewis-Williams might disagree with this assessment. He (2000: 36) writes of Watson's poems that 'it is hard for a reader to know how much of the resulting "poems" are Watson and how much are Bleek and Lloyd — let alone IXam'. Presumably, however, Lewis-Williams is referring to a reader who has only read Watson's poems rather than to someone who has read Watson's poems, the notebooks and *Specimens of Bushman Folklore*.

5 The majority of Markowitz's pieces, it should be noted, are presented in prose form. Where he chooses poetry, it is often the case that the version used in the source was already presented in poetry. He does, however, also rework into poetry some of the texts that appear in *Specimens of Bushman Folklore* and his other sources in prose form. Unlike Watson, Markowitz does not rely exclusively on the Bleek and Lloyd materials, although they are his most common source (Markowitz 1956: 9). He does not supply references for each piece or attempt to acknowledge the individual Bushman narrators, with the exception of a piece that recounts ||Kabbo's arrest (72–74).

6 Otto Spohr was the only scholar 'outside the Bleek family' before Hewitt to exhibit an

interest in the actual collection, and even he, according to Bank (2006: 390), 'appears not to have consulted the notebooks at all'. Writers who had previously used the |Xam materials that were collected by Bleek and Lloyd relied on Bleek and Lloyd's *Specimens of Bushman Folklore* (1911), Dorothea Bleek's *The Mantis and His Friends* (1923) and her articles in *Bantu Studies*, which appeared in the 1930s. While Watson was the first poet to work directly with the notebooks, he was not the first writer to do so. David Lewis-Williams's reading of the notebooks informed his interpretation of Bushman rock art, which was published in 1981.

7   Krog (2004), too, by her own admission (2006a), worked mostly with material from *Specimens of Bushman Folklore*. Watson charges that Krog's choice of material often parallels his own. Krog argues that this was inevitable, because they both relied on the same source. James (2001), in contrast to both Watson and Krog, bases most of his poems on previously unpublished material.

8   Despite these criticisms, Watson continues to regard his work as translation (2005: 49).

9   Cf. James's (2001: 24) assertion that poetry has the ability to 'highlight an aspect, such as a structure or imagery, that might be passed over if it were not emphasized'. Presumably, James's poetry project escapes Watson's censure because he (James 2001: 20) acknowledges Watson as a predecessor, along with Arthur Markowitz (1956; 1971) and Gideon von Wielligh (1919–21). James also draws much more extensively than Krog does on previously unpublished materials in the notebooks. Although his stated aim is to remain close to the notebooks, he intervenes significantly in the texts. He modernises the language, includes some 'authorial comment' and highlights 'particular textual elements' (James 2001: 25). He also adds 'a measure of aesthetic qualities, albeit of a Western literary character' (James 2001: 24). In addition, his volume is characterised by the sort of meticulous scholarship whose absence Watson (2005: 50–51) abhors in Krog's work. Extensive notes on each poem are provided and each piece is cross-referenced with other materials from the collection. Like Watson, James also discusses the methods and ethics of his enterprise in his introduction. He notes the danger of making poems out of the |Xam texts. Such a project could, for example, contribute to the 'romanticizing' and 'other-ing' of the |Xam (James 2001: 21–22). It would be 'opportunistic', in James's opinion, to make poems out of the texts 'simply for the sake of making poems' (James 2001: 25). Each piece should, in his opinion, 'acknowledge the individual narrators and transcriber-translators' (James 2001: 25). Krog's project is similar to James's in this respect. Like Krog, James (2001: 25) does not wish to 'undervalue the primacy and worth of the texts and mask the poems' dependence on the texts'. James's project, however, is closer to Watson's in several other important ways. Most significantly, in terms of the concerns of this chapter, both poets believe that the texts need to be substantially reworked, aestheticised and accompanied by notes if they are to speak meaningfully to contemporary readers and 'live again as part of daily life' (James 2001: 23). James elaborates his position regarding translation, poetry, appropriation and the |Xam materials in an interview conducted by Brown (2002).

10 Watson (2005: 50) points out in his *New Contrast* article that Krog repeats the observations he made concerning repetition in oral literature in the introduction to *Return of the Moon*. She might, however, equally have been echoing James (2001: 23–25) or Markowitz (1956: 10).

11 Frances Vosloo's (2006) analysis of several of Krog's Afrikaans translations of the
   |Xam poems provides a detailed account of Krog's strategies of intervention.
12 'Afrikaans writers know South Africa, [Krog] asserts; English writers only jerk off on
   it' (Eaton 2006).
13 See Barnard (1996: 239–47) for a discussion of Van der Post's Bushman writing.
14 Watson himself concedes that this contention is probably wrong. Krog, he maintains,
   repeats it, without acknowledgement, some two decades after he first wrote it (Watson
   2005: 49). Krog (2006a), in response, claims to have arrived at the figure by following the logic of Theal's linking of the Bushmen with Egypt in his introduction to
   Specimens of Bushman Folklore (1911). Although Theal does maintain that the
   Bushmen once inhabited the whole of Africa and beyond, the link he makes between
   the people of southern Africa and Egypt concerns the Hottentots and not the
   Bushmen. Nor can Theal's speculations seriously be considered as history. They have
   to be understood in terms of his notions of racial evolution.
15 Examples of this syndrome abound in the literature of an earlier era. Markowitz, for
   example, remarks on the physical smallness of the Bushman. He finds the space in his
   brief introduction to mention that 'the average height of the adult male Bushman is
   56.85 inches — within an inch of the average height of the Congo pygmy' (Markowitz
   1956: 11). Phillip Tobias's foreword to Markowitz is fixated on the Bushman's physical stature, which he conflates with simplicity, childishness and the primitive: 'in a
   world of men, the Bushmen were children. … "Peter Pans" of humanity they have
   been called and well do these baby-faced, pygmoid, yellow-skinned huntsmen deserve
   the title.' Their stories belong to 'a vanishing phase in the dawning of human culture'
   (Tobias 1956: 5–6). Watson (1991: 17) mentions the presence of the 'little Bushman
   syndrome' specifically in relation to Tobias's work.
16 Brown's own writing admirably escapes the complex I am identifying in Krog's work.
   He consistently treats the materials as discourse rather than as timeless myth.

CONCLUSION

In the course of this book, I have concentrated on the body of inter-
pretation that exists in relation to the |Xam narratives of the Bleek and
Lloyd Collection. I have, in addition, attempted the analysis of some of
these narratives. It has been my contention that much of the interpretation
of the stories reflects the intellectual tradition from which it has emerged
rather than the |Xam materials themselves. I have followed Derrida in
characterising this tradition as predicated on the myth of the lost origin
and a metaphysics of presence. I have detected this complex in the interest
in the figure of the 'Bushman' in its various manifestations and the way in
which this figure has been constructed as a pre-historical, pure hunter-
gatherer with little relationship to the heterogeneity of colonial or post-
colonial space. In the interpretation of the materials, I have especially
discovered the metaphysics of presence in the use of universal, cross-
cultural, comparative discourses involving, particularly, the trickster and
the idea of the myth of origin, as well as in the concentration on the
function of the stories. I have also argued that the lack of attention to the
detail of individual stories points to a hermeneutic practice that is more
interested in overarching or underlying patterns and structures than it is in
the signifying practices of the |Xam discursive tradition itself.

I have attempted in a discussion of a number of narratives to offer a
mode of interpretation that concentrates on their details. I have discussed
these stories in terms of their own modes of signification, situated within

the wider circuits of IXam discursive practice. The details of the stories, I maintain, are not subordinate to a hidden social function, nor are the clusters of elements in the stories mere variations on universal themes. The stories do, however, signify in the wider intertextual field of IXam discursive practice. For reasons I make clear at different points in the book, my interpretation cannot elude the interpretations I criticise, and I cannot pretend to evade their shortcomings. I have tried to compensate for this inescapable feature of intellectual practice by opting for a self-reflexive, ironic and tentative mode of analysis. I put new statements about the narratives into play rather than claim to reveal new truths about them. This does not mean, however, that these statements are random and arbitrary. They have emerged from a process of close engagement with the materials and make carefully considered strategic claims about them. My analysis tries, however, to maintain a high degree of awareness as to its status as a type of discourse that exists within a historically delimited regime of truth.

I hope that the body of interpretation that exists in relation to the narratives and also to other aspects of the field will in the future be subjected to even closer critical scrutiny than I have managed in this study. The materials in the Bleek and Lloyd Collection become better known by the year and will inevitably continue to receive attention. I hope that some of this attention, at least, will consist of close textual analysis. In this book, I discuss several stories in some detail. Each of these stories offers much scope for further discussion, however, and there are hundreds of narratives in the collection that offer the opportunity for similar treatment. I have hardly touched, for example, on the animal narratives that comprise as rich a body of texts as the IKaggen narratives do. And this does not even take into account the other sorts of materials in the collection: the wealth of informative matter about daily living or the historical and biographical materials that form a rare indigenous commentary, as Brown (1998) observes, on the colonial situation. There are a great many aspects of those narratives on which I have focused that I have not attempted to explore, such as their formal, aesthetic and generic characteristics. These all await close investigation.

The sorts of questions I raise in the pages of this book could be expanded almost indefinitely and the sorts of answers in whose direction I have gestured could similarly be multiplied in numerous ways. The answers that earlier generations of critics wished to glean from the materials regarding human evolution or universal structures or the functions of stories can be shown to reside to some degree in the nature of the questions themselves. The sort of approach I am advocating here endeavours to remain more faithful to the narratives' own modes of textuality. It resists the temptation, for example, to use them to provide evidence about earlier phases of human history or to employ them as materials for a comparative mythology. Inevitably, however, it is as much a product of its time and discursive context as the viewpoints it deconstructs.

BIBLIOGRAPHY

Adair, B. 2006. 'Speaking through the mask of culture', LitNet, 13 March, <http://www.oulitnet.co.za/seminarroom/krog_adair.asp>.

Althusser, L. 1971. *Lenin and Philosophy, and Other Essays*. New York: Monthly Review Press.

Bakhtin, M.M. 1968. *Rabelais and His World*. Cambridge, Mass.: M.I.T. Press.

——. 1981. *The Dialogic Imagination: Four Essays*. Austin: University of Texas Press.

Bank, A. 1999. 'Anthropology, race and evolution: Rethinking the legacy of Wilhelm Bleek', paper presented at a seminar at the University of the Western Cape, 14 April, <http:www.history.und.ac.za/sempapers/bank%20 on%20bleek.pdf>.

——. 2002. 'From pictures to performance: Early learning at the hill', *Kronos: Journal of Cape History* 28: 66–101.

——. 2006. *Bushmen in a Victorian World: The Remarkable Story of the Bleek-Lloyd Collection of Bushman Folklore*. Cape Town: Double Storey.

Barber, K. 1991. *I Could Speak until Tomorrow: Oriki, Women and the Past in a Yoruba Town*. Edinburgh: Edinburgh University Press.

——. 1999. 'Obscurity and exegesis in African oral praise poetry', in *Oral Literature and Performance in Southern Africa*, edited by D. Brown, pp. 27–49. Oxford: James Currey.

Barnard, A. 1992. *Hunters and Herders: A Comparative Ethnology of the Khoisan Peoples*. Cambridge: Cambridge University Press.

——. 1996. 'Laurens van der Post and the Kalahari debate', in *Miscast: Negotiating the Presence of the Bushmen*, edited by P. Skotnes, pp. 239–47. Cape Town: UCT Press.

Barthes, R. 1986. *Mythologies*. London: Paladin.

Bascom, W.R. 1965. 'The forms of folklore: Prose narratives', *Journal of American Folklore* 78: 3–20.

——. 1984. 'The forms of folklore; prose narratives', in *Sacred Narrative: Readings in the Theory of Myth*, edited by A. Dundes, pp. 5–29. Berkeley: University of California Press.

Bassnett, S. & H. Trivedi. 1999. 'Introduction: Of colonies, cannibals and vernaculars', in *Post-colonial Translation: Theory and Practice*, edited by S. Bassnett & H. Trivedi, pp. 1–18. London: Routledge.

Baudrillard, J. 2001. *Selected Writings*, edited by M. Poster, 2nd ed. Cambridge: Polity Press.

Bauman, Z. 1997. *Postmodernity and Its Discontents*. Cambridge: Polity Press.

———. 2002. *Society under Siege*. Cambridge: Polity Press.

Beidelman, T. 1993. 'The moral imagination of the Kaguru: some thoughts on tricksters, translation and comparative analysis', in *Mythical Trickster Figures: Contours, Contexts, and Criticisms*, edited by W. Hynes & W. Doty, pp. 174–92. Tuscaloosa: University of Alabama Press.

Bennun, N. 2005. *The Broken String: The Last Words of an Extinct People*. London: Penguin.

Bhabha, H.K. 1994. *The Location of Culture*. London: Routledge.

Biesele, M. 1976. 'Aspects of !Kung folklore', in *Kalahari Hunter-gatherers: Studies of the !Kung San and Their Neighbours*, edited by R.B. Lee & I. de Vore, pp. 303–24. Cambridge, Mass.: Harvard University Press.

———. 1993. *Women Like Meat: The Folklore and Foraging Ideology of the Kalahari Jul'hoan*. Johannesburg: Wits University Press.

Biesele, M.A., R. Katz & V. St. Denis. 1997. *Healing Makes Our Hearts Happy: Spirituality and Cultural Transformation among the Kalahari Ju/'Hoansi*. Rochester: Inner Traditions International.

Bleek, D.F. 1923. *The Mantis and His Friends: Bushman Folklore*. Cape Town: Maskew Miller.

———. 1929. 'Bushman folklore', *Africa: Journal of the International African Institute* 2(3): 302–13.

———. 1956. *A Bushman Dictionary*. New Haven: American Oriental Society.

Bleek, D.F. & G.W. Stow. 1930. *Rock Paintings in Southern Africa*. London: Methuen.

Bleek, W.H.I. 1857. 'Researches into the relations between Hottentots and Kafirs'. *Cape Monthly Magazine* 1: 199–208; 289–296.

———. 1858. 'South African philology', *Cape Monthly Magazine* 3: 21–27.

———. 1862. *A Comparative Grammar of South African Languages*. London: Trübner.

———. 1869. *On the Origin of Language*, edited by E. Haeckel. New York: L.W. Schmidt.

——— 1873a. 'Scientific reasons for the study of the Bushman language', *Cape Monthly Magazine* 7: 149–53.

———. 1873b. 'Report concerning his researches into the Bushman languages and customs', in *Cape Parliamentary Papers* A 17-'73. Cape Town: Parliament of the Cape Colony.

——— 1874a. 'On resemblances in Bushman and Australian mythology', *Cape Monthly Magazine* 8: 98–102.

———. 1874b. 'Remarks', in J.M. Orpen, 'A glimpse into the mythology of the Maluti Bushmen', *Cape Monthly Magazine* 9: 10–13.

———. 1875a. 'Bushman researches', *Cape Monthly Magazine* 11: 104–15, 150–55.

———. 1875b. *A Brief Account of Bushman Folklore and Other Texts*.

Bleek, W.H.I. & L.C. Lloyd. 1911. *Specimens of Bushman Folklore*. London: George Allen.

Bourdieu, P. 2001. *Masculine Domination*. Stanford: Stanford University Press.

Bourdieu, P. & L. Wacquant. 1992. *An invitation to Reflexive Sociology*. Cambridge: Polity Press.

Bower, C. 2006. 'What about the reader?', <http://www.chico.mweb.co.za/art/2006mar/060303-readers.html>.

Bregin, E. 1998. 'The identity of difference: A critical study of representations of the Bushmen.' MA dissertation, University of Natal, Durban.

———. 2000. 'Representing the Bushmen through the colonial lens', *English in Africa* 27(1): 37–54.

Brinton, D. 1868. *The Myths of the New World: A Treatise on the Symbolism and Methodology of the Red Race of America*. New York: Leipoldt & Holt.

Brown, D. 1995. 'The society of the text: The oral literature of the |Xam Bushmen', *Critical Arts* 9(2): 76–108.

———. 1998. *Voicing the Text: South African Oral Poetry and Performance*. Cape Town: Oxford University Press.

——— (ed.). 1999. *Oral literature and Performance in Southern Africa*. Oxford: James Currey.

———. 2002. 'Reflections on the First Bushman's path: Stories, songs and testimonies of the |Xam of the Northern Cape, interview with Alan James', *Current Writing* 14(2): 155–73.

———. 2006. *To Speak of This Land: Identity and Belonging in South Africa and Beyond*. Pietermaritzburg: University of KwaZulu-Natal Press.

Calvino, I. 1996. *Six Memos for the Next Millennium*. London: Vintage.

Campbell, J. 1959. *The Masks of God: Primitive Mythology*. New York: Viking.

Campion, N. 1994. *The Great Year: Astrology, Millenarianism and History in the Western Tradition*. London: Arkana.

Carroll, M. 1984. 'The trickster as selfish-buffoon and culture hero', *Ethos*, 12(2): 105–31.

Chidester, D. 1996a. *Savage Systems: Colonialism and Comparative Religion in Southern Africa*. Charlottesville: University Press of Virginia.

———. 1996b. 'Bushman religion: Open, closed, and new frontiers', in *Miscast: Negotiating the Presence of the Bushmen*, edited by P. Skotnes, pp. 51–59. Cape Town: UCT Press.

Cope, J. & U. Krige (eds). 1968. *The Penguin Book of South African Verse*. Harmondsworth: Penguin.

Coupe, L. 1997. *Myth*. London: Routledge.

Csapo, E. 2005. *Theories of Mythology*. Oxford: Blackwell.

Cupitt, D. 1982. *The World to Come*. London: SCM Press.

Deacon, J. 1992. *Arrows as Agents of Belief amongst the /Xam Bushmen*. Cape Town: South African Museum.

———. 1996. 'A tale of two families: Wilhelm Bleek, Lucy Lloyd and the |Xam San of the Northern Cape', in *Miscast: Negotiating the Presence of the Bushmen*, edited by P. Skotnes, pp. 93–114. Cape Town: UCT Press.

Deacon, J. & T.A. Dowson (eds). 1996. *Voices from the Past: /Xam Bushmen and the Bleek and Lloyd Collection*. Johannesburg: Wits University Press.

De Certeau, M. 1986. *Heterologies: Discourse on the Other*. Minneapolis: University of Minnesota Press.

De Jager, N. 2006. 'Kwela responds', LitNet, 19 February, <http://www.oulitnet.co.za/seminarroom/krog_kwela.asp>.

De Lange, J. 2006. 'Stephen Watson and Antjie Krog, or the return of the repressed', LitNet, 21 February, <http://www.oulitnet.co.za/seminarroom/krog_delange.asp>.

Dentith, S. 1995. *Bakhtinian Thought: An Introductory Reader*. London: Routledge.

Derrida, J. 1976. *Of Grammatology*. Trans. G.C. Spivak. Baltimore: Johns Hopkins University Press.

——. 1985. *Derrida and Difference*, edited by D. Wood & R. Bernasconi. Coventry: Parousia Press.

——. 1992. *Acts of Literature*, edited by D. Attridge. New York: Routledge.

De Waal, S. 2006. 'Much ado', *Mail & Guardian*, 3–10 March.

Doueihi, A. 1984. 'Trickster: On inhabiting the space between discourse and story', *Soundings: An Interdisciplinary Journal* 67(3): 283–311.

——. 1993. 'Inhabiting the space between discourse and story in trickster narratives', in *Mythical Trickster Figures: Contours, Contexts, and Criticisms*, edited by W. Hynes & W. Doty, pp. 193–201. Tuscaloosa: University of Alabama Press.

Douglas, M. 1966. *Purity and Danger: An analysis of the Concept of Pollution and Taboo*. London: Routledge & Kegan Paul.

Dubow, S. 1995. *Illicit Union: Scientific Racism in Modern South Africa*. Johannesburg: Wits University Press.

Dundes, A. (ed.). 1984. *Sacred Narrative: Readings in the Theory of Myth*. Berkeley: University of California Press.

——. 1997. 'Binary opposition in myth: The Propp/Lévi-Strauss debate in retrospect', *Western Folklore* 56(1): 39–50.

Durkheim, É. 2001. *The Elementary Forms of Religious Life*. Oxford: Oxford University Press.

Eaton, T. 2006. 'Koeksusters vs cream pies', *Mail & Guardian*, 3–10 March, <http://www.chico.mweb.co.za/art/2006/2006mar/060303-eaton.html>.

Eliade, M. 1961. *The Sacred and the Profane: The Nature of Religion*. New York: Harper & Row.

——. 1972. *Shamanism: Archaic Techniques of Ecstasy*. New York: Routledge & Kegan Paul.

Evans-Pritchard, E.E. (ed.) 1967. *The Zande Trickster*. Oxford: Clarendon Press.

Finnegan, R. 1976. *Oral Literature in Africa*. Nairobi: Oxford University Press.

Firth, R. 1961. *History and Traditions of Tikopia*. Wellington: Polynesian Society.

Foucault, M. 1970. *The Order of Things: An Archaeology of the Human Sciences*. London: Tavistock.

——. 1972. *The Archaeology of Knowledge*. London: Tavistock.

——. 1973. *Madness and Civilisation: A History of Insanity in the Age of Reason*. New York: Vintage Books.

——. 1975. *The Birth of the Clinic: An Archaeology of Medical Perception*. New York: Vintage Books.

——. 1977. *Discipline and Punish: The Birth of the Prison*. London: Allen Lane.

——. 1980. *Power/knowledge: Selected Interviews and Other Writings 1972–1977*, edited by C. Gordon. New York: Pantheon Books.

——. 1985. *The Use of Pleasure*. New York: Pantheon Books.

——. 1987. *The Foucault Reader*, edited by P. Rabinow. Harmondsworth: Penguin.

Gagiano, A. 1992. 'Just a touch of the cultural trophy-hunter', *Die Suid-Afrikaan* 78.

——. 1999. 'By what authority? Presentations of the Khoisan in South African English poetry', *Alternation*. 6(1): 155–73.

——. 2006. 'Just a touch of the cultural trophy-hunter', LitNet, 21 February, <http://www.oulitnet.co.za/seminarroom/krog_gagiano.asp>.

Gates, H.L. 1988. *The Signifying Monkey: A Theory of Afro-American Literary Criticism*. New York: Oxford University Press.

Glenn, I. 1996. 'The Bushman in early South African literature', in *Miscast: Negotiating the Presence of the Bushmen*, edited by P. Skotnes, pp. 41–49. Cape Town: UCT Press.

Godby, M. 1996. 'Images of ‖Kabbo', in *Miscast: Negotiating the Presence of the Bushmen*, edited by P. Skotnes, pp. 115–27. Cape Town: UCT Press.

Godzich, W. 1986. 'The further possibility of knowledge', foreword in M. de Certeau, *Heterologies: Discourse on the Other*. Minneapolis: University of Minnesota Press.

Gordon, R. J. 1992. *The Bushman Myth: The Making of a Namibian Underclass*. Boulder: Westview Press.

Gray, E. 2006. 'Commentary on Stephen Watson's *New Contrast* article', LitNet, 19 February, <http://www.litnet.co.za/seminarroom/krog_eve_gray.asp>.

Guenther, M.G. 1986. *The Nharo Bushmen of Botswana: Tradition and Change*. Hamburg: Helmut Buske Verlag.

———. 1989. *Bushman Folktales: Oral Traditions of the Nharo of Botswana and the /Xam of the Cape*. Stuttgart: Franz Steiner Verlag, Wiesbaden.

———. 1995. 'Contested images, contexted texts: The politics of representing the Bushmen of Southern Africa', *Critical Arts* 9(2): 110–18.

———. 1996. 'Attempting to contextualise |Xam oral tradition', in *Voices from the Past: |Xam Bushmen and the Bleek and Lloyd Collection*, edited by J. Deacon & T. Dowson, pp. 77–99. Johannesburg: Wits University Press.

———. 1999. *Tricksters and Trancers: Bushman Religion and Society*. Bloomington: Indiana University Press.

———. 2002. 'The Bushman trickster: Protagonist, divinity and agent of creativity', *Marvels & Tales: Journal of Fairy-Tale Studies* 16 (1): 13–28.

———. 2006. '*N‖àe* ("talking"): The oral and rhetorical base of San culture', *Journal of Folklore Research* 43(3): 241–61.

Hall, M. 1996. 'The proximity of Dr. Bleek's Bushmen', in *Miscast: Negotiating the Presence of the Bushmen*, edited by P. Skotnes, pp. 143–59. Cape Town: UCT Press.

Hewitt, R.L. 1986. *Structure, Meaning and Ritual in the Narratives of the Southern San*. Hamburg: Helmut Buske Verlag.

———. 2007. 'Reflections on narrative', in *Claim to the Country: The Archive of Wilhelm Bleek and Lucy Lloyd*, edited by P. Skotnes, pp. 161–69. Johannesburg: Jacana.

———. 2008. *Structure, Meaning and Ritual in the Narratives of the Southern San*. Johannesburg: Wits University Press.

Hoff, A. 1998. 'The water bull of the |Xam', *South African Archaeological Bulletin* 53: 109–24.

———. 2007. *Medicine Experts and the /Xam San: The !Kwa-ka!gi:ten who Controlled the Rain and Water*. Cologne: Rüdiger Köppe Verlag.

Hofmeyr, I. 1993. *We Spend Our Years as a Tale that Is Told: Oral Historical Narrative in a South African Chiefdom*. Johannesburg: Wits University Press.

Hollmann, J.C. (ed.). 2004. *Customs and Beliefs of the /Xam Bushmen*. Johannesburg: Wits University Press.

Hultkrantz, A. 1997. 'Theories on the North American trickster', *ACTA Americana* 5(2): 5–24.

Hyde, L. 1998. *Trickster Makes This World: Mischief, Myth and Art*. New York: Farrar, Straus & Giroux.

Hynes, W.J. 1993. 'Mapping the characteristics of mythic tricksters: A heuristic guide', in *Mythical Trickster Figures: Contours, Contexts, and Criticisms*, edited by W.J. Hynes & W.G. Doty, pp. 33–45. Tuscaloosa: University of Alabama Press.

Hynes, W.J. & W.G. Doty (eds). 1993. *Mythical Trickster Figures: Contours, Contexts, and Criticisms*. Tuscaloosa: University of Alabama Press.

———. 1993. 'Historical overview of theoretical issues: the problem of the trickster', in *Mythical Trickster Figures: Contours, Contexts, and Criticisms*, edited by W. J. Hynes & W.G. Doty, pp. 13–32. Tuscaloosa: University of Alabama Press.

James, A. 2001. *The First Bushman's Path: Stories, Songs and Testimonies of the /Xam of the Northern Cape*. Pietermaritzburg: University of Natal Press.

Jeursen, B. 1994. 'Gender in |Xam narratives: Towards an unidealised reading of the community.' MA dissertation, University of Natal, Durban.

———. 1995 '!Khwa and menstruation in narratives of the |Xam Bushmen', *Alternation*. 2(2): 40–54.

Johnson, S. 2006. 'Statement in response to charges that Antjie Krog plagiarised Ted Hughes in *Country of My Skull* (Random House, Johannesburg 1998)', LitNet, 19 February, <http://www.oulitnet.co.za/seminarroom/krog_random_house.asp>.

Jolly, P. 1994. 'Strangers to brothers: Interaction between South-Eastern San and Southern Nguni/Sotho communities.' MA dissertation, University of Cape Town.

Jung, C. 1972. 'On the psychology of the trickster', in *The Trickster: A Study in American Indian Mythology*, by P. Radin, pp. 195–211. New York: Schocken Books.

Kirk, G. 1974. *The Nature of Greek Myths*. Harmondsworth: Penguin.

Kristeva, J. 1986. *The Kristeva Reader*, edited by T. Moi. Oxford: Blackwell.

Kroeber, K. 1977. 'Deconstructionist criticism and American Indian literature', *Boundary 2*, 7(3): 73–89.

Krog, A. 1998. *Country of My Skull: Guilt, Sorrow, and the Limits of Forgiveness in the New South Africa*. Johannesburg: Random House.

———. 2004. *The Stars Say 'Tsau': /Xam Poetry of Dia!kwain, Kweiten-Ta//Ken, /A!kunta, /Han#kass'o, and //Kabbo*. Cape Town: Kwela Books.

———. 2006a. 'Stephen Watson in the annals of plagiarism', LitNet, 19 February, <http://www.oulitnet.co.za/seminarroom.Krog_Krog.asp>.

———. 2006b. 'Last time, this time', LitNet, 20 March, <http://www.oulitnet.co.za/seminarroom.Krog_Krog2.asp>.

———. 2006c. 'From ||Kabbo to Zapiro: A foreword', in *To Speak of This Land: Identity and Belonging in South Africa and Beyond*, by D. Brown, pp. xiii–xx. Pietermaritzburg: University of KwaZulu-Natal Press.

Leach, E.R. 1989. *Claude Lévi-Strauss*. Chicago: University of Chicago Press.

Lee, R.B. & M.G. Guenther. 1993. 'Problems in the Kalahari historical ethnography and the tolerance of error', *History in Africa* 20:185–235.

Le Vaillant, F. 1790. *Travels into the Interior Parts of Africa*, 2 vols. London: Robinson.

Lévinas, E. 1989. *The Levinas Reader*, edited by S. Hand. Oxford: Blackwell.

Lévi-Strauss, C. 1955. 'The structural study of myth', *Journal of American Folklore* 68: 428–44.

———. 1960. 'L'Analyse morphologique des contes russes', *International Journal of Slavic Linguistics and Poetics* 3:122–49.

——. 1961. *Tristes Tropiques*. Trans. J. Russell. New York: Atheneum.

——. 1966. *The Savage Mind*. London: Weidenfeld & Nicolson.

——. 1969. *The Raw and the Cooked: Introduction to a Science of Mythology*, vol. 1. New York: Harper & Row.

——. 1973. *From Honey to Ashes: Introduction to a Science of Mythology*, vol. 2. New York: Harper & Row.

——. 1979. *The Origin of Table Manners: Introduction to a Science of Mythology*, vol. 3. New York: Harper & Row.

——. 1981. *The Naked Man: Introduction to a Science of Mythology*, vol. 4. New York: Harper & Row.

Lewis-Williams, J.D. 1981. *Believing and Seeing: Symbolic Meanings in Southern San Rock Paintings*. London: Academic Press.

——. 1996a. '"A Visit to the Lion's House": The structures, metaphors and sociopolitical significance of a nineteenth-century Bushman myth', in *Voices from the Past: /Xam Bushmen and the Bleek and Lloyd Collection*, edited by J. Deacon & T. Dowson, pp. 122–41. Johannesburg: Wits University Press.

——. 1996b. "The ideas generally entertained with regard to the Bushmen and their mental condition", in *Miscast: Negotiating the Presence of the Bushmen*, edited by P. Skotnes, pp. 307–13. Cape Town: UCT Press.

——. 1998a. 'The mantis, the eland and the meerkats: Conflict and mediation in a nineteenth-century San myth', *African Studies* 26: 195–216.

——. 1998b. 'Quanto? The issue of many meanings in southern African San rock art', *South African Archaeological Bulletin* 53: 86–97.

—— (ed.). 2000. *Stories that Float from Afar: Ancestral Folklore of the San of Southern Africa*. Cape Town: David Philip.

——. 2007. 'Wilhelm Bleek, Lucy Lloyd and Dorothea Bleek: A personal tribute', in *Claim to the Country: The Archive of Wilhelm Bleek and Lucy Lloyd*, edited by P. Skotnes, pp. 176–81. Johannesburg: Jacana.

Lewis-Williams, J.D. & T. Dowson. 1989. *Images of Power: Understanding Bushman Rock Art*. Johannesburg: Southern Book Publishers.

—— (eds). 1994. *Contested Images: Diversity in Southern African Rock Art Research*. Johannesburg: Wits University Press.

Lewis-Williams, J.D. & D. Pearce. 2004. *San Spirituality: Roots, Expressions, and Social Consequences*. Cape Town: Double Storey.

——. 2005. *Inside the Neolithic Mind: Consciousness, Cosmos and the Realm of the Gods*. London: Thames & Hudson.

Lloyd, L.C. 1889. *A Short Account of Further Bushman Material Collected: Third Report Concerning Bushman Researches, Presented to Both Houses of Parliament of the Cape of Good Hope, by Command of His Excellency the Governor*. London: Nutt.

Makarius, L. 1993. 'The myth of the trickster: The necessary breaker of taboos', in *Mythical Trickster Figures: Contours, Contexts, and Criticisms*, edited by W. Hynes & W. Doty, pp. 66–86. Tuscaloosa: University of Alabama Press.

Malinowski, B. 1926. *Myth in Primitive Psychology*. London: Routledge & Kegan Paul.

——. 1948. *Magic, Science, Religion and Other Essays*. Boston: Beacon Press.

——. 2001. *Argonauts of the Western Pacific: An Account of Native Enterprise and*

Adventure in the Archipelagoes of Melanesian New Guinea. London: Routledge.

Marais, E. 1959 [1927]. *Dwaalstories*. Cape Town: Human & Rousseau.

Markowitz, A.1956. *With Uplifted Tongue: Stories, Myths and Fables of the South African Bushmen Told in Their Manner*. Johannesburg: CNA.

Marshall, L. 1962. '!Kung Bushman religious beliefs', *Africa* 32: 221–52

Martin, J. 2008. *A Millimetre of Dust*. Cape Town: Kwela Books.

Mason-Jones, C. 2006. 'The google of my skull', LitNet, 24 March, <http://www.oulitnet. co.za/seminarroom/krog_masonjones.asp>.

Maughan Brown, D. 1983 'The noble savage in Anglo-Saxon colonial ideology, 1950–1980: "Masai" and "Bushmen" in popular fiction', *English in Africa* 10(2): 55–77.

Monsma, B. 1996. '"Active readers … observe tricksters": Trickster, texts and cross-cultural reading', *Modern Language Studies* 26(4): 83–98.

Moran, S. 1995. 'White mythology: What use is deconstruction?', *Alternation*. 2(1): 16–36.

———. 2001. 'Specimens of "Bushman" studies', *Wasafiri* 34: 46–51.

———. 2009. *Representing Bushmen: South Africa and the Origin of Language*. Rochester: University of Rochester Press.

Okpewho, I. 1983. *Myth in Africa*. Cambridge: Cambridge University Press.

Orpen, J.M. 1874. 'A glimpse into the mythology of the Maluti Bushmen', *Cape Monthly Magazine* 9: 1–13.

Parkington, J. 1996. '"What is an eland?" *N!ao* and the politics of age and sex in the paintings of the western Cape', in *Miscast: Negotiating the Presence of the Bushmen*, edited by P. Skotnes, pp. 281–89. Cape Town: UCT Press.

———. 2002. *The Mantis, the Eland and the Hunter*. Cape Town: Krakadouw Trust.

Peires, J.B. 1989. *The Dead Will Arise: Nongqawuse and the Great Xhosa Cattle-Killing Movement of 1856–57*. Johannesburg: Ravan Press.

Pelton, R. 1980. *The Trickster in West Africa: A Study of Mythic Irony and Sacred Delight*. Berkeley: University of California Press.

Penn, N. 1996. '"Fated to perish": The destruction of the Cape San', in *Miscast: Negotiating the Presence of the Bushmen*, edited by P. Skotnes, pp. 81–91. Cape Town: UCT Press.

———. 2005. *The Forgotten Frontier: Colonist and Khoisan on the Cape's Northern Frontier in the 18th Century*. Cape Town: Double Storey.

Propp, V. 1968. *Morphology of the Folktale*, 2nd ed. Austin: University of Texas Press.

———. 1984. *Theory and History of Folklore*. Minneapolis: University of Minnesota Press.

Radin, P. 1924. *Monotheism among Primitive Peoples*. London: Allen & Unwin.

———. 1956. *The Trickster: A Study in American Indian Mythology*. London: Routledge & Kegan Paul.

———. 1972. *The Trickster: A Study in American Indian Mythology*. New York: Schocken Books.

Ricketts, M.L. 1966. 'The North American Indian trickster', *History of Religions* 5(2): 327–50.

———. 1993. 'The shaman and the trickster', in *Mythical Trickster Figures: Contours, Contexts, and Criticisms*, edited by W. Hynes & W. Doty, pp. 87–105. Tuscaloosa: University of Alabama Press.

Ricoeur, P. 1991. *A Ricoeur Reader: Reflection and Imagination*. New York: Harvester/Wheatsheaf.

Riley, E. 2007. 'The hunting ground's doings: IXam narratives of animals, hunting and the veld', in *Claim to the Country: The Archive of Wilhelm Bleek and Lucy Lloyd*, edited by P. Skotnes, pp. 290–311. Johannesburg: Jacana.

Said, E. 1991. *Orientalism: Western Conceptions of the Orient*. Harmondsworth: Penguin.

——. 1993. *Culture and Imperialism*. London: Chatto & Windus.

Scheub, H. 1998. *Story*. Madison: University of Wisconsin Press.

Schmidt, S. 1989. *Catalogue of the Khoisan Folktales of Southern Africa*. Hamburg: Helmut Buske Verlag.

——. 1996. 'The relevance of the Bleek/Lloyd folktales to the general Khoisan traditions', in *Voices from the Past: /Xam Bushmen and the Bleek and Lloyd Collection*, edited by J. Deacon & T. Dowson, pp. 100–21. Johannesburg: Wits University Press.

——. 2001. *Tricksters, Monsters and Clever Girls: African Folktales–Texts and Discussions*. Köln: Rüdiger Köppe Verlag.

Schoeman, K. 1997. *A Debt of Gratitude: Lucy Lloyd and the 'Bushman work' of G.W. Stow*. Cape Town: South African Library.

Skotnes, P. (ed.). 1996a. *Miscast: Negotiating the Presence of the Bushmen*. Cape Town: UCT Press.

——. 1996b. 'The thin black line: Diversity in the paintings of the southern San and the Bleek and Lloyd Collection', in *Voices from the Past: /Xam Bushmen and the Bleek and Lloyd Collection*, edited by J. Deacon & T. Dowson, pp. 234–44. Johannesburg: Wits University Press.

——. 2007. *Claim to the Country: The Archive of Wilhelm Bleek and Lucy Lloyd*. Johannesburg: Jacana.

Smit, J., J. van Wyk & J.-P. Wade (eds). 1996. *Rethinking South African Literary History*. Durban: Y-Press.

Solomon, A.C. 1997. 'The myth of ritual origins? Ethnography, mythology and interpretation of San rock art', *South African Archaeological Bulletin* 52: 3–13.

——. 1999. 'The quest for mind via San rock art', unpublished paper presented at the 4th World Archaeological Congress, Cape Town.

——. 2007. 'Images, words and worlds: The IXam testimonies and the rock arts of the southern San', in *Claim to the Country: The Archive of Wihelm Bleek and Lucy Lloyd*, edited by P. Skotnes, pp. 148–59. Johannesburg: Jacana.

—— 2008. 'Myths, making, and consciousness: Differences and dynamics in San rock arts', *Current Anthropology* 49(1): 59–86.

——. 2009. 'Broken strings: Interdisciplinarity and IXam oral literature', *Critical Arts* 23(1): 26–41.

——. n.d. *The Imagination of the San*. Unpublished ms.

Spivak, G.C. 1976. 'Translator's preface', in *Of Grammatology* by J. Derrida. Baltimore: Johns Hopkins University Press.

——. 1988. 'Can the subaltern speak?', in *Marxism and the Interpretation of Culture*, edited by C. Nelson & L. Grossberg, pp. 271–313. Chicago: University of Illinois Press.

——. 1999. *A Critique of Post-Colonial Reason: Toward a History of the Vanishing Present*. Cambridge, Mass.: Harvard University Press.

Spohr, O.H. 1962. *Wilhelm Heinrich Immanuel Bleek: A Bibliographical Sketch*. Cape Town: UCT Library.

Street, B. 1972. 'The trickster theme: Winnebago and Azande', in *Zande Themes: Essays Presented to Sir Edward Evans-Pritchard*, edited by A. Singer & B. Street, pp. 82–104. Oxford: Blackwell.

Strenski, I. 1987. *Four Theories of Myth in Twentieth-Century History: Cassirer, Eliade, Lévi-Strauss and Malinowski*. Iowa City: University of Iowa Press.

Swart, S. 2003. 'Mythic Bushmen in Afrikaans literature: The '*Dwaalstories*' of Eugène N. Marais', *Current Writing* 15(2): 91–108.

Szalay, M. 1995. *The San and the Colonization of the Cape 1770–1879: Conflict, Incorporation, Acculturation*. Köln: Rüdiger Köppe Verlag.

Theal, G.M. 1911. 'Introduction', in *Specimens of Bushman Folklore*, edited by W. Bleek & L. Lloyd, pp. xxv–xl. London: George Allen.

Thomas, E.M. 1959. *The Harmless People*. Harmondsworth: Penguin.

Thornton, R.J. 1983a. 'The elusive unity of Sir George Grey's library', *African Studies* 42(1): 79–80.

——. 1983b. '"This dying out race": W.H.I. Bleek's approach to the languages of southern Africa', *Social Dynamics* 9(2): 1–10.

Tobias, P. 1956. 'Foreword', in *With Uplifted Tongue: Stories, Myths and Fables of the South African Bushmen Told in Their Manner*, by A. Markowitz. Johannesburg: CNA.

Traill, A. 1996. '!Khwa-ka hhouiten hhouiten, "The rush of the storm": The linguistic death of |Xam', in *Miscast: Negotiating the Presence of the Bushmen*, edited by P. Skotnes, pp. 161–83. Cape Town: UCT Press.

Van der Post, L. 1958. *The Lost World of the Kalahari*. Harmondsworth: Penguin.

——. 1961. *The Heart of the Hunter*. Harmondsworth: Penguin.

Van Vuuren, H. 1994. 'Forgotten territory: The oral tradition of the |Xam', *Alternation: International Journal for the Study of Southern African Literature and Language* 1(2): 57–70.

——. 1995. 'Die mondelinge tradisie van die |Xam en 'n herlees van Von Wielligh se *Boesman-Stories* (vier dele, 1919–1921)', *Tydskrif vir Letterkunde* 33(1): 25–35.

——. 1996. 'Orality in the margins of literary history: Prolegomena to a study of interaction between Bushmen orality and Afrikaans literature', in *Rethinking South African Literary History*, edited by J. Smit, J. van Wyk & J.-P. Wade, pp. 129–35. Durban: Y-Press.

Vecsey, C. 1993. 'The exception who proves the rules: Ananse the Akan trickster', in *Mythical Trickster Figures: Contours, Contexts, and Criticisms*, edited by W. Hynes & W. Doty, pp. 106–21. Tuscaloosa: University of Alabama Press.

Von Wielligh, G. 1919–21. *Boesman Stories*, 4 vols. Cape Town: Nasionale Pers.

Vosloo, F. 2006. 'Antjie Krog se vertaling *die sterre sê* '*Tsau*': 'n Deskriptiewe analise.' MA dissertation, University of Stellenbosch.

Voss, A.E. 1987. 'The image of the Bushman in South African English writing of the nineteenth and twentieth centuries', *English in Africa* 14(1): 21–40.

——. 1990. 'Die Bushie is dood. Long live the Bushie: Black South African writers on the San'. *African Studies* 49(1): 59–70.

——. 1995. 'Re-recuperating the San', *Critical Arts* 9(2): 147–53.

Watson, S. 1991. *Return of the Moon: Versions from the /Xam*. Cape Town: Carrefour Press.

——. 2005. 'Annals of plagiarism, or: Antjie Krog and the Bleek and Lloyd Collection', *New Contrast* 33(2): 48–61.

Webb, J., T. Schirato & G. Danaher. 2002. *Understanding Bourdieu*. London: Sage.

Webster, C. 2000. 'The portrait cabinet of Dr Bleek: Anthropometric photographs by early Cape photographers', *Critical Arts* 14(1): 1–15.

Wilmsen, E.N. 1989. *Land Filled with Flies: A Political Economy of the Kalahari*. Chicago: University of Chicago Press.

——. 1995. 'First people?: Images and imaginations in South African iconography', *Critical Arts* 9(2): 1–27.

——. 1996. 'Decolonising the mind: Steps towards cleansing the Bushman stain from southern African history', in *Miscast: Negotiating the Presence of the Bushmen*, edited by P. Skotnes, pp. 185–89. Cape Town: UCT Press.

Wilmsen, E.N. & J. Denbow. 1990. 'A paradigmatic history of San-speaking peoples and current attempts at revision', *Current Anthropology* 31(5): 489–524.

Zizek, S. 2001. *On Belief*. London: Routledge.

INDEX

Prepositions in subheadings are not used for alphabetical ordering. Words that include non-Roman letters are listed by their first Roman letter.

shoes 86-90, 131, 147, 285
sidereal stories 198, 199, 200, 219
sidereal worship 19, 188
signifiers xii, 167-173, 195-196, 207,
212-215
cosmic entities 222
crows 213
lions 280-282
springbok 213, 252-259
sun 219-222, 225, 235
Skotnes, Pippa 10, 122, 178, 277
social conflict 163
Social Darwinism 54, 70, 189
Solomon, Anne 12, 90, 138, 184-185,
221, 258, 276-277
South African historiography 54
South African literature 54
speech 224
and writing 50, 55, 56-61, 164, 173
spirits of the dead 6, 16, 201-206, 231,
246, 252, 254, 258-259
Spivak, Gayatri 32, 42-45
springbok 88, 110, 113-115, 132, 140,
213, 252-259, 280
stars 37, 114, 242-248, 253-254, 258-260,
268
stories (specific) 3-4, 199-200, 207-213
see also IXam narratives
Children are sent to throw the
sleeping sun into the sky 195-237
Dasse's and crow's 207-214
Girl of the Early Race who made
stars 241-261, 165-173
Mantis assumes the form of a
hartebeest 126-149, 161, 166
Mantis, eland and meerkats 85-91
moon and hare 200-206, 235 see also
origin of death
analysis 223-230, 232-236,
242-252
of IKaggen 4, 19-21
of sun, moon, stars 19-21, 68,
197, 218-219
Son of the Mantis 165-172

Visit to the lion's house 270-287
story (term), critique of 74-75
structured, unstructured societies 156
structuralism 25, 28, 47, 48, 49, 62, 70,
90, 152-153 see also Lévi-Strauss,
Claude; functionalism
anti-structuralism156, 162
post-structuralism 47, 71
reductive nature 158, 165, 173
sun 88-89, 199, 206, 217-237, 242, 244,
267, 304, 225, 235
symbolic capital 40
symbols 86-90
Bushmen 51
crows 212
eland 88, 89
moon 89
rain 257-258
shoes 86-90
springbok 252-259

T

taboos 115, 170, 172, 242, 260
baboons 171, 172
incest 172
menarcheal 245, 248-252
tappings 112-113, 116
Third World intellectuals 42
traditional (term), critique 72
traditional nature 73
trances 89, 90
trickster, the see also IKaggen 26, 44, 48,
49, 93-117, 155
Akan 103
archetype 99-102, 108, 109
as culturally specific 105-107
deconstructed 106-108
typologies 105
West African 103-104
trickster literature 93-98, 100-109
tales 127-129, 138
Trobiand society 26
typology 181